TORQUATO TASSO

JERUSALEM DELIVERED

Being a translation into English verse by
EDWARD FAIRFAX
of Tasso's GERUSALEMME LIBERATA

WITH AN INTRODUCTION BY
JOHN CHARLES NELSON
Associate Professor of Italian, Columbia University

CAPRICORN BOOKS
NEW YORK

Fourth Impression

SBN: 399-50119-3

Manufactured in the United States of America

PLOT SUMMARY

BOOK I

Introduction.—Invocation of the Heavenly Muse.—Address to Alphonso II, Duke of Ferrara, the poet's patron.—Summary of the conquests of the Christians during their six years' stay in Asia.—In the spring of the seventh year, the Supreme Being sends the Archangel Gabriel to Godfrey of Bouillon, ordering him to assemble the Chiefs of the Crusaders, and encourage them to march without further delay to Jerusalem, assuring him at the same time that he shall be elected their leader.—Speeches of Godfrey and of Peter the Hermit to the assembly.—Godfrey is elected chief of the expedition.—He reviews his troops.—Catalogue of the Christian forces.—They commence their march.—Submission of the Prince of Tripoli.—Consternation of the inhabitants of Jerusalem, and of the King Aladine.—His character, and cruelty to his Christian subjects; his preparations for resistance.   1

BOOK II

Aladine seizes an image of the Virgin Mary, that was concealed in one of the Christian churches, and places it in the royal mosque, instigated thereto by Ismeno the sorcerer, who promises to render it, by means of his incantations, a magical safeguard to Jerusalem.—In the course of the night, the statue is taken away from the mosque.—The king, enraged at not being able to discover the author of the removal, resolves upon a general massacre of his Christian subjects.—Sophronia, a young Christian lady of great beauty and virtue, determines to sacrifice herself for her countrymen, and accuses herself to the king, as the perpetrator of the theft.—She is ordered to be burnt alive.—Olindo, her lover, contradicts the confession she had made, takes the charge upon himself, and desires to suffer in her stead.—They are both tied to the stake, but are released by the timely arrival and intercession of Clorinda.—The Christian army arrives at Emaus, where they are met by Alethes and Argantes, ambassadors from the King of Egypt.—Speech of Alethes.—Godfrey's reply—Reciprocal defiance and declaration of war by Godfrey and Argantes.—Godfrey dismisses the am-

BOOK III

BOOK IV

BOOK V

BOOK X

BOOK XI

BOOK XII

BOOK XVI

BOOK XVII

BOOK XVIII

INTRODUCTION

The first thirty-one years of the life of Torquato Tasso are marked by precocity and brilliant achievement, the remaining twenty by intense mental illness and diminished poetic verve, by depression and by disappointment.

Tasso, a precocious child, reputedly was speaking at the age of six months. When he was eighteen he published his *Rinaldo,* a narrative poem in twelve cantos, and was soon enjoying a secure and honored position, with no duties other than to write poetry, at the magnificent Este court in Ferrara, at which Ariosto had lived and flourished earlier in the century, and which still patronized the leading poets of Tasso's day. At twenty-nine, Tasso's pastoral poem *Aminta* was an immediate and unqualified success; two years later he had completed the composition of the finest epic poem of the Italian Renaissance. But from that point his life is such a morass of troubles and sorrows as to be painful even in the telling.

Tasso was born of a noble Bergamasque family in Sorrento, March 11, 1544. His father Bernardo, author of the narrative poem *Amadigi* (*Amadis*) and secretary to Ferrante Sanseverino, prince of Salerno, followed the latter into exile and poverty in 1552. When Torquato was eight, he entered a Jesuit school in Naples; by ten he had learned both Latin and Greek. His Mother, Porzia de' Rossi, a gentlewoman of Pistoia, died in 1556. The following year his father gained the favor of Guidobaldo II della Rovere, duke of Urbino, who appointed Torquato companion and perhaps tutor to his son Francesco Maria, enabling the future poet to study with the young prince's masters and thereby allowing young Torquato to acquire the knowledge and appreciation of the chivalric arts he later displayed in the *Gerusalemme Liberata.* Tasso's early taste for court life and his pride in associating with the upper nobility were never to leave him.

In 1559 Torquato joined his father in Venice and helped him to copy and revise the *Amadigi,* a re-elaboration of Garcia de Montalvo's version of *Amadis de Gaula.* There and in Padua, where he was enrolled in the university, he became known in literary circles, cultivating Sperone Speroni and Paolo and Aldo Manuzio and learning Aristotelian precepts from lectures on the *Poetics* by the learned classicist Carlo Guido Sigonio. The *Rinaldo,* published in Venice in 1562,

won him a considerable reputation. For his third year of
university studies Tasso, aided by a subsidy from the Duke of
Urbino, followed Sigonio to Bologna, but had to leave hur-
riedly the following year after being charged with writing an
offensive *pasquinata* ridiculing fellow students and faculty
members. In 1564 the hospitality of the young prince
Scipione Gonzaga enabled him to return to Padua and to con-
tinue his studies of philosophy and eloquence, although there
is no evidence that he earned a degree. He entered Gon-
zaga's *Accademia degli Eterei* (Academy of the Ethereal)
with the name of *Pentito* (he "repented" having left Padua
for Bologna) and composed poems to Laura Peperara and
Lucrezia Bendidio. The following year he entered the service
of Cardinal Luigi d'Este in Ferrara. For several years he was
engaged in writing his epic on the liberation of Jerusalem, in
preparing his three *Discourses on Poetic Art,* in writing
lyrical and occasional poetry and in studying classical and
Italian literature. His father died in 1569 in Ostiglia, and
young Torquato mourned him deeply.

In 1570 Tasso accompanied the cardinal to Paris, where he
may have met Ronsard. Returning to Ferrara in April 1571,
he wrote his incisive *Observations on the State of France,* and
soon after for obscure reasons left the service of the cardinal.
That very year he was employed by Duke Alfonso II, the
cardinal's brother, on a temporary basis until January 1572,
when he was assigned a regular salary and a personal servant.
He was very proud of the fact that, unlike the other poets at
court, Battista Guarini (author of the *Pastor Fido,* 1590), and
Giambattista Pigna, he was given no other duties than to write
verse. He firmly anticipated that his studies and writing
would bring him glory; his declared goal was "pleasure and
honor." In 1573 he composed his pastoral *Aminta,* an im-
mediate success which was to be translated and imitated
throughout Europe for generations to come. Tasso was re-
warded with the honorary title of lecturer on geometry.

The *Aminta* (1573), which Tasso called a "pastoral fable,"
is lyrical in inspiration, dramatic in form. It was written in
two months at a time when Tasso felt more dominant than
dominated at court. Extremely musical, consistently excel-
lent and more nearly perfect in its genre than the *Gerusa-
lemme,* it presents a series of exquisite pictures: Aminta falling
in love with Silvia, whose kisses he artfully steals; Silvia
admiring her reflection in a pool; again Silvia, shy and hostile,

freed by Aminta from the satyr who has bound her nude to a tree; and her pity at last for Aminta, which quickly becomes love. The play is an idealization of — rather than a flight from — life at court with its civility and refined sensibility, projected into a world of myth where only gentle and delicate sentiments can survive. Even the satyr, ostensibly the embodiment of feral lust, is a sensitive, madrigalizing creature. Among these noble emotions the dominant one is love, the supreme law of life. Contrasting with Aminta's quest for Silvia's affection is the bantering, yet voluptuous dialogue of Tirsi (Thyrsis), a disillusioned epicure, and Dafne. The will toward pleasure in both characters and chorus goes beyond any restrictive norm. The expression of love both in dialogue and in plot, combined with the poem's rare lyricism and charming simplicity, creates an unsurpassed example of the idyllic and hedonistic ideal of the Renaissance.

Tasso completed the writing of the *Gerusalemme* in 1575. Thus at the age of thirty-one he was riding the lustrous crest of a superb career. Yet in the same year of 1575 a certain restlessness seemed to foreshadow the onset of his psychosis. The duke had firmly prohibited his courtiers to seek other service without his permission. Tasso, however, tried unsuccessfully to negotiate his entry into the Medici court in Florence — the court with which the Este family was in sharpest rivalry.

For some reason, perhaps as a result of the Jesuit stress on obedience, he never completely trusted his own mental faculties, whether in religion, in philosophy, or in poetry; he once complained that philosophy taught him not "to live, but to question." He submitted the text of his epic poem to the judgment of friends and critics. As a poet he could only partially accept their cavilling criticisms; but as a theorist who shared their Neo-Aristotelian orientation he took their niggling commentaries to heart in an effort to avoid public criticism. Fearing that the imprimatur might be denied him because of religious or moral objections or the excessive representation of love and magic in the *Gerusalemme*, he attempted to justify such episodes in the *Allegory of the Jerusalem Delivered* which he wrote in June of 1576. Actually the poem's sensuality is innocuous by Ariosto's standards or our own; but an avowedly religious epic was naturally subject to post-Tridentine religious censure. One of his critics, Silvio Antoniano, professor of eloquence in Rome and a future cardinal, wrote

Tasso, "If you wished to write a religious poem, you should have written a poem that could go even into the hands of nuns."

From about 1576 until his death in 1595 Tasso suffered from a mental illness which was characterized by depression, delusions of persecution, occasional hallucinations, and the fear that he was guilty of heresy. He suspected that enemies and spies were everywhere, that his room was ransacked by an evil genie, that his correspondence was intercepted. He guessed nervously that the Inquisitor who examined him in Ferrara at his own request had absolved him falsely so as to leave him in a state of sin. A letter which he wrote during this period to the Cardinals of the Inquisition in Rome illustrates the extent of his suspicion and fear:

> Torquato Tasso, the most humble servant of Your Most Illustrious Lordships, entered during the past months into the firmest opinion that he had been accused to the Holy Office, because he noticed that by subtle ruses he had been made to possess beyond any intention of his, certain forbidden books. Beyond that the suppliant was himself aware of having said to certain persons — who later were revealed as his enemies, the confidants and employees of persons of great importance, by whom he has been much persecuted — certain very scandalous words which could occasion some doubt concerning his faith. Now the suppliant having presented himself, he was absolved rather as erring [*peccante*] by a melancholy humor than as one suspected of heresy . . . He believes that the Father Inquisitor did not wish to forward his trial documents, in order that the lord Duke of Ferrara, his Lord, might not learn of the persecutions suffered by the suppliant in his State, His Highness wishing not only to see the witnesses, but the names also of those who depose against anyone in the Holy Office. Whence at last for this reason, and for another dependent upon it, the suppliant has been confined as one transgressing in melancholy humor and has been purged against his will. Fearing to be poisoned in that purge and fearing further that some grave imputation concerning him may be made to His Highness to prevent his [the latter's] becoming aware of the uncertainty of the sentence, he entreats Your Most Illustrious Lordships to inform His Highness, so that having been accused and not being entirely absolved by the sentence given in Ferrara, he may again have his freedom and abandon his continual suspicion of death and come to Rome . . . to cleanse himself and satisfy his honor and peace . . .

This unhappy letter is cogent documentation of his incipient paranoia. He is surrounded by his accusers; and to make matters worse, he himself has doubts regarding his faith which only the Inquisitors of the Eternal City can judge and absolve, and perhaps not even they. On June 17, 1577, thinking, perhaps with some reason, that a servant was spying on him, he attacked him with a knife. Though confined in the convent of St. Francis, he succeeded the following month in escaping. Having made his way to Sorrento, he greeted his sister Cornelia, who did not recognize him in his shepherd's clothing, with the news that her brother Torquato was dead. Reassured of her affection for him (she fainted) he then revealed his identity. From Rome in 1578 he negotiated a re-entry into the Este court, conditional upon his recognition that his suspicions of persecution were a result of his illness, a disorder which required medical treatment. Duke Alfonso argued that he certainly was not trying to murder Tasso; to do so, he said, would have presented little difficulty —a declaration which could not have reassured the nervous poet greatly. Within a few months Tasso left Ferrara for Turin. Returning in February 1579 during the festivities of Duke Alfonso's third marriage (to Margherita Gonzaga), he felt offended that no one was paying attention to him and burst out with violent insults directed at the duke and his court. He was promptly imprisoned in the *Ospedale di Sant'Anna*.

The details of Tasso's seven-year imprisonment have been the subject of much speculation. From the dubious conjectures of an early biographer, Gianbattista Manso (*Vita di Torquato Tasso, Venice,* 1621), there arose the romantic myth of the poet's passionate love for Leonora d'Este, the Duke's sister, which inspired among other works Goethe's fine Romantic drama *Torquato Tasso* (1790). For the entire nineteenth century throughout all of Europe, until the publication of Angelo Solerti's exhaustive biography in 1895, Tasso was the personification of the poet-genius unjustly incarcerated by a wicked tyrant for daring to love the latter's sister. There is scant evidence that Tasso loved any woman — let alone the princess Leonora — beyond the limits of courtly gallantry. The only reason for his commitment to Sant'Anna was his insanity. There is well-founded suspicion, however, that

Duke Alfonso had another reason for fearing Tasso's release. Tasso wished to take his religious doubts to Rome; he suspected not only himself, but others at the Este court, of heresy. The duke's mother, Renée of Valois, daughter of Louis XII, had been exiled from Ferrara in 1560 after her conversion to Calvinism. Any renewal of the Curia's suspicions of heresy could have adversely affected the succession in Ferrara which in the absence of direct heirs Alfonso was trying to secure against Papal encroachment. It is noteworthy that after Tasso's imprisonment the duke never wished to see him again. The poet's lucidity, evidenced by a continual literary output, as well as the docility of his behavior following his eventual release, suggest that the confinement was excessively long for the severity of his condition.

The conditions of detention during the first year were harsh. He wrote to Scipione Gonzaga, ". . . I am able neither to write nor to act. And the fear of continuous imprisonment greatly increases my sadness, as do the indignity that I have to undergo and the squalor of my beard and hair and clothes; the dirt and filth bother me terribly. Above all I am afflicted by solitude, my cruel and persistent enemy . . . And I am sure that if he [Duke Alfonso] who has so scantly returned my affection saw me in such a state and in such affliction, he would feel some compassion for me." Thereafter he was treated more as a sick person than as a dangerous prisoner; in 1582, he was again sent food from the ducal kitchen. Incidentally, he was allowed visitors and occasional outings, thus belying the romantic legend of a Tasso enchained in a horrid cell for seven years. The following year he was allowed more frequent outings and even appearances in court. He was visited at Sant'Anna by princes, friends and famous literati. (Solerti disputes Montaigne's assertion that he visited Tasso, however.)

During his imprisonment the poet complained of "human and diabolic disorders." "The human ones," he wrote in a letter of October 18, 1581, "are shouts of men and particularly of women and children, and mocking laughter and various animal voices . . . and noises of inanimate things." Elsewhere he wrote, "I have heard frightful noises, and in my ears I often hear whistles, clinking, bells and a noise as of clocks [orologi da corda]; and often an hour is struck; and while I was sleeping it seemed to me that a horse fell upon me, and I felt somewhat bruised." In a letter of June 28, 1583, to the physician Girolamo Mercuriale he expressed the opinion that he had been "bewitched" [*ammaliato*].

Tasso was powerless to prevent the piracy of his *Gerusalemme* by unscrupulous publishers and well-meaning friends. In 1580 Celio Malespini published in Venice fourteen cantos of the *Gerusalemme Liberata* under the title *Il Goffredo* [*Godfrey*], after the central figure, Godfrey of Boulogne, leader of the First Crusade. Tasso's friend Angelo Ingegneri was thereby induced to publish the entire poem from one of many manuscript copies already in circulation, entitling it (against the author's wishes) *Gerusalemme Liberata*. The same year Febo Bonnà, another friend of Tasso, who had access to the autograph, published an edition in Ferrara. Five other editions followed in less than a year. It soon surpassed the *Orlando Furioso* in public favor and long remained the most popular of Italian narrative poems. (It was not until the nineteenth century that Dante, after centuries of relative obscurity, came into his own.) Not only was poor Tasso cheated of income; he saw his life's work published in shabby and incorrect editions before he could complete the polishing of his verses and the revision of the plot itself. It is indeed ironic that we owe to these piracies our possession of Tasso's masterpiece in the form in which successive generations have acclaimed it. The only version of the poem which Tasso ever willingly authorized was the sternly "corrected," not to say "emasculated," *Gerusalemme Conquistata* published in 1593.

The widespread acclaim which greeted the *Gerusalemme* in Italy and abroad was soon accompanied by carping and pedantic criticism. The Accademia della Crusca, most famous of the Italian academies, first became known because of its founders' criticisms of Tasso's epic. The Romantics with some justification portray the Academy as Tasso's second executioner, matching the "tyranny" of Alfonso with their own equally vicious "pedantry." Francesco de Sanctis wrote as follows in his *History of Italian Literature*:

> It was then that the Accademia della Crusca [Academy of Chaff] was formed, and it was the Council of Trent of our language. It too excommunicated writers and posited dogmas. And there came from it a disorder conceivable only in that idleness of minds.

> . . . The Accademia della Crusca considered the [Italian] language like Latin, that is to say as a language finished and closed in itself, so that there was nothing left to do except to make an inventory . . .

In a dialogue entitled *Il Carrafa o vero dell'epica poesia* [*Carrafa, or Of Epic Poetry*] (November 1584) Camillo Pellegrino, a canon of Capua, though finding some faults in Tasso's epic, asserted its superiority to the *Orlando furioso*. The fiercest of many literary quarrels in cinquecento Italy then began, with the refutation of Pellegrino's assertion in February 1585 by Leonardo Salviati and Bastiano de' Rossi in their *Difesa dell'Orlando furioso degli accademici della Crusca*, subtitled *Stacciata prima* (*First sifting*); in defending Ariosto they emphasized the defects of Tasso. (Salviati, it should be noted, wished at the time to enter the service of Duke Alfonso.) Francesco Patrizi, the leading Platonist of the day, refrained from disparaging Tasso directly, and confined himself to attacking points of Aristotelian theory. Orazio Ariosto generously defended not only his great-uncle Ludovico, but Tasso as well; he even defended old Bernardo Tasso, for good measure. And when the academicians were earning a bad reputation for their assault on Tasso, Bastiano de' Rossi drew attention to the harsh words about Florentines in Tasso's dialogue *Piacere onesto* (*Honest pleasure*).

In his *Apology* Tasso praised especially his father's *Amadigi*, leaving the defense of his own poem mainly to others. He pointed out that the critical words in his dialogue were spoken by an anti-Medici exile and that another character in it defended Florence and its people. In his *Discorso sopra il parere del Signor Francesco Patricio* he defended Aristotle against Patrizi's censures.

Lombardelli in his *Discorso intorno ai contrasti che si fanno sopra la Gerusalemme Liberata* [*Discourse about the quarrels over the Jerusalem Delivered*, 1956] summarized the charges of Pellegrino and the academicians, indicating by the letter "D" Pellegrino's charges in his *Dialogo*, by "C" those of the Crusca academy.

> I. That the *Jerusalem Delivered* is mere history without a plot [*favola*]. (C)
> II. That it is defiled by filth, carnal vices, homicides, affections and sins in saintly men and martyrs. (C)

III. That the poem is disproportionate, narrow, thin, sterile, dry, boring and unpleasant. (C)

IV. That it is void of marvelous inventions. (D)

V. That it is exceedingly obscure because of its laconic, distorted, forced, unusual and harsh style, whence it cannot be understood by the public at large. (D,C)

VI. That its language is excessively cultivated, especially in the rude and enamored characters. (D)

VII. That it is a mixture of Latin, pedantic, foreign, Lombard, new, compound, improper and makeshift words and modes, producing laughable sounds. (D,C)

VIII. That the verse is harsh and jerky . . . (C)

IX. That it could have a clearer and more florid diction. (D)

X. That it is inefficacious in its maxims. (D)

XI. That it sought to compete with Ariosto, Poliziano and Dante, but lost to all three. (C)

XII. That in moving the affections it is unsuccessful, lacking in imitation, dry, forced, cold, invalid, inept and strained. (C)

XIII. That in its similes it is low and pedantic. (C)

XIV. That it could demonstrate better morals. (D)

XV. That Rinaldo is too young and that there are lapses of memory. (D)

XVI. That it will never be imitated; it will soon be neglected, and if discussion about it ceases, it cannot be revived. (C)

Most of these allegations are patently spurious. History has belied the last charge; an unhurried reading of the poem will refute most of the others. Tasso thought Lombardelli's defense weak at points, and he declared in an embittered letter, "Nothing must be conceded to them, because they have wanted everything."

The harsh and uncompromising conduct of the quarrel by the chief Crusca disputants, Salviati and de' Rossi, showing no consideration for a stricken and unhappy man who by then was recognized as Italy's greatest living poet, is certainly open to criticism. Salviati later admitted that he had written "solely for punctilio" — and not always his true opinions! There is, however, a deeply rooted historical reason for their polemic. Tasso in temperament and intent and frequently in language represented a challenge to Florentine hegemony in Italian poetry. Though both Ariosto and Tasso were non-Tuscans who wrote for Este patrons in Ferrara, the finely attuned Florentine ear could accept the *Orlando furioso* with an enthusiasm which the occasional provincialisms and flaws of diction in the *Gerusalemme* did not permit.° Galilei among others preferred the simplicity and naturalness of Ariosto to the declamatory style, the antitheses and the baroque conceits of Tasso. Yet Tasso's verses are more musical than Ariosto's — an important reason for his wider popularity. Ariosto was more urbane, his vocabulary richer and, in the last edition of the *Orlando* (1532), more Florentine. For all of Tasso's popularity, Ariosto was and is the poet of the intellectual elite; the *Orlando Furioso,* devoid of strong patriotic and religious ideals, achieves in its marvelously unreal world of enchanted castles and deluded knights a unique poetic expression of human wisdom.

Although the onset of Tasso's psychosis marked the end of his finest creativity, he continued to write a great deal. Twenty-two of his thirty-one *Dialogues* were written during his confinement in Sant'Anna. He wrote a great many letters and poems to princes and prelates in hope of liberation. In the seven-year period he composed some six hundred and fifty poems.

Finally, in July 1586 Vincenzo Gonzaga of Mantua, Duke Alfonso's brother-in-law, secured the conditional release of Tasso into his custody, promising to take precautions against the poet's escape. Tasso at first took great pleasure in going about the city of Mantua under the surveillance of a single servant. Spells of depression, however, kept recurring. In 1587 he declined an offer to teach Aristotle's *Ethics* and *Poetics* at the *Accademia degli Addormentati* (Academy of the Sleeping) of Genoa. In the same year he published a slow-moving tragedy, the *Re Torrismondo,* modeled upon Sophocles' *Oedipus Rex.* He made brief trips to Bergamo, Modena, Bologna and Loreto before going to Rome, from where Vincenzo Gonzaga, now Duke of Mantua, sought to recall him. A return by force was prevented by Pope Sixtus V; Duke Alfonso, probably believing that the Holy Office would not now take seriously any charges of heresy which the poet might

---

° By 1691, a century and more after the quarrel, the definitive Crusca *Dictionary* had incorporated a great many of Tasso's expressions.

bring against his court, renounced his claim to the custody of
Tasso.

In 1588 the poet expressed his gratitude for the hospitality
of the monks of Monte Oliveto in Naples with an unfinished
poem in *ottava rima* on the origins of the monastery, *Il Monte
Oliveto,* published posthumously in 1605. His efforts in
Naples to recover his maternal inheritance proved fruitless.
Still unhappy and suspicious, Tasso in his declining years un-
ashamedly sought recognition and monetary rewards for the
encomiastic poems which he addressed to every prospective
protector. He experienced an imbalance between his social
condition and his high ambitions and humanistic self-esteem;
as a poet for all ages who could render his patrons immortal,
he found any recompense no more than adequate. From
November 1588 until May 1592 he was frequently the guest
of his long-time friend and protector, Scipione Gonzaga, now
a cardinal. In 1591 during a period of illness in Mantua he
wrote in *ottava rima* the *Genealogia di casa Gonzaga,* pub-
lished in 1666. In gratitude for the hospitality of Pope
Clement VIII, he dedicated the *Gerusalemme Conquistata*
to him upon its publication in 1593. Frequently ill, he de-
scribed himself as "dead," and said that while philosophy
might counsel liberation through suicide, his hand was stayed
by the Christian faith. During the last three years of his life
he composed the *Sette giorni del mondo creato* (*Seven days
of the created world*), in blank verse, and other sacred poems.

While in Naples he received an invitation from Clement
VIII to return to Rome in order to be crowned poet laureate.
He spent several months in the Vatican, and was rewarded
at last with an adequate pension. Ill health prevented the
coronation. His last weeks were spent in the monastery of
Sant'Onofrio on the Janiculum.

From Sant'Onofrio during his last days he penned a moving
letter to Antonio Costanini, a literary friend and admirer:

> What will my Sir Anthony say when he hears of the death
> of his Tasso? And in my opinion the news will not be long
> in coming, because I feel that I am at the end of my life, no
> remedy having ever been found for this troublesome indis-
> position of mine, added to my usual ills. I clearly see that
> I am carried away as though by a rapid torrent against which
> there can be no impediment. It is no longer a time for me to

speak of my obstinate fortune, not to mention the ingratitude of the world which has indeed wished to achieve the victory of taking me penniless to my grave. I thought that the glory which, despite those who wish otherwise, this age will derive from my writings, would not leave me without any sort of reward. I have caused myself to be brought to this monastery of Sant'Onofrio not only because its air is praised by the physicians more than that of any other part of Rome, but as if to begin from this eminent place and with the conversation of these devout fathers my conversation in heaven. Pray God for me, and be sure that just as I have always honored you in the present life, so will I do for you in the other and truer life that which pertains to true and unfeigned charity. To divine grace I recommend you and myself.

His troubled life came to an end on April 25, 1595. The Pope decreed highest honors for his funeral, which was attended by all of the literati in Rome; the laurel crown was placed on his coffin.

Tasso's biography is significant as a social barometer of late sixteenth-century Italy. Psychoanalysts today observe in the mentally ill exaggerated reactions to the pressures to which all men are subjected.° For all of his manifest desire to conform scrupulously to the rules of poetic composition and of religious conduct, his inner spirit rebelled against fixed rules. In theory and to an extent in practice he upheld the Aristotelian unities; yet his most genuine poetry is episodic. He inclined now toward Lorenzo's gaiety and hedonism, now toward Savonarola's repression, personifying the post-Tridentine conflict between sensuality and rigid authority. He sought and then resented the advice of critical "authorities." The same ambivalence is discernible in his wavering and irresolute attitude toward the court — both the abstract *inique corti* (wicked courts, *Gerus. Lib.* VII, 12) and the court of Ferrara where he now effusively courted Duke Alfonso's favor, now inveighed against him.

There was, in Tasso's time, a growing dependence on rigor and rigidity in human relations. The saints of the Counter Reformation are not known to be revolutionaries: St. Ignatius of Loyola (1491-1556) and St. Teresa of Avila

° The analysis of mental illnesses has even been employed as an instrument for determining societal characteristics. See Herbert Hendin, *Suicide in Scandinavia,* New York, 1963.

(1515-1582) stressed obedience to authority. Giovanni Botero's *Ragion di stato* (1589) emphasized the preservation of the state rather than its creation, as in Machiavelli's *Prince* (1513). The Council of Trent (1545-1563) increased the authority of the Pope, emphasized the power of the sacraments *per se,* instituted vigorous disciplinary reforms and established the Index on a regular and unitary basis.

Neither in literature nor in religion nor in life at court, then, could the rules of conduct be broken lightly. In each case Tasso vehemently declared his desire to conform; yet the strictness of the rules exacted a heavy toll from the unfortunate poet, who actually courted trouble with both religious and literary authorities. Historians are still debating whether the triumph of authority in the sixteenth century stifled philosophical and scientific and literary creativity in Italy in the decades and centuries which followed.

Tasso's most spontaneous poetry in the *Gerusalemme* is sensual and sentimental. The earlier *Aminta* is openly hedonistic: the rule of nature in the Golden Age, unworried by *onore* ("honor" in the sense of chastity), is *"S'ei piace, ei lice"* [If it is pleasurable, it is lawful]. Tasso's jovial letter of April 9, 1577 to his friend Scalabrini, reveals his predilection for the life of pleasure:

> . . . A plague on ill humor! Except that I'm a Christian in the main, I want to be completely epicurean in that which is not contrary to Christianity, and I say *Pereat qui crastina curat* [Let him perish who cares for tomorrow]. I study certain hours; the rest of the time I spend laughing, singing, trifling, but being familiar with very few persons; for I can tell you that I'm careful about my rank [*sto su la mia*]. And there's neither baron nor minister of the Duke, however great, who finds me ready with homage . . . People say, "Whence a countenance so gay and such reputation? Has he found a treasure?" Twice since I returned from Rome I've gone out to dine; and I can tell you I let them coax me. And then without any argument I accepted the chair at the head of table. I've had my nativity taken by three astrologers, all of whom, without knowing who I was, paint me *uno ore* [unanimously] as a great man of letters and promise me a very long life and the highest fortune . . . All agree in saying that I shall have great benefits from women.

Yet five days later, with a sudden darkening of mood, he wrote to his friend Scipione Gonzaga, urging him not to read "the amorous part" of the *Gerusalemme*:

I'm sure of having my poem printed in Venice, without changing anything, with the change of only a few words: but I am frightened by the example of Sigonio, who went into print with the license of the Inquisitor, and then his book was suspended; another example of Muzio related to me by Borghesi frightens me; the severity of Silvio Antoniano [the severest of the poem's would-be revisers] frightens me, as I imagine that there are many like him in Rome . . .

The half-century that elapsed between Ariosto's *Orlando* and Tasso's epic witnessed two events of singular importance for the latter: the creation of a large body of poetic theory based on the rediscovered *Poetics* of Aristotle, and the Council of Trent. Tasso wrote for an audience which was critically oriented toward "rules of poetry," rules of which his great predecessor was happily unaware; his generation generally considered poetry an instrument of moral philosophy. Tasso himself was a theorist of epic poetry even before he began writing the *Gerusalemme.* Following his father Bernardo, who had attempted to "elevate" the chivalric *Amadigi* to the rank of a heroic poem according to Aristotelian precepts by basing a unitary action upon a single "perfect" hero and by eliminating sensual allurements, Torquato took religion and history seriously, he stripped the supernatural of its aura of romance and referred it to celestial and infernal action, on which the plot was made to turn as in Homer. His conception of poetry was strongly influenced by the humanist tradition. The choice of an epic theme in itself, though made in accordance with Christian criteria, denotes a wish to emulate Virgil and Homer. He abandoned the technique which Ariosto took over from Boiardo of interweaving episodes to create suspense.

His six discourses *Del poema eroico* (1594), an amplification with erudite documentation of his three earlier discourses *Dell'arte poetica* (1570), declare that the end of heroic poetry is "to profit men with the example of human actions"; that the means for so doing is pleasure [*il diletto*], "but only that which is joined with honesty." The epic should be based on history that is neither very ancient nor very recent; the readers must be able to recognize themselves in the characters. The poet may alter the facts to suit his convenience, but must retain the final results as traditionally believed; he should be "rather an artful poet than a true historian." Some variety of episodes is not only permissible, but necessary. Ariosto's *Orlando* with the multiplicity of its plot is read by everyone; Giangiorgio Trissino's *Italia liberata dai Goti* (*Italy liberated from the Goths*) is neglected. The marvelous is a legitimate and necessary ingredient, but should be based upon the true faith, not only for religious reasons, but for the sake of verisimilitude. As history focuses upon the individual, so poetry embraces the universal. Hence the heroic world of the poet must present characters who are either "at the height of virtue" or "the excess of vice." In the name of decorum not only obscenity but humor is banned. The diction must be magnificent, the vocabulary "not common, but rare and removed from popular usage."

Although the discourses contain nothing novel and are quite typical of their time, their clear and programmatic statement exerted wide influence both in Italy and abroad. Their traditional character was indicative of Tasso's desire to conform to the most authoritative rules literarily and morally.

Despite the variety of episodes and passions, the poem envisioned by Tasso before he began its composition was to constitute a unitary world:

> . . . I judge that an excellent poet (who is called divine for the sole reason that resembling the supreme Artificer in his operations, he comes to participate in His divinity) can fashion a poem in which, as in a little world, one reads here of the disposition of armies, here of land and naval battles, the storming of cities, skirmishes and duels, here jousts, descriptions of famine and thirst, tempests, fires, prodigies; there may be found celestial and infernal councils, there may be seen sedition, discord, errors, adventures, enchantments; works of cruelty, audacity, courtesy, generosity; there incidents of love, now happy now unhappy, now joyful now pitiable; but that nevertheless the poem be one, although it contain such variety of materials; one its form and plot; and that all these things be composed in such fashion that . . . the one necessarily or verisimilarly depend on the other; so that a single part being either taken away or changed in place, the whole must ruin.

The *Gerusalemme* narrates the story of the First Crusade, led by Godfrey of Boulogne, which captured Jerusalem in July 1099. Its main outlines are historical, as are also the major warriors. Rinaldo is the poet's invention; the instrument of divine providence, he is also the mythical ancestor of Tasso's Este patrons. The choice of subject was appropriate to its time: the Counter-Reformation was in full operation and the battle of Lepanto (October 7, 1571) was a recent memory. The first canto opens when the war is already in its sixth year (historically, the third). Virgilian and Homeric reminiscences abound throughout the poem. As Jove sends Mercury to order Aeneas to leave Carthage, so the Almighty sends the archangel Gabriel to instruct Goffredo, who with the aid of Pier l'Eremita [Peter the Hermit] is elected supreme commander.

The episode of Olindo and Sofronia in the second canto illustrates Tasso's resourcefulness in transforming history and legend into poetry. William of Tyre relates that the Moslems, indignant at finding a dead dog in a mosque in Jerusalem, wanted to massacre the Christian community, until a young Christian came forward to declare his guilt. In the *Gerusalemme* it is the disappearance of an image of the Virgin, previously taken from the Christians at the behest of the magician Ismeno to protect the city, which prompts Sofronia's spurious confession, soon contradicted by that of her timid admirer, Olindo.

As Virgil's Trojans rejoice when they first see the Italian shore, so the Christians in Canto III greet the sight of Jerusalem with pious shouts of joy. And as Helen in the *Iliad* points out to Priam the warriors of Greece, so Erminia identifies the Christians for Aladino.

Tasso noted in a letter that "all the episodes derive" from the fourth canto. The appearance of the enchantress Armida in the Christian camp, asking Godfrey for ten knights to reconquer her kingdom from an alleged usurper, causes a breakdown in discipline, diabolically aggravated, which extends over many cantos and leads to the alienation of Rinaldo.

Canto VI thrusts the epic into the background and transports the reader into the chivalric and romantic world of Boiardo and Ariosto. Erminia, burning with love for the Christian knight Tancredi who has been wounded in a daylong duel with Argante, the fierce and sarcastic Circassian, leaves Jerusalem in disguise during the night in an unsuccessful attempt to reach her hero. Her pastoral interlude in the following canto takes us still further from the epos: the princess Erminia divests herself of royal attire, leads sheep to pasture, shapes cheese with her own hands, and carves the story of her love into the bark of beeches and laurels.

The war resumes in earnest in Canto IX as the Christians repel Solimano's nocturnal attack. As always in the battle scenes, classical reminiscences abound. The humanists' predilection for imitation still strongly influenced the taste of Tasso's courtly audience; and the monotonous thrusts of lance and sword which he described with careful attention to correctness of weapon-handling form were doubtless enjoyed by his contemporaries. The assault on Jerusalem in Canto XI following the return (Canto IX) of fifty Christian warriors liberated by Rinaldo (Canto X) from Circean bondage to Armida, incorporates more history, if less poetry, than most of the cantos.

Godfrey's wound and divinely effected cure are modeled upon the experience of *pius Aeneas* in Book XII of the *Aeneid*. The classical epics also suggested the foray beyond the city walls of Clorinda and Argante, who burn the Christians' assault tower. Mortally wounded by the unwitting Tancredi, who loves her passionately, Clorinda asks for baptism and achieves an affecting, Petrarchan "beautiful death." The building of a new tower, hampered by Ismeno's enchantment of the woods, must await the return of Rinaldo, whose sojourn with Armida in a sensual paradise in the Fortunate Isles is narrated in Cantos XIV, XV and XVI. Despite a structural flaw whereby Tasso tells parts of the story twice (in Cantos XIV and XVI), this episode of seduction and immoral bliss embodies Tasso's most brilliant poetry. It strongly influenced the second book of *The Faerie Queene*. Spenser in the "Bower of Bliss" (II, xii, 74-75) translates verbatim the famous description of the rose (XVI, 14-15) in which Tasso vied with Poliziano (*Stanze per la giostra* I, 78) and Ariosto (*Orlando furioso* I, 42-43). Even in this hedonistic setting, where echoes of Lorenzo's *"Quant' è bella giovinezza"* are still audible, there is a pervasive melancholy — the rose "then languisheth and dies in last extremes" (Fairfax) — which distinguishes Tasso's metaphor from Ariosto's and to a lesser degree from Poliziano's. As C. M. Bowra has ably demonstrated in *From Virgil to Milton*, Chap. IV, Spenser retells the story from a Puritanical point of view which denies Acrasie (his Armida) the reconciliation which Tasso permitted Armida. To Tasso's Latin mind, her sin was not so reprehensible as for Spenser; Counter Reformation morality demanded simply that her love be legitimized. In the final canto, despite her earlier rage at his return to duty (Canto XVI and following), he dissuades her from suicide. To his wish that Heaven would lift her "veil of paganism" she replies with words that presage her conversion — "*Ecco l'ancella tua*" ("Behold your handmaid"; Fairfax). As in Canto II Tasso intermixes religion and sensuality. After Rinaldo breaks the enchantment of the woods he and Godfrey storm the walls of Jerusalem (Canto XVIII); Tancredi slays Argante and, severely wounded, is attended by Erminia. A huge Egyptian army arriving in aid of Jerusalem's hard-pressed defenders is defeated in Canto XX, and Godfrey and his knights adore the Holy Sepulchre.

Although the Holy War provides the poem's formal framework, the poetic foci are undeniably the love stories. Godfrey is drawn consistently according to Tasso's concept of the Crusade's leader. For that very reason he appears negative and passionless in comparison with the other warriors. He stands, a saint, above the battle between pleasure and duty which animates Rinaldo and Tancredi — and which the author fought in his own soul.

Love in Ariosto's poem is healthy and physical; the *dolce stil nuovo* and Platonism are forgotten and perhaps occasionally mocked in the portrayal of Angelica, ironically named, and the knights who pursue her. In Tasso's poetry love is imaginative, voluptuous, dolorous, unsatisfied, almost a "sick love." His sensuality is studied and sometimes masked: one critic has characterized Ariosto as a painter of nude women, Tasso as a painter of half-dressed women. Ariosto depicts boldly the complete nudity first of Angelica and later of Olimpia bound to the reef as intended victims of the orc. One of the few brief passages in Tasso's epic which has been subject to censorship in Italian school editions is the description of a nymph rising before Rinaldo's eyes from a stream on Alcina's island (XIV, 60; repeated with variations in XV, 59):.

> Whence first he saw, with golden tresses, peep
> The rising visage of a virgin bright,
> And then her neck, her breasts, and all, as low
> As he for shame could see, or she could show.

For all his fervent desire to sing the faith of his times, he ends by singing his own credo: pleasure. This dichotomy ultimately produced two poems: the great *Liberata* and the un-read *Conquistata*.

While Rinaldo as Godfrey's ablest warrior is the epic hero, Tancredi, into whom Tasso infused more of himself than into any other character, is clearly the poem's sentimental hero:

No shameful vice his worth had overgone,
His fault was love, by unadvised sight,
Bred in the dangers of adventurous arms,
And nursed with griefs, with
          sorrows, woes, and harms.   (I,45)

Among the feminine characters Sofronia is perhaps the least successful. She has too much of the saint, too little feminin-ity; she never really comes alive as do Erminia, Armida, and even the Amazonian Clorinda. Armida is a more complete woman, certainly less of a witch, than Ariosto's Alcina. The duel between Honor and Love in Erminia (VI, 70-77) as she yearns for Tancredi supplies the element of conflict lacking in the representative women of earlier Italian literature.

There are elements of autobiography in many aspects of the *Gerusalemme*: the yearning for primacy and for boundless pleasure, tempered by stern moral restrictions; the transcend-ing of everyday life in choreographic spectacle, foreign ad-venture, idyllic retreat, and the quest of the unattainable; the tendency especially of the feminine characters toward self-pity; and the ubiquitous shadow of death.

Petrarch's pleasure in cherished sorrow reappears in Tasso, whose world is peopled by rebuffed or unknown lovers who live in their desperate dreams: Olindo, who is too timid to declare his love to Sofronia; Erminia, of whom Tancredi, enamored of the hostile Clorinda, is unaware; Armida, stung to vengeance by Rinaldo's abandonment, yet destined for rec-onciliation. Tasso's melancholy, as De Sanctis said, is deeper than Petrarch's. Elegiac renunciation prevails also in non-amatory situations: the Moslem warriors Argante and Soli-mano fight desperately against their irrevocable destiny, an-ticipating the heroes of Romantic literature. Tasso's best poetry is sentimental and pre-romantic. In his strained an-titheses and *bisticci* (puns and juxtapositions of words similar in sound) he heralds the arrival of *secentismo* (the "seven-teenth-century" affectation which began in the latter part of the sixteenth century). He is a poet of supreme mastery, whose theoretical framework and architecture in the *Gerusalemme* do not permit him a free range of creativity. However, the loves of Tancredi for Clorinda and of Erminia for Tancredi, dwelling like Petrarch's love of Laura in the bittersweet realm of contemplation, reach their heights in idyllic interludes tinged with sadness which presage Leopardi, and the eroticism of the *Aminta* and of Armida's island foreshadows Leopardi's immense desire for pleasure. Living in an age of rapid transition at the end of the Renaissance, Tasso brought to Italian poetry a new amorous sensibility: love which contemplates itself, not joyously but with a refined and sometimes tired sensuality (Dafne and Tirsi); a subjective and self-conscious love. More often in the *Aminta* than in the *Gerusalemme* it becomes tearful sentimentality. Woman is no longer wrapped in the angelic aura of an earlier period, and is the object of covetous lovers, but the love of woman fights hard in Tasso's divided soul for mastery over the epic quest; and almost wins.

Notes on the Translation

The *Gerusalemme Liberata* was translated in English octaves by Edward Fairfax (c. 1575-1635) in 1600. Fairfax's unit of translation is not the verse, but the stanza. Within that unit he takes extensive liberties in diction; yet the narrative remains unaltered. Tasso's refined comparisons and the conceits which delighted contemporary taste are generally rendered. For example, he writes of Clorinda and Tancredi, III, 23, "And so at once she threats to kill him twice" [with love and with the sword]. In the epic moment of the storming of Jerusalem Rinaldo replies to Solimano's challenge: "If here my life be spent,/I spend and spill . . . my blood in vain!" As English words and sentences are generally shorter than their Italian equivalents, Fairfax frequently resorts to doubling and tripling Tasso's nouns and adjectives. He takes the further liberty of adding mythological embellishments which Tasso excluded on principle from his Christian epic.

Fairfax was a poet in his own right, as good verse translators must be. He wrote twelve eclogues, only three of which survive, but he is best known for the Tasso translation which he dedicated to Queen Elizabeth and which was later valued highly by King James. Spenser's *Faerie Queene*, which borrows freely from Tasso's poem, was published in

1590 and 1596: Fairfax in turn borrows words and images from Spenser and like the latter makes use of archaic words. Dryden praised him highly, coupling his name with Spenser's. There are traces of him in Milton and in Edmund Waller's *Instructions to a Painter* (1666).

January 31, 1963

John Charles Nelson
Columbia University

Select Bibliography (Compiled by Joann Soloff)

WORKS IN ITALIAN

Albertazzo, Adolfo, *Torquato Tasso* 2nd Ed. Roma. Formiggini, 1926

Belloni, Antonio, *Gli epigoni della Gerusalemme Liberata,* Padova. A. Draghi, 1893

Capasso, Aldo, *Studi sul Tasso minore,* Roma. Albrighi e Segati, 1940

Capuani, Antonio, *Torquato Tasso.* Milano. Fratelli Treves, 1935

Cardarelli, Vincenzo, "Il Tasso uomo," *Fiera letteraria* (Roma) July 2, 1950

Caretti, Lanfranco, "Sul Gierusalemme" *Filologia e critica* (Milano-Napoli, R. Ricciardi, 1955)

Caterbi, Giuseppe, *La chiesa di S. Onofrio e le sue tradizioni religiose, storiche, artistiche e letterarie.* Roma. Tipografia forense, 1858, partequinta, pp. 147-223

Di Pietro, Antonio, *Il noviziato di T. Tasso.* Milano, Malfassi, 1953

Donadoni, Eugenio, *Torquato Tasso.* Firenze, La Nuova Italia, 1946

Flora, Francesco, *I discorsi del poema eroico di T. Tasso.* Milano, Malfasi, 1951

Fubino, Mario, "Il Rinaldo del Tasso" Leonardo VIII (1937) pp. 185-194

Getto, Giovanni, *Interpretazione del Tasso.* Napoli. Edizioni scientifiche italiane, 1951

Guerrieri-Crocetti, Camillo, *Il Rinaldo di T. Tasso..* Firenze. Vallechi, 1924

Iseo, Giuseppe, *Discorso . . . sopra il poema di M. Torquato Tasso* in Galilei, *Considerazioni al Tasso,* pp. 106-202

Manso, Giovanni Battista, *Vita di Torquato Tasso; divisa in tre parte.* Roma. Cavelli, 1634

Pico, Puglisi, *Il Tasso nella critica francese.* Acireale. Donzuso, 1896

Pool, Franco, *Desiderio e realtà nella poesia del Tasso, Padova.* Liviana editrici, 1960 (includes bibliography)

Raya, Gino, *Poeta del rinascimento . . .* Catania, Guaitolini, 1929

Scuderi, E., "La conscienza critica del Tasso," *La Voce Repubblicana* (Rome) January 16 and 17, 1954

Serassi, Pietro Antonio, *La vita di Torquato Tasso . . .* Roma. Stamperia Pagliarini, 1785

Solerti, Angelo, *Vita di Torquato Tasso.* Roma. Loescher, 1895

Sozzi, B. T., *Studi sul Tasso.* Pisa. Nistri-Lischi, 1954

Tonelli, Luigi, . . . *Tasso.* Torino, G. B. Paravia & c., 1935 (bibliography p. 349)

Vailati, M., *Il tormento artistico del Tasso dalla Liberata alla Conquistata.*

Milano. C. Marzorati, 1950

Vismara, Felici, *L'animo di Torquato Tasso rispecchiato ne suoi scritti; . . .* Milano. Hoepli, 1895 (includes bibliography)

Vivaldi, Vincenzo, *Prolegomeni ad uno studio completo sulle fonti della Gerusalemme Liberata.* Trani. V. Vecchi, 1904

Additional bibliographical materials may be found in *Studi tassiani.*

WORKS IN GERMAN

Geisel, Judith, *Tasso und sein Gefolge.* Berlin, Paul, 1911

Koeppel, Emil, "Die englischen Tassoubersetzungen des XVI Jahrhunderts" *Anglia* XI (1889) pp. 341-362

Leo, Ulrich, *Ritterepos-Gottesepos: Torquato Tassos Weg als Dichter,* Kolh. Bohlau, 1958

————,*Torquato Tasso: studien zur Vorgeschichte des Secentismo, Bern.* A. Francke, 1951

Pommrich, Ewald, *Miltons Verhaltnis zu Torquato Tasso.* Halle a.S., Karras, 1902

Tribolet, Hans, *Wielands Verhaltnis zur Ariost und Tasso,* Bern. Francke, 1919

Wagner, Hedwig, *Tasso daheim und in Deutschland,* Berlin, 1905

WORKS IN FRENCH

Beall, Chandler Baker, *Chateaubriand et le Tasse* Baltimore, Johns Hopkins Press, 1934 (also Oxford U. Press) (includes bibliography) (see also Johns Hopkins Press *Studies in Romantic Literatures and Languages* v. XXIV

————, "La Fortune de Tasse en France" in *University of Oregon Monographs, Studies in Literature and Philology* No. 4 pp. 1-308 (bibliography pp. 277-299)

Cottaz, Joseph, *L'influence des theories du Tasse sur l'epopee en France,* Paris, R. Foulon, 1942 (includes bibliography)

————, *Le Tasse et la conception epique,* Paris. Foulton, 1942 (includes bibliography)

WORKS IN ENGLISH

Aguzzi, Danilo L., *Allegory in the Heroic Poetry of the Renaissance,* unpublished thesis, Columbia, 1959

Black, John, *Life of Torquato Tasso; with an historical and critical account of his writings,* 2v. Edinburgh, 1910

Boulting, William, *Tasso and his Times,* New York. G. Putnam and Sons, 1907

Bowra, Cecil Maurice, *From Virgil to Milton,* London, Macmillan and Co., 1957

Blanchard, H. S., *Imitations from Tasso in the Fairie Queene,* Berkley, 1925

————, "Gerusalemme Liberata" *PMLA XLV* (1930)

Grillo, Giacomo, *Poets at the Court of Ferrara,* Boston. The Excelsior Press, Inc., 1943 (includes bibliography)

Hoole, John, trans., *Jerusalem Delivered with life of Tasso* (various prefaces, in the 1788 v.l, the 1797 v.i, the 1803 v.l.)

Weinberg, Bernard, *History of Literary Criticism in the Italian Renaissance* 2 v. U. of Chicago, 1961

Wilde, R. H., *Conjectures and researches concerning the love, madness and imprisonment of Torquato Tasso,* N.Y., Blake, 1942

BOOK I.

THE ARGUMENT.

God sends his Angel to Tortosa down,
  Godfrey unites the Christian peers and knights,
And all the Lords and Princes of renown
  Choose him their Duke, to rule the wars and fights;
He mustereth all his host, whose number known
  He sends them to the fort that Sion heights;
The aged Tyrant Judah's land that guides
In fear and trouble to resist provides.

I.

THE sacred armies and the godly knight
  That the great sepulchre of Christ did free
I sing; much wrought his valor and foresight,
  And in that glorious war much suffer'd he:
In vain 'gainst him did hell oppose her might,
  In vain the Turks and Morians armed be;
His soldiers wild, to brawls and mutines prest,
Reduced he to peace; so heaven him blest.

II.

O heavenly muse, that not with fading bays
  Deckest thy brow by th' Heliconian spring,
But sittest, crown'd with stars' immortal rays,
  In heaven, where legions of bright angels sing,
Inspire life in my wit, my thoughts upraise,
  My verse ennoble, and forgive the thing,
If fictions light I mix with truth divine,
And fill these lines with others' praise than thine.

2

III.

Thither thou know'st the world is best inclined
   Where luring Parnass most his sweet imparts,
And truth convey'd in verse of gentle kind,
   To read perhaps will move the dullest hearts;
So we, if children young diseas'd we find,
   Anoint with sweets the vessel's foremost parts,
To make them taste the potions sharp we give;
They drink deceived; and so deceiv'd they live.

IV.

Ye noble princes, that protect and save
   The pilgrim muses, and their ship defend
From rock of ignorance and error's wave,
   Your gracious eyes upon this labor bend;
To you these tales of love and conquests brave
   I dedicate, to you this work I send,
My muse hereafter shall perhaps unfold
Your fights, your battles, and your combats bold.

V.

For if the Christian princes ever strive
   To win fair Greece out of the tyrant's hands,
And those usurping Ismaelites deprive
   Of woful Thrace, which now captived stands,
You must from realms and seas the Turks forth drive,
   As Godfrey chased them from Judah's lands,
And in this legend, all that glorious deed
Read, whilst you arm you: arm you, whilst you read.

VI.

Six years were run, since first, in martial guise,
   The Christian lords warray'd the eastern land,
Nice by assault, and Antioch by surprise,
   Both fair, both rich, both won, both conquer'd stand,
And this defended they, in noblest wise,
   'Gainst Persian knights and many a valiant band;
Tortosa won, lest winter might them shend,
They drew to holds, and coming spring attend.

VII.

The sullen season now was come and gone,
   That forc'd them, late, cease from their noble war,
When God Almighty from his lofty throne,
   Set in those parts of heaven that purest are,

As far above the clear stars every one,
　　As it is hence up to the highest star,
Look'd down, and all at once this world behield,
Each land, each city, country, town and field.

VIII.

All things he view'd, at last in Syria stay'd
　　Upon the Christian lords, his gracious eye ;
That wondrous look wherewith he oft survey'd
　　Men's secret thoughts that most concealed lie,
He cast on puissant Godfrey, that assay'd
　　To drive the Turks from Sion's bulwarks high,
And, full of zeal and faith, esteemed light
All worldly honor, empire, treasure, might.

IX.

In Baldwin next he spied another thought,
　　Whom spirits proud to vain ambition move :
Tancred he saw his life's joy set at naught,
　　So wo-begone was he with pains of love :
Boemond the conquer'd folk of Antioch brought
　　The gentle yoke of Christian rule to prove,
He taught them laws, statutes, and customs new,
Arts, crafts, obedience, and religion true ;

X.

And with such care his busy work he plied,
　　That to naught else his acting thoughts he bent.
In young Rinaldo fierce desires he spied,
　　And noble heart, of rest impatient,
To wealth or sovereign power he naught applied
　　His wits, but all to virtue excellent,
Patterns and rules of skill and courage bold
He took from Guelpho, and his fathers old.

XI.

Thus, when the Lord discover'd had and seen
　　The hidden secrets of each worthy's breast,
Out of the hierarchies of angels sheen
　　The gentle Gabriel called he from the rest ;
'Twixt God and souls of men that righteous been
　　Ambassador is he, for ever blest,
The just commands of heaven's eternal King,
'Twixt skies and earth, he up and down doth bring.

XII.

To whom the Lord thus spake, Godfredo find,
  And in my name ask him, why doth he rest ?
Why be his arms to ease and peace resign'd ?
  Why frees he not Jerusalem distress'd ?
His peers to counsel call, each baser mind
  Let him stir up ; for, chieftain of the rest
I choose him here, the earth shall him allow,
His fellows late shall be his subjects now.

XIII.

This said, the angel swift himself prepar'd
  To execute the charge impos'd aright :
In form of airy members fair embar'd,
  His spirits pure were subject to our sight ;
Like to a man in show and shape he far'd,
  But full of heav'nly majesty and might,
A stripling seem'd he thrice five winters old,
And radiant beams adorn'd his locks of gold.

XIV.

Of silver wings he took a shining pair,
  Fringed with gold, unwearied, nimble, swift,
With these he parts the winds, the clouds, the air,
  And over seas and earth himself doth lift ;
Thus clad, he cuts the spheres and circles fair,
  And the pure skies with sacred feathers clift,
On Libanon at first his foot he set,
And shook his wings with rory May-dews wet.

XV.

Then to Tortosa's confines swiftly sped
  The sacred messenger, with headlong flight :
Above the eastern wave appeared red
  The rising sun, yet scantly half in sight ;
Godfrey e'en then his morn devotions said,
  As was his custom, when, with Titan bright,
Appear'd the angel, in his shape divine,
Whose glory far obscured Phœbus' shine.

XVI.

Godfrey (quoth he), behold the season fit
  To war, for which thou waited hast so long,
Now serves the time, if thou o'erslip not it,
  To free Jerusalem from thrall and wrong :

Thou with thy lords in counsel quickly sit,
  Comfort the feeble, and confirm the strong,
The Lord of Hosts their general doth make thee,
And for their chieftain they shall gladly take thee.

XVII.

I, messenger from everlasting love,
  In his great name thus his behests do tell,
Oh! what sure hope of conquest ought thee move!
  What zeal, what love, should in thy bosom dwell!
This said, he vanish'd to those seats above,
  In height and clearness which the rest excel;
Down fell the Duke, his joints dissolv'd asunder,
Blind with the light, and stricken dead with wonder.

XVIII.

But, when recover'd, he consider'd more
  The man, his manner, and his message said;
If erst he wished, now he longed sore
  To end that war, whereof he lord was made:
Nor swell'd his breast with uncouth pride therefore,
  That heav'n on him above this charge had laid,
But, for his great Creator would the same,
His will increas'd; so fire augmenteth flame.

XIX.

The captains called forthwith from every tent,
  Unto the rendezvous he them invites,
Letter on letter, post on post he sent,
  Entreatance fair with counsel he unites;
All, what a noble courage could augment,
  The sleeping spark of valor what incites,
He us'd, that all their thoughts to honor rais'd,
Some prais'd, some prayed, some counselled, all pleas'd.

XX.

The captains, soldiers, all (save Boemond) came,
  And pitch'd their tents, some in the fields without,
Some of green boughs their slender cabins frame,
  Some lodged were Tortosa's streets about;
Of all the host the chief of worth and name
  Assembled been, a senate grave and stout,
Then Godfrey, after silence kept a space,
Lift up his voice, and spake with princely grace.

XXI.

Warriors, whom God himself elected hath
  His worship true in Sion to restore,
And still preserv'd from danger, harm, and scath,
  By many a sea and many an unknown shore,
You have subjected lately to his faith
  Some provinces rebellious long before ;
And, after conquests great, have in the same
Erected trophies to his cross and name.

XXII.

But not for this our homes we first forsook,
  And from our native soil have march'd so far :
Nor us to dangerous seas have we betook,
  Exposed to hazard of so far-sought war,
Of glory vain to gain an idle smook,
  And lands possessed that wild and barbarous are :
That for our conquests were too mean a prey,
To shed our blood, to work our souls' decay.

XXIII.

But this the scope was of our former thought,
  Of Sion's fort to scale the noble wall,
The Christian folk from bondage to have brought,
  Wherein, alas, they long have lived thrall,
In Palestine an empire to have wrought
  Where godliness might reign perpetual,
And none be left, that pilgrims might denay
To see Christ's tomb, and promis'd vows to pay.

XXIV.

What to this hour successively is done
  Was full of peril, to our honor small ;
Naught to our first designment, if we shun
  The purpos'd end, or here lie fixed all :
What boots it us these wars to have begun,
  Or Europe rais'd to make proud Asia thrall,
If our beginnings have this ending known,
Not kingdoms rais'd, but armies overthrown ?

XXV.

Not as we list erect we empires new
  On frail foundations, laid in earthly mould,
Whereof our faith and country be but few,
  Among the thousands stout of pagans bold,

Where naught behoves us trust to Greece untrue,
 And western aid we far remov'd behold ;
Who buildeth thus, methinks, so buildeth he,
As if his work should his sepulchre be.

XXVI.

Turks, Persians, conquer'd, Antiochia won,
 Be glorious acts, and full of glorious praise,
By heav'n's mere grace, not by our prowess, done,
 Those conquests were achiev'd by wondrous ways :
If now from that directed course we run
 The God of battles thus before us lays,
His loving kindness shall we lose, I doubt,
And be a by-word to the lands about.

XXVII.

Let not these blessings then, sent from above,
 Abûsed be, or spilt in profane wise,
But let the issue correspondent prove
 To good beginnings of each enterprise ;
The gentle season might our courage move,
 Now every passage plain and open lies :
What lets us then the great Jerusalem
 With valiant squadrons round about to hem ?

XXVIII.

Lords, I protest ; and hearken all to it,
 Ye times and ages, future, present, past ;
Hear all ye blessed in the heavens that sit,
 The time for this achievement hasteneth fast :
The longer rest worse will the season fit,
 Our surety shall with doubts be overcast,
If we foreslow the siege, I well foresee
From Egypt will the pagans succor'd be.

XXIX.

This said, the hermit Peter rose and spake
 (Who sat in counsel those great lords among),
At my request this war was undertake,
 In private cell who erst liv'd closed long ;
What Godfrey wills, of that no question make,
 There cast no doubts where truth is plain and strong,
Your acts, I trust, will correspond his speech,
Yet one thing more I would you gladly teach.

XXX.

These strifes, unless I far mistake the thing,
  And discords rais'd, oft in disorder'd sort,
Your disobedience, and ill-managing
  Of actions, lost for want of due support,
Refer I justly to a further spring,
  Spring of sedition, strife, oppression, tort,
I mean commanding power to sundry given,
In thought, opinion, worth, estate, uneven.

XXXI.

Where divers Lords divided empire hold,
  Where causes be by gifts, not justice, tried,
Where offices be falsely bought and sold,
  Needs must the lordship there from virtue slide.
Of friendly parts one body then uphold,
  Create one head the rest to rule and guide,
To one the regal power and sceptre give,
That henceforth may your king and sovereign live

XXXII.

And therewith stayed his speech.   O gracious muse,
  What kindling motions in their breasts do fry !
With grace divine the hermit's talk infuse,
  That in their hearts his words may fructifie ;
By this a virtuous concord they did choose,
  And all contentions then began to die ;
The princes with the multitude agree,
That Godfrey ruler of those wars should be.

XXXIII.

This power they gave him, by his princely right
  All to command, to judge all, good and ill,
Laws to impose to lands subdued by might,
  To maken war both when and where he will,
To hold in due subjection every wight,
  Their valors to be guided by his skill ;
This done, report displays her tell-tale wings,
And to each ear the news and tidings brings.

XXXIV.

She told the soldiers, who allow'd him meet,
  And well deserving of that sovereign place ;
Their first salutes and acclamations sweet
  Received he, with love and gentle grace ;

After, their reverence done, with kind regreet
   Requited was: with mild and cheerful face,
He bids his armies should, the following day,
On those fair plains, their standards proud display.

XXXV.

The golden sun rose from the silver wave,
   And with his beams enamel'd every green,
When up arose each warrior bold and brave,
   Glist'ring in filed steel and armors sheen,
With jolly plumes their crests adorn'd they have,
   And all tofore their chieftain muster'd been:
He, from a mountain, cast his curious sight
On every footman, and on every knight.

XXXVI.

My mind, time's enemy, oblivion's foe,
   Disposer true of each note-worthy thing,
O let thy virtuous might avail me so,
   That I each troop and captain great may sing,
That in this glorious war did famous grow,
   Forgot till now, by time's evil handling:
This work, derived from thy treasures dear,
Let all times hearken, never age out-wear.

XXXVII.

The French came foremost battailous and bold,
   Late led by Hugo, brother to their king,
From France the isle that rivers four enfold
   With rolling streams descending from their spring;
But Hugo dead, the lily fair of gold,
   Their wonted ensign, they tofore them bring
Under Clotharius great, a captain good,
And hardy knight, ysprung of princes' blood.

XXXVIII.

A thousand were they in strong armors clad;
   Next whom there marched forth another band,
That number, nature, and instruction had,
   Like them, to fight far off, or charge at hand,
All valiant Normans, by Lord Robert lad,
   The native Duke of that renowned land,
Two Bishops next their standards proud upbear,
Call'd reverend William, and good Ademare.

xxxix.

Their jolly notes they chanted loud and clear,
   On merry mornings, at the mass divine,
And horrid helms high on their heads they bear,
   When their fierce courage they to war incline ;
The first four hundred horsemen gathered near
   To Orange town, and lands that it confine :
But Ademare the Poggian youth brought out,
In number like, in hard assays as stout.

xl.

Baldwin his ensign fair did next despread
   Among his Boulougniers of noble fame,
His brother gave him all his troops to lead
   When he commander of the field became.
The Count Carinto did him straight succeed,
   Grave in advice, well skill'd in Mars his game,
Four hundred brought he ; but so many thrice
Led Baldwin, clad in gilden arms of price.

xli.

Guelpho next them the land and place possess'd,
   Whose fortunes good with his great acts agree,
By his Italian sire, from th' house of Est
   Well could he bring his noble pedigree,
A German born, with rich possessions blest,
   A worthy branch sprung from the Guelphian tree ;
'Twixt Rhine and Danubie the land contain'd
He rul'd, where Suaves and Rhetians whilom reign'd.

xlii.

His mother's heritage was this and right,
   To which he added more by conquest got,
From thence approved men of passing might,
   He brought, that death or danger feared not ;
It was their wont in feasts to spend the night,
   And pass cold days in baths and houses hot,
Five thousand late, of which now scantly are
The third part left, such is the chance of war.

xliii.

The nation then, with crisped locks and fair,
   That dwell between the seas and Ardenne wood,
Where Moselle streams and Rhene the meadows wear,
   A batten soil, for grain, for pasture good,

Their islanders with them, who oft repair
　　Their earthen bulwarks 'gainst the ocean flood,
The flood, elsewhere that ships and barks devours,
But there drowns cities, countries, towns, and towers.

XLIV.

Both in one troop, and but a thousand all,
　　Under another Robert fierce they run ;
Then th' English squadron, soldiers stout and tall,
　　By William led, their sovereign's younger son,
These archers be, and with them come withal,
　　A people near the northern pole that won,
Whom Ireland sent from loughs and forests hoar
Divided far by sea from Europe's shore.

XLV.

Tancredie next, nor 'mongst them all was one,
　　Rinald except, a prince of greater might ;
With majesty his noble count'nance shone,
　　High were his thoughts, his heart was bold in fight,
No shameful vice his worth had overgone,
　　His fault was love, by unadvised sight,
Bred in the dangers of adventurous arms,
And nurs'd with griefs, with sorrows, woes, and harms.

XLVI.

Fame tells, that on that ever-blessed day,
　　When Christian swords with Persian blood were dyed,
The furious prince Tancredie from that fray
　　His coward foes chased through forests wide,
Till tired with the fight, the heat, the way,
　　He sought some place to rest his weary side,
And drew him near a silver stream, that play'd
Among wild herbs, under the greenwood shade.

XLVII.

A Pagan damsel there unwares he met,
　　In shining steel, all save her visage fair,
Her hair unbound she made a wanton net
　　To catch sweet breathing from the cooling air.
On her at gaze his longing looks he set,
　　Sight, wonder ; wonder, love ! love bred his care ;
O love, O wonder ; love new born, new bred,
Now grown, now arm'd, this champion captive led.

XLVIII.

Her helm the virgin don'd, and but some wight
  She fear'd might come to aid him as they fought,
Her courage yearn'd to have assail'd the knight,
  Yet thence she fled, uncompanied, unsought,
And left her image in his heart ypight,
  Her sweet idea wander'd through his thought;
Her shape, her gesture, and her place in mind
He kept, and blew love's fire with that wind.

XLIX.

Well might you read his sickness in his eyes,
  Their banks were full, their tide was at the flow,
His help far off, his hurt within him lies,
  His hopes unsprung, his cares were fit to mow.
Eight hundred horse, from Champaign came, he guies,
  Champaign, a land where wealth, ease, pleasure grow,
Rich nature's pomp and pride, the Tirrhene main
There woos the hills, hills woo the valleys plain.

L.

Two hundred Greeks came next, in fight well tried,
  Not surely arm'd in steel or iron strong,
But each a glaive had pendant by his side,
  Their bows and quivers at their shoulders hung,
Their horses well inured to chace and ride,
  In diet spare, untir'd with labor long,
Ready to charge and to retire at will,
Though broken, scatter'd, fled, they skirmish still.

LI.

Tatine their guide, and except Tatine, none
  Of all the Greeks went with the Christian host:
O sin, O shame, O Greece accurs'd alone!
  Did not this fatal war affront thy coast?
Yet sattest thou an idle looker-on,
  And glad attendest which side won or lost:
Now if thou be a bond slave vile become
No wrong is that, but God's most righteous doom.

LII.

In order last, but first in worth and fame,
  Unfear'd in fight, untir'd with hurt or wound,
The noble squadron of adventurers came,
  Terrors to all that tread on Asian ground;

Cease Orpheus of thy Minois, Arthur shame
  To boast of Launcelot, or thy table round,
For these whom antique times with laurel drest,
These far exceed, them, thee, and all the rest.

LIII.

Dudon of Consa was their guide and lord,
  And for of worth and birth alike they been,
They chose him captain, by their free accord,
  For he most acts had done, most battles seen ;
Grave was the man in years, in looks, in word,
  His locks were grey, yet was his courage green,
Of worth and might the noble badge he bore,
Old scars of grievous wounds received of yore.

LIV.

After came Eustace, well esteemed man
  For Godfrey's sake his brother, and his own ;
The King of Norway's heir, Gernando, then,
  Proud of his father's titles, sceptre, crown ;
Roger of Balnavill, and Engerlan
  For hardy knights approved were and known ;
Besides were number'd, in that warlike train,
Rambald, Gentonio, and the Gerards twain.

LV.

Ubaldo, then, and puissant Rosimond
  Of Lancaster the heir, in rank succeed ;
Let none forget Obizo of Tuscan lond,
  Well worthy praise for many a worthy deed,
Nor those three brethren, Lombards fierce and yond,
  Achilles, Sforza, and stern Palameed ;
Nor Otton's shield he conquer'd in those stowers,
In which a snake a naked child devours.

LVI.

Guascher and Raiphe in valor like there was,
  The one and other Guido, famous both ;
Gernier and Eberard to overpass
  In foul oblivion would my muse be loth ;
With his Gildippes dear, Edward, alas,
  A loving pair, to war among them, go'th,
In bond of virtuous love together tied,
Together serv'd they, and together died.

LVII.

In school of love are all things taught we see,
    There learn'd this maid of arms the ireful guise,
Still by his side a faithful guard went she,
    One truelove knot their lives together ties,
No wound to one alone could dang'rous be,
    But each the smart of other's anguish tries,
If one were hurt, the other felt the sore,
She lost her blood, he spent his life therefore.

LVIII.

But these and all Rinaldo far exceeds,
    Star of this sphere, the diamond of this ring,
The nest, where courage with sweet mercy breeds;
    A comet, worthy each eye's wondering;
His years are fewer than his noble deeds,
    His fruit is ripe soon as his blossoms spring,
Armed, a Mars might coyest Venus move,
And if disarm'd, then God himself of Love.

LIX.

Sophïa by Adige flowery bank him bore,
    Sophia the fair, spouse to Bertolda great,
Fit mother for that pearle, and before
    The tender imp was weaned from the teat,
The Princess Maud him took; in virtue's lore
    She brought him up, fit for each worthy feat.
Till of these wars the golden trump he hears,
That soundeth glory, fame, praise in his ears.

LX.

And then, though scantly three times five years old,
    He fled alone, by many an unknown coast,
O'er Ægean seas, by many a Greekish hold,
    Till he arrived at the Christian host;
A noble flight, adventurous, brave, and bold,
    Whereon a valiant prince might justly boast,
Three years he serv'd in field, when scant begin
Few golden hairs to deck his ivory chin.

LXI.

The horsemen past, their void-left stations fill
    The bands on foot, and Raymond them beforn,
Of Toulouse lord; from lands near Piræne hill,
    By Garonne streams and salt sea billows worn,

Four thousand foot he brought, well arm'd, and skill
　　Had they all pains and travel to have born,
Stout men of arms, and with their guide of power
Like Troy's old town, defenc'd with Ilion's tower.

LXII.

Next Stephen of Amboise did five thousand lead
　　The men he press'd from Tours and Blois but late,
To hard assays unfit, unsure at need,
　　Yet arm'd to point in well attemper'd plate,
The land did like itself the people breed,
　　The soil is gentle, smooth, soft, delicate;
Boldly they charge, but soon retire for doubt,
Like fire of straw soon kindled, soon burnt out.

LXIII.

The third Alcasto marched, and with him
　　The boaster brought six thousand Switzers bold;
Audacious were their looks, their faces grim,
　　Strong castles on the Alpine cliffs they hold;
Their shares and culters broke, to armors trim
　　They change that metal, cast in warlike mould;
And with this band late herds and flocks that guide,
Now kings and realms he threaten'd and defied.

LXIV.

The glorious standard last to heav'n they spread,
　　With Peter's keys ennobled, and his crown,
With it seven thousand stout Camillo had,
　　Embattailed in walls of iron brown;
In this adventure and occasion, glad
　　So to revive the Romans' old renown,
Or prove at least to all of wiser thought
Their hearts were fertile land, although unwrought.

LXV.

But now was passed every regiment,
　　Each band, each troop, each person, worth regard,
When Godfrey with his lords to counsel went,
　　And thus the Duke his princely will declar'd:
I will, when day next clears the firmament,
　　Our ready host in haste be all prepar'd,
Closely to march to Sion's noble wall,
Unseen, unheard, or undescried at all.

LXVI.

Prepare you then, for travail strong and light,
  Fierce to the combat, glad to victory :
And with that word and warning soon was dight
  Each soldier, longing for near coming glory ;
Impatient be they of the morning bright,
  Of honor so them prick'd the memory.
But yet their chieftain had conceiv'd a fear
Within his heart, but kept it secret there.

LXVII.

For he by faithful spiall was assur'd,
  That Egypt's king was forward on his way,
And to arrive at Gaza old procur'd
  A fort, that on the Syrian frontiers lay ;
Nor thinks he that a man to wars enur'd
  Will aught forslow, or in his journey stay,
For well he knew him for a dang'rous foe ;
An herald call'd he then, and spake him so :

LXVIII.

A pinnace take thee, swift as shaft from bow
  And speed thee, Henry, to the Greekish main,
There should arrive, as I by letters know
  From one that never aught reports in vain,
A valiant youth, in whom all virtues flow,
  To help us this great conquest to obtain,
The Prince of Danes he is, and brings to war
A troop with him from under th' Arctic star.

LXIX.

And, for I doubt the Greekish monarch sly,
  Will use with him some of his wonted craft,
To stay his passage, or divert awry
  Elsewhere his forces, his first journey laft,
My herald good, and messenger well try,
  See that these succors be not us beraft,
But send him thence with such convenient speed,
As with his honor stands, and with our need.

LXX.

Return not thou, but legier stay behind,
  And move the Greekish prince to send us aid,
Tell him his kingly promise doth him bind
  To give us succors, by his covenant made.

This said, and thus instruct, his letters sign'd
  The trusty herald took, nor longer stay'd,
But sped him thence to done his lord's behest,
And thus the Duke reduc'd his thoughts to rest.

LXXI.

Aurora bright her crystal gates unbarr'd,
  And bridegroom-like forth-step'd the glorious sun,
When trumpets loud and clarions shrill were heard,
  And every one to rouse him fierce begun,
Sweet music to each heart for war prepar'd,
  The soldiers glad by heaps to harness run ;
So, if with drought endanger'd be their grain,
Poor ploughmen joy, when thunders promise rain.

LXXII.

Some shirts of mail, some coats of plate put on,
  Some don'd a cuirass, some a corslet bright,
An hawberk some, and some a habergeon,
  So every one in arms was quickly dight,
His wonted guide each soldier tends upon,
  Loose in the wind waved their banners light,
Their standard royal towards heaven they spread,
The cross triumphant on the Pagans dead.

LXXIII.

Meanwhile the car that bears the light'ning brand,
  Upon the eastern hill was mounted high,
And smote the glist'ring armies as they stand,
  With quiv'ring beams which daz'd the wond'ring eye,
That Phaeton-like it fired sea and land,
  The sparkles seem'd up to the skies to fly ;
The horses neigh, and clatt'ring armors sowne,
Pursue the echo over dale and down.

LXXIV.

Their general did with due care provide
  To save his men from ambush and from train ;
Some troops of horse that lightly armed ride,
  He sent to scour the woods and forests main,
His pioneers their busy work applied,
  To even the paths and make the highways plain,
They fill'd the pits, and smooth'd the rougher ground,
And open'd every strait they closed found.

3

LXXV.

They meet no forces gathered by their foe,
  No towers, defenc'd with rampire, mote, or wall,
No stream, no wood, no mountain could forslow
  Their hasty pace, or stop their march at all:
So when his banks the prince of rivers, Po,
  Doth overswell, he breaks, with hideous fall,
The mossy rocks and trees o'ergrown with age,
Nor aught withstands his fury and his rage.

LXXVI.

The king of Tripoli in every hold
  Shut up his men, munition, and his treasure,
The straggling troops sometimes assail he would,
  Save that he durst not move them to displeasure,
He stay'd their rage with presents, gifts, and gold,
  And led them through his land at ease and leisure ;
To keep his realm in peace and rest he chose,
With what conditions Godfrey list impose.

LXXVII.

Those of Mount Seir, that neighboreth by east
  The holy city, faithful folk each one,
Down from the hill descended most and least,
  And to the Christian Duke by heaps they gone,
And welcome him and his, with joy and feast,
  On him they smile, on him they gaze alone,
And were his guides, as faithful, from that day,
As Hesperus, that leads the sun his way.

LXXVIII.

Along the sands his armies safe they guide,
  By ways secure, to them well known before ;
Upon the tumbling billows fraughted ride
  The armed ships, coasting along the shore,
Which for the camp might every day provide
  To bring munition good, and victuals' store,
The Isles of Greece sent in provision meet,
And store of wine from Scios came and Crete.

LXXIX.

Great Neptune grieved underneath the load
  Of ships, hulks, galleys, barks, and brigantines,
In all the mid-earth seas was left no road,
  Wherein the Pagan his bold sails untwines,

Spread was the huge Armado wide and broad,
  From Venice, Genes, and towns which them confines,
From Holland, England, France, and Sicill sent,
And all for Judah ready bound and bent ;

LXXX.

All these together were combin'd, and knit
  With surest bonds of love and friendship strong,
Together sail'd they, fraught with all things fit
  To service done by land that might belong,
And when occasion serv'd disbarked it ;
  Then sail'd the Asian coasts and isles along ;
Thither with speed their hasty course they plied,
Where Christ the Lord for our offences died.

LXXXI.

The brazen trump of iron-winged fame
  That mingleth faithful troth with forged lies,
Foretold the Heathen how the Christians came,
  How thitherward the conquering army hies,
Of every knight it sounds the worth and name,
  Each troop, each band, each squadron it descries,
And threat'neth death to those, fire, sword and slaughter,
Who held captived Israel's fairest daughter.

LXXXII.

The fear of ill exceeds the evil we fear,
  For so our present harms still most annoy us,
Each mind is press'd, and open every ear
  To hear new tidings, though they no way joy us.
This secret rumor whisper'd everywhere
  About the town, these Christians will destroy us ;
The aged king his coming evil that knew,
Did cursed thoughts in his false heart renew.

LXXXIII.

This aged prince, ycieped Aladine,
  Ruled in care, new sovereign of this state ;
A tyrant erst, but now his fell engine
  His graver age did somewhat mitigate ;
He heard the western lords would undermine
  His city's wall, and lay his towers prostrate.
To former fear he adds a new-come doubt,
Treason he fears within, and force without.

LXXXIV.

For nations twain inhabit there and dwell,
  Of sundry faith, together in that town,
The lesser part on Christ believed well,
  On Termagant the more, and on Mahowne :
But when this king had made his conquest fell,
  And brought that region subject to his crown,
Of burdens all he set the Paynims large,
And on poor Christians laid the double charge.

LXXXV.

His native wrath reviv'd with this new thought,
  With age and years that weaken'd was of yore ;
Such madness in his cruel bosom wrought,
  That now, than ever, blood he thirsteth more ;
So stings a snake that to the fire is brought,
  Which harmless lay benumb'd with cold before ;
A lion, so, his rage renewed hath,
Though tame before, if he be mov'd to wrath.

LXXXVI.

I see, quoth he, some expectation vain,
  In these false Christians, and some new content ;
Our common loss they trust will be their gain,
  They laugh, we weep ; they joy, while we lament ;
And more, perchance by treason or by train,
  To murder us they secretly consent,
Or otherwise to work us harm and wo,
To ope the gates, and so let in our foe.

LXXXVII.

But, lest they should effect their cursed will,
  Let us destroy this serpent on his nest ;
Both young and old, let us this people kill,
  The tender infants at their mothers' breast ;
Their houses burn, their holy temples fill
  With bodies slain, of those that lov'd them best ;
And on that tomb they hold so much in price,
Let 's offer up their priests in sacrifice.

LXXXVIII.

Thus thought the tyrant in his trait'rous mind,
  But durst not follow what he had decreed ;
Yet, if the innocents some mercy find,
  From cowardice, not ruth, did that proceed.

His noble foes durst not his craven kind
   Exasperate, by such a bloody deed ;
For if he need, what grace could then be got,
If thus of peace he broke, or loos'd the knot ?

LXXXIX.

His villain heart his cursed rage restrain'd,
   To other thoughts he bent his fierce desire :
The suburbs, first, flat with the earth he plain'd,
   And burnt their buildings with devouring fire ;
Loth was the wretch the Frenchmen should have gain'd
   Or help, or ease, by finding aught intire ;
Cedron, Bethsaida, and each wat'ring els,
Empoison'd he, both fountain, springs, and wells.

XC.

So wary-wise this child of darkness was,
   The city's self he strongly fortifies ;
Three sides by scite it well defensed has,
   That 's only weak that to the northward lies ;
With mighty bars of long enduring brass,
   The steel-bound doors, and iron gates he ties,
And lastly, legions armed well provides,
Of subjects born, and hired aid besides.

BOOK II.

I.

WHILE thus the tyrant bends his thoughts to arms,
   Ismeno 'gan tofore his sight appear,
Ismen, dead bones laid in cold graves that warms,
   And makes them speak, smell, taste, touch, see, and hear ;
Ismen, with terror of his mighty charms,
   That makes great Dis in deepest hell to fear,
That binds and looseth souls condemn'd to wo,
And sends the devils on errands to and fro.

II.

A Christian once, Macon he now adores,
   Nor could he quite his wonted faith forsake,
But in his wicked arts both oft implores
   Help from the Lord, and aid from Pluto blake ;
He, from deep caves by Acheron's dark shore,
   Where circles vain and spells he us'd to make,
T' advise his king in these extremes is come ;
Architophell so counsell'd Absalom.

III.

My liege, he says, the camp fast hither moves,
   The axe is laid unto this cedar's root ;
But let us work as valiant men behoves,
   For boldest hearts good fortune helpeth out :

Your princely care your kingly wisdom proves,
  Well have you labor'd, well foreseen about,
If each perform his charge and duty so,
Naught but his grave here conquer shall your foe.

IV.

From surest castle of my secret cell
  I come, partaker of your good and ill ;
What counsel sage or magic's sacred spell
  May profit us, all that perform I will :
The sprites impure, from bliss that whilom fell,
  Shall to your service bow, constrain'd by skill :
But how we must begin this enterprise,
I will your highness thus in brief advise.

V.

Within the Christians' church, from light of skies,
  An hidden altar stands, far out of sight,
On which the image consecrated lies
  Of Christ's dear mother, call'd a virgin bright ;
An hundred lamps aye burn before her eyes ;
  She, in a slender veil of tinsel dight,
On every side great plenty doth behold
Of offerings brought, myrrh, frankincense, and gold.

VI.

This idol would I have remov'd away
  From thence, and by your princely hand transport,
In Macon's sacred temple safe it lay,
  Which then I will enchant in wond'rous sort,
That while the image in that church doth stay,
  No strength of arms shall win this noble fort,
Or shake this puissant wall ; such passing might
Have spells and charms, if they be said aright.

VII.

Advised thus, the king impatient
  Flew in his fury to the house of God,
The image took, with words unreverent
  Abus'd the prelates, who that deed forbod ;
Swift with his prey away the tyrant went,
  Of God's sharp justice naught he fear'd the rod,
But in his chapel vile the image laid,
On which th' enchanter charms and witchcrafts said.

VIII.

When Phœbus next unclos'd his wakeful eye,
   Uprose the sexton of that place prophane,
And miss'd the image where it us'd to lie ;
   Each-where he sought in grief, in fear, in vain ;
Then to the king his loss he 'gan descrie,
   Who sore enraged kill'd him for his pain,
And straight conceiv'd, in his malicious wit,
Some Christian bade this great offence commit.

IX.

But whether this were act of mortal hand,
   Or else the Prince of Heav'n's eternal pleasure,
That of his mercy would this wretch withstand,
   Nor let so vile a chest hold such a treasure,
As yet conjecture hath not fully scann'd ;
   By godliness let us this action measure,
And truth of purest faith will fitly prove,
That this rare grace came down from heav'n above.

X.

With busy search the tyrant 'gan invade
   Each house, each hold, each temple, and each tent,
To them the fault or faulty one bewrai'd,
   Or hid, he promis'd gifts or punishment ;
His idle charms the false enchanter said,
   But in this maze still wander'd and mis-went,
For heaven decreed to conceal the same,
To make the miscreant more to feel his shame.

XI.

But when the angry king discover'd not
   What guilty hand this sacrilege had wrought,
His ireful courage boil'd in vengeance hot
   Against the Christians, whom he faulters thought ;
All ruth, compassion, mercy, he forgot,
   A staff to beat that dog he long had sought :
Let them all die, quoth he, both great and small,
So shall the offender perish sure withall.

XII.

To spill the wine with poison mix'd who spares ?
   Slay then the righteous with the faulty-one,
Destroy this field, that yieldeth naught but tares,
   With thorns this vineyard all is overgone ;

Among these wretches is not one that cares
  For us, our laws, or our religion,
Up, up, dear subjects, fire and weapon take,
Burn, murder, kill, these traitors, for my sake.

XIII.

This Herod thus would Bethlem's infants kill;
  The Christians soon these direful news receive,
The trump of death sounds in their hearing shrill,
  Their weapon, faith; their fortress was the grave,
They had no courage, time, devise, or will,
  To fight, to flie, excuse, or pardon crave,
But stood prepar'd to die, yet help they find
Whence least they hope, such knots can heav'n unbind.

XIV.

Among them dwelt, her parents' joy and pleasure,
  A maid, whose fruit was ripe, not over-year'd,
Her beauty was her not-esteemed treasure;
  The field of love, with plough of virtue ear'd.
Her labor goodness, godliness her leisure;
  Her house the heav'n by this full moon aye clear'd,
For there, from lover's eyes withdrawn, alone
With virgin beams this spotless Cinthia shone.

XV.

But what avail'd her resolution chaste,
  Whose soberest looks were whetstones to desire?
Nor love consents that beauty's field lie waste;
  Her visage set Olindo's heart on fire:
O subtle love! a thousand wiles thou hast,
  By humble suit, by service, or by hire,
To win a maiden's hold, a thing soon done,
For nature fram'd all women to be won.

XVI.

Sophronia she, Olindo hight the youth,
  Both of one town, both in one faith were taught,
She fair, he full of bashfulness and truth,
  Lov'd much, hop'd little, and desired naught;
He durst not speak, by suit to purchase ruth,
  She saw not, mark'd not, wist not what he sought;
Thus lov'd, thus serv'd he long, but not regarded,
Unseen, unmark'd, unpitied, unrewarded.

XVII.

To her came message of the murderment,
  Wherein her guiltless friends should hopeless serve,
She that was noble, wise, as fair and gent,
  Cast how she might their harmless lives preserve ;
Zeal was the spring whence flow'd her hardiment,
  From maiden's shame yet was she loth to swerve :
Yet had her courage ta'en so sure a hold,
That boldness, shamefast ; shame had made her bold.

XVIII.

And forth she went, a shop for merchandize,
  Full of rich stuff, but none for sale exposed,
A veil obscur'd the sun-shine of her eyes,
  The rose within herself her sweetness closed,
Each ornament about her seemly lies,
  By curious chance, or careless art, composed ;
For what the most neglects, most curious prove,
So beauty's help'd by nature, heaven, and love.

XIX.

Admir'd of all on went this noble maid
  Until the presence of the king she gained,
Nor, for he swelled with ire, was she afraid,
  But his fierce wrath with fearless grace sustained ;
I come, quoth she (but be thine anger stay'd,
  And causeless rage 'gainst faultless souls restrained),
I come to show thee and to bring thee both
The wight, whose fact hath made thy heart so wroth.

XX.

Her modest boldness, and that light'ning ray
  Which her sweet beauty streamed on his face,
Had strook the prince with wonder and dismay,
  Changed his cheer and clear'd his moody grace,
That had her eyes dispos'd their looks to play,
  The king had snared been in love's strong lace ;
By wayward beauty doth not fancy move,
A frown forbids, a smile engendereth love.

XXI.

It was amazement, wonder and delignt,
  Although not love, that moved his cruel sense,
Tell on, quoth he, unfold the chance aright,
  Thy people's lives I grant for recompense.

Then she, Behold the faulter here in sight,
    This hand committed that suppos'd offence,
It took the image, mine that fault, that fact,
Mine be the glory of that virtuous act.

XXII.

This spotless lamb thus offered up her blood
    To save the rest of Christ's selected fold ;
O noble lie ! was ever truth so good ?
    Blest be the lips that such a leasing told :
Thoughtful awhile remain'd the tyrant wood,
    His native wrath he 'gan a space withhold,
And said, That thou discover soon I will,
What aid ? what counsel hadst thou in that ill ?

XXIII.

My lofty thoughts, she answer'd him, envied
    Another's hand should work my high desire,
The thirst of glory can no partner bide,
    With mine own self I did alone conspire.
On thee alone, the tyrant then replied,
    Shall fall the vengeance of my wrath and ire.
'Tis just and right, quoth she, I yield consent,
Mine be the honor, mine the punishment.

XXIV.

The wretch of new enraged at the same,
    Ask'd where she hid the image so convey'd :
Not hid, quoth she, but quite consum'd with flame,
    The idol is of that eternal maid,
For so at least I have preserv'd the same
    With hands profane from being eft betray'd.
My lord, the thing thus stolen demand no more ;
Here see the thief, that scorneth death therefore.

XXV.

And yet no theft was this, yours was the sin,
    I brought again what you unjustly took ;
This heard, the tyrant did for rage begin
    To whet his teeth, and bend his frowning look ;
No pity, youth ; fairness, no grace could win ;
    Joy, comfort, hope, the virgin all forsook ;
Wrath kill'd remorse, vengeance stopped mercy's breath,
Love's thrall to hate, and beauty slave to death.

XXVI.

Ta'en was the damsel, and without remorse,
    The king condemn'd her, guiltless, to the fire ;
Her veil and mantle pluck'd they off by force,
    And bound her tender arms in twisted wire :
Dumb was this silver dove, while from her corse
    These hungry kites pluck'd off her rich attire,
And for some-deal perplexed was her sprite,
Her damask late now chang'd to purest white.

XXVII.

The news of this mishap spread far and near,
    The people ran, both young and old, to gase ;
Olindo also ran, and 'gan to fear
    His lady was some partner in this case :
But when he found her bound, stripp'd from her gear,
    And vile tormentors ready saw in place,
He broke the throng, and into present brast,
And thus bespake the king in rage and haste :

XXVIII.

Not so, not so this girl shall bear away
    From me the honor of so noble feat,
She durst not, did not, could not, so convey
    The massy substance of that idol great ;
What sleight had she the wardens to betray ?
    What strength to heave the goddess from her seat ?
No, no, my lord, she sails but with my wind
(Ah thus he lov'd, yet was his love unkind).

XXIX.

He added further, Where the shining glass
    Lets in the light amid your temple's side,
By broken by-ways did I inward pass,
    And in that window made a postern wide,
Nor shall therefore the ill-advised lass
    Usurp the glory should this fact betide,
Mine be these bonds, mine be these flames so pure,
O glorious death, more glorious sepulture.

XXX.

Sophronia rais'd her modest looks from ground,
    And on her lover bent her eye-sight mild ;
Tell me what fury, what conceit unsound,
    Presenteth here to death so sweet a child ?

Is not in me sufficient courage found
    To bear the anger of this tyrant wild ?
Or hath fond love thy heart so overgone ?
Wouldst thou not live, not let me die alone ?

XXXI.

Thus spake the nymph, yet spake but to the wind,
    She could not alter his well-settled thought:
O miracle ! O strife of wondrous kind !
    Where love and virtue such contention wrought,
    Where death the victor had for meed assign'd,
    Their own neglect each other's safety sought ;
But thus the king was more provok'd to ire,
Their strife for bellows serv'd to anger's fire.

XXXII.

He thinks (such thoughts self-guiltiness finds out)
    They scorn'd his power, and therefore scorn'd the pain :
Nay, nay, quoth he, let be your strife and doubt,
    You both shall win, and fit reward obtain.
With that the serjeant bent the young man stout,
    And bound him likewise in a worthless chain,
Then back to back fast to a stake both ties,
Two harmless turtles, dight for sacrifice.

XXXIII.

About the pile of faggots, sticks and hay,
    The bellows rais'd the newly-kindled flame,
When thus Olindo, in a doleful lay,
    Begun too late his bootless plaints to frame :
Be these the bonds ?   Is this the hop'd-for day
    Should join me to this long-desired dame ?
Is this the fire alike should burn our hearts ?
Ah ! hard reward for lovers' kind desarts !

XXXIV.

Far other flames and bonds kind lovers prove,
    But thus our fortune casts the hapless die ;
Death hath exchang'd again his shafts with love,
    And Cupid thus lets borrow'd arrows fly.
O Hymen say, what fury doth thee move
    To lend thy lamps to light a tragedy ?
Yet this contents me that I die for thee,
Thy flames, not mine, my death and torment be.

XXXV.

Yet happy were my death, mine ending blest,
  My torments easy, full of sweet delight,
If this I could obtain, that breast to breast
  Thy bosom might receive my yielded sprite;
And thine with it, in heav'n's pure clothing drest,
  Through clearest skies might take united flight.
Thus he complain'd, whom gently she reprov'd,
And sweetly spake him thus, that so her lov'd:

XXXVI.

Far other plaints, dear friend, tears and laments,
  The time, the place, and our estates require;
Think on thy sins, which man's old foe presents
  Before that judge that quites each soul his hire;
For his name suffer, for no pain torments
  Him, whose just prayers to his throne aspire:
Behold the heavens, thither thine eyesight bend,
Thy looks, sighs, tears, for intercessors send.

XXXVII.

The pagans loud cried out to God and man,
  The Christians mourn'd in silent lamentation;
The tyrant's self, a thing unus'd, began
  To feel his heart relent, with mere compassion,
But not dispos'd to ruth or mercy than,
  He sped him thence, home to his habitation:
Sophronia stood not griev'd nor discontented,
By all that saw her, but herself, lamented.

XXXVIII.

The lovers, standing in this doleful wise,
  A warrior bold unwares approached near,
In uncouth arms yclad, and strange disguise,
  From countries far but new arrived there;
A savage tigress on her helmet lies,
  The famous badge Clorinda us'd to bear;
That wonts in every warlike stour to win,
By which bright sign well known was that fair inn.

XXXIX.

She scorn'd the arts these seely women use,
  Another thought her nobler humor fed;
Her lofty hand would of itself refuse
  To touch the dainty needle, or nice thread:

She hated chambers, closets, secret mews,
    And in broad fields preserv'd her maidenhead :
Proud were her looks, yet sweet, though stern and stout,
Her dame a dove thus brought an eagle out.

XL.

While she was young, she us'd with tender hand
    The foaming steed with froarie bit to steer ;
To tilt and tournay, wrestle in the sand,
    To leave with speed Atlanta swift arreare ;
Through forests wild and unfrequented land
    To chase the lion, boar, or rugged bear ;
The satyrs rough, the fawns and fairies wild,
She chased oft, oft took, and oft beguil'd.

XLI.

This lusty lady came from Persia late,
    She with the Christians had encountered eft,
And in their flesh had opened many a gate
    By which their faithful souls their bodies left ;
Her eye at first presented her the state
    Of these poor souls, of hope and help bereft,
Greedy to know, as is the mind of man,
Their cause of death, swift to the fire she ran.

XLII.

The people made her room, and on them twain
    Her piercing eyes their fiery weapons dart ;
Silent she saw the one, the other plain,
    The weaker body lodg'd the nobler heart :
Yet him she saw lament, as if his pain
    Were grief and sorrow for another's smart ;
And her keep silence so, as if her eyes
Dumb orators were to entreat the skies.

XLIII.

Clorinda chang'd to ruth her warlike mood,
    Few silver drops her vermeil cheeks depaint,
Her sorrow was for her that speechless stood,
    Her silence more prevail'd than his complaint ;
She ask'd an aged man, seem'd grave and good,
    Come say me sire, quoth she, what hard constraint
Would murder here love's queen, and beauty's king ?
What fault or fate doth to this death them bring ?

XLIV.

Thus she inquir'd, and answer short he gave,
    But such as all the chance at large disclosed;
She wondered at the case, the virgin brave
    That both were guiltless of the fault supposed;
Her noble thought cast how she might them save,
    The means on suit or battle she reposed;
Quick to the fire she ran, and quench'd it out,
And thus bespake the serjeants and the rout:

XLV.

Be there not one among you all that dare
    In this your hateful office aught proceed,
Till I return from court, nor take you care
    To reap displeasure for not making speed:
To do her will the men themselves prepare,
    In their faint hearts her looks such terror breed;
To court she went, their pardon would she get,
But on the way the courteous king she met.

XLVI.

Sir king, quoth she, my name Clorinda hight,
    My fame perchance hath pierc'd your ears ere now,
I come to try my wonted power and might,
    And will defend this land, this town, and you;
All hard assays esteem I eath and light,
    Great acts I reach to, to small things I bow,
To fight in field, or to defend this wall,
Point what you list, I naught refuse at all.

XLVII.

To whom the king: What land so far remote,
    From Asia's coasts, or Phœbus' glist'ring rays,
O glorious virgin, that recordeth not
    Thy fame, thine honor, worth, renown and praise?
Since on my side I have thy succors got,
    I need not fear in these mine aged days;
For in thine aid more hope, more trust, I have,
Than in whole armies of these soldiers brave.

XLVIII.

Now Godfrey stays too long, he fears I ween;
    Thy courage great keeps all our foes in awe;
For thee all actions far unworthy been,
    But such as greatest danger with them draw;

Be you commandress, therefore, princess, queen,
  Of all our forces, be thy word a law.
This said, the virgin 'gan her beavoir vale,
And thank'd him first, and thus began her tale:

XLIX.

A thing unus'd, great monarch, may it seem,
  To ask reward for service yet to come;
But so your virtuous bounty I esteem,
  That I presume for to entreat, this groom
And seely maid from danger to redeem,
  Condemn'd to burn by your unpartial doom,
I not excuse, but pity much their youth,
And come to you for mercy and for ruth.

L.

Yet give me leave to tell your highness this,
  You blame the Christians, them my thoughts acquite,
Nor be displeas'd, I say you judge amiss,
  At every shot look not to hit the white;
All what th' enchanter did persuade you is
  Against the lore of Macon's sacred right;
For us commandeth mighty Mahomet,
No idols in his temples pure to set.

LI.

To him therefore this wonder done refar,
  Give him the praise and honor of the thing;
Of us the gods benign so careful are,
  Lest customs strange into their church we bring:
Let Ismen with his squares and trigons war,
  His weapons be the staff, the glass, the ring;
But let us manage war with blows, like knights,
Our praise in arms, our honor lies in fights.

LII.

The virgin held her peace when this was said:
  And though to pity never fram'd his thought,
Yet, for the king admir'd the noble maid,
  His purpose was not to deny her aught;
I grant them life, quoth he; your promis'd aid
  Against these Frenchmen hath their pardon bought;
Nor further seek what their offences be,
Guiltless I quite; guilty, I set them free.

4

LIII.

Thus were they loos'd, happiest of human kind ;
  Olindo, blessed be this act of thine ;
True witness of thy great and heav'nly mind ;
  Where sun, moon, stars, of love, faith, virtue, shine.
So forth they went, and left pale death behind,
  To joy the bliss of marriage-rites divine ;
With her he would have died, with him content
Was she to live, that would with her have brent.

LIV.

The king, as wicked thoughts are most suspicious,
  Suppos'd too fast this tree of virtue grew ;
O blessed Lord ! why should this Pharaoh vicious
  Thus tyrannize upon thy Hebrews true ?
Who to perform his will, vile and malicious,
  Exiled these, and all the faithful crew,
All that were strong of body, stout of mind ;
But kept their wives and children pledge behind.

LV.

A hard division, when the harmless sheep
  Must leave their lambs to hungry wolves in charge,
But labor 's virtue's watching, ease her sleep,
  Trouble best wind that drives salvation's barge ;
The Christians fled, whither they took no keep,
  Some strayed wild among the forests large,
Some to Emmaus, to the Christian host,
And conquer would again their houses lost.

LVI.

Emmaus is a city small, that lies
  From Sion's walls distant a little way ;
A man that early on the morn doth rise,
  May thither walk ere third hour of the day.
Oh ! when the Christian lords this town espies,
  How merry were their hearts, how fresh, how gay !
But, for the sun inclined fast to west,
That night there would their chieftain take his rest.

LVII.

Their canvas castles up they quickly rear,
  And build a city in an hour's space ;
When lo ! disguised in unusual gear,
  Two barons bold approachen 'gan the place ;

Their semblance kind, and mild their gestures were,
　Peace in their hands, and friendship in their face;
From Egypt's king ambassadors they come,
Them many a 'squire attends, and many a groom.

LVIII.

The first Aletes, born in lowly shed
　Of parents base, a rose sprung from a brier,
That now his branches over Egypt spread,
　No plant in Pharaoh's garden prospered higher;
With pleasing tales his lord's vain ears he fed,
　A flatterer, a pickthank, and a liar;
Curst be estate got with so many a crime,
Yet this is oft the stair by which men climb.

LIX.

Argantes called is that other knight,
　A stranger came he late to Egypt's land,
And there advanced was to honor's height,
　For he was stout of courage, strong of hand;
Bold was his heart, and restless was his sprite,
　Fierce, stern, outrageous, keen as sharpen'd brand,
Scorner of God, scant to himself a friend,
And prick'd his reason on his weapon's end.

LX.

These two entreatance made they might be heard,
　Nor was their just petition long denied;
The gallants quickly made their court of guard,
　And brought them in where sat their famous guide;
Whose kingly look his princely mind declared,
　Where noblesse, virtue, troth, and valor bide:
A slender courtsie made Argantes bold,
So as one prince salute another would.

LXI.

Aletes laid his right hand on his heart,
　Bent down his head, and cast his eyes full low;
And rev'rence made with courtly grace and art,
　For all that humble lore to him was know;
His sober lips then did he softly part,
　Whence of pure rhetoric whole streams outflow,
And thus he said, while on the Christian lords
Down fell the mildew of his sugar'd words:

LXII.

O, only worthy, whom the earth all fears!
　　High God defend thee, with his heav'nly shield;
And humble so the hearts of all thy peers,
　　That their stiff necks to thy sweet yoke may yield;
These be the sheaves that honor's harvest bears,
　　The seed thy valiant acts, the world the field,
Egypt the headland is, where heaped lies
Thy fame, worth, justice, wisdom, victories.

LXIII.

These, altogether, doth our sovereign hide
　　In secret storehouse of his princely thought,
And prays he may in long accordance bide
　　With that great worthy, which such wonders wrought,
Nor that oppose against the coming tide
　　Of proffered love, for that he is not taught
Your Christian faith, for, though of divers kind,
The loving vine about her elm is twin'd.

LXIV.

Receive, therefore, in that unconquered hand,
　　The precious handle of this cup of love,
If not religion, virtue be the band
　　'Twixt you to fasten friendship, not to move:
But, for our mighty king doth understand,
　　You mean your power 'gainst Judah land to prove,
He would, before this threat'ned tempest fell,
I should his mind and princely will first tell.

LXV.

His mind is this; he prays thee be contented
　　To joy in peace the conquests thou hast got,
Be not thy death, or Sion's fall lamented,
　　Forbear this land, Judea trouble not;
Things done in haste at leisure be repented;
　　Withdraw thine arms, trust not uncertain lot,
For oft we see what least we think betide;
He is thy friend 'gainst all the world beside.

LXVI.

True labor in the vineyard of thy Lord,
　　Ere prime thou hast th' imposed day-work done;
What armies conquer'd, perish'd with thy sword!
　　What cities sack'd! what kingdoms hast thou won!

All ears are 'maz'd, while tongues thine acts record.
   Hands quake for fear, all feet for dread do run ;
And though new realms you may to thraldom bring,
No higher can your praise, your glory spring.

LXVII.

Thy sun is in his Apogæon placed,
   And when it moveth next must needs descend ;
Chance is uncertain, fortune double-faced,
   Smiling at first, she frowneth in the end ;
Beware thine honor be not then disgraced,
   Take heed thou mar not, when thou think'st to mend,
For this the folly is of fortune's play,
'Gainst doubtful, certain ; much, 'gainst small, to lay.

LXVIII.

Yet still we sail, while prosp'rous blows the wind,
   Till on some secret rock un'wares we light ;
The sea of glory hath no banks assign'd ;
   They who are wont to win in every fight,
Still feed the fire that so enflames thy mind,
   To bring mo nations subject to thy might ;
This makes thee, blessed peace, so light to hold,
Like summer's flies that fear not winter's cold.

LXIX.

They bid thee follow on the path, now made
   So plain and easy, enter fortune's gate,
Nor in thy scabbard sheathe that famous blade,
   Till settled be thy kingdom, and estate,
Till Macon's sacred doctrine fall and fade,
   Till woful Asia all lie desolate ;
Sweet words, I grant, baits and allurements sweet,
But greatest hopes oft greatest crosses meet.

LXX.

For, if thy courage do not blind thine eyes,
   If clouds of fury hide not reason's beams,
Then may'st thou see this desp'rate enterprise,
   The field of death water'd with danger's streams :
High state the bed is where misfortune lies,
   Mars most unfriendly when most kind he seems ;
Who climbeth high on earth he hardest lights,
And lowest falls attend the highest flights.

LXXI.

Tell me, if, great in counsel, arms, and gold,
   The Prince of Egypt war 'gainst you prepare;
What if the valiant Turks and Persians bold
   Unite their forces with Cassano's heir?
Oh! then, what marble pillar shall uphold
   The falling trophies of your conquests fair?
Trust you the monarch of the Greekish land?
That reed will break; and breaking, wound your hand.

LXXII.

The Greekish faith is like that half-cut tree,
   By which men take wild elephants in Ind,
A thousandth time it hath beguiled thee,
   As firm as waves in seas, or leaves in wind.
Will they, who erst denied you passage free
   (Passage to all men free, by use and kind),
Fight for your sake? or on them do you trust
To spend their blood, that could scarce spare their dust?

LXXIII.

But all your hope and trust perchance is laid
   In these strong troops, which thee environ round;
Yet foes unite are not so soon dismay'd,
   As when their strength you erst divided found:
Besides, each hour thy bands are weaker made,
   With hunger, slaughter, lodging on cold ground;
Meanwhile the Turks seek succors from our king;
Thus fade thy helps, and thus thy cumbers spring.

LXXIV.

Suppose no weapon can thy valor's pride
   Subdue, that by no force thou may'st be won;
Admit no steel can hurt or wound thy side,
   And be it heav'n hath thee such favor done;
'Gainst famine yet what shield canst thou provide?
   What strength resist? what sleight her wrath can shun?
Go, shake thy spear, and draw thy flaming blade,
And try if hunger so be weaker made.

LXXV.

Th' inhabitants each pasture and each plain
   Destroyed have, each field to waste is laid,
In fenced towers bestowed is their grain,
   Before thou cam'st this kingdom to invade;

These horse and foot how canst thou then sustain ?
　Whence comes thy store ? whence thy provision made ?
Thy ships to bring it are, perchance, assign'd,
Oh ! that you live so long as please the wind !

LXXVI.

Perhaps thy fortune doth control the wind,
　Doth loose or bind their blasts in secret cave ;
The sea, pardie, cruel, and deaf by kind,
　Will hear thy call, and still her raging wave :
But if our armed galleys be assign'd
　To aid those ships, which Turks and Persians have,
Say then, what hope is left thy slender fleet ?
Dare flocks of crows a flight of eagles meet ?

LXXVII.

My lord, a double conquest must you make,
　If you achieve renown by this emprise :
For if our fleet your navy chase or take,
　For want of victuals all your camp then dies ;
Or if by land the field you once forsake,
　Then vain by sea were hope of victories :
Nor could your ships restore your lost estate ;
For steed once stolen, we shut the door too late.

LXXVIII.

In this estate, if thou esteemest light
　The proffer'd kindness of th' Egyptian king,
Then give me leave to say, this oversight
　Beseems thee not, in whom such virtues spring :
But heav'ns vouchsafe to guide thy mind aright
　To gentle thoughts, that peace and quiet bring ;
So that poor Asia her complaints may cease,
And you enjoy your conquest got, in peace.

LXXIX.

Nor ye that part in these adventures have,
　Part in his glory, partners in his harms,
Let not blind fortune so your minds desave,
　To stir him more to try these fierce alarms ;
But, like the sailor, 'scaped from the wave,
　From further peril, that his person arms
By staying safe at home, so stay you all ;
Better sit still, men say, than rise to fall.

LXXX.

This said Aletes; and a murmur rose
  That show'd dislike among the Christian peers,
Their angry gestures with mislike disclose
  How much his speech offends their noble ears.
Lord Godfrey's eye three times environ goes,
  To view what count'nance every warrior bears,
And lastly on th' Egyptian baron stay'd,
To whom the duke thus, for his answer, said:

LXXXI.

Ambassador, full both of threats and praise,
  Thy doubtful message hast thou wisely told,
And, if thy sovereign love us, as he says,
  Tell him he sows to reap an hundred-fold;
But where thy talk the coming storm displays
  Of threat'ned warfare, from the Pagans bold,
To that I answer, as my custom is,
In plainest phrase, lest mine intent thou miss.

LXXXII.

Know, that till now, we suff'red have much pain,
  By lands and seas, where storms and tempests fall,
To make the passage easy, safe, and plain,
  That leads us to this venerable wall;
That so we might reward from heav'n obtain,
  And free this town, from being longer thrall;
Nor is it grievous to so good an end,
Our honors, kingdoms, lives, and goods to spend.

LXXXIII.

Not hope of praise, nor thirst of worldly good,
  Enticed us to follow this emprise:
The heav'nly father keep his sacred brood
  From foul infection of so great a vice:
But by our zeal aye be that plague withstood,
  Let not those pleasures us to sin entice;
His grace, his mercy, and his powerful hand
Will keep us safe from hurt, by sea and land.

LXXXIV.

This is the spur that makes our coursers run;
  This is our harbor, safe from danger's floods;
This is our beild, the blust'ring winds to shun;
  This is our guide, through deserts, forests, woods;

This is our summer's shade, our winter's sun ;
    This is our wealth, our treasure, and our goods ;
This is our engine, towers that overthrows ;
Our spear that hurts, our sword that wounds our foes.

LXXXV.

Our courage hence, our hope, our valor springs,
    Not from the trust we have in shield or spear ;
Not from the succors France or Grecia brings,
    On such weak posts we list no buildings rear :
He can defend us from the power of kings,
    From chance of war, that makes weak hearts to **fear** :
He can these hungry troops with manna feed,
And make the seas—land, if we passage need.

LXXXVI.

But if our sins us of his help deprive,
    Or his high justice let no mercy fall :
Yet should our deaths us some contentment give,
    To die, where Christ receiv'd his burial ;
So might we die, not envying them that live ;
    So would we die, not unrevenged all :
Nor Turks, nor Christians, if we perish such,
Have cause to joy, or to complain too much.

LXXXVII.

Think not that wars we love, and strife affect ;
    Or that we hate sweet peace, or rest denay ;
Think not your sovereign's friendship we reject,
    Because we list not in our conquests stay :
But, for it seems he would the Jews protect,
    Pray him from us that thought aside to lay,
Nor us forbid this town and realm to gain,
And he in peace, rest, joy, long mote he reign.

LXXXVIII.

This answer given, Argantes wild drew nar,
    Trembling for ire, and waxing pale for rage,
Nor could he hold, his wrath increas'd so far,
    But thus, enflam'd, bespake the captain sage :
Who scorneth peace shall have his fill of war ;
    I thought thy wisdom should thy fury 'swage,
But well you show what joy you take in fight,
Which makes you prize our love and friendship light.

LXXXIX.

This said, he took his mantle's foremost part,
　　And 'gan the same together fold and wrap ;
Then spake again, with fell and spiteful heart
　　(So lions roar, enclos'd in train or trap) :
Thou proud despiser of inconstant Mart,
　　I bring thee war and peace clos'd in this lap,
Take quickly one, thou hast no time to muse ;
If peace, we rest ; we fight, if war thou chuse.

XC.

His semblant fierce and speeches proud provoke
　　The soldiers all, War, war, at once to cry ;
Nor could they tarry till their chieftain spoke ;
　　But, for the knight was more enflam'd hereby,
His lap he open'd, and spread forth his cloak :
　　To mortal wars, he says, I you defy ;
And this he utter'd with fell rage and hate,
And seem'd of Janus' church t' undo the gate.

XCI.

It seemed fury, discord, madness fell,
　　Flew from his lap, when he unfolds the same ;
His glaring eyes with anger's venom swell,
　　And like the brand of foul Alecto flame,
He looked like huge Typhœus loos'd from hell
　　Again to shake heav'n's everlasting frame ;
Or him that built the tower on Shinaar,
Which threat'neth battle 'gainst the morning star.

XCII.

Godfredo then : depart, and bid your king
　　Haste hitherward, or else, within short while
(For gladly we accept the war you bring),
　　Let him expect us on the banks of Nile.
He entertain'd them then with banqueting,
　　And gifts presented to those Pagans vile ;
Aletes had a helmet, rich and gay,
Late found at Nice, among the conquer'd prey ;

XCIII.

Argant a sword, whereof the web was steel,
　　Pummel, rich stone ; hilts, gold, approv'd by touch,
With rarest workmanship all forged weel,
　　The curious art excell'd the substance much :

Thus fair, rich, sharp, to see, to have, to feel,
   Glad was the Painim to enjoy it such,
And said, How I this gift can use and wield
Soon shall you see, when first we meet in field.

XCIV.

Thus took they congee, and the angry knight
   Thus to his fellow parlied on their way,
Go thou by day, but let me walk by night,
   Go thou to Egypt, I at Sion stay,
The answer given thou canst unfold aright;
   No need of me, what I can do or say;
Among these arms I will go wreak my spite,
Let Paris court it, Hector lov'd to fight.

XCV.

Thus he, who late arriv'd a messenger,
   Departs a foe, in act, in word, in thought;
The law of nations, or the lore of war,
   If he transgress, or no, he recketh naught.
Thus parted they, and ere he wander'd far
   The friendly starlight to the walls him brought:
Yet his fell heart thought long that little way,
Griev'd with each stop, tormented with each stay.

XCVI.

Now spread the night her spangled canopy,
   And summon'd every restless eye to sleep:
On beds of tender grass the beasts down lye,
   The fishes slumb'red in the silent deep,
Unheard was serpent's hiss, and dragon's cry,
   Birds left to sing, and Philomene to weep,
Only that noise heav'n's rolling circles kest,
Sung lullaby, to bring the world to rest.

XCVII.

Yet neither sleep, nor ease, nor shadows dark,
   Could make the faithful camp or captain rest,
They long'd to see the day, to hear the lark
   Record her hymns and chant her carols blest,
They yearn'd to view the walls, the wished mark
   To which their journeys long they had address'd;
Each heart attends, each longing eye beholds
What beam the eastern window first unfolds.

BOOK III.

THE ARGUMENT.

The camp at great Jerusalem arrives:
  Clorinda gives them battle. In the breast
Of fair Erminia Tancred's love revives;
  He justs with her unknown, whom he lov'd best;
Argant th' adventurers of their guide deprives;
  With stately pomp they lay their Lord in chest:
Godfrey commands to cut the forest down,
And make strong engines to assault the town.

I.

THE purple morning left her crimson bed,
  And don'd her robe of pure vermilion hue ;
Her amber locks she crown'd with roses red,
  In Eden's flowery gardens gathered new ;
When through the camp a murmur shrill was spread ;
  Arm, arm, they cried ; arm, arm, the trumpets blew ;
Their merry noise prevents the joyful blast,
So hum small bees, before their swarms they cast.

II.

Their captain rules their courage, guides their heat,
  Their forwardness he stay'd with gentle rein ;
And yet more easy, haply, were the feat,
  To stop the current near Charybdis' main,
Or calm the blust'ring winds on mountains great,
  Than fierce desires of warlike hearts restrain ;
He rules them yet, and ranks them in their haste,
For well he knows disord'red speed makes waste.

III.

Feath'red their thoughts, their feet in wings were dight,
  Swiftly they march'd, yet were not tir'd thereby,
For willing minds make heaviest burdens light ;
  But when the gliding sun was mounted high,

Jerusalem, behold, appear'd in sight,
   Jerusalem they view, they see, they spy ;
Jerusalem with merry noise they greet,
With joyful shouts, and acclamations sweet.

IV.

As when a troop of jolly sailors row,
   Some new found land and country to descry ;
Through dang'rous seas and under stars unknow,
   Thrall to the faithless waves, and trothless sky ;
If once the wished shore begin to show,
   They all salute it with a joyful cry,
And each to other show the land in haste,
Forgetting quite their pains and perils past.

V.

To that delight which their first sight did breed,
   That pleased so the secret of their thought,
A deep repentance did forthwith succeed,
   That rev'rend fear and trembling with it brought.
Scantly they durst their feeble eyes dispread
   Upon that town, where Christ was sold and bought,
Where for our sins he, faultless, suff'red pain,
There where he died, and where he liv'd again.

VI.

Soft words, low speech, deep sobs, sweet sighs, salt tears,
   Rose from their breasts, with joy and pleasure mixt ;
For thus fares he the Lord aright that fears,
   Fear on devotion, joy on faith is fixt :
Such noise their passions make, as when one hears
   The hoarse sea-waves roar hollow rocks betwixt ;
Or as the wind in hoults and shady greaves
A murmur makes, among the boughs and leaves.

VII.

Their naked feet trod on the dusty way,
   Following th' ensample of their zealous guide ;
Their scarfs, their crests, their plumes, and feathers gay,
   They quickly doft, and willing laid aside ;
Their molten hearts their wonted pride alay,
   Along their watery cheeks warm tears down slide,
And then such secret speech as this, they us'd,
While to himself, each one himself accused :

VIII.

Flower of goodness, root of lasting bliss,
   Thou well of life, whose streams were purple blood
That flowed here, to cleanse the foul amiss
   Of sinful man, behold this brinish flood,
That from my melting heart distilled is ;
   Receive in gree these tears, O lord so good,
For never wretch with sin so overgone,
Had fitter time, or greater cause to moan.

IX.

This while the wary watchman looked over,
   From tops of Sion's towers, the hills and dales,
And saw the dust the fields and pastures cover,
   As when thick mists arise from moory vales :
At last the sun-bright shields he 'gan discover,
   And glist'ring helms, for violence none that fails ,
The metal shone like lightning bright in skies,
And man and horse amid the dust descries.

X.

Then loud he cries, Oh, what a dust ariseth !
   Oh, how it shines with shields and targets clear !
Up, up, to arms, for valiant heart despiseth
   The threat'ned storm of death, and danger near ,
Behold your foes : then further thus deviseth ;
   Haste, haste, for vain delay increaseth fear,
These horrid clouds of dust, that yonder fly,
Your coming foes do hide, and hide the sky.

XI.

The tender children, and the fathers old,
   The aged matrons, and the virgin chaste,
That durst not shake the spear, nor target hold,
   Themselves devoutly in their temples plac'd ;
The rest, of members strong and courage bold,
   On hardy breasts their harness don'd in haste,
Some to the walls, some to the gates them dight ;
Their king meanwhile directs them all aright.

XII.

All things well ord'red, he withdrew with speed
   Up to a turret high, two ports between,
That so he might be near at every need,
   And overlook the lands and furrows green ;

Thither he did the sweet Erminia lead,
　That in his court had entertained been,
Since Christians Antioch did to bondage bring,
And slew her father, who thereof was king.

XIII.

Against their foes Clorinda sallied out,
　And many a baron bold was by her side;
Within the postern stood Argantes stout
　To rescue her, if ill mote here betide:
With speeches brave she cheer'd her warlike rout,
　And with bold words them heart'ned as they ride,
Let us by some brave act, quoth she, this day
Of Asia's hopes the ground-work found and lay.

XIV.

While to her folk thus spake the virgin brave,
　Thereby, behold, forth past a Christian band,
Towards the camp that herds of cattle drave;
　For they that morn had forraid all the land;
The fierce virago would that booty save,
　Whom their commander singled hand for hand,
A mighty man at arms, who Guardo hight,
But far too weak to match with her in fight.

XV.

They met, and low in dust was Guardo laid,
　'Twixt either army, from his sell down kest;
The Pagans shout for joy, and hopeful said,
　Those good beginnings would have endings blest:
Against the rest on went the noble maid,
　She broke the helm, and pierc'd the armed breast;
Her men the paths rode through made by her sword,
They pass the stream where she had found the ford.

XVI.

Soon was the prey out of their hands recov'red;
　By step and step the Frenchmen 'gan retire,
Till on a little hill at last they hov'red,
　Whose strength preserv'd them from Clorinda's ire:
When, as a tempest that hath long been cov'red
　In watery clouds, breaks out with sparkling fire,
With his strong squadron Lord Tancredie came;
His heart with rage, his eyes with courage flame:

XVII.

Mast-great the spear was which the gallant bore,
　　That in his warlike pride he made to shake,
As winds tall cedars toss on mountains hoar ;
　　The king, that wond'red at his brav'ry, spake
To her, that near him seated was before,
　　Who felt her heart with love's hot fever quake,
Well should'st thou know, quoth he, each Christian **knight**
By long acquaintance, though in armor dight.

XVIII.

Say, who is he shows so great worthiness,
　　That rides so rank, and bends his lance so fell ?
To this the princess said nor more nor less,
　　Her heart with sighs, her eyes with tears did swell ;
But sighs and tears she wisely could suppress,
　　Her love and passion she dissembled well,
And strove her love and hot desire to cover,
Till heart with sighs, and eyes with tears ran over.

XIX.

At last she spake, and with a crafty sleight
　　Her secret love disguis'd in clothes of hate ;
Alas, too well, she says, I know that knight,
　　I saw his force and courage proved late ;
Too late I viewed when his power and might
　　Shook down the pillar of Cassano's state ;
Alas, what wounds he gives ! how fierce, how fell !
No physic helps them cure, nor magic's spell.

XX.

Tancred he hight ; O Macon, would he wear
　　My thrall, ere fates him of this life deprive !
For to his hateful head such spite I bear,
　　I would him reave his cruel heart on live.
Thus said she ; they, that her complainings hear,
　　In other sense her wishes credit give.
She sigh'd withall, they construed all amiss,
And thought she wish'd to kill, who long'd to kiss.

XXI.

This while forth prick'd Clorinda from the throng,
　　And 'gainst Tancredie set her spear in rest ;
Upon their helms they crack'd their lances long,
　　And from her head her guilden casque he kest,

For every lace he broke and every thong,
   And in the dust threw down her plumed crest,
About her shoulders shone her golden locks,
Like sunny beams on alabaster rocks.

XXII.

Her looks with fire, her eyes with lightning blaze,
   Sweet was her wrath, what then would be her smile ?
Tancred, whereon think'st thou ? what dost thou gaze ?
   Hast thou forgot her in so short a while ?
The same is she, the shape of whose sweet face
   The god of love did in thy heart compile :
The same that left thee by the cooling stream,
Safe from sun's heat, but scorch'd with beauty's beam.

XXIII.

The prince well knew her, though her painted shield
   And golden helm he had not mark'd before ;
She sav'd her head, and with her axe, well steel'd,
   Assail'd the knight: but her the knight forbore ;
'Gainst other foes he prov'd him through the field,
   Yet she for that refrained ne'er the more,
But following, Turn thee, cried, in ireful wise ;
And so at once she threats to kill him twice.

XXIV.

Not once the baron lift his armed hand
   To strike the maid, but gazing on her eyes,
Where lordly Cupid seem'd in arms to stand,
   No way to ward or shun her blows he tries ;
But softly says, No stroke of thy strong hand
   Can vanquish Tancred, but thy conquest lies
In those fair eyes, which fiery weapons dart,
That find no lighting-place except this heart.

XXV.

At last resolv'd, although he hop'd small grace,
   Yet ere he died to tell how much he loved,
For pleasing words in women's ears find place,
   And gentle hearts with humble suit are moved :
O thou, quoth he, withhold thy wrath a space,
   For if thou long to see my valor proved,
Were it not better, from this warlike rout
Withdrawn, somewhere, alone to fight it out ?

XXVI.

So singled, may we both our courage try.
  Clorinda to that motion yielded glad,
And helmless to the forestward 'gan hie,
  Whither the prince right pensive went and sad,
And there the virgin 'gan him soon defy,
  One blow she strucken and he warded had,
When he cried, Hold, and ere we prove our might,
First hear thou some conditions of the fight.

XXVII.

She stay'd, and desp'rate love had made him bold:
  Since from the fight thou wilt no respite give,
The cov'nants be, he said, that thou unfold
  This wretched bosom, and my heart out rive,
Giv'n thee long since, and if thou, cruel, would
  I should be dead, let me no longer live,
But pierce this breast, that all the world may say,
The eagle made the turtle-dove her prey.

XXVIII.

Save with thy grace, or let thine anger kill,
  Love hath disarm'd my life of all defence ;
An easy labor harmless blood to spill,
  Strike then, and punish where is none offence.
This said the prince, and more perchance had will
  To have declar'd, to move her cruel sense ;
But, in ill time, of Pagans thither came
A troop, and Christians that pursu'd the same.

XXIX.

The Pagans fled before their valiant foes,
  For dread or craft, it skills not that we knew ;
A soldier wild, careless to win or lose,
  Saw where her locks about the damsel flew,
And at her back he proffereth, as he goes,
  To strike where her he did disarmed view :
But Tancred cry'd, Oh, stay thy cursed hand,
And, for to ward the blow, lift up his brand.

XXX.

But yet the cutting steel arrived there,
  Where her fair neck adjoin'd her noble head ;
Light was the wound, but through her amber hair,
  The purple drops down railed bloody red ;

So rubies set in flaming gold appear:
  But Lord Tancredie pale with rage, as lead,
Flew on the villain, who to flight him bound;
  The smart was his, though she receiv'd the wound:

XXXI.

The villain flies; he, full of rage and ire,
  Pursues, she stood and wond'red on them both,
But yet to follow them show'd no desire;
  To stray so far she would perchance be loth,
But quickly turn'd her, fierce as flaming fire,
  And on her foes wreaked her anger wroth;
On every side she kills them down amain,
And now she flies, and now she turns again;

XXXII.

As the swift ure, by Volga's rolling flood,
  Chas'd through the plains the mastiff curs toforn,
Flies to the succor of some neighbor wood,
  And often turns again his dreadful horn,
Against the dogs imbru'd in sweat and blood,
  That bite not, till the beast to flight retorn;
Or as the Moors at their strange tennis run
Defenc'd, the flying balls unhurt to shun:

XXXIII.

So ran Clorinda, so her foes pursued,
  Until they both approach'd the city's wall;
When, lo, the Pagans their fierce wrath renewed,
  Cast, in a ring, about they wheeled all,
And 'gainst the Christians' backs and sides they showed
  Their courage fierce, and to new combat fall;
When down the hill Argantes came to fight,
Like angry Mars to aid the Trojan knight;

XXXIV.

Furious, tofore the foremost of his rank,
  In sturdy steel forth stept the warrior bold;
The first he smote down from his saddle sank,
  The next, under his steed, lay on the mould;
Under the Sar'cen's spear the worthies shrank,
  No breast-plate could that cursed tree outhold,
When that was broke, his precious sword he drew,
And whom he hit, he felled, hurt, or slew.

XXXV.

Clorinda slew Ardelio, aged knight,
    Whose graver years would for no labor yield ;
His age was full of puissance and might,
    Two sons he had to guard his noble eild ;
The first, far from his father's care and sight,
    Called Alicandro, wounded lay in field,
And Poliphern, the younger, by his side
Had he not nobly fought, had surely died.

XXXVI.

Tancred by this, that strove to overtake
    The villain that had hurt his only dear,
From vain pursuit at last returned back,
    And his brave troop discomfit saw well near ;
Thither he spurr'd, and 'gan huge slaughter make,
    His shock no steed, his blow no knight could bear ;
For dead he strikes him whom he lights upon,
So thunders break high trees on Libanon.

XXXVII.

Dudon his squadron of adventurers brings,
    To aid the worthy and his tired crew ;
Before the res'due young Rinaldo flings,
    As swift as fiery lightning kindled new :
His argent eagle with her silver wings
    In field of azure, fair Erminia knew ;
See there, sir king, she says, a knight as bold
And brave, as was the son of Peleus old.

XXXVIII.

He wins the prize in just and tournament,
    His acts are numberless, though few his years ;
If Europe six like him to war had sent
    Among these thousands strong of Christian peers,
Syria were lost, lost were the Orient,
    And all the lands the Southern Ocean wears ;
Conquer'd were all hot Afric's tawny kings,
And all that dwell by Nilus' unknown springs.

XXXIX.

Rinaldo is his name ; his armed fist
    Breaks down stone walls, when rams and engines fail ;
But turn your eyes, because I would you wist
    What lord that is, in green and golden mail ;

Dudon he hight, who guideth as him list
   Th' adventurers' troop, whose prowess seld doth fail ;
High birth, grave years, and practice long in war,
And fearless heart, make him renowned far.

XL.

See that big man, that all in brown is bound,
   Gernando call'd, the king of Norway's son,
A prouder knight treads not on grass or ground,
   His pride hath lost the praise his prowess won ;
And that kind pair in white all armed round,
   Is Edward and Gildippes, who begone
Through love the hazard of fierce war to prove,
Famous for arms, but famous more for love.

XLI.

While thus they tell their foemen's worthiness,
   The slaughter rageth in the plain at large ;
Tancred and young Rinaldo break the press,
   They bruise the helm, and pierce the sevenfold targe ;
The troop by Dudon led perform'd no less,
   But in they come and give a furious charge ;
Argantes self, fell'd at one single blow,
Inglorious, bleeding, lay on earth full low.

XLII.

Nor had the boaster ever risen more,
   But that Rinaldo's horse ev'n then down fell,
And with the fall his leg oppress'd so sore,
   That for a space there must he algates dwell.
Meanwhile the pagan troops were nigh forlore,
   Swiftly they fled, glad they escap'd so well ;
Argantes, and with him Clorinda stout,
For bank and bulwark serv'd to save the rout.

XLIII.

These fled the last, and with their force sustained
   The Christians' rage, that followed them so near ;
Their scatt'red troops to safety well they trained,
   And while the res'due fled the brunt these bear ;
Dudon pursu'd the victory he gained,
   And on Tigranes nobly broke his spear,
Then with his sword headless to ground him cast,
So gard'ners branches lop that spring too fast.

XLIV.

Algazer's breastplate, of fine temper made,
   Nor Corban's helmet, forg'd by magic art,
Could save their owners, for Lord Dudon's blade
   Cleft Corban's head, and pierc'd Algazer's heart ;
And their proud souls down to th' infernal shade,
   From Amurath and Mahomet depart ;
Nor strong Argantes thought his life was sure,
He could not safely fly, nor fight secure.

XLV.

The angry pagan bit his lips for teen ;
   He ran, he stay'd, he fled, he turn'd again ;
Until at last unmark'd, unview'd, unseen,
   When Dudon had Almansor newly slain,
Within his side he sheath'd his weapon keen,
   Down fell the worthy on the dusty plain,
And lifted up his feeble eyes unneath,
Oppress'd with leaden sleep of iron death.

XLVI.

Three times he strove to view heav'n's golden ray,
   And rais'd him on his feeble elbow thrice,
And thrice he tumbled on the lowly lay,
   And three times clos'd again his dying eyes ;
He speaks no word, yet makes he signs to pray ;
   He sighs, he faints, he groans, and then he dies :
Argantes proud to spoil the corpse disdain'd,
But shook his sword with blood of Dudon stain'd.

XLVII.

And turning to the Christian knights, he cried,
   Lordings, behold, this bloody reeking blade
Last night was given me by your noble guide ;
   Tell him what proof thereof this day is made ;
Needs must this please him well that is betide,
   That I so well can use this martial trade,
To whom so rare a gift he did present ;
Tell him the workman fits the instrument.

XLVIII.

If further proof hereof he long to see,
   Say it still thirsts, and would his heart-blood drink ;
And I he haste not to encounter me,
   Say I will find him when he least doth think :

The Christians at his words enraged be,
  But he to shun their ire doth safely shrink
Under the shelter of the neighbor wall,
Well guarded with his troops and soldiers all.

XLIX.

Like storms of hail the stones fell down from high,
  Cast from the bulwarks, flankers, ports and towers,
The shafts and quarries from their engines fly,
  As thick as falling drops in April showers:
The French withdrew, they list not press too nigh,
  The Saracens escaped all the powers.
But now Rinaldo from the earth up-lept,
Where by the leg his steed had long him kept.

L.

He came and breathed vengeance from his breast,
  'Gainst him that noble Dudon late had slain,
And being come, thus spake he to the rest:
  Warriors, why stand you gazing here in vain?
Pale death our valiant leader hath oppress'd,
  Come wreak his loss, whom bootless you complain.
These walls are weak, they keep but cowards out,
No rampier can withstand a courage stout.

LI.

Of double iron, brass, or adamant,
  Or, if this wall were built of flaming fire,
Yet should the pagan vile a fortress want,
  To shroud his coward head safe from mine ire:
Come follow then, and bid base fear avaunt,
  The harder work deserves the greater hire:
And with that word close to the walls he starts,
Nor fears he arrows, quarries, stones, or darts.

LII.

Above the waves as Neptune lift his eyes
  To chide the winds, that Trojan ships oppress'd,
And with his count'nance calm'd seas, winds, and skies,
  So look'd Rinaldo, when he shook his crest
Before those walls; each pagan fears and flies
  His dreadful sight, or trembling stay'd at lest:
Such dread his awful visage on them cast,
So seem poor doves at goshawks' sight aghast.

LIII.

The herald Sigier now from Godfrey came,
  To will them stay and calm their courage hot ;
Retire, quoth he, Godfrey commands the same,
  To wreak your ire this season fitteth not :
Though loth, Rinaldo stay'd and stopt the flame
  That boiled in his hardy stomach hot ;
His bridled fury grew thereby more fell,
So rivers stopp'd above their banks do swell.

LIV.

The bands retire, nor dang'red by their foes
  In their retreat, so wise were they and wary ;
To murder'd Dudon each lamenting goes,
  From wonted use of ruth they list not vary ;
Upon their friendly arms they soft impose
  The noble burden of his corpse to carry :
Meanwhile Godfredo from a mountain great
Beheld the sacred city and her seat.

LV.

Jerusalem is seated on two hills
  Of height unlike, and turned side to side,
The space between a gentle valley fills,
  From mount to mount expansed fair and wide ;
Three sides are sure imbar'd, with crags and hills,
  The rest is easy, scant to rise espied :
But mighty bulwarks fence that plainer part,
So art helps nature, nature strengtheneth art.

LVI.

The town is stor'd of troughs and cisterns, made
  To keep fresh water, but the country seems
Devoid of grass, unfit for ploughmen's trade,
  Not fertile, moist with rivers, wells, and streams.
There grow few trees, to make the summer's shade,
  To shield the parched land from scorching beams,
Save that a wood stands six mile from the town,
With aged cedars dark, and shadows brown.

LVII.

By east, among the dusty valleys, glide
  The silver streams of Jordan's crystal flood ;
By west, the midland sea, with bounders tied
  Of sandy shores, where Joppa whilom stood ;

By north, Samaria stands, and on that side
   The golden calf was rear'd in Bethel wood ;
Bethlem by south, where Christ incarnate was,
A pearl in steel, a diamond set in brass.

LVIII.

While thus the Duke on every side descried
   The city's strength, the walls and gates about,
And saw where least the same was fortified,
   Where weakest seem'd the walls to keep him out ;
Erminia, as he armed rode, him spyed,
   And thus bespake the heathen tyrant stout :
See Godfrey there, in purple clad and gold,
His stately port, and princely look behold :

LIX.

Well seems he born to be with honor crown'd,
   So well the lore he knows of regiment ;
Peerless in fight, in counsel grave and sound,
   The double gift of glory excellent ;
Among these armies is no warrior found
   Graver in speech, bolder in tournament ;
Raimond pardie in counsel match him might ;
Tancred and young Rinaldo like in fight.

LX.

To whom the king ; he likes me well therefore,
   I knew him whilom in the court of France ;
When I from Egypt went ambassador,
   I saw him there break many a sturdy lance ;
And yet his chin no sign of manhood bore,
   His youth was forward, but with governance ;
His words, his actions, and his portance brave,
Of future virtue timely tokens gave.

LXI.

Presages, ah, too true ; with that a space
   He sigh'd for grief, then said, Fain would I know
The man in red, with such a knightly grace,
   A worthy lord he seemeth by his show ;
How like to Godfrey looks he in the face !
   How like in person ! but some deal more low.
Baldwin, quoth she, that noble baron hight,
By birth his brother, and his match in might.

LXII.

Next look on him that seems for council fit,
  Whose silver locks bewray his store of days;
Raimond he hight, a man of wondrous wit,
  Of Tholouse lord, his wisdom is his praise,
What he forethinks doth (as he looks for) hit,
  His stratagems have good success always:
With gilden helm beyond him rides the mild
And good Prince William, England's king's dear child.

LXIII.

With him is Guelpho as his noble mate,
  In birth, in acts, in arms alike the rest,
I know him well, since I beheld him late,
  By his broad shoulders and his squared breast;
But my proud foe that quite hath ruinate
  My high estate, and Antioch opprest,
I see not, Boemond, that to death did bring
Mine aged lord, my father, and my king.

LXIV.

Thus talked they: meanwhile Godfredo went
  Down to the troops that in the valley stay'd,
And, for in vain he thought the labor spent,
  T' assail those parts that to the mountains laid,
Against the northern gate his force he bent,
  'Gainst it he camp'd, 'gainst it his engines play'd;
All felt the fury of his angry power,
That from those gates lies to the corner tower.

LXV.

The town's third part was this, or little less,
  'Fore which the Duke his glorious ensigns spread,
For so great compass had that forteress,
  That round it could not be environed,
With narrow siege (nor Babel's king, I guess,
  That whilome took it, such an army led);
But all the ways he kept, by which his foe
Might to or from the city come or go.

LXVI.

His care was next to cast the trenches deep,
  So to preserve his resting camp by night,
Lest from the city, while his soldiers sleep,
  They might assail them with untimely fight.

This done, he went where lords and princes weep,
  With dire complaint, about the murder'd knight,
Where Dudon dead lay slaughter'd on the ground,
And all the soldiers sate lamenting round.

LXVII.

His wailing friends adorn'd the mournful bier
  With woful pomp, whereon his corpse they laid ;
And when they saw the Bulloigne prince draw near,
  All felt new grief, and each new sorrow made ;
But he, withouten show or change of cheer,
  His springing tears within their fountains stay'd ;
His rueful looks upon the corpse he cast
Awhile, and thus bespake the same at last :

LXVIII.

We need not mourn for thee, here laid to rest,
  Earth is thy bed, and not thy grave ; the skies
Are for thy soul the cradle and the nest,
  There live, for here thy glory never dies :
For like a Christian knight and champion blest,
  Thou didst both live and die ; now feed thine eyes
With thy Redeemer's sight, where crown'd with bliss
Thy faith, zeal, merit, well deserving is.

LXIX.

Our loss, not thine, provokes these plaints and tears,
  For when we lost thee, then our ship her mast,
Our chariot lost her wheels, their points our spears,
  The bird of conquest her chief feather cast :
But though thy death far from our army bears
  Her chiefest earthly aid, in heav'n yet plac'd
Thou wilt procure us help divine ; so reaps
He that sows godly sorrow, joy by heaps.

LXX.

For if our God the Lord Armipotent
  Those armed angels in our aid down send
That were at Dothan to his prophet sent,
  Thou wilt come down with them, and well defend
Our host, and with thy sacred weapons bent
  'Gainst Sion's fort, these gates and bulwarks rend,
That so thy hand may win this hold, and we
May in these temples praise our Christ for thee.

LXXI.

Thus he complain'd ; but now the sable shade
    Ycleped night, had thick enveloped
The sun, in veil of double darkness made :
    Sleep eased care ; rest brought complaint to bed.
All night the wary Duke devising laid
    How that high wall should best be battered ;
How his strong engines he might aptly fràme,
And whence get timber fit to build the same.

LXXII.

Up with the lark the sorrowful Duke arose,
    A mourner chief at Dudon's burial ;
Of cypress sad a pile his friends compose
    Under a hill, o'ergrown with cedars tall ;
Beside the hearse a fruitful palm-tree grows,
    Ennobled since by this great funeral,
Where Dudon's corpse they softly laid in ground ;
The priests sung hymns, the soldiers wept around.

LXXIII.

Among the boughs they here and there bestow
    Ensigns and arms, as witness of his praise,
Which he from pagan lords, that did them owe,
    Had won in prosp'rous fights and happy frays :
His shield they fixed on the bole below,
    And there this distich under-writ, which says—
This palm with stretched arms doth overspread
The champion Dudon's glorious carcase dead.

LXXIV.

This work performed with advisement good,
    Godfrey his carpenters, and men of skill
In all the camp, sent to an aged wood,
    With convoy meet to guard them safe from ill :
Within a valley deep this forest stood,
    To Christian eyes unseen, unknown, until
A Syrian told the Duke, who thither sent
Those chosen workmen that for timber went.

LXXV.

And now the axe rag'd in the forest wild,
    The echo sighed in the groves unseen,
The weeping nymphs fled from their bowers exil'd,
    Down fell the shady tops of shaking treen ;

Down came the sacred palms, the ashes wild,
    The funeral cypress, holly ever green,
The weeping fir, thick beech, and sailing pine,
The married elm fell with his fruitful vine.

LXXVI.

The shooter yew, the broad-leav'd sycamore,
    The barren plantain, and the walnut sound,
The myrrh that her foul sin doth still deplore,
    The alder owner of all wat'rish ground,
Sweet juniper, whose shadow hurteth sore,
    Proud cedar, oak the king of forests crown'd.
Thus fell the trees, with noise the deserts roar,
The beasts their caves, the birds their nests forlore.

BOOK IV.

I.

WHILE thus their work went on with lucky speed,
　And reared rams their horned fronts advance,
The ancient foe to man and mortal seed
　His wannish eyes upon them bent askance ;
And when he saw their labors well succeed,
　He wept for rage, and threat'ned dire mischance,
He chok'd his curses, to himself he spake,
Such noise wild bulls that softly bellow make.

II.

At last, resolving in his damned thought
　To find some let to stop their warlike feat,
He gave command his princes should be brought
　Before the throne of his infernal seat.
O fool ! as if it were a thing of naught
　God to resist, or change his purpose great,
Who on his foes doth thunder in his ire,
Whose arrows hail-stones be and coals of fire.

III.

The dreary trumpet blew a dreadful blast,
　And rumbled through the lands and kingdoms under,
Through wasteness wide it roar'd, and hollows vast,
　And fill'd the deep with horror, fear, and wonder ;

Not half so dreadful noise the tempests cast,
    That fall from skies with storms of hail and thunder,
Nor half so loud the whistling winds do sing,
Broke from the earthen prisons of their king.

IV.

The Peers of Pluto's realm assembled been
    Amid the palace of their angry king,
In hideous forms and shapes 'tofore unseen,
    That fear, death, terror, and amazement bring;
With ugly paws some trample on the green,
    Some gnaw the snakes that on their shoulders hing,
And some their forked tails stretch forth on high,
And tear the twinkling stars from trembling sky.

V.

There were Sileno's foul and loathsome rout,
    There Sphinxes, Centaurs, there were Gorgons fell,
There howling Scyllas yawling round about,
    There serpents hiss, there seven-mouthed Hydras yell,
Chimera there spews fire and brimstone out,
    And Polyphemus blind supporteth hell;
Besides ten thousand monsters therein dwells,
Mis-shap'd, unlike themselves, and like naught else.

VI.

About their Prince each took his wonted seat
    On thrones red hot, ybuilt of burning brass,
Pluto in middest heav'd his trident great,
    Of rusty iron huge that forged was;
The rocks on which the salt sea billows beat,
    And Atlas tops the clouds in height that pass,
Compar'd to his huge person, mole-hills be,
So his rough front, his horns so lifted he.

VII.

The tyrant proud frown'd from his lofty cell,
    And with his looks made all his monsters tremble,
His eyes, that full of rage and venom swell,
    Two beacons seem, that men to arms assemble,
His feltred locks, that on his bosom fell,
    On rugged mountains briars and thorns resemble,
His yawning mouth that foamed clotted blood,
Gap'd like a whirlpool wide in Stygian flood.

VIII.

And as mount Ætna vomits sulphur out,
    With clifts of burning crags, and fire, and smoke,
So from his mouth flew kindled coals about,
    Hot sparks and smells that man and beast would choke.
The gnarring porter durst not whine for doubt,
    Still were the Furies while their Sovereign spoke,
And swift Cocytus stay'd his murmur shrill,
While thus the murderer thund'red out his will:

IX.

Ye powers infernal, worthier far to sit
    Above the sun, whence you your offspring take,
With me that whilome through the welkin flit,
    Down tumbled headlong to this empty lake,
Our former glory still remember it,
    Our bold attempts and war we once did make
'Gainst Him that rules above the starry sphere,
For which like traitors we lie damned here.

X.

And now, instead of clear and gladsome sky,
    Of Titan's brightness that so glorious is,
In this deep darkness, lo! we helpless lie,
    Hopeless again to joy our former bliss;
And more, which makes my griefs to multiply,
    That sinful creature man elected is,
And in our place the heavens possess he must,
Vile man! begot of clay, and born of dust.

XI.

Nor this suffic'd, but that he also gave
    His only Son, his darling, to be slain,
To conquer so hell, death, sin, and the grave,
    And man condemned to restore again;
He brake our prisons, and would algates save
    The souls that here should dwell in wo and pain,
And now in Heav'n with Him they live always,
With endless glory crown'd and lasting praise.

XII.

But why recount I thus our passed harms?
    Remembrance fresh makes weak'ned sorrows strong,
Expulsed were we with injurious arms,
    From those due honors us of right belong.

But let us leave to speak of these alarms,
  And bend our forces 'gainst our present wrong;
Ah! see you not how He attempted hath
To bring all lands, all nations to his faith!

XIII.

Then let us careless spend the day and night,
  Without regard what haps, what comes or goes;
Let Asia subject be to Christians' might,
  A prey be Sion to her conquering foes;
Let her adore again her Christ aright,
  Who her before all nations whilome chose,
In brazen tables be his lore ywrit,
And let all tongues and lands acknowledge it.

XIV.

So shall our sacred altars all be his,
  Our holy idols tumbled in the mold,
To him the wretched man, that sinful is,
  Shall pray, and offer incense, myrrh, and gold;
Our temples shall their costly deckings miss,
  With naked walls and pillars freezing cold,
Tribute of souls shall end and our estate,
Or Pluto reign in kingdoms desolate.

XV.

Oh! be not then the courage perish'd clean
  That whilome dwelt within your haughty thought,
When, arm'd with shining fire and weapons keen,
  Against the angels of proud heav'n we fought:
I grant we fell on the Phlegrean green,
  Yet good our cause was, though our fortune naught;
For chance assisteth oft th' ignobler part,
We lost the field, yet lost we not our heart.

XVI.

Go then, my strength, my hope, my spirits, go,
  These western rebels with your power withstand,
Pluck up these weeds, before they overgrow
  The gentle garden of the Hebrews' land;
Quench out this spark before it kindle so
  That Asia burn, consumed with the brand.
Use open force, or secret guile unspied;
For craft is virtue 'gainst a foe defied.

6

XVII.

Among the knights and worthies of their train,
  Let some like out-laws wander uncouth ways,
Let some be slain in field, let some again
  Make oracles of women's yeas and nays,
And pine in foolish love ; let some complain
  On Godfrey's rule, and mutines 'gainst him raise ;
Turn each one's sword against his fellow's heart ;
Thus kill them all, or spoil the greatest part.

XVIII.

Before his words the tyrant ended had,
  The lesser devils arose with ghastly roar,
And thronged forth about the world to gad ;
  Each land they filled, river, stream, and shore,
The goblins, fairies, fiends, and furies mad,
  Ranged in flow'ry dales, and mountains hoar,
And under every trembling leaf they sit,
Between the solid earth and welkin flit:

XIX.

About the world they spread both far and wide,
  Filling the thoughts of each ungodly heart
With secret mischief, anger, hate, and pride,
  Wounding lost souls with sin's empoison'd dart.
But say, my Muse, recount whence first they tried
  To hurt the Christian lords, and from what part ;
Thou know'st of things perform'd so long agone,
This latter age hears little troth or none.

XX.

The town Damascus and the lands about
  Rul'd Hidraort, a wizard grave and sage,
Acquainted well with all the damned rout
  Of Pluto's reign, ev'n from his tender age ;
Yet of this war he could not figure out
  The wished ending, or success presage ;
For neither stars above, nor powers of hell,
  Nor skill, nor art, nor charm, nor devil could tell.

XXI.

And yet he thought, O vain conceit of man !
  Which as thou wishest judgest things to come,
That the French host to sure destruction ran,
  Condemned quite by heav'n's eternal doom :

He thinks no force withstand or vanquish can
    Th' Egyptian strength, and therefore would that some
Both of the prey and glory of the fight,
Upon his Syrian folk should haply light.

XXII.

But for he held the Frenchmen's worth in prise,
    And fear'd the doubtful gain of bloody war
He, that was closely false and slily wise,
    Cast how he might annoy them most from far :
And as he 'gan upon this point devise
    (As counsellors in ill still nearest are),
At hand was Satan, ready ere men need,
If once they think to make them do the deed.

XXIII.

He counsel'd him how best to hunt his game,
    What dart to cast, what net, what toil to pitch :
A niece he had, a nice and tender dame,
    Peerless in wit, in nature's blessings rich,
To all deceit she could her beauty frame,
    False, fair, and young, a virgin and a witch ;
To her he told the sum of this emprise,
And prais'd her thus, for she was fair and wise :

XXIV.

My dear, who underneath these locks of gold,
    And native brightness of thy lovely hue,
Hidest grave thoughts, ripe wit, and wisdom old,
    More skill than I, in all mine arts untrue,
To thee my purpose great I must unfold,
    This enterprise thy cunning must pursue,
Weave thou to end this web which I begin,
I will the distaff hold, come thou and spin.

XXV.

Go to the Christians' host, and there assay
    All subtle sleights that women use in love,
Shed brinish tears, sob, sigh, entreat, and pray,
    Wring thy fair hands, cast up thine eyes above,
For mourning beauty hath much power, men say,
    The stubborn hearts with pity frail to move ;
Look pale for dread, and blush sometime for shame,
In seeming troth thy lies will soonest frame.

XXVI.

Take with the bait Lord Godfrey, if thou may'st,
　　Frame snares of looks, trains of alluring speech ;
For if he love, the conquest then thou hast :
　　Thus purpos'd war thou may'st with ease impeach ;
Else lead the other lords to deserts waste,
　　And hold them slaves far from their leader's reach.
This taught he her, and for conclusion saith,
All things are lawful for our lands and faith.

XXVII.

The sweet Armida took this charge on hand,
　　A tender piece, for beauty, sex and age.
The sun was sunken underneath the land
　　When she began her wanton pilgrimage ;
In silken weeds she trusteth to withstand,
　　And conquer knights in warlike equipage.
Of their night-ambling dame the Syrians prated,
Some good, some bad, as they her lov'd or hated.

XXVIII.

Within few days the nymph arrived there,
　　Where puissant Godfrey had his tents ypight ;
Upon her strange attire, and visage clear,
　　Gazed each soldier, gazed every knight :
As when a comet doth in skies appear,
　　The people stand amazed at the light,
So wonder'd they, and each at other sought,
What mister wight she was, and whence ybrought.

XXIX.

Yet never eye to Cupid's service vow'd
　　Beheld a face of such a lovely pride ;
A tinsel veil her amber locks did shroud,
　　That strove to cover what it could not hide ;
The golden sun, behind a silver cloud,
　　So streameth out his beams on every side ;
The marble goddess, set at Guido's, naked,
She seem'd, were she uncloth'd, or that awaked.

XXX.

The gamesome wind among her tresses plays,
　　And curleth up those glowing riches short ;
Her spareful eye to spread his beams denays,
　　But keeps his shot where Cupid keeps his fort ;

The rose and lily on her cheek assays
　　To paint true fairness out in bravest sort ;
Her lips, where blooms naught but the single rose,
Still blush, for still they kiss while still they close.

XXXI.

Her breasts, two hills o'erspread with purest snow,
　　Sweet, smooth and supple, soft and gently swelling,
Between them lies a milken dale below,
　　Where love, youth, gladness, whiteness make their dwelling ;
Her breasts half hid, and half were laid to show ;
　　Her envious vesture greedy sight repelling :
So was the wanton clad, as if thus much
Should please the eye, the rest unseen the touch.

XXXII.

As when the sunbeams dive through Tagus' wave,
　　To spy the storehouse of his springing gold,
Love-piercing thought so through her mantle drave,
　　And in her gentle bosom wander'd bold :
It view'd the wondrous beauty virgins have,
　　And all to fond desire with vantage told :
Alas ! what hope is left to quench the fire,
That kindled is by sight, blown by desire.

XXXIII.

Thus past she, praised, wish'd, and wond'red at,
　　Among the troops who there encamped lay,
She smil'd for joy, but well dissembled that
　　Her greedy eye chose out her wished prey ;
On all her gestures seeming virtue sat,
　　Towards th' imperial tent she ask'd the way :
With that she met a bold and lovesome knight,
Lord Godfrey's youngest brother, Eustace hight.

XXXIV.

This was the fowl that first fell in the snare,
　　He saw her fair, and hop'd to find her kind ;
The throne of Cupid hath an easy stair,
　　His bark is fit to sail with every wind,
The breach he makes no wisdom can repair.
　　With rev'rence meet the baron low inclin'd,
And thus his purpose to the virgin told,
For youth, use, nature, all had made him bold :

XXXV.

Lady, if thee beseem a stile so low,
  In whose sweet looks such sacred beauties shine,
For never yet did heav'n such grace bestow
  On any daughter born of Adam's line,
Thy name let us, though far unworthy, know,
  Unfold thy will, and whence thou art in fine,
Lest my audacious boldness learn too late,
What honors due become thy high estate.

XXXVI.

Sir knight, quoth she, your praises reach too high
  Above her merit you commenden so,
A hapless maid I am, both born to die,
  And dead to joy, that live in care and wo,
A virgin helpless, fugitive pardie,
  My native soil and kingdom thus forego
To seek Duke Godfrey's aid, such store men tell
Of virtuous ruth doth in his bosom dwell.

XXXVII.

Conduct me then that mighty Duke before,
  If you be courteous, sir, as well you seem,—
Content, quoth he; since of one womb ybore,
  We brothers are, your fortune good esteem
T' encounter me, whose word prevaileth more
  In Godfrey's hearing than you haply deem,
Mine aid I grant, and his I promise too,
All that his sceptre, or my sword, can do.

XXXVIII.

He led her eas'ly forth when this was said,
  Where Godfrey sat among his lords and peers;
She rev'rence did, then blush'd as one dismay'd
  To speak, for secret wants and inward fears;
It seem'd a bashful shame her speeches stay'd.
  At last the courteous Duke her gently cheers;
Silence was made, and she began her tale.
They sit to hear, thus sung the nightingale:

XXXIX.

Victorious prince, whose honorable name
  Is held so great among our pagan kings,
That to those lands thou dost by conquest tame,
  That thou hast won them some content it brings

Well known to all is thy immortal fame.
  The earth thy worth, thy foe thy praises sings,
And painims wronged come to seek thine aid,
So doth thy virtue, so thy power persuade.

XL.

And I, though bred in Macon's heath'nish lore,
  Which thou oppressest with thy puissant might,
Yet trust thou wilt an helpless maid restore,
  And repossess her in her father's right :
Others in their distress do aid implore
  Of kin and friends ; but I in this sad plight
Invoke thy help my kingdom to invade,
So doth thy virtue, so my need persuade.

XLI.

In thee I hope, thy succors I invoke,
  To win the crown whence I am dispossest ;
For like renown awaiteth on the stroke .
  To cast the haughty down, or raise th' opprest ;
Nor greater glory brings a sceptre broke,
  Than doth deliv'rance of a maid distress'd :
And since thou canst at will perform the thing,
More is thy praise to make than kill a king.

XLII.

But if thou wouldst thy succors due excuse,
  Because in Christ I have no hope nor trust,
Ah ! yet for virtue's sake thy virtue use ;
  Who scorneth gold because it lies in dust ?
Be witness, heav'n, if thou to grant refuse,
  Thou dost forsake a maid in cause most just,
And for thou shalt at large my fortunes know,
I will my wrongs, and their great treasons show.

XLIII.

Prince Arbilan, that reigned in his life
  On fair Damascus, was my noble sire,
Born of mean race he was, yet got to wife
  The queen Chariclia, such was the fire
Of her hot love ; but soon the fatal knife
  Had cut the thread that kept their joys entire,
For so mishap her cruel lot had cast,
My birth her death, my first day was her last.

XLIV.

And ere five years had fully come and gone
    Since his dear spouse to hasty death did yield,
My father also died, consum'd with moan,
    And sought his love amid the Elysian field,
His crown and me, poor orphan, left alone.
    Mine uncle govern'd in my tender eild;
For well he thought, if mortal men have faith,
In brother's breast true love his mansion hath.

XLV.

He took the charge of me, and of the crown,
    And with kind shows of love so brought to pass,
That through Damascus great report was blown
    How good, how just, how kind mine uncle was;
Whether he kept his wicked hate unknown,
    And hid the serpent in the flow'ring grass,
Or that true faith did in his bosom won,
Because he meant to match me with his son.

XLVI.

Which son, within short while, did undertake
    Degree of knighthood, as beseem'd him well,
Yet never durst he, for his lady's sake,
    Break sword or lance, advanc'd in lofty cell:
As fair he was as Citherea's make,
    As proud as he that signoriseth hell,
In fashions wayward, and in love unkind,
For Cupid deigns not wound a currish mind.

XLVII.

This paragon should queen Armida wed,
    A goodly swain to be a princess' pheer,
A lovely partner of a lady's bed,
    A noble head a golden crown to wear!
His glosing sire his errand daily said,
    And sugar'd speeches whisper'd in mine ear,
To make me take this darling in mine arms,
But still the adder stopp'd her ears from charms.

XLVIII.

At last he left me with a troubled grace,
    Through which transparent was his inward spite;
Methought I read the story in his face
    Of these mishaps that on me since have light.

Since that, foul spirits haunt my resting place,
   And ghastly visions break my sleep by night;
Grief, horror, fear, my fainting soul did kill,
For so my mind foreshow'd my coming ill.

XLIX.

Three times the shape of my dear mother came,
   Pale, sad, dismay'd, to warn me in my dream:
Alas! how far transformed from the same,
   Whose eyes shone erst like Titan's glorious beam.—
Daughter, she says, fly, fly, behold thy dame,
   Foreshows the treasons of thy wretched eame,
Who poison 'gainst thy harmless life provides.—
This said, to shapeless air unseen she glides.

L.

But what avail high walls or bulwarks strong,
   Where fainting cowards have the peece to guard?
My sex too weak, mine age was all too young,
   To undertake alone a work so hard;
To wander wild the desert woods among,
   A banish'd maid, of wonted ease debarr'd,
So grievous seem'd, that leifer were my death,
And there t' expire where first I drew my breath.

LI.

I feared deadly evil if long I stay'd,
   And yet to fly had neither wit nor power;
Nor durst my heart declare it wax'd afraid,
   Lest so I hasten might my dying hour;
Thus restless waited I, unhappy maid!
   What hand should first pluck up my springing flow'r;
Even as the wretch, condemn'd to lose his life,
Awaits the falling of the murd'ring knife.

LII.

In these extremes (for so my fortune would
   Perchance preserve me to my further ill),
One of my noble father's servants old,
   That for his goodness bore his child good will,
With store of tears this treason 'gan unfold,
   And said, my guardian would his pupil kill;
And that himself, if promise made he kept,
Should give me poison dire ere next I slept.

LIII.

And further told me, if I wish'd to live,
    I must convey myself by secret flight ;
And offer'd then all succors he could give
    To aid his mistress, banish'd from her right.
His words of comfort fear to exile drive,
    The dread of death made lesser dangers light ;
So we concluded, when the shadows dim
Obscur'd the earth, I should depart with him.

LIV.

Of close escapes the aged patroness,
    Blacker than erst, her sable mantle spread,
When with two trusty maids, in great distress,
    Both from my uncle and my realm I fled.
Oft look'd I back, but hardly could suppress
    Those streams of tears mine eyes uncessant shed ;
For when I looked on my kingdom lost,
It was a grief, a death, an hell almost.

LV.

My steeds drew on the burden of my limbs,
    But still my looks, my thoughts, drew back as fast ;
So fare the men that, from the haven's brims,
    Far out to sea by sudden storm are cast.
Swift o'er the grass the rolling chariot swims,
    Through ways unknown, all night, all day, we haste
At last, nigh tir'd, a castle strong we fand,
The utmost border of my native land ;

LVI.

The fort Arontes was, for so the knight
    Was call'd that my deliv'rance thus had wrought.
But when the tyrant saw, by mature flight
    I had escap'd the treasons of his thought,
The rage increased in the cursed wight,
    'Gainst me, and him that me to safety brought ;
And us accus'd, we would have poisoned
Him ; but descried, to save our lives we fled ;

LVII.

And that, in lieu of his approved truth,
    To poison him I hired had my guide ;
That he dispatched, mine unbridled youth
    Might range at will, in no subjection tied,

And that each night I slept (O foul untruth !)
   Mine honor lost, by this Arontes' side :—
But heaven I pray send down revenging fire,
When so base love shall change my chaste desire !

LVIII.

Not that he sitteth on my regal throne,
   Nor that he thirst to drink my lukewarm blood,
So grieveth me as this despite alone,
   That my renown, which ever blameless stood,
Hath lost the light wherewith it always shone,
   With forged lies he makes his tale so good,
And holds my subjects' hearts in such suspense,
That none take armor for their queen's defence.

LIX.

And though he doth my regal throne possess,
   Clothed in purple, crown'd with burnish'd gold ;
Yet is his hate, his rancor, ne'er the less,
   Since naught assuageth malice when 'tis old :
He threats to burn Arontes' forteress,
   And murder him unless he yield the hold ;
And me, and mine, threats not with war, but death ;
Thus causeless hatred endless is uneath.

LX.

And so he trusts to wash away the stain,
   And hide his shameful fact with mine offence ;
And saith he will restore the throne again,
   To its late honor and due excellence ;
And therefore would I should be algates slain,
   For while I live his right is in suspense.—
This is the cause my guiltless life is sought,
For on my ruin is his safety wrought.

LXI.

And let the tyrant have his heart's desire,
   Let him perform the cruelty he meant,
My guiltless blood must quench the ceaseless fire,
   On which my endless tears were bootless spent,
Unless thou help.   To thee, renowned sire,
   I fly, a virgin, orphan, innocent ;
And let these tears that on thy feet distil,
Redeem the drops of blood he thirsts to spill.

LXII.

By these thy glorious feet that tread secure
  On necks of tyrants, by thy conquests brave,
By that right hand, and by those temples pure
  Thou seek'st to free from Macon's lore, I crave
Help for this sickness, none but thou canst cure;
  My life and kingdom let thy mercy save
From death and ruin: but in vain I prove thee,
If right, if truth, if justice cannot move thee.

LXIII.

Thou, who dost all thou wishest at thy will,
  And never willest aught but what is right,
Preserve this guiltless blood they seek to spill;
  Thine be my kingdom, save it with thy might.
Among these captains, lords, and knights of skill,
  Appoint me ten approved most in fight,
Who, with assistance of my friends and kin,
May serve my kingdom lost again to win.

LXIV.

For lo, a knight that hath a gate to ward,
  A man of chiefest trust about his king,
Hath promised so to beguile the guard,
  That me and mine he undertakes to bring
Safe where the tyrant haply sleepeth hard.
  He counsell'd me to undertake this thing,
Of thee some little succor to entreat,
Whose name alone accomplish can the feat.—

LXV.

This said, his answer did the nymph attend;
  Her looks, her sighs, her gestures all did pray him;
But Godfrey wisely did his grant suspend,
  He doubts the worst, and that awhile did stay him;
He knows, who fears no God, he loves no friend,
  He fears the heathen false would thus betray him:
But yet such ruth dwelt in his princely mind,
That, 'gainst his wisdom, pity made him kind.

LXVI.

Besides the kindness of his gentle thought,
  Ready to comfort each distressed wight,
The maiden's offer profit with it brought;
  For if the Syrian kingdom were her right,

That won, the way were easy which he sought,
   To bring all Asia subject to his might;
There might he raise munition, arms, and treasure,
To work th' Egyptian king and his displeasure.

LXVII.

Thûs was his noble heart long time betwixt
   Fear and remorse, not granting nor denaying,
Upon his eyes the dame her lookings fix'd,
   As if her life and death lay on his saying;
Some tears she shed, with sighs and sobbings mix'd,
   As if her hope were dead through his delaying.
At last her earnest suit the Duke denay'd,
But with sweet words thus would content the maid:

LXVIII.

If not in service of our God we fought,
   In meaner quarrel if this sword were shaken,
Well might thou gather in thy gentle thought,
   So fair a Princess should not be forsaken;
But since these armies, from the world's end brought,
   To free this sacred town have undertaken,
It were unfit we turned our strength away,
And victory, even in her coming, stay.

LXIX.

I promise thee, and on my princely word
   The burden of thy wish and hope repose,
That when this chosen temple of the Lord
   Her holy doors shall to his saints unclose
In rest and peace, then this victorious sword
   Shall execute due vengeance on thy foes:
But if, for pity of a worldly dame,
I left this work, such pity were my shame.—

LXX.

At this the Princess bent her eyes to ground,
   And stood unmov'd, though not unmark'd, a space;
The secret bleeding of her inward wound
   Shed heav'nly dew upon her angel's face.
Poor wretch, quoth she, in tears and sorrows drown'd,
   Death be thy peace, the grave thy resting-place,
Since such thy hap, that, lest thou mercy find,
The gentlest heart on earth is prov'd unkind.

LXXI.

Where none attends what boots it to complain ?
    Men's froward hearts are mov'd with women's tears,
As marble stones are pierc'd with drops of rain ;
    No plaints find passage through unwilling ears.
The tyrant haply would his wrath restrain,
    Heard he these prayers ruthless Godfrey hears ;
Yet not thy fault is this ; my chance, I see,
Hath made ev'n pity pitiless in thee.

LXXII.

So both thy goodness and good hap denay'd me,
    Grief, sorrow, mischief, care, hath overthrown me ,
The star that rul'd my birth-day hath betray'd me,
    My genius sees his charge, but dares not own me ;
Of queen-like state my flight hath disarray'd me ;
    My father died ere he five years had known me ;
My kingdom lost, and lastly resteth now ;
Down with the tree sith broke is every bough.

LXXIII.

And, for the modest lore of maidenhood
    Bids me not sojourn with these armed men,
O ! whither shall I flie ?   What secret wood
    Shall hide me from the tyrant ?   Or what den,
What rock, what vault, what cave can do me good
    No, no, where death is sure, it resteth then
To scorn his power, and be it therefore seen,
Armida liv'd, and died, both like a queen.—

LXXIV.

With that she look'd as if a proud disdain
    Kindled displeasure in her noble mind ;
The way she came she turn'd her steps again,
    With gestures sad, but in disdainful kind ;
A tempest railed down her cheeks amain,
    With tears of wo, and sighs of anger's wind ;
The drops her footsteps wash whereon she treads,
And seems to step on pearls or crystal beads.

LXXV.

Her cheeks on which this streaming nectar fell,
    'Still'd through the limbeck of her diamond eyes,
The roses white and red resembled well,
    Whereon the rory May-dew sprinkled lies,

When the fair morn first blusheth from her cell,
   And breatheth balm from opened paradise :
Thus sigh'd, thus mourn'd, thus wept, this lovely queen,
And in each drop bathed a grace unseen.

LXXVI.

Thrice twenty Cupids unperceived flew
   To gather up this liquor, ere it fall,
And of each drop an arrow forged new ;
   Else, as it came, snatch'd up the crystal ball,
And at rebellious hearts for wild-fire threw.
   O wondrous love ! thou makest gain of all ;
For if she weeping sit, or smiling stand,
She bends thy bow, or kindleth else thy brand.

LXXVII.

This forged plaint drew forth unfeigned tears
   From many eyes, and pierc'd each worthy's heart ;
Each one condoleth with her that her hears,
   And of her grief would help her bear the smart :
If Godfrey aid her not, not one but swears
   Some tygress gave him suck, on roughest part,
'Midst the rude crags, on Alpine cliffs aloft :
Hard is that heart which beauty makes not soft.

LXXVIII.

But jolly Eustace, in whose breast the brand
   Of love and pity kindled had the flame,
While others softly whisper'd under hand,
   Before the Duke, with comely boldness, came :—
Brother and lord, quoth he, too long you stand
   In your first purpose, yet vouchsafe to frame
Your thoughts to ours, and lend this virgin aid :
Thanks are half lost when good turns are delayed.

LXXIX.

And think not that Eustace's talk assays
   To turn these forces from this present war,
Or that I wish you should your armies raise
   From Sion's walls ; my speech tends not so far ;
But we that venture all for fame and praise,
   That to no charge nor service bounden are,
Forth of our troop may ten well spared be
To succor her, which naught can weaken thee.

LXXX.

And know they shall in God's high service fight,
   That virgins innocent save and defend;
Dear will the spoils be in the heaven's sight,
   That from a tyrant's hateful head we rend;
Nor seem I forward in this lady's right,
   With hope of gain or profit in the end;
But, for I know he arms unworthy bears,
To help a maiden's cause that shuns or fears.

LXXXI.

Ah! be it not pardie declared in France,
   Or elsewhere told where court'sy is in prize,
That we forsook so fair a chevisance,
   For doubt or fear that might from fight arise:
Else, here surrender I both sword and lance,
   And swear no more to use this martial guise;
For ill deserves he to be termed a knight,
That bears a blunt sword in a lady's right.—

LXXXII.

Thus parled he, and with confused sound
   The rest approved what the gallant said.
Their general the knights encompass'd round;
   With humble grace and earnest suit they pray'd.—
I yield, quoth he, and be it happy found
   What I have granted; let her have your aid;
Yours be the thanks, for yours the danger is
If aught succeed, as much I fear, amiss.

LXXXIII.

But, if with you my words may credit find,
   Oh! temper then this heat misguides you so.—
Thus much he said: but they with fancy blind,
   Accept his grant and let his counsel go.
What works not beauty! man's relenting mind
   Is eath to move with plaints and shows of wo:
Her lips cast forth a train of sugar'd words,
That captive led most of the Christian lords.

LXXXIV.

Eustace recall'd her, and bespake her thus:—
   Beauty's chief darling, let these sorrows be,
For such assistance shall you find in us,
   As with your need or will may best agree.—

With that she cheer'd her forehead dolorous,
    And smil'd for joy that Phœbus blush'd to see ;
And had she deign'd her veil for to remove,
The god himself once more had fallen in love.

LXXXV.

With that she broke the silence once again,
    And gave the knight great thanks in little speech ;
She said she would his handmaid poor remain,
    So far as honor's laws receiv'd no breach.
Her humble gestures made the res'due plain,
    Dumb eloquence persuading more than speech.
This women know, and thus they use the guise
T' enchant the valiant, and beguile the wise.

LXXXVI.

And when she saw her enterprise had got
    Some wished mean of quick and good proceeding,
She thought to strike the iron that was hot ;
    For every action hath its hour of speeding.
Medea or false Circe changed not
    So far the shapes of men, as her eyes spreeding
Alter'd their hearts, and with her siren's sound,
In lust their minds, their hearts in love, she drown'd.

LXXXVII.

All wily sleights that subtle women know,
    Hourly she us'd to catch some lover new.
None ken'd the bent of her unsteadfast bow,
    For with the time her thoughts her looks renew :
From some she cast her modest eyes below,
    At some her gazing glances roving flew ;
And while she thus pursued her wanton sport,
She spurr'd the slow, and rein'd the forward short.

LXXXVIII.

If some, as hopeless that she would be won,
    Forbore to love, because they durst not move her,
On them her gentle looks to smile begun,
    As who say, she is kind, if you dare prove her.
On ev'ry heart thus shone this lustful sun,
    All strove to serve, to please, to woo, to love her :
And in their hearts that chaste and bashful were,
Her eye's hot glance dissolved th' frost of fear.

7

LXXXIX.

On them, who durst with fing'ring bold assay
　　To touch the softness of her tender skin,
She look'd as coy as if she list not play,
　　And made as things of worth were hard to win;
Yet temper'd so her 'dainful looks alway,
　　That outward scorn show'd store of grace within:
Thus with false hope their longing hearts she fir'd,
For hardest gotten things are most desir'd.

XC.

Alone sometimes she walk'd in secret, where
　　To ruminate upon her discontent;
Within her eyelids sat the swelling tear,
　　Not poured forth, though sprung from sad lament;
And with this craft a thousand souls well near
　　In snares of foolish ruth and love she hent,
And kept as slaves; by which we fitly prove,
That witless pity breedeth fruitless love.

XCI.

Sometimes, as if her hope unloosed had
　　The chains of grief wherein her thoughts lay fetter'd
Upon her minions look'd she blithe and glad;
　　In that deceitful lore so was she letter'd.
Not glorious Titan, in his brightness clad,
　　The sunshine of her face in lustre better'd;
For when she list to cheer her beauties so,
She smil'd away the clouds of grief and wo.

XCII.

Her double charm of smiles and sugar'd words
　　Lulled on sleep the virtue of their senses;
Reason small aid 'gainst those assaults affords,
　　Wisdom no warrant from those sweet offences;
Cupid's deep rivers have their shallow fords,
　　His griefs bring joys, his losses recompenses;
He breeds the sore, and cures us of the pain;
Achilles' lance, that wounds and heals again.

XCIII.

While thus she them torments 'twixt frost and fire,
　　'Twixt joy and grief, 'twixt hope and restless fear,
The sly enchantress felt her gain the nigher;
　　These were her flocks that golden fleeces bear:

But if some one durst utter his desire,
   And by complaining make his griefs appear ;
He labored hard rocks with plaints to move,
She had not learn'd the gamut then of love.

XCIV.

For down she bent her bashful eyes to ground,
   And donn'd the weed of women's modest grace ;
Down from her eyes welled the pearles round
   Upon the bright enamel of her face :
Such honey drops on springing flow'rs are found,
   When Phœbus holds the crimson morn in chace :
Full seem'd her looks of anger and of shame,
Yet pity shone transparent through the same.

XCV.

If she perceived by his outward cheer,
   That any would his love by talk bewray,
Sometimes she heard him, sometimes stop'd her ear,
   And played fast and loose the live-long day :
Thus all her lovers kind deluded were,
   Their earnest suit got neither yea nor nay ;
But like the sort of weary huntsmen fare,
That hunt all day and lose at night the hare.

XCVI.

These were the arts by which she captived
   A thousand souls of young and lusty knights ;
These were the arms wherewith love conquered
   Their feeble hearts subdued in wanton fights.
What wonder if Achilles were misled,
   Or great Alcides, at their ladies' sights,
Since these true champions of the Lord Above
Were thralls to beauty, yielden slaves to love ?

BOOK V.

THE ARGUMENT.

Gernando scorns Rinaldo should aspire
   To rule that charge for which he seeks and strives,
And slanders him so far, that in his ire
   The wronged knight his foe of life deprives.
Far from the camp the slayer doth retire,
   Nor lets himself be bound in chains or gyves.
Armide departs content; and from the seas
Godfrey hears news which him and his displease.

I.

WHILE thus Armida false the knights misled
   In wand'ring errors of deceitful love ;
And thought, besides the champions promised,
   The other lordings in her aid to move ;
In Godfrey's thought a strong contention bred
   Who fittest were this hazard great to prove ;
For all the worthies of th' advent'rers' band
Were like in birth, in power, in strength of hand.

II.

But first the Prince, by grave advice, decreed,
   They should some knight choose at their own election,
That in his charge Lord Dudon might succeed,
   And of that glorious troop should take protection ;
So none should grieve, displeased with the deed,
   Nor blame the causer of their new subjection :
Besides, Godfredo show'd by this device,
How much he held that regiment in price.

III.

He call'd the worthies then, and spake them so :—
   Lordings, you know I yielded to your will,
And gave you licence with this dame to go,
   To win her kingdom, and that tyrant kill :

But now again I let you further know,
   In following her it may betide you ill ;
Refrain therefore, and change this forward thought,
For death unsent for, danger comes unsought.

IV.

But if to shun these perils, sought so far,
   May seem disgraceful to the place you hold ;
If grave advice and prudent counsel are
   Esteem'd detractors from your courage bold ;
Then know, I none against his will debar,
   Nor what I granted erst I now withhold ;
But be mine empire, as it ought of right,
Sweet, easy, pleasant, gentle, meek, and light.

V.

Go then or tarry, each as likes him best,
   Free pow'r I grant you on this enterprise ;
But first, in Dudon's place, now laid in chest,
   Choose you some other captain stout and wise :
Then ten appoint among the worthiest,
   But let no more attempt this hard emprise ;
In this my will content you that I have,
For pow'r constrain'd is but a glorious slave.—

VI.

Thus Godfrey said ; and thus his brother spake,
   And answer'd for himself and all his peers :—
My Lord, as well it fitteth thee to make
   These wise delays, and cast these doubts and fears ;
So 'tis our part at first to undertake,
   Courage and haste beseem our might and years ;
And this proceeding with so grave advice,
Wisdom in you, in us were cowardice.

VII.

Since then the feat is easy, danger none,
   All set in battle and in hardy fight,
Do thou permit the chosen ten to gone,
   And aid the damsel.—Thus devis'd the knight,
To make men think the sun of honor shone
   There where the lamp of Cupid gave the light.
The rest perceive his guile, and it approve,
And call that knighthood which was childish love.

VIII.

But loving Eustace, that with jealous eye
  Beheld the worth of Sophia's noble child,
And his fair shape did secretly envie,
  Besides the virtues in his breast compil'd ;
And, for in love he would no company,
  He stor'd his mouth with speeches smoothly fil'd,
Drawing his rival to attend his word ;
Thus with fair sleight he laid the knight aboard :—

IX.

Of great Bertoldo thou far greater heir,
  Thou star of knighthood, flow'r of chivalry,
Tell me who now shall lead this squadron fair,
  Since our late guide in marble cold doth lie ?
I, that with famous Dudon might compare
  In all but years, hoar locks, and gravity,
To whom should I, Duke Godfrey's brother, yield,
Unless to thee, the Christian army's shield ?

X.

Thee, whom high birth makes equal with the best,
  Thine acts prefer both me and all beforne,
Nor that in fight thou both surpass the rest
  And Godfrey's worthy self, I hold in scorn :
Thee to obey then am I only press'd ;
  Before these worthies be thine eagle borne.
This honor haply thou esteemest light,
Whose day of glory never yet found night.

XI.

Yet may'st thou further, by this means, display
  The spreading wings of thy immortal fame ;
I will procure it, if thou say'st not nay,
  And all their wills to thine election frame :
But, for I scantly am resolv'd which way
  To bend my force, or where employ the same,
Leave me, I pray, at my discretion free
To help Armida, or serve here with thee.—

XII.

This last request, for love is evil to hide,
  Impurpled both his cheeks with scarlet red ;
Rinaldo soon his passions had descried,
  And, gently smiling, turn'd aside his head ;

And, for weak Cupid was too feeble-ey'd
   To strike him sure, the fire in him was dead ;
So that of rivals was he naught afraid,
   Nor car'd he for the journey or the maid :

XIII.

But in his noble thought revolv'd he oft
   Dudon's high prowess, death and burial ;
And how Argantes bore his plumes aloft,
   Praising his fortune for that worthy's fall :
Besides, the knight's sweet words and praises soft
   To his due honor did him fitly call,
And made his heart rejoice ; for well he knew,
Though much he prais'd him, all his words were true.—

XIV.

Degrees, quoth he, of honors high to hold,
   I would them first deserve, and then desire ;
And were my valor such as you have told,
   Would I for that to higher place aspire ;
But if to honors due raise me you would,
   I will not of my works refuse the hire ;
And much it glads me that my pow'r and might
Ypraised is by such a valiant knight.

XV.

I neither seek it, nor refuse the place,
   Which if I get, the praise and thanks be thine.—
Eustace, this spoken, hied thence apace
   To know which way his fellows' hearts incline.
But Prince Gernando coveted the place,
   Whom though Armida sought to undermine,
'Gainst him yet vain did all her engines prove,
His pride was such there was no place for love.

XVI.

Gernando was the King of Norway's son,
   That many a realm and region had to guide,
And, for his elders lands and crowns had won,
   His heart was puffed up with endless pride :
The other boasts more what himself had done
   Than all his ancestors' great acts beside :
Yet his forefathers old before him were
Famous in war and peace five hundred year.

XVII.

This barb'rous Prince, who only vainly thought
    That bliss in wealth and kingly pow'r doth lie,
And in respect esteem'd all virtue naught,
    Unless it were adorn'd with titles high,
Could not endure that to the place he sought,
    A simple knight should dare to prease so nigh ;
And in his breast so boiled fell despight,
That ire and wrath exiled reason quite.

XVIII.

The hidden devil that lies in close await
    To win the fort of unbelieving man,
Found entry there where ire undid the gate,
    And in his bosom unperceived ran ;
It fill'd his heart with malice, strife, and hate,
    It made him rage, blaspheme, swear, curse, and ban,
Invisible it still attends him near,
And thus each minute whisp'reth in his ear :

XIX.

What, shall Rinaldo match thee ? Dares he tell
    Those idle names of his vain pedigree ?
Then let him say, if thee he would excel,
    What lands, what realms his tributaries be ;
If his forefathers, in the graves that dwell,
    Were honored like thine that live, let see :
Oh how dares one so mean aspire so high,
Born in that servile country Italy ?

XX.

Now, if he win, or if he lose the day,
    Yet is his praise and glory hence derived,
For that the world will to his credit say,
    Lo, this is he that with Gernando strived.
The charge some deal thee haply honor may,
    That noble Dudon had while here he lived ;
But laid on him he would the office shame,
Let it suffice he durst desire the same.

XXI.

If when this breath from man's frail body flies,
    The soul take keep, or know the things done here,
Oh ! how looks Dudon from the glorious skies !
    What wrath, what anger in his face appear,

On this proud youngling while he bends his eyes,
  Marking how high he doth his feathers rear,
Seeing his rash attempt, how soon he dare,
Though but a boy, with his great worth compare!

XXII.

He dares not only, but he strives, and proves,
  Where chastisement were fit, there wins he praise:
One counsels him, his speech him forward moves;
  Another fool approveth all he says:
If Godfrey favor him more than behoves,
  Why then he wrongeth thee an hundred ways:
Nor let thy state so far disgraced be,
  But what thou art, and can'st, let Godfrey see.—

XXIII.

With such false words the kindled fire began
  To ev'ry vein its poison'd heat to reach,
It swell'd his scornful heart, and forth it ran
  At his proud looks, and too audacious speech:
All that he thought blame-worthy in the man
  To his disgrace, that would he each-where preach;
He term'd him proud and vain, his worth in fight
He call'd fool-hardice, rashness, madness right:

XXIV.

All that in him was rare or excellent,
  All that was good, all that was princely found,
With such sharp words as malice could invent,
  He blam'd, such power hath wicked tongue to wound.
The youth (for everywhere those rumors went)
  Of these reproaches heard sometimes the sound;
Nor did for that his tongue the fault amend,
Until it brought him to his woful end.

XXV.

The cursed fiend that set his tongue at large,
  Still bred more fancies in his idle brain,
His heart with slanders new did overcharge,
  And soothed him still in his angry vein.
Amid the camp a place was broad and large,
  Where one fair regiment might eas'ly train;
And there, in tilt and harmless tournament,
Their days of rest the youths and gallants spent:

XXVI.

There, as his fortune would it should betide,
  Amid the prease Gernando 'gan retire,
To vomit out his venom unespy'd,
  Wherewith foul envy did his heart inspire.
Rinaldo heard him as he stood beside,
  And, as he could not bridle wrath and ire,—
Thou liest,—cried he loud ; and, with that word,
About his head he tost his flaming sword.

XXVII.

Thunder his voice, and lightning seem'd his brand,
  So fell his look and furious was his cheare ;
Gernando trembled, for he saw at hand
  Pale death, and neither help nor comfort near ;
Yet, for the soldiers all to witness stand,
  He made proud sign as though he naught did fear,
But bravely drew his little-helping blade,
And valiant show of strong resistance made.

XXVIII.

With that a thousand blades of burnish'd steel
  Glist'red on heaps, like flames of fire in sight :
Hundreds, that knew not yet the quarrel weel,
  Ran thither, some to gaze and some to fight :
The empty air a sound confus'd did feel
  Of murmurs low and outcries loud on height,
Like rolling waves and Boreas' angry blasts,
When roaring seas against the rocks he casts.

XXIX.

But not for this the wronged warrior stay'd
  His just displeasure and incensed ire,
He car'd not what the vulgar did or said,
  To vengeance did his courage fierce aspire :
Among the thickest weapons way he made,
  His thund'ring sword made all on heaps retire,
So that of a near thousand stay'd not one,
But Prince Gernando bore the brunt alone.

XXX.

His hand, too quick to execute his wrath,
  Performed all as pleas'd his eye and heart,
At head and breast oft-times he strucken hath,
  Now at the right, now at the other part :

On ev'ry side thus did he harm and scath,
    And oft beguil'd his sight with nimble art;
That no defence the Prince of wounds acquits,
Where least he thinks or fears, there most he hits.

XXXI.

Nor ceased he till in Gernando's breast
    He sheathed once or twice his furious blade;
Down fell the hapless Prince with death oppress'd,
    A double way to his weak soul was made.
His bloody sword the victor wip'd and dress'd,
    Nor longer by the slaughter'd body stay'd,
But sped him thence, and soon appeased hath
His hate, his ire, his rancor, and his wrath.

XXXII.

Call'd by the tumult Godfrey drew him near,
    And there beheld a sad and rueful sight,
The signs of death upon his face appear,
    With dust and blood his locks were loathly dight:
Sighs and complaints on each side might he hear,
    Made for the sudden death of that great knight
Amaz'd, he ask'd who durst and did so much;
For yet he knew not whom the fault would touch.

XXXIII.

Arnoldo, minion of the Prince thus slain,
    Augments the fault in telling it; and saith—
This prince is murder'd, for a quarrel vain,
    By young Rinaldo in his desp'rate wrath;
And with that sword, that should Christ's law maintain,
    One of Christ's champions bold he killed hath;
And this he did, in such a place and hour,
As if he scorn'd your rule, despis'd your power.—

XXXIV.

And further adds, that he deserved death
    By law, and law should be inviolate;
That none offence could greater be uneath,
    And yet the place the fault did aggravate:
If he escap'd, that mischief would take breath,
    And flourish bold in spite of rule and state;
And that Gernando's friends would 'venge the wrong,
Although to justice that should first belong.

XXXV.

And by that means should discord, hate, and strife,
   Raise mutinies, and what thereof ensu'th :
Lastly, he prais'd the dead, and still had rife
   All words he thought could veng'ance move or ruth.
Against him Tancred argued for life,
   With honest reasons to excuse the youth.
The Duke heard all, but with such sober cheer
As banish'd hope, and still increased fear.—

XXXVI.

Grave Prince, quoth Tancred, set before thine eyes
   Rinaldo's worth and courage, what it is,
How much our hope of conquest in him lies ;
   Regard that princely house and race of his :
He that correcteth every fault he spies,
   And judgeth all alike, doth all amiss ;
For faults, you know, are greater thought or less,
   As is the person's self that doth transgress.—

XXXVII.

Godfredo answer'd him—If high and low
   Of sov'reign power alike should feel the stroke,
Then, Tancred, ill you counsel us, I trow ;
   If lords should know no law, as erst you spoke,
How vile and base our empire were, you know ;
   If none but slaves and peasants bear the yoke,
Weak is the sceptre, and the pow'r is small,
That such provisoes brings annex'd withal ;

XXXVIII.

But mine was freely given ere it was sought,
   Nor that it lessen'd be I now consent ;
Right well know I both when and where I ought
   To give condign reward and punishment :
Since you are all in like subjection brought,
   Both high and low, obey and be content.—
This heard, Tancredie wisely stay'd his words ;
Such weight the sayings have of kings and lords.

XXXIX.

Old Raymond prais'd his speech, for old men think
   They ever wisest seem when most severe :—
'Tis best, quoth he, to make these great ones shrink,
   The people love him whom the nobles fear :

There must the rule to all disorders sink,
　　Where pardons, more than punishments, appear ;
For feeble is each kingdom, frail and weak,
Unless its basis be this fear I speak.—

XL.

These words Tancredie heard and ponder'd well,
　　And by them wist how Godfrey's thoughts were bent ;
Nor list he longer with these old men dwell,
　　But turn'd his horse and to Rinaldo went ;
Who, when his noble foe death-wounded fell,
　　Withdrew him softly to his gorgeous tent ;
There Tancred found him, and at large declar'd
The words and speeches sharp which late he heard.

XLI.

And said,—Although I wot the outward show
　　Is not true witness of the secret thought,
For that some men so subtle are, I trow,
　　That when they purpose most, appeareth naught ;
Yet dare I say Godfredo means, I know,
　　Such knowledge hath his looks and speeches wrought,
You shall first pris'ner be, and then be tried,
As he shall deem it good, and law provide.—

XLII.

With that a bitter smile well might you see
　　Rinaldo cast, with scorn and high disdain.—
Let them in fetters plead their cause, quoth he,
　　That are base peasants, born of servile strain ;
I was free born, I live and will die free,
　　Before these feet be fetter'd in a chain :
These hands were made to shake sharp spears and swords,
Not to be tied in gyves and twisted cords.

XLIII.

If my good service reap this recompence,
　　To be clapp'd up in close and secret mew,
And as a thief be after dragg'd from thence,
　　To suffer punishment as law finds due ;
Let Godfrey come or send, I will not hence,
　　Until we know who shall this bargain rue ;
That of our tragedy, the late done fact
May be the first, and this the second act :

XLIV.

Give me mine arms, he cried :—His 'squire them brings,
     And clad his head and breast in iron strong ;
About his neck his silver shield he flings,
     Down by his side a cutting sword there hung.
Among this earth's brave lords, and mighty kings,
     Was none so stout, so fierce, so fair, so young.
God Mars he seem'd descending from his sphere,
Or one whose looks could make great Mars to fear.

XLV

Tancredie labor'd with some pleasing speech
     His spirits fierce and courage to appease :—
Young prince, thy valor (thus he 'gan to preach)
     Can chastise all that do thee wrong, at ease ;
I know your virtue can your en'mies teach
     That you can 'venge you when and where you please :
But God forbid this day you lift your arm
To do this camp, and us, your friends, such harm !

XLVI.

Tell me, what will you do ? why would you stain
     Your noble hands in our unguilty blood ?
By wounding Christians, will you again
     Pierce Christ, whose parts they are and members good ?
Will you destroy us for your glory vain,
     Unstaid as rolling waves in ocean flood ?
Far be it from you so to prove your strength,
But let your zeal appease your rage at length ;

XLVII.

For God's love stay your heat and just displeasure,
     Appease your wrath, your courage fierce assuage,
Patience a praise, forbearance is a treasure ;
     Suff'rence an angel is, a monster rage :
At least your actions by ensample measure,
     And think how I, in mine unbridled age,
Was wronged ; yet I nould revengement take
On all this camp, for one offender's sake.

XLVIII.

Cilicia conquer'd I, as all men wot,
     And there the glorious cross on high I rear'd ;
But Baldwin came, and what I nobly got
     Bereft me falsely, when I least him fear'd ;

He seem'd my friend, and I discover'd not
   His secret covetise which since appear'd:
Yet strive I not to get mine own by fight,
Or civil war, although perchance I might.

XLIX.
If then you scorn to be in prison pent;
   If bonds, as high disgrace, your hands refuse;
Or if your thoughts still to maintain are bent
   Your liberty, as men of honor use;
To Antioch what if forthwith you went;
   And leave me here your absence to excuse;
There with Prince Boemond live in ease and peace,
Until this storm of Godfrey's anger cease;

L.
For soon, if forces come from Egypt land,
   Or other nations that us here confine,
Godfrey will beaten be with his own wand,
   And feel he wants that valor great of thine;
Our camp may seem an arm without a hand,
   Amid our troops unless thy eagle shine.—
With that came Guelpho, and these words approved,
And pray'd him go, if him he fear'd or loved.

LI.
Their speeches soften much the warrior's heart,
   And make his wilful thoughts at last relent,
So that he yields, and saith he will depart,
   And leave the Christian camp incontinent.
His friends, whose love did never shrink or start,
   Proffer'd their aid, what way soe'er he went.
He thank'd them all, but left them all, besides
Two bold and trusty 'squires, and so he rides;

LII.
He rides, revolving in his noble spright
   Such haughty thoughts as fill the glorious mind;
On hard adventures was his whole delight,
   And now to wondrous acts his will inclin'd;
Alone against the pagans would he fight,
   And kill their kings from Egypt unto Inde;
From Cinthia's hills, and Nilus' unknown spring,
He would fetch praise, and glorious conquest bring.

LIII.

But Guelpho, when the prince his leave had take,
   And now had spurr'd his courser on his way,
No longer tarriance with the rest would make,
   But hastes to find Godfredo, if he may :
Who seeing him approaching, forthwith spake,—
   Guelpho, quoth he, for thee I only stay,
For thee I sent my heralds all about,
In ev'ry tent to seek and find thee out.—

LIV.

This said, he softly drew the knight aside
   Where none might hear, and then bespake him thus :
How chanceth it thy nephew's rage and pride
   Makes him so far forget himself and us ?
Hardly could I believe what is betide,
   A murder done for cause so frivolous !
How I have lov'd him thou and all can tell :
But Godfrey lov'd him but whilst he did well.

LV.

I must provide that ev'ry one have right,
   That all be heard, each cause be well discuss'd ;
As far from partial love, or free from spight,
   I hear complaints, yet naught but proofs I trust :
Now, if Rinaldo weigh our rule so light,
   And have the sacred lore of war so brust,
Take you the charge that he before us come,
To clear himself and hear our upright doom :

LVI.

But let him come withouten bond or chain,
   For still my thoughts to do him grace are framed :
But if our power he haply shall disdain,
   As well I know his courage yet untamed,
To bring him by persuasion take some pain ;
   Else, if I prove severe, both you be blamed,
That force my gentle nature ('gainst my thought)
To rigor, lest our laws return to naught.—

LVII.

Lord Guelpho answered thus :—What heart can bear
   Such slanders false, devis'd by hate and spight ;
Or with staid patience reproaches hear,
   And not revenge by battle and by fight ?

The Norway prince hath bought his folly dear,
　But who with words could stay the angry knight ?
A fool is he that comes to preach or prate,
When men with swords their right and wrong debate.

LVIII.

And where you wish he should himself submit
　To hear the censure of your upright laws,
Alas ! that cannot be, for he is flit
　. Out of this camp, withouten stay or pause.
There take my gage, behold I offer it
　To him that first accus'd him in this cause,
Or any else that dare, and will maintain
That for his pride the prince was justly slain :

LIX.

I say with reason Lord Gernando's pride
　He hath abated : if he have offended
'Gainst your commands, who are his lord and guide,
　Oh, pardon him, that fault shall be amended.—
If he be gone, quoth Godfrey, let him ride
　And brawl elsewhere, here let all strife be ended :
And you, Lord Guelpho, for your nephew's sake,
Breed us no new, nor quarrels old awake.—

LX.

This while, the fair and false Armida striv'd
　To get her promis'd aid in sure possession,
The day to end with endless plaint she driv'd ;
　Wit, beauty, craft, for her made intercession :
But when the earth was once of light depriv'd,
　And western seas felt Titan's hot impression,
'Twixt two old knights and matrons twain she went,
　Where pitched was her fair and curious tent.

LXI.

But this false queen of craft and sly invention
　(Whose looks Love's arrows were ; whose eyes his quivers ;
Whose beauty matchless, free from reprehension,
　A wonder left by heav'n to after-livers),
Among the Christian lords had bred contention,
　Who first should quench his flames in Cupid's rivers ;
With all her weapons and her darts rehears'd,
Had not Godfredo's constant bosom pierc'd.

8

LXII.

To change his modest thought the dame procureth,
   And proff'reth heaps of love's enticing treasure :
But as the falcon, newly gorg'd, endureth
   Her keeper lure her oft, but comes at leisure ;
So he, whom fulness of delight assureth
   What long repentance comes of love's short pleasure,
Her crafts, her arts, herself and all despiseth ;
So base affections fall when virtue riseth ;

LXIII.

And not one foot his steadfast foot was moved
   Out of that heav'nly path wherein he paced,
Yet thousand wiles and thousand ways she proved,
   To have that castle fair of goodness razed :
She used those looks and smiles that most behoved
   To melt the frost which his hard heart embraced,
And 'gainst his breast a thousand shot she ventur'd,
Yet was the fort so strong it was not enter'd.

LXIV.

The dame, who thought that one blink of her eye
   Could make the chastest heart feel love's sweet pain,
Oh, how her pride abated was hereby,
   When all her sleights were void, her crafts were vain !
Some other where she would her forces try,
   Where at more ease she might more vantage gain ;
As tired soldiers, whom some fort keeps out,
   Thence raise their siege, and spoil the towns about.

LXV.

But yet all ways the wily witch could find
   Could not Tancredie's heart to loveward move ;
His sails were filled with another wind,
   He list no blast of new affection prove :
For as one poison doth exclude by kind
   Another's force, so love excludeth love.
These two alone nor more nor less the dame
   Could win, the rest all burnt in her sweet flame.

LXVI.

The princess, though her purpose would not frame
   As late she hoped and as still she would,
Yet, for the lords and knights of greatest name
   Became her prey, as erst you heard it told ;

She thought, ere truth-revealing time or fame
    Bewray'd her act, to lead them to some hold,
Where chains and bands she meant to make them prove,
Compos'd by Vulcan, not by gentle Love.

LXVII.

The time prefix'd at length was come and past,
    Which Godfrey had set down, to lend her aid,
When at his feet herself to earth she cast,—
    The hour is come, my lord, she humbly said;
And if the tyrant haply hear at last
    His banish'd niece hath your assistance pray'd,
He will in arms to save his kingdom rise,
So shall we harder make this enterprise.

LXVIII.

Before report can bring the tyrant news,
    Or his espials certify their king,
Oh let thy goodness these few champions chuse,
    That to her kingdom should thy handmaid bring;
Who, except heaven to aid the right refuse,
    Recover shall her crown, from whence shall spring
Thy profit; for betide thee peace or war,
Thine all her cities, all her subjects are.—

LXIX.

The captain sage the damsel fair assured
    His word was past, and should not be recanted;
And she with sweet and humble grace endured
    To let him point those ten, which late he granted.
But to be one each one sought and procured,
    No suit, entreaty, intercession wanted:
Their envy each at other's love exceeded,
And all importunate made more than needed.

LXX.

She, that well saw the secret of their hearts,
    And knew how best to warm them in their blood,
Against them threw the cursed poison'd darts
    Of jealousy, and grief at other's good;
For love she wist was weak without those arts,
    And slow; for jealousy is Cupid's food;
For the swift steed runs not so fast alone,
As when some strain, some strive him to outgone.

LXXI.

Her words in such alluring sort she framed,
  Her looks enticing, and her wooing smiles,
That every one his fellow's favors blamed,
  That of their mistress he receiv'd erewhiles:
This foolish crew of lovers, unashamed,
  Mad with the poison of her secret wiles,
Ran forward still in this disorder'd sort,
Nor could Godfredo's bridle rein them short.

LXXII.

He, that would satisfy each good desire,
  Withouten partial love, of ev'ry knight,
Although he swell'd with shame, with grief, and ire,
  To see these follies and these fashions light ;
Yet since by no advice they would retire,
  Another way he sought to set them right :—
Write all your names, quoth he, and see whom chance
Of lot to this exploit will first advance.—

LXXIII.

Their names were writ, and in a helmet shaken,
  While each did Fortune's grace and aid implore ;
At last they drew them, and the foremost taken
  The Earl of Pembroke was, Artemidore ;
Doubtless the County thought his bread well baken.
  Next Gerrard follow'd ; then, with tresses hoar,
Old Wenceslaus, that felt Cupid's rage
Now in his doting and his dying age.

LXXIV.

Oh how contentment in their foreheads shined,
  Their looks with joy, thoughts swell'd with secret pleasure !
These three it seemed good success designed
  To make the lords of love and beauty's treasure.
Their doubtful fellows at their hap repined,
  And with small patience wait fortune's leisure,
Upon his lips that read the scrolls attending,
As if their lives were on his words depending.

LXXV.

Guascar the fourth, Ridolpho him succeeds,
  Then Uldericke whom love list so advance,
Lord William of Ronciglion next he reads,
  Then Eberard, and Henry born in France ;

Rambaldo last, whom wicked lust so leads,
   That he forsook his Saviour with mischance ;
This wretch the tenth was, who was thus deluded,
The rest to their huge grief were all excluded.

LXXVI.

O'ercome with envy, wrath, and jealousy,
   The rest blind fortune curse, and all her laws,
And mad with love, yet out on love they cry,
   That in his kingdom let her judge their cause :
And, for man's mind is such, that oft we try
   Things most forbidden, without stay or pause,
In spite of fortune, purpos'd many a knight
To follow fair Armida when 't was night ;

LXXVII.

To follow her, by night or else by day,
   And in her quarrel venture life and limb.
With sighs and tears she 'gan them softly play
   To keep that promise when the skies were dim ;
To this and that knight did she plain, and say
   What grief she felt to part withouten him.
Meanwhile the ten had don'd their armor best,
And taken leave of Godfrey and the rest.

LXXVIII.

The Duke advis'd them every one apart,
   How light, how trustless was the pagans' faith ;
And told what policy, what wit, what art,
   Avoids deceit, which heedless men betray'th.
His speeches pierce their ear, but not their heart ;
   Love calls it folly, what so wisdom saith.
Thus warn'd he leaves them to their wanton guide,
Who parts that night ; such haste had she to ride.

LXXIX.

The conqueress departs, and with her led
   These prisoners whom love would captive keep ;
The hearts of those she left behind her bled,
   With point of sorrow's arrow pierced deep.
But when the night her drowsy mantle spread,
   And fill'd the earth with silence, shade, and sleep,
In secret sort then each forsook his tent,
And as blind Cupid led them, blind they went.

LXXX.

Eustatio first, who scantly could forbear
    Till friendly night might hide his haste and shame,
He rode in post, and let his beast him bear
    As his blind fancy would his journey frame:
All night he wand'red and he wist not where,
    But with the morning he espied the dame,
That with her guard up from a village rode,
Where she and they that night had made abode.

LXXXI.

Thither he gallop'd fast, and drawing near,
    Rambaldo knew the knight, and loudly cried—
Whence comes young Eustace, and what seeks he here?
    I come (quoth he) to serve the queen Armide,
If she accept me; would we all were there
    Where my goodwill and faith might best be tried.
Who (quoth the other) chooseth thee to prove
This high exploit of hers?—He answer'd, Love:

LXXXII.

Love hath Eustatio chosen, fortune thee;
    In thy conceit which is the best election?—
Nay then these shifts are vain, replied he,
    These titles false serve thee for no protection,
Thou canst not here for this admitted be,
    Our fellow servant, in this sweet subjection.—
And who (quoth Eustace angry) dares deny
My fellowship?—Rambaldo answered, I.—

LXXXIII.

And with that word his cutting sword he drew,
    That glist'red bright and sparkled flaming fire:
Upon his foe the other champion flew,
    With equal courage and with equal ire.
The gentle Princess (who the danger knew)
    Between them stept and pray'd them both retire.—
Rambald (quoth she) why should you grudge or plain,
If I a champion, you an helper gain?

LXXXIV.

If me you love, why wish you me deprived
    (In so great need) of such a puissant knight?
But welcome, Eustace, in good time arrived,
    Defender of my state, my life, my right;

I wish my hapless self no longer lived,
  When I esteem such good assistance light.—
Thus talk'd they on and travell'd on their way,
Their fellowship increasing every day.

LXXXV.

From every side they come, yet wist there none
  Of others' coming or of others' mind;
She welcomes all, and telleth every one
  What joy her thoughts in his arrival find.
But when Duke Godfrey wist his knights were gone,
  Within his breast his wiser soul divin'd
Some hard mishap upon his friends should light,
For which he sigh'd all day, and wept all night.

LXXXVI.

A messenger (while thus he mus'd) drew near,
  All soil'd with dust and sweat, quite out of breath;
It seem'd the man did heavy tidings bear,
  Upon his looks sat news of loss and death,—
My lord, quoth he, so many ships appear
  At sea, that Neptune bears the load uneath;
From Egypt come they all, this lets thee weet,
William, Lord Admiral of the Genoa fleet.

LXXXVII.

Besides, a convoy coming from the shore,
  With vittaile for this noble camp of thine,
Surprised was, and lost is all that store,
  Mules, horses, camels laden, corn and wine.
Thy servants fought till they could fight no more,
  For all were slain or captives made in fine:
Th' Arabian outlaws them assail'd by night,
When least they fear'd, and least they look'd for fight.

LXXXVIII.

Their frantic boldness doth presume so far,
  That many Christians have they falsely slain;
And like a raging flood they 'spersed are,
  And overflow each country, field and plain;
Send therefore some strong troops of men of war,
  To force them hence, and drive them home again;
And keep the ways between these tents of thine
And those broad seas, the seas of Palestine.

LXXXIX.

From mouth to mouth the heavy rumor spread
　　Of these misfortunes, which dispersed wide
Among the soldiers, great amazement bred ;
　　Famine they doubt, and new-come foes beside.
The Duke (that saw their wonted courage fled,
　　And in the place thereof weak fear espied),
With merry looks these cheerful words he spake,
To make them heart again and courage take.

XC.

You champions bold, with me that 'scaped have
　　So many dangers, and such hard assays,
Whom still your God did keep, defend, and save.
　　In all your battailes, combats, fights, and frays ;
You that subdued the Turks and Persians brave,
　　That thirst and hunger held in scorn always,
That vanquish'd hills and seas, with heat and cold,
Shall vain reports appal your courage bold ?

XCI.

That Lord, who help'd you out at every need,
　　When aught befel this glorious camp amiss,
Shall fortune all your actions well to speed,
　　On whom his mercy large extended is ;
Tofore his tomb when conquering hands you spreed,
　　With what delight will you remember this !
Be strong therefore, and keep your valors high,
To honor, conquest, fame, and victory.

XCII.

Their hopes half dead, and courage well-nigh lost,
　　Reviv'd, with these brave speeches of their guide ;
But in his breast a thousand cares he toss'd,
　　Although his sorrows he could wisely hide ;
He studied how to feed that mighty host,
　　In so great scarceness ; and what force provide
He should against th' Egyptian warriors sly,
And how subdue those thieves of Arabie.

BOOK VI.

~~~~~~~~~~

~~~~~~~~~~

I.

But better hopes had them recomforted
  That lay besieged in the sacred town ;
With new supply late they were vittailed,
  When night obscur'd the earth with shadows brown ;
Their arms and engines on the walls they spread,
  Their slings to cast, and stones to tumble down ;
And all that side which to the northward lies,
High rampires and strong bulwarks fortifies.

II.

Their wary king commands, now here, now there,
  To build this tower, to make that bulwark strong ;
Whether the sun, the moon, or stars appear,
  To give them light, to work no time comes wrong :
In every street new weapons forged were
  By cunning smiths, sweating with labor long.
While thus the careful Prince provision made,
To him Argantes came, and boasting said—

III.

How long shall we, like prisoners in chains,
  Captived lie inclos'd within this wall !
I see your workmen taking endless pains
  To make new weapons, for no use at all ;

Meanwhile these western thieves destroy the plains,
  Your towns are burnt, your forts and castles fall,
Yet none of us dares at these gates out-peep,
Or sound one trumpet shrill to break their sleep.

IV.

Their time in feasting and good cheer they spend,
  Nor dare we once their banquets sweet molest ;
The days and nights they bring likewise to end,
  In peace, assurance, quiet, ease, and rest :
But we must yield, whom hunger soon will shend,
  And make for peace, to save our lives, request ;
Else, if th' Egyptian army stay too long,
Like cowards die within this fortress strong.

V.

Yet never shall my courage great consent
  So vile a death should end my noble days ;
Nor on mine arms, within these walls ypent,
  To-morrow's sun shall spread his timely rays :
Let sacred heavens dispose as they are bent
  Of this frail life, yet not withouten praise
Of valor, prowess, might, Argantes shall
Inglorious die, or unrevenged fall.

VI.

But if the roots of wonted chivalry
  Be not quite dead your princely breast within,
Devise not how with fame and praise to die,
  But how to live, to conquer, and to win ;
Let us together at these gates out-fly,
  And skirmish bold, and bloody fight begin ;
For when last need to desperation driveth,
Who dareth most he wisest counsel giveth.

VII.

But if in field your wisdom dare not venture
  To hazard all your troops to doubtful fight,
Then bind yourself to Godfrey by indenture,
  To end your quarrels by one single knight :
And, for the Christian this accord shall enter
  With better will, say such you know your right,
That he the weapons, place, and time, shall chuse,
And let him for his best that 'vantage use.

VIII.

For though your foe had hands like Hector strong,
　　With heart unfear'd and courage stern and stout,
Yet no misfortune can your justice wrong,
　　And what that wanteth shall this arm help out;
In spite of fate shall this right hand ere long
　　Return victorious: if hereof you doubt,
Take it for pledge, wherein if trust you have,
It shall yourself defend and kingdom save.—

IX.

Bold youth (the tyrant thus began to speak),
　　Although I with'red seem with age and years,
Yet are not these old arms so faint and weak,
　　Nor this hoar head so full of doubts and fears;
But when as death this vital thread shall break,
　　He shall my courage hear, my death who hears;
And Aladine, that liv'd a king and knight,
To his fair morn will have an evening bright.

X.

But that (which yet I nould have farther blaised)
　　To thee in secret shall be told and spoken;
Great Soliman of Nice, so far ypraised,
　　To be revenged for his sceptre broken,
The men of arms of Arabie hath raised,
　　From Inde to Afric; and, when we give token,
Attends the favor of the friendly night,
To vittaile us and with our foes to fight.

XI.

Now, though Godfredo hold by warlike feat
　　Some castles poor and forts in vile oppression,
Care not for that; for still our princely seat,
　　This stately town, we keep in our possession;
But thou appease and calm that courage great
　　Which in thy bosom makes so hot impression,
And stay fit time, which will betide ere long
T' increase thy glory, and revenge our wrong.—

XII.

The Saracine at this was inly spited,
　　Who Soliman's great worth had long envied;
To hear him praised thus he naught delighted,
　　Nor that the king upon his aid relied.—

Within your power, Sir King (he says), united
  Are peace and war, nor shall that be denied ;
But for the Turk and his Arabian band,
He lost his own ; shall he defend your land ?

XIII.

Perchance he comes some heavenly messenger,
  Sent down to set the Pagan people free ;
Then let Argantes for himself take care,
  This sword, I trust, shall well safeconduct me ;
But while you rest and all your forces spare,
  That I go forth to war at least agree,
Though not your champion, yet a private knight,
I will some Christian prove in single fight.—

XIV.

The king replied—Though thy force and might
  Should be reserv'd to better time and use,
Yet that thou challenge some renowned knight
  Among the Christians bold, I not refuse.
The warrior, breathing out desire of fight,
  An herald call'd, and said—Go tell these news
To Godfrey's self, and to the Western Lords,
And in their hearings boldly say these words :

XV.

Say that a knight who holds in great disdain
  To be thus closed up in secret mew,
Will with his sword in open field maintain,
  If any dare deny his words for true ;
That no devotion, as they falsely feign,
  Hath mov'd the French these countries to subdue ;
But vile ambition, and pride's hateful vice,
Desire of rule and spoil, and covetice ;

XVI.

And that to fight I am not only prest
  With one or two that dare defend the cause,
But come the fourth or fifth, come all the rest,
  Come all that will, and all that weapons draws,
Let him that yields obey the victor's hest,
  As wills the lore of mighty Mars his laws.—
This was the challenge that fierce Pagan sent ;
The herald don'd his coat of arms, and went.

XVII.

And when the man before the presence came
 Of princely Godfrey and his captains bold ;—
My Lord, quoth he, may I withouten blame
 Before your grace my message brave unfold ?—
Thou may'st, he answer'd, we approve the same,
 Withouten fear be thine ambassage told.—
Then, quoth the herald, shall your Highness see
If this ambassage sharp or pleasing be.—

XVIII.

The challenge 'gan he then at large expose,
 With mighty threats, high terms, and glorious words ;
On every side an angry murmur rose,
 To wrath so moved were the knights and lords.
Then Godfrey spake and said—The man hath chose
 An hard exploit, but when he feels our swords,
I trust we shall so fair entreat the knight
As to excuse the fourth or fifth of fight.

XIX.

But let him come and prove, the field I grant,
 Nor wrong nor treason let him doubt or fear ;
Some here shall pay him for his glorious vaunt,
 Without or guile or 'vantage, that I swear.—
The herald turn'd when he had ended scant,
 And hasted back the way he came whilere ;
Nor stay'd he aught, nor once foreslow'd his pace,
Till he bespake Argantes face to face.—

XX.

Arm you, my Lord, he said, your bold defies
 By your brave foes accepted boldly been ;
This combat neither high nor low denies,
 Ten thousand wish to meet you on the green ;
A thousand frown'd with angry flaming eyes,
 And shak'd for rage their swords and weapons keen ;
The field is safely granted by their guide.—
This said, the champion for his armor cried.

XXI.

While he was arm'd, his heart for ire nigh brake,
 So yearn'd his courage hot his foe to find.
The King, to fair Clorinda present, spake :—
 If he go forth, remain not you behind,

But of our soldiers best a thousand take,
 To guard his person and your own assign'd ;
Yet let him meet alone the Christian knight,
And stand yourself aloof, while they two fight.—

XXII.

Thus spake the king, and soon without abode
 The troop went forth in shining armor clad :
Before the rest the Pagan champion rode,
 His wonted arms and ensigns all he had.
A goodly plain displayed wide and broad
 Between the city and the camp was sprad ;
A place like that wherein proud Rome beheld
Her forward young men manage spear and shield.

XXIII.

There all alone Argantes took his stand,
 Defying Christ and all his servants true,
In stature, stomach, and in strength of hand,
 In pride, presumption, and in dreadful shew,
Encelade like, on the Phlegrean strand,
 Or that huge giant Jesse's infant slew :
But his fierce semblance they esteemed light,
For most not knew, or else not fear'd his might.

XXIV.

As yet not one had Godfrey singled out
 To undertake this hardy enterprise,
But on Prince Tancred saw he all the rout
 Had fix'd their wishes and had cast their eyes ;
On him he spied them gazing round about,
 As though their honor on his prowess lies ;
And now they whisper'd louder what they meant,
Which Godfrey heard and saw, and was content.

XXV.

The rest gave place, for every one descried
 To whom their chieftain's will did most incline.—
Tancred (quoth he), I pray thee calm the pride,
 Abate the rage of yonder Saracine.—
No longer would the chosen champion bide,
 His face with joy, his eyes with gladness shine ;
His helm he took, and ready steed bestrode,
And, guarded with his trusty friends, forth rode.

XXVI.

But scantly had he spurr'd his courser swift
  Near to that plain where proud Argantes stay'd,
When unawares his eyes he chanc'd to lift,
  And on the hill beheld the warlike maid ;
As white as snow upon the Alpine clift
  The virgin shone, in silver arms array'd,
Her ventail up so high that he descried
Her goodly visage and her beauty's pride.

XXVII.

He saw not where the Pagan stood, and stared,
  As if with looks he would his foeman kill ;
But full of other thoughts he forward fared,
  And sent his looks before him up the hill ;
His gesture such his troubled soul declared ;
  At last as marble rock he standeth still ;
Stone-cold without, within burnt with love's flame ;
And quite forgot himself and why he came.

XXVIII.

The challenger, that yet saw none appear
  That made or sign or show he came to just—
How long, cried he, shall I attend you here ?
  Dares none come forth ? Dares none his fortune trust ?
The other stood amaz'd, love stopp'd his ear ;
  He thinks on Cupid, think of Mars who lust ;
But forth starts Otho bold, and took the field,
A gentle knight, whom God from danger shield !

XXIX.

This youth was one of those who late desired
  With that vain-glorious boaster to have fought ;
But Tancred chosen, he and all retired ;
  Yet to the field the valiant prince they brought :
Now, when his slackness he awhile admired,
  And saw elsewhere employed was his thought,
Nor that to just (though chosen) once he proffer'd,
He boldly took that fit occasion offer'd.

XXX.

No tiger, panther, spotted leopard,
  Runs half so swift the forests wild among,
As this young champion hasted thitherward,
  Where he attending saw the Pagan strong.

Tancredie started with the noise he heard,
  As wak'd from sleep where he had dreamed long ;—
Oh stay, he cried, to me belongs this war :—
But cried too late, Otho was gone too far.

XXXI.

Then full of fury, anger, and despite,
  He stay'd his horse, and waxed red for shame ;
The fight was his, but now disgraced quite
  Himself he thought, another play'd his game.
Meanwhile the Saracine did hugely smite
  On Otho's helm ; who, to requite the same,
His foe quite through his sev'n-fold targe did bear,
And in his breast-plate stuck and broke his spear.

XXXII.

Th' encounter such, upon the tender grass
  Down from his steed the Christian backward fell ;
Yet his proud foe so strong and sturdy was,
  That he nor shook nor stagger'd in his sell,
But to the knight, that lay full low, alas !
  In high disdain his will thus 'gan he tell :—
Yield thee my slave, and this thine honor be,
Thou mayst report thou hast encounter'd me.—

XXXIII.

Not so, quoth he, pardie it 's not the guise
  Of Christian knights, tho' fall'n, so soon to yield ;
I can my fall excuse in better wise,
  And will revenge this shame, or die in field.—
The great Circassian bent his frowning eyes,
  Like that grim visage in Minerva's shield :—
Then learn, quoth he, what force Argantes useth
Against that fool that proffer'd grace refuseth.—

XXXIV.

With that he spurr'd his horse with speed and haste
  (Forgetting what good knights to virtue owe) :
Otho his fury shunn'd, and, as he pass'd,
  At his right side he reach'd a noble blow :
Wide was the wound, the blood outstreamed fast,
  And from his side fell to his stirrup low.
But what avails to hurt, if wounds augment
Our foe's fierce courage, strength, and hardiment ?

XXXV.

Argantes nimbly turn'd his ready steed,
   And, ere his foe was wist or well aware,
Against his side he drove his courser's head;
   What force could he 'gainst so great might prepare?
Weak were his feeble joints, his courage dead,
   His heart amaz'd, his paleness show'd his care;
His tender side 'gainst the hard earth he cast,
Sham'd with the first fall; bruised with the last.

XXXVI.

The victor spurr'd again his light-foot steed,
   And made his passage over Otho's heart;
And cried—These fools thus under foot I tread,
   That dare contend with me in equal mart.—
Tancred for anger shook his noble head,
   So was he griev'd with that unknightly part:
The fault was his, he was so slow before,
With double valor would he salve that sore.

XXXVII.

Forward he gallop'd fast, and loudly cried—
   Villain! (quoth he) thy conquest is thy shame?
What praise, what honor shall this fact betide?
   What gain, what guerdon shall befal the same?
Among th' Arabian thieves thy face go hide,
   Far from resort of men of worth and fame;
Or else in woods and mountains wild, by night,
On savage beasts employ thy savage might.—

XXXVIII.

The Pagan patience never knew, nor used;
   Trembling for ire his sandy locks he tore,
Out from his lips flew such a sound confused
   As lions make in deserts thick which roar;
Or as when clouds, together crush'd and bruised,
   Pour down a tempest by the Caspian shore:
So was his speech imperfect, stop'd, and broken,
He roar'd and thund'red when he should have spoken.

XXXIX.

But when with threats they both had whetted keen
   Their eager rage, their fury, spite and ire,
They turn'd their steeds and left large space between,
   To make their forces greater 'proaching nigher.

With terms that warlike and that worthy been,
  O sacred muse ! my haughty thoughts inspire,
And make a trumpet of my slender quill,
To thunder out this furious combat shrill.

XL.

These sons of Mavors bore, instead of spears,
  Two knotty masts, which none but they could lift ;
Each foaming steed so fast his master bears,
  That never beast, bird, shaft, flew half so swift :
Such was their fury, as when Boreas tears
  The shatter'd crags from Taurus' northern clift :
Upon their helms their lances long they broke,
And up to heav'n flew splinters, sparks, and smoke.

XLI.

The shock made all the towers and turrets quake,
  And woods and mountains all nigh-hand resound ;
Yet could not all that force and fury shake
  The valiant champions, nor their persons wound :
Together hurtled both their steeds, and brake
  Each other's neck ; the riders lay on ground :
But they (great masters of war's dreadful art)
Pluck'd forth their swords, and soon from earth upstart.

XLII.

Close at his surest ward each warrior lieth ;
  He wisely guides his hand, his foot, his eye ;
This blow he proveth, that defence he trieth ;
  He traverseth, retireth, preaseth nigh ;
Now strikes he out, and now he falsifieth ;
  This blow he wardeth, that he lets slip by ;
And for advantage oft he lets some part
Discover'd seem ; thus art deludeth art.

XLIII.

The Pagan, ill defenc'd with sword or targe
  Tancredie's thigh, as he suppos'd, espied,
And reaching forth 'gainst it his weapon large,
  Quite naked to his foe leaves his left side :
Tancred avoideth quick his furious charge,
  And gave him eke a wound, deep, sore, and wide ;
That done, himself safe to his ward retired,
His courage prais'd by all, his skill admired.

XLIV.

The proud Circassian saw his streaming blood
    Down from his wound, as from a fountain, running;
He sigh'd for rage, and trembled as he stood,
    He blamed his fortune, folly, want of cunning;
He lift his sword aloft, for ire nigh wood,
    And forward rush'd;—Tancred, his fury shunning,
With a sharp thrust once more the Pagan hit,
To his broad shoulder where his arm is knit.

XLV.

Like as a bear through-pierced with a dart,
    Within the secret woods no further flieth,
But bites the senseless weapon, mad with smart,
    Seeking revenge till unreveng'd she dieth;
So mad Argantes far'd, when his proud heart
    Wound upon wound and shame on shame espieth;
Desire of vengeance so o'ercame his senses,
That he forgot all dangers, all defences.

XLVI.

Uniting force extreme with endless wrath,
    Supporting both with youth and strength untired;
His thund'ring blows so fast about he la'th,
    That skies and earth the flying sparkles fired:
His foe to strike one blow no leisure hath,
    Scantly he breathed, though he oft desired;
His warlike skill and cunning all was waste,
Such was Argantes', force, and such his haste.

XLVII.

Long time Tancredie had in vain attended
    When this huge storm could overblow and pass;
Some blows his mighty target well defended,
    Some fell beside and wounded deep the grass;
But when he saw the tempest never ended,
    Nor that the Painim's force aught weaker was,
He high advanc'd his cutting sword at length,
And rage to rage oppos'd, and strength to strength.

XLVIII.

Wrath bore the sway, both art and reason fail,
    Fury new force and courage new supplies;
Their armors forged were of metal frail;
    On every side thereof huge cantles flies;

The land was strewed all with plate and mail,
  That on the earth, on that their warm blood lies,
And at each rush and every blow they smote,
Thunder the noise, the sparks seem'd lightning hote.

XLIX.

The Christian people and the Pagans gazed,
  On this fierce combat, wishing oft the end ;
'Twixt hope and fear they stood long time amazed,
  To see the knights assail and eke defend :
Yet neither sign they made nor noise they raised,
  But for the issue of the fight attend,
And stood as still as life and sense they wanted,
Save that their hearts within their bosoms panted.

L.

Now were they tired both, and well nigh spent,
  Their blows show'd greater will than power to wound ;
But night her gentle daughter, darkness, sent
  With friendly shade to overspread the ground.
Two heralds to the fighting champions went,
  To part the fray, as law of arms them bound ;
Aridens born in France, and wise Pindore,
The man that brought the challenge proud before.

LI.

These men their sceptres interpose between
  The doubtful hazards of uncertain fight ;
For such their privilege hath ever been,
  The law of nations doth defend their right :
Pindore began—Stay, stay, you warriors keen,
  Equal your honor, equal is your might ;
Forbear this combat, so we deem it best,
Give night her due, and grant your persons rest :

LII.

Man goeth forth to labor with the sun,
  But with the night all creatures draw to slee p ;
Nor yet of hidden praise, in darkness won,
  The valiant heart of noble knight takes keep.—
Argantes answer'd him—The fight begun
  Now to forbear doth wound my heart right deep :
Yet will I stay, so that this Christian swear,
Before you both, again to meet me here.—

LIII.

I swear, quoth Tancred; but swear thou likewise
    To make return thy pris'ner eke with thee,
Else for achievement of this enterprise
    None other time but this expect of me.—
Thus sware they both; the heralds both devise
    What time for this exploit should fittest be;
And, for their wounds of rest and cure hath need,
To meet again the sixth day was decreed.

LIV.

This fight was deep imprinted in their hearts
    That saw this bloody fray to ending brought,
An horror great possest their weaker parts,
    Which made them shrink who on this combat thought:
Much speech was of the praise and high desarts
    Of these brave champions that so nobly fought;
But which for knightly worth was most ypraised,
Of that was doubt and disputation raised.

LV.

All long to see them end this doubtful fray,
    And as they favor, so they wish success;
These hope true virtue shall obtain the day;
    Those trust on fury, strength, and hardiness;
But on Erminia most this burthen lay,
    Whose looks her trouble and her fear express;
For on this dang'rous combat's doubtful end,
Her joy, her comfort, hope, and life, depend.

LVI.

Her, the sole daughter of that hapless king
    That of proud Antioch late wore the crown,
The Christian soldiers to Tancredie bring,
    When they had sack'd and spoil'd that glorious town
But he, in whom all good and virtue spring,
    The virgin's honor sav'd and her renown;
And when her city and her state was lost,
Then was her person lov'd and honor'd most.

LVII.

He honor'd her, serv'd her, and leave her gave,
    And will'd her go whither and when she list;
Her gold and jewels had he care to save,
    And them restored all; she nothing miss'd:

She (that beheld his youth and person brave)
    When, by this deed, his noble mind she wist,
Laid ope her heart for Cupid's shaft to hit,
    Who never knots of love more surer knit.

LVIII.

Her body free, captived was her heart,
    And love the keys did of that prison bear;
Prepar'd to go, it was a death to part
    From that kind Lord, and from that prison dear:
But thou, O Honor, which esteemed art
    The chiefest vesture noble ladies wear,
Enforcest her against her will to wend
To Aladine, her mother's dearest friend.

LIX.

At Sion was this princess entertained
    By that old tyrant, and her mother dear,
Whose loss too soon the woful damsel plained;
    Her grief was such she liv'd not half the year;
Yet banishment nor loss of friends constrained
    The hapless maid her passions to forbear;
For though exceeding were her wo and grief,
Of all her sorrows yet her love was chief.

LX.

The seely maid in secret longing pined,
    Her hope a mote drawn up by Phœbus' rays;
Her love a mountain seem'd, whereon bright shined
    Fresh memory of Tancred's worth and praise:
Within her closet if herself she shrined,
    A hotter fire her tender heart assays:
Tancred at last, to raise her hope nigh dead,
Before those walls did his broad ensign spread.

LXI.

The rest to view the Christian army feared,
    Such seem'd their number, such their power and
But she alone her troubled forehead cleared,
    And on them spread her beauty shining bright;
In every squadron when it first appeared,
    Her curious eye sought out her chosen knight;
And every gallant that the rest excels,
The same seems him; so love and fancy tells.

LXII.

Within the kingly palace, builded high,
  A turret standeth near the city's wall,
From which Erminia might at ease descry
  The western host, the plains and mountains all;
And there she stood all the long day to spy,
  From Phœbus' rising to his evening fall;
And with her thoughts disputed of his praise,
And every thought a scalding sigh did raise.

LXIII.

From hence the curious combat she survey'd,
  And felt her heart tremble with fear and pain;
Her secret thought thus to her fancy said,
  Behold thy dear in danger to be slain;
So with suspect, with fear, and grief dismay'd,
  Attended she her darling's loss or gain;
And ever when the Pagan lift his blade,
The stroke a wound in her weak bosom made.

LXIV.

But when she saw the end, and wist withal
  Their strong contention should eftsoons begin;
Amazement strange her courage did appal,
  Her vital blood was icy cold within;
Sometimes she sighed, sometimes tears let fall,
  To witness what distress her heart was in;
Hopeless, dismay'd, pale, sad, astonished,
Her love was fear, her fear her torment bred.

LXV.

Her idle brain unto her soul presented
  Death, in an hundred ugly fashions painted;
And if she slept, then was her grief augmented,
  With such sad visions were her thoughts acquainted;
She saw her lord with wounds and hurts tormented,
  How he complain'd, call'd for her help, and fainted;
And found, awak'd from that unquiet sleeping,
Her heart with panting sore, eyes red with weeping.

LXVI.

Yet these presages of his coming ill
  Not greatest cause of her discomfort were;
She saw his blood from his deep wounds distil,
  Nor what he suffer'd could she bide or bear:

Besides, report her longing ear did fill,
  Doubling his danger, doubling so her fear,
That she concludes, so was her courage lost,
Her wounded lord was weak, faint, dead almost.

LXVII.

And, for her mother had her taught before
  The secret virtue of each herb that springs,
Besides fit charms for every wound or sore
  Corruption breedeth, or misfortune brings
(An art esteemed in those times of yore
  Beseeming daughters of great lords and kings),
She would herself be surgeon to her knight,
And heal him with her skill, or with her sight.

LXVIII.

Thus would she cure her love, and cure her foe
  She must, that had her friends and kinsfolk slain:
Some cursed weeds her cunning hand did know,
  That could augment his harm, increase his pain;
But she abhorr'd to be revenged so,
  No treason should her spotless person stain,
And virtueless she wish'd all herbs and charms
Wherewith false men increase their patients' harms:

LXIX.

Nor feared she among the bands to stray
  Of armed men, for often had she seen
The tragic end of many a bloody fray;
  Her life had full of haps and hazards been;
This made her bold in every hard assay,
  More than her feeble sex became, I ween;
She feared not the shake of every reed,
So cowards are courageous made through need.

LXX.

Love,—fearless, hardy, and audacious love,—
  Embold'ned had this tender damsel so,
That where wild beasts and serpents glide and move,
  Through Afric's deserts durst she ride or go,
Save that her honor (she esteem'd above
  Her life and body's safety) told her no;
For in the secret of her troubled thought
  A doubtful combat love and honor fought.—

LXXI.

O spotless virgin (Honor thus begon),
  That my true lore observed firmly hast,
When with thy foes thou didst in bondage won,
  Remember then I kept thee pure and chaste;
At liberty, now whither wouldst thou ron,
  To lay that field of princely virtue waste,
Or lose that jewel ladies hold so dear?
Is maidenhood so great a load to bear?

LXXII.

Or deem'st thou it a praise of little price
  The glorious title of a virgin's name?
That thou wilt gad by night in giglet-wise
  Amid thine armed foes to seek thy shame?
O fool! a woman conquers when she flies,
  Refusal kindleth, proffers quench the flame:
Thy lord will judge thou sinnest beyond measure,
If vainly thus thou waste so rich a treasure.—

LXXIII.

The sly deceiver, Cupid, thus beguil'd
  The simple damsel with his filed tongue :—
Thou wert not born (quoth he) in deserts wild,
  The cruel bears and savage beasts among,
That thou shouldst scorn fair Citherea's child,
  Or hate those pleasures that to youth belong,
Nor did the gods thy heart of iron frame;
To be in love is neither sin nor shame:

LXXIV.

Go then, go, whither sweet desire inviteth;
  How can thy gentle knight so cruel be?
Love in his heart thy grief and sorrows writeth,
  For thy laments how he complaineth see.
Oh cruel woman, whom no care exciteth
  To save his life that sav'd and honor'd thee!
He languisheth, one foot thou wilt not move
To succor him, yet say'st thou art in love.

LXXV.

No, no, stay here Argantes' wounds to cure,
  And make him strong to shed thy darling's blood;
Of such reward he may himself assure,
  That doth a thankless woman so much good :—

Ah, may it be thy patience can endure
  To see the strength of this Circassian wood,
And not with horror and amazement shrink,
When on their future fight thou hap'st to think ?

LXXVI.

Besides the thanks and praises for the deed,
  Suppose what joy, what comfort shalt thou win,
When thy soft hand doth wholesome plasters spread
  Upon the breaches in his ivory skin ;
Thence to thy dearest lord may health succeed,
  Strength to his limbs, blood to his cheeks so thin ;
And his rare beauties, now half dead and more,
Thou may'st to him, him to thyself restore :

LXXVII.

So shall some part of his adventures bold
  And valiant acts henceforth be held as thine ;
His dear embracements shall thee strait enfold,
  Together join'd in marriage rites divine ;
Lastly, high place of honor shalt thou hold
  Among the matrons sage and dames Latine,
In Italy, a land (as each one tells)
Where valor true and true religion dwells.—

LXXVIII.

With such vain hopes the seely maid abused,
  Promis'd herself mountains and hills of gold ;
Yet were her thoughts with doubts and fears confused,
  How to escape unseen out of that hold ;
Because the watchmen every minute used
  To guard the walls against the Christians bold ;
And in such fury and such heat of war,
The gates or seld or never open'd are.

LXXIX.

With strong Clorinda was Erminia sweet
  In surest links of dearest friendship bound ;
With her she us'd the rising sun to greet,
  And her (when Phœbus glided under ground)
She made the lovely partner of her sheet ;
  In both their hearts one will, one thought was found ;
Nor aught she hid from that virago bold,
Except her love ; that tale to none she told ;

LXXX.

That kept she secret; if Clorinda heard
  Her make complaints, or secretly lament,
To other cause her sorrow she referr'd;
  Matter enough she had of discontent:
Like as the bird, that having close imbarr'd
  Her tender young ones in the springing bent,
To draw the searcher farther from her nest,
Cries and complains most, where she needeth least

LXXXI.

Alone, within her chamber's secret part,
  Sitting one day upon her heavy thought,
Devising by what means, what sleight, what art,
  Her close departure should be safest wrought;
Assembled in her unresolved heart,
  A hundred passions strove and ceaseless fought;
At last she saw high hanging on the wall
Clorinda's silver arms; and sigh'd withal:—

LXXXII.

And sighing, softly to herself she said,
  How blessed is this virgin in her might!
How envy I the glory of the maid,
  Yet envy not her shape or beauty's light;
Her steps are not with trailing garments stay'd,
  Nor chambers hide her valor's shining bright;
But arm'd she rides, and breaketh sword and spear,
Nor is her strength restrain'd by shame or fear.

LXXXIII.

Alas! why did not heav'n these members frail
  With lively force and vigor strengthen so,
That I this silken gown and slender veil
  Might for a breastplate and an helm forego?
Then should not heat, nor cold, nor rain, nor hail,
  Nor storms that fall, nor blust'ring winds that blow,
Withhold me, but I would both day and night
In pitched field or private combat fight.

LXXXIV.

Nor haddest thou, Argantes, first begun
  With my dear lord that fierce and cruel fight,
But I to that encounter would have run,
  And haply ta'en him captive by my might;

Yet should he find (our furious combat done)
    His thraldom easy, and his bondage light;
For fetters mine embracements should he prove;
For diet, kisses sweet; for keeper, love:

LXXXV.

Or else my tender bosom opened wide,
    And heart through-pierced with his cruel blade,
The bloody weapon in my wounded side
    Might cure the wound, which love before had made;
Then should my soul in rest and quiet slide
    Down to the valleys of th' Elysian shade,
And my mishap the knight perchance would move
To shed some tears upon his murdered love.

LXXXVI.

Alas! impossible are all these things;
    Such wishes vain afflict my woful sprite.
Why yield I thus to plaints and sorrowings,
    As if all hope and help were perish'd quite?
My heart dares much, it soars with Cupid's wings.
    Why use I not for once these armors bright?
I may sustain awhile this shield aloft,
Though I be tender, feeble, weak, and soft.

LXXXVII.

Love, strong, bold, mighty, never-tired love,
    Supplieth force to all his servants true;
The fearful stags he doth to battaile move,
    Till each his horns in other's blood embrue;
Yet mean not I the haps of war to prove,
    A stratagem I have devised new;
Clorinda-like, in this fair harness dight,
I will escape out of the town this night.

LXXXVIII.

I know the men that have the gate to ward,
    If she command, dare not her will deny;
In what sort else could I beguile the guard?
    This way is only left, this will I try.
O gentle love, in this adventure hard
    Thine handmaid guide, assist, and fortify!
The time, the hour, now fitteth best the thing,
While stout Clorinda talketh with the king.—

LXXXIX.

Resolved thus, without delay she went,
  As her strong passion did her rashly guide,
And those bright arms down from the rafter hent,
  Within her closet did she closely hide:
That might she do unseen; for she had sent
  The rest on sleeveless errands from her side;
And night her stealths brought to their wished end;
Night, patroness of thieves, and lovers' friend.

XC.

Some sparkling fires on heav'n's bright visage shone,
  His azure robe the orient blueness lost,
When she, whose wit and reason both were gone,
  Call'd for a squire she lov'd and trusted most;
To whom, and to a maid (a faithful one),
  Part of her will she told; how that in post
She would depart from Judah's king; and feign'd
That other cause her sudden flight constrain'd.

XCI.

That trusty squire provided needments meet,
  As for their journey fitting most should be;
Meanwhile her vesture (pendent to her feet)
  Erminia doft, as erst determin'd she;
Stript to her petticoat, the virgin sweet
  So slender was, that wonder was to see;
Her handmaid, ready at her mistress' will,
To arm her help'd, though simple were her skill.

XCII.

The rugged steed oppressed and offended
  Her dainty neck and locks of shining gold;
Her tender arm so feeble was, it bended
  When that huge target it presum'd to hold;
The burnish'd steel bright rays far off extended;
  She feigned courage, and appeared bold:
Fast by her side unseen smiled Venus' son,
As erst he laughed when Alcides spun.

XCIII.

Oh, with what labor did her shoulders bear
  That heavy burden, and how slow she went!
Her maid, to see that all the coasts were clear,
  Before her mistress through the streets was sent.

Love gave her courage, love exiled fear,
  Love to her tired limbs new vigor lent,
Till she approached where the squire abode,
There took they horse forthwith, and forward rode :

XCIV.

Disguis'd they went, and by unused ways
  And secret paths they strove unseen to gone ;
Until the watch they meet, which sore affrays
  These soldiers new, when swords and weapons shone ;
Yet none to stop their journey once assays,
  But place and passage yielded every one ;
For that white armor and that helmet bright
Were known and feared in the darkest night.

XCV.

Erminia (though some deal she were dismay'd)
  Yet went she on, and goodly count'nance bore ;
She doubted lest her purpose were bewray'd ;
  Her too-much boldness she repented sore.
But now the gate her fear and passage stay'd,
  The heedless porter she beguil'd therefore :—
I am Clorinda, ope the gates, she cried,
Whereas the king commands, thus late I ride.—

XCVI.

Her woman's voice and terms all framed been
  Most like the speeches of the princess stout.
Who would have thought on horseback to have seen
  That feeble damsel armed round about ?
The porter her obey'd ; and she (between
  Her trusty squire and maiden) sallied out,
And through the secret dales they silent pass,
Where danger least, least fear, least peril was.

XCVII.

But when these fair advent'rers entered were
  Deep in a vale, Erminia stay'd her haste ;
To be recall'd she had no cause to fear,
  This foremost hazard had she trimly past ;
But dangers new (tofore unseen) appear,
  New perils she descried, new doubts she cast ;
The way that her desire to quiet brought
More difficult now seem'd than erst she thought.

XCVIII.

Armed to ride among her angry foes,
   She now perceiv'd it were great oversight;
Yet would she not, she thought, herself disclose,
   Until she came before her chosen knight;
To him she purpos'd to present the rose,
   Pure, spotless, clean, untouch'd of mortal wight;
She stay'd therefore, and in her thoughts more wise,
She called her 'squire, whom thus she 'gan advise:—

XCIX.

Thou must, quoth she, be mine ambassador;
   Be wise, be careful, true, and diligent;
Go to the camp, present thyself before
   The prince Tancredie, wounded in his tent;
Tell him thy mistress comes to cure his sore,
   If he to grant her peace and rest consent,
'Gainst whom fierce love such cruel war hath raised;
So shall his wound be cur'd, her torments eased:

C.

And say, in him such hope and trust she hath,
   That in his powers she fears no shame nor scorn;
Tell him thus much; and whatsoe'er he saith,
   Unfold no more, but make a quick return:
I (for this place is free from harm and scath)
   Within this valley will meanwhile sojourn.—
Thus spake the princess; and her servant true
To execute the charge imposed flew;

CI.

And was receiv'd (he so discreetly wrought)
   First of the watch that guarded in their place;
Before the wounded prince then was he brought,
   Who heard his message kind with gentle grace;
Which told, he left him tossing in his thought
   A thousand doubts, and turn'd his speedy pace
To bring his lady and his mistress word
She might be welcome to that courteous lord.

CII.

But she impatient, to whose desire
   Grievous and harmful seem'd each little stay,
Recounts his steps, and thinks, now draws he nigher,
   Now enters in, now speaks, now comes his way;

And that which griev'd her most, the careful squire
   Less speedy seem'd than e'er before that day:
Lastly she forward rode with love to guide,
Until the Christian tents at hand she spied.

CIII.

Invested in her starry veil, the night
   In her kind arms embraced all this round;
The silver moon from sea uprising bright,
   Spread frosty pearl upon the candied ground:
And Cinthia-like for beauty's glorious light,
   The love-sick nymph threw glist'ring beams around;
And counsellors of her old love she made
Those valleys dumb, that silence, and that shade.

CIV.

Beholding then the camp, quoth she,—O fair ·
   And castle-like pavilions, richly wrought,
From you how sweet methinketh blows the air,
   How comforts it my heart, my soul, my thought!
Through heav'n's fair grace, from gulf of sad despair
   My tossed bark to port well nigh is brought;
In you I seek redress for all my harms,
Rest 'midst your weapons, peace amongst your arms;

CV.

Receive me then, and let me mercy find,
   As gentle love assureth me I shall;
Among you had I entertainment kind,
   When first I was the Prince Tancredie's thrall:
I covet not, led by ambition blind,
   You should me in my father's throne instal;
Might I but serve in you my lord so dear,
That my content, my joy, my comfort were.

CVI.

Thus parlied she (poor soul), and never feared
   The sudden blow of fortune's cruel spite;
She stood where Phœbe's splendent beam appeared
   Upon her silver armor doubly bright;
The place about her round the shining cleared
   Of that pure white wherein the nymph was dight;
The tigress great that on her helmet laid,
Bore witness where she went, and where she stay'd.

CVII.

So, as her fortune would, a Christian band
  Their secret ambush there had closely framed,
Let by two brothers of Italia land,
  Young Polipherne and Alicandro named ;
These with their forces watched to withstand
  Those that brought vittailes to their foes untamed,
And kept that passage ; them Erminia spied,
And fled as fast as her swift steed could ride.

CVIII.

But Polipherne, before whose watery eyes
  His aged father strong Clorinda slew,
When that bright shield and silver helm he spies,
  The championess he thought he saw and knew ;
Upon his hidden mates for aid he cries
  'Gainst his supposed foe, and forth he flew ;
As he was rash and heedless in his wrath,
Bending his lance—Thou art but dead, he saith.

CIX.

As when a chased hind her course doth bend
  To seek by soil to find some ease or good,
Whether from craggy rock the spring descend,
  Or softly glide within the shady wood,
If there the dogs she meet where late she wend
  To comfort her weak limbs in cooling flood,
Again she flies swift as she fled at first,
Forgetting weakness, weariness, and thirst :

CX.

So she, that thought to rest her weary spright,
  And quench the endless thirst of ardent love,
With dear embracements of her lord and knight,
  But such as marriage rites should first approve ;
When she beheld her foe, with weapon bright,
  Threat'ning her death, his hasty courser move,
Her love, her lord, herself abandoned,
She spurr'd her speedy steed, and swift she fled.

CXI.

Erminia fled, scantly the tender grass
  Her Pegasus with his light footsteps bent,
Her maiden's beast for speed did likewise pass ;
  Yet divers ways (such was their fear) they went.
10

The squire, who all too late return'd, alas!
    With tardy news from Prince Tancredie's tent,
Fled likewise, when he saw his mistress gone;
    booted not to sojourn there alone.

CXII.

But Alicandro, wiser than the rest,
    Who this suppos'd Clorinda saw likewise,
To follow her yet was he nothing press'd,
    But in his ambush still and close he lies;
A messenger to Godfrey he address'd,
    That should him of this accident advise;
How that his brother chas'd with naked blade
Clorinda's self, or else Clorinda's shade;

CXIII.

Yet that it was, or that it could be she,
    He had small cause or reason to suppose,
Occasion great and weighty must it be
    Should make her ride by night among her foes:
What Godfrey willed that observed he,
    And with his soldiers lay in ambush close.
These news through all the Christian army went,
In every cabin talk'd, and every tent.

CXIV.

Tancred, whose thoughts the squire had filled with doubt,
    By his sweet words, suppos'd now, hearing this—
Alas! the virgin came to seek me out,
    And for my sake her life in danger is.—
Himself forthwith he singled from the rout,
    And rode in haste, though half his arms he miss;
Among those sandy fields and valleys green,
To seek his love, he gallop'd fast unseen.

BOOK VII.

THE ARGUMENT.

A shepherd fair Erminia entertains,
  Whom whilst Tancredie seeks in vain to find,
He is entrapped in Armida's trains.
  Raymond with strong Argantes is assign'd
To fight : an Angel to his aid he gains.
  Satan, that sees the Pagan's fury blind
And hasty wrath turn to his loss and harm,
Doth raise new tempest, uproar, and alarm.

I.

ERMINIA's steed this while his mistress bore
  Through forests thick among the shady treen,
Her feeble hand the bridle reins forlore,
  Half in a swoon she was for fear, I ween ;
But her fleet courser spared ne'er the more
  To bear her through the desert woods unseen
Of her strong foes, that chas'd her through the plain,
And still pursu'd, but still pursu'd in vain.

II.

Like as the weary hounds at last retire,
  Windless, displeased, from the fruitless chace,
When the sly beast tapish'd in bush and briar,
  No art nor pains can rouse out of his place ;
The Christian knights so full of shame and ire
  Returned back, with faint and weary pace ;
Yet still the fearful dame fled swift as wind,
Nor ever stay'd nor ever look'd behind.

III.

Through thick and thin all night, all day, she drived,
  Withouten comfort, company, or guide ;
Her plaints and tears with every thought revived,
  She heard and saw her griefs, but naught beside :

But when the sun his burning chariot dived
   In Thetis' wave, and weary team untied,
On Jordan's sandy banks her course she stay'd
At last, there down she light, and down she laid.

IV.

Her tears her drink, her food her sorrowings,
   This was her diet that unhappy night:
But sleep, that sweet repose and quiet brings
   To ease the griefs of discontented wight,
Spread forth his tender, soft, and nimble wings,
   In his dull arms folding the virgin bright;
And love, his mother, and the graces kept
Strong watch and ward, while this fair lady slept.

V.

The birds awak'd her with their morning song,
   Their warbling music pierc'd her tender ear;
The murmuring brooks and whistling winds among
   The rattling boughs and leaves their parts did bear;
Her eyes unclos'd beheld the groves along
   Of swains and shepherd grooms that dwellings were;
And that sweet noise, birds, winds, and waters sent,
Provok'd again the virgin to lament.

VI.

Her plaints were interrupted with a sound
   That seem'd from thickest bushes to proceed;
Some jolly shepherd sung a lusty round,
   And to his voice had tun'd his oaten reed;
Thither she went; an old man there she found,
   At whose right hand his little flock did feed,
Sat making baskets, his three sons among,
That learn'd their father's art, and learn'd his song.

VII.

Beholding one in shining arms appear,
   The seely man and his were sore dismay'd;
But sweet Erminia comforted their fear,
   Her ventail up, her visage open laid.—
You happy folk, of heav'n beloved dear,
   Work on, quoth she, upon your harmless trade;
These dreadful arms I bear no warfare bring
To your sweet toil, nor those sweet tunes you sing:

VIII.

But, father, since this land, these towns and towers,
    Destroyed are with sword, with fire, and spoil,
How may it be, unhurt that you and yours
    In safety thus apply your harmless toil ?—
My son, quoth he, this poor estate of ours
    Is ever safe from storm of warlike broil ;
This wilderness doth us in safety keep,
No thund'ring drum, no trumpet breaks our sleep :

IX.

Haply just heav'ns, defence and shield of right,
    Doth love the innocence of simple swains ;
The thunderbolts on highest mountains light,
    And seld or never strike the lower plains ;
So kings have cause to fear Bellona's might,
    Not they whose sweat and toil their dinner gains,
Nor ever greedy soldier was enticed
By poverty, neglected and despised :

X.

O poverty ! chief of the heav'nly brood,
    Dearer to me than wealth or kingly crown,
No wish for honor, thirst of other's good,
    Can move my heart, contented with mine own :
We quench our thirst with water of this flood,
    Nor fear we poison should therein be thrown ;
These little flocks of sheep and tender goats
Give milk for food, and wool to make us coats :

XI.

We little wish, we need but little wealth,
    From cold and hunger us to clothe and feed ;
These are my sons, their care preserves from stealth
    Their father's flocks, nor servants more I need :
Amid these groves I walk oft for my health,
    And to the fishes, birds, and beasts give heed,
How they are fed in forest, spring and lake,
And their contentment for ensample take :

XII.

Time was (for each one hath his doting time,
    These silver locks were golden tresses then)
That country life I hated as a crime,
    And from the forest's sweet contentment ran ;

To Memphis' stately palace would I climb,
   And there became the mighty caliph's man,
And though I but a simple gardener were,
Yet could I mark abuses, see and hear :

XIII.

Enticed on with hope of future gain,
   I suffer'd long what did my soul displease :
But when my youth was spent, my hope was vain ;
   I felt my native strength at last decrease ;
I 'gan my loss of lusty years complain,
   And wish'd I had enjoy'd the country's peace ;
I bade the court farewell, and with content
My later age here have I quiet spent.—

XIV.

While thus he spake, Erminia, hush'd and still,
   His wise discourses heard with great attention ;
His speeches grave those idle fancies kill,
   Which in her troubled soul bred such dissension.
After much thought reformed was her will ;
   Within those woods to dwell was her intention,
Till fortune should occasion new afford,
To turn her home to her desired lord.

XV.

She said therefore—O shepherd fortunate !
   That troubles some didst whilom feel and prove,
Yet livest now in this contented state,
   Let my mishap thy thoughts to pity move,
To entertain me as a willing mate
   In shepherd's life, which I admire and love ;
Within these pleasant groves perchance my heart
Of her discomforts may unload some part :

XVI.

If gold or wealth, of most esteemed dear,
   If jewels rich thou diddest hold in prize,
Such store thereof, such plenty have I here,
   As to a greedy mind might well suffice.—
With that down trickled many a silver tear,
   Two crystal streams fell from her watery eyes ;
Part of her sad misfortunes then she told,
And wept, and with her wept that shepherd old.

XVII.

With speeches kind he 'gan the virgin dear
 Towards his cottage gently home to guide ;
His aged wife there made her homely cheer,
 Yet welcom'd her, and plac'd her by her side.
The princess don'd a poor pastora's gear,
 A 'kerchief coarse upon her head she tied ;
But yet her gestures and her looks, I guess,
Were such as ill beseem'd a shepherdess :

XVIII.

Not those rude garments could obscure and hide
 The heav'nly beauty of her angel's face,
Nor was her princely offspring damnified
 Or aught disparag'd by those labors base :
Her little flocks to pasture would she guide,
 And milk her goats, and in their folds them place ;
Both cheese and butter could she make, and frame
Herself to please the shepherd and his dame.

XIX.

But oft, when underneath the green-wood shade
 Her flocks lay hid from Phœbus' scorching rays,
Unto her knight she songs and sonnets made,
 And them engrav'd in bark of beech and bays ;
She told how Cupid did her first invade,
 How conquer'd her, and ends with Tancred's praise :
And when her passion's writ she over read,
Again she mourn'd, again salt tears she shed.—

XX.

You happy trees, for ever keep (quoth she)
 This woful story in your tender rind :
Another day under your shade, may be,
 Will come to rest again some lover kind,
Who if these trophies of my griefs he see,
 Shall feel dear pity pierce his gentle mind.
With that she sigh'd, and said—Too late I prove
There is no truth in fortune, trust in love :

XXI.

Yet may it be (if gracious heav'ns attend
 The earnest suit of a distressed wight)
At my entreat they will vouchsafe to send
 To these huge deserts that unthankful knight ;

That when to earth the man his eyes shall bend,
  And see my grave, my tomb, and ashes light,
My woful death his stubborn heart may move,
With tears and sorrows to reward my love:

XXII.

So, though my life hath most unhappy been,
  At least yet shall my spirit dead be blest;
My ashes cold shall, buried on this green,
  Enjoy that good the body ne'er possest.—
Thus she complained to the senseless treen,
  Floods in her eyes, and fires were in her breast;
But he for whom these streams of tears she shed,
Wander'd far off, alas! as chance him led.

XXIII.

He follow'd on the footsteps he had traced,
  Till in high woods and forests old he came,
Where bushes, thorns, and trees so thick were placed,
  And so obscure the shadows of the same,
That soon he lost the track wherein he paced;
  Yet went he on, which way he could not aim;
But still attentive was his longing ear,
If noise of horse or noise of arms he hear:

XXIV.

If with the breathing of the gentle wind
  An aspen leaf but shaked on the tree,
If bird or beast stirr'd in the bushes blind,
  Thither he spurr'd, thither he rode to see;
Out of the wood, by Cinthia's favor kind,
  At last with travail great and pains got he,
And following on a little path, he heard
A rumbling sound, and hasted thitherward:

XXV.

It was a fountain from the living stone
  That poured down clear streams in noble store,
Whose conduit pipes, united all in one,
  Throughout a rocky channel ghastly roar:
Here Tancred stay'd, and call'd, yet answer'd none,
  Save babbling echo from the crooked shore;
And there the weary knight at last espies
The springing day-light red and white arise.

XXVI.

He sighed sore, and guiltless heaven 'gan blame,
  That wish'd success to his desires deny'd,
And sharp revenge protested for the same,
  If aught but good his mistress fair betide :
Then wish'd he to return the way he came,
  Although he wist not by what path to ride ;
And time drew near when he again must fight
With proud Argantes, that vain-glorious knight.

XXVII.

His stallworth steed the champion stout bestrode,
  And pricked fast to find the way he lost ;
But through a valley as he musing rode,
  He saw a man, that seem'd for haste a post ;
His horn was hung between his shoulders broad,
  As is the guise with us.   Tancredie crost
His way, and gently pray'd the man to say,
To Godfrey's camp how he should find the way.—

XXVIII.

Sir, in the Italian language, answer'd he,
  I ride where noble Boemond hath me sent.—
The Prince thought this his uncle's man should be,
  And after him his course with speed he bent.
A fortress stately built at last they see,
  'Bout which a muddy stinking lake there went ;
There they arriv'd when Titan went to rest
His weary limbs in night's untroubled nest.

XXIX.

The courier gave the fort a warning blast ;
  The drawbridge was let down by them within.—
If thou a Christian be (quoth he) thou may'st
  Till Phœbus shine again here take thine inn ;
The County of Cosenza (three days past)
  This castle from the Turks did nobly win.
The Prince beheld the peece, which site and art
Impregnable had made on every part ;

XXX.

He fear'd within a pile so fortified
  Some secret treason or enchantment lay ;
But had he known even there he should have died,
  Yet should his looks no sign of fear bewray ;

For wheresoever will or chance him guide,
　His strong victorious hand still made him way ;
Yet, for the combat he must shortly make,
No new adventures list he undertake.

XXXI.

Before the castle,' in a meadow plain,
　Beside the bridge's end he stay'd and stood,
Nor was entreated by the speeches vain
　Of his false guide to pass beyond the flood.
Upon the bridge appear'd a warlike swain,
　From top to toe all clad in armor good,
Who, brandishing a broad and cutting sword,
Thus threat'ned death with many an idle word :—

XXXII.

O thou, whom chance or will brings to the soil
　Where fair Armida doth the sceptre guide,
Thou canst not fly, of arms thyself despoil,
　And let thy hands with iron chains be tied ;
Enter and rest thee from thy weary toil ;
　Within this dungeon shalt thou safe abide,
And never hope again to see the day,
Or that thy hair for age shall turn to grey,

XXXIII.

Except thou swear her valiant knights to aid
　Against those traitors of the Christian crew.—
Tancred at this discourse a little stay'd,
　His arms, his gesture, and his voice he knew ;
It was Rambaldo, who for that false maid
　Forsook his country and religion true,
And of that fort defender chief became,
And those vile customs 'stablish'd in the same.

XXXIV.

The warrior answer'd (blushing red for shame)—
　Cursed apostate and ungracious wight,
I am that Tancred, who defend the name
　Of Christ, and have been aye his faithful knight ;
His rebel foes can I subdue and tame,
　As thou shalt find before we end this fight ;
And thy false heart, cleft with this vengeful sword,
Shall feel the ire of thy forsaken Lord.—

XXXV.

When that great name Rambaldo's ears did fill,
     He shook for fear and looked pale for dread,
Yet proudly said—Tancred, thy hap was ill
     To wander hither where thou art but dead,
Where naught can help thy courage, strength, and skill ;
     To Godfrey will I send thy cursed head,
That he may see how, for Armida's sake,
Of him and of his Christ a scorn I make.—

XXXVI.

This said, the day to sable night was turned,
     That scant one could another's arms descry ;
But soon a hundred lamps and torches burned,
     That cleared all the earth and all the sky ;
The castle seem'd a stage with lights adorned,
     On which men play some pompous tragedy :
Within a terrace sat on high the Queen,
And heard and saw, and kept herself unseen.

XXXVII.

The noble Baron whet his courage hot,
     And busk'd him boldly to the dreadful fight ;
Upon his horse long while he tarried not,
     Because on foot he saw the Pagan knight,
Who underneath his trusty shield was got,
     His sword was drawn, clos'd was his helmet bright ;
'Gainst whom the Prince march'd on a stately pace,
Wrath in his voice, rage in his eyes and face.

XXXVIII.

His foe, his furious charge not well abiding,
     Travers'd his ground, and started here and there,
But he (though faint and weary both with riding)
     Yet followed fast, and still oppress'd him near,
And on what side he felt Rambaldo sliding,
     On that his forces most employed were ;
Now at his helm, now at his hauberk bright,
He thundered blows, now at his face and sight ;

XXXIX.

Against those members battery chief he maketh
     Wherein man's life keeps chiefest residence :
At his proud threats the Gascoine warrior quaketh,
     An uncouth fear appalled every sense ;

To nimble shifts the knight himself betaketh,
　　And skippeth here and there for his defence ;
Now with his targe, now with his trusty blade,
Against his blows he good resistance made ;

XL.

Yet no such quickness for defence he used,
　　As did the Prince to work him harm and scaith ;
His shield was cleft in twain, his helmet bruised,
　　And in his blood his other arms did bathe ;
On him he heaped blows, with thrusts confused,
　　And more or less each stroke annoy'd him hath ;
He fear'd, and in his troubled bosom strove
Remorse of conscience, shame, disdain, and love :

XLI.

At last so careless foul despair him made,
　　He meant to prove his fortune ill or good ;
His shield cast down, he took his helpless blade
　　In both his hands, which yet had drawn no blood,
And with such force upon the Prince he laid,
　　That neither plate nor mail the blow withstood ;
The wicked steel scis'd deep in his right side,
And with his streaming blood his bases dyed.

XLII.

Another stroke he lent him on the brow,
　　So great that loudly rung the sounding steel ;
Yet pierc'd he not the helmet with the blow,
　　Although the owner twice or thrice did reel.
The Prince (whose looks his 'sdainful anger show)
　　Now meant to use his puissance every deal ;
He shak'd his head and crash'd his teeth for ire,
His lips breath'd wrath, eyes sparkled shining fire.

XLIII.

The Pagan wretch no longer could sustain
　　The dreadful terror of his fierce aspect,
Against the threat'ned blow he saw right plain
　　No temper'd armor could his life protect ;
He leap'd aside, the stroke fell down in vain
　　Against a pillar near the bridge erect,
Thence flaming fire and thousand sparks out start,
And kill with fear the coward Pagan's heart.

XLIV.

Toward the bridge the fearful Painim fled,
    And in swift flight his hope of life reposed ;
Himself fast after Lord Tancredie sped,
    And now in equal pace almost they closed,
When, all the burning lamps extinguished,
    The shining fort his goodly splendor losed,
And all those stars on heaven's blue face that shone,
With Cinthia's self, dis'peared were and gone.

XLV.

Amid those witchcrafts and that ugly shade
    No further could the Prince pursue the chace,
Nothing he saw, yet forward still he made,
    With doubtful steps, and ill-assured pace ;
At last his foot upon a threshold trade,
    And ere he wish'd he entered had the place ;
With ghastly noise the door-leaves shut behind,
And clos'd him fast in prison dark and blind.

XLVI.

As in our seas, in the Comachian bay,
    A seely fish, with streams enclosed, striveth
To shun the fury and avoid the sway
    Wherewith the current in that whirlpool driveth ;
Yet seeketh all in vain, but finds no way
    Out of that watery prison where she diveth ;
For with such force there be the tides in-brought,
There entereth all that will, thence issueth naught :

XLVII.

This prison so entrapp'd that valiant knight,
    Of which the gate was fram'd by subtle train,
To close, without the help of human wight,
    So sure, none could undo the leaves again :
Against the doors he bended all his might,
    But all his forces were employ'd in vain :
At last a voice 'gan to him loudly call—
Yield thee (quoth it), thou art Armida's thrall ;

XLVIII.

Within this dungeon buried shalt thou spend
    The res'due of thy woful days and years,—
The champion list not more with words contend,
    But in his heart kept close his griefs and fears ;

He blamed love, chance 'gan he reprehend,
   And gainst enchantments huge complaints he rears:
It were small loss (softly he thus begun)
To lose the brightness of the shining sun ;

XLIX.

But I, alas! the golden beam forego
   Of my far brighter sun ; nor can I say
If these poor eyes shall ere be blessed so,
   As once again to view that shining ray.—
Then thought he on his proud Circassian foe,
   And said—Ah! how shall I perform that fray ?
He (and the world with him) will Tancred blame ;
This is my grief, my fault, my endless shame.—

L.

While those high spirits of this champion good
   With love and honor's care are thus oppress'd,
While he torments himself, Argantes wood
   Wax'd weary of his bed and of his rest ;
Such hate of peace, and such desire of blood,
   Such thirst of glory, boiled in his breast,
That though he scant could stir or stand upright,
Yet long'd he for th' appointed day to fight.

LI.

The night, which that expected day fore-went,
   Scantly the Pagan clos'd his eyes to sleep,
He told how night her sliding hours spent,
   And rose ere springing day began to peep ;
He call'd for armor, which incontinent
   Was brought by him that used the same to keep ;
That harness rich old Aladine him gave,
A worthy present for a champion brave.

LII.

He don'd them on, nor long their riches ey'd,
   Nor did he aught with so great weight incline,
His wonted sword upon his thigh he tied,
   The blade was old and tough, of temper fine.
As when a comet, far and wide descried,
   In scorn of Phœbus 'midst bright heav'n doth shine,
And tidings sad of death and mischief brings
To mighty lords, to monarchs, and to kings ;

LIII.

So shone the Pagan in bright armor clad,
   And roll'd his eyes great swoll'n with ire and blood,
His dreadful gestures threat'ned horror sad,
   And ugly death upon his forehead stood;
Not one of all his squires the courage had
   T' approach their master in his angry mood;
Above his head he shook his naked blade,
And 'gainst the subtile air vain battle made.—

LIV.

That Christian thief (quoth he) that was so bold
   To combat me in hard and single fight,
Shall wounded fall inglorious on the mould,
   His locks with clods of blood and dust bedight,
And living shall with wat'ry eyes behold
   How from his back I tear his harness bright,
Nor shall his dying words me so entreat,
But that I'll give his flesh to dogs for meat.

LV.

Like as a bull, when prick'd with jealousy
   He spies the rival of his hot desire,
Through all the fields doth bellow, roar, and cry,
   And with his thund'ring voice augments his ire,
And threat'ning battle to the empty sky,
   Tears with his horn each tree, plant, bush and briar,
And with his foot casts up the sand on height,
Defying his strong foe to deadly fight:

LVI.

Such was the Pagan's fury, such his cry;
   An herald call'd he then, and thus he spake:—
Go to the camp, and in my name defy
   The man that combats for his Jesus' sake.—
This said, upon his steed he mounted high,
   And with him did his noble prisoner take,
The town he thus forsook, and on the green
He ran as mad or frantic he had been.

LVII.

A bugle small he winded loud and shrill,
   That made resound the fields and valleys near;
Louder than thunder from Olympus' hill
   Seemed that dreadful blast to all that hear.

The Christian lords of prowess, strength, and skill,
  Within th' imperial tent assembled were,
The herald there in boasting terms defied
Tancredie first, and all that durst beside.

LVIII.

With sober cheer Godfredo look'd about,
  And view'd at leisure every lord and knight,
But yet for all his looks not one stept out
  With courage bold to undertake the fight:
Absent were all the Christian champions stout,
  No news of Tancred since his secret flight;
Boemond far off, and banished from the crew
Was that strong Prince who proud Gernando slew:

LIX.

And eke those ten which chosen were by lot,
  And all the worthies of the camp beside,
After Armida false were follow'd hot,
  When night was come their secret flight to hide;
The rest their hands and hearts that trusted not
  Blushed for shame, yet silent still abide;
For none there was that sought to purchase fame
In so great peril; fear exiled shame.

LX.

The angry Duke their fear discovered plain,
  By their pale looks and silence, from each part,
And as he moved was with just disdain,
  These words he said and from his seat upstart:—
Unworthy life I judge that coward swain
  To hazard it e'en now that wants the heart,
When this vile Pagan with his glorious boast
Dishonors and defies Christ's sacred host.

LXI.

But let my camp sit still in peace and rest,
  And my life's hazard at their ease behold,
Come bring me here my fairest arms and best;—
  And they were brought sooner than could be told.
But gentle Raymond, in his aged breast
  Who had mature advice and counsel old,
Than whom in all the camp were none or few
Of greater might, before Godfredo drew,

LXII.

And gravely said—Ah let it not betide
  On one man's hand to venture all this host!
No private soldier thou, thou art our guide,
  If thou miscarry all our hope were lost;
By thee must Babel fall and all her pride,
  Of our true faith thou art the prop and post;
Rule with thy sceptre, conquer with thy word,
Let others combat make with spear and sword.

LXIII.

Let me this Pagan's glorious pride assuage,
  These aged arms can yet their weapons use,
Let others shun Bellona's dreadful rage,
  These silver locks shall not Raymondo 'scuse.
Oh that I were in prime of lusty age,
  Like you that this adventure brave refuse,
And dare not once lift up your coward eyes
'Gainst him that you and Christ himself defies!

LXIV.

Or as I was, when all the lords of fame
  And German princes great stood by to view,
In Conrad's court (the second of that name)
  When Leopold in single fight I slew;
A greater praise I reaped by the same,
  So strong a foe in combat to subdue,
Than he should do who all alone should chase
Or kill a thousand of these Pagans base.

LXV.

Within these arms had I that strength again,
  This boasting Painim had not liv'd till now;
Yet in this breast doth courage still remain,
  For age or years these members shall not bow;
And if I be in this encounter slain,
  Scotfree Argantes shall not 'scape, I vow;
Give me mine arms, this battle shall with praise
Augment mine honor got in younger days.—

LXVI.

The jolly Baron old thus bravely spake,
  His words are spurs to virtue; every knight
That seem'd before to tremble and to quake,
  Now talked bold, ensample hath such might;

11

Each one the battle fierce would undertake,
   Now strove they all who should begin the fight ;
Baldwin and Roger both would combat fain,
Stephen, Guelpho, Gernier, and the Gerrards twain :

LXVII.

And Pyrrhus, who, with help of Boemond's sword,
   Proud Antioch by cunning sleight oppress'd ;
The battle eke, with many a lowly word,
   Ralph, Rosimond, and Eberard request,
A Scotch, an Irish, and an English lord,
   Whose lands the sea divides far from the rest ;
And for the fight did likewise humbly sue,
   Edward and his Gildippes, lovers true.

LXVIII.

But Raymond more than all the rest doth sue
   Upon that Pagan fierce to wreak his ire :
Now wants he naught of all his armors due
   Except his helm, that shone like flaming fire.
To whom Godfredo thus : O mirror true
   Of antique worth ! thy courage doth inspire
New strength in us ; of Mars in thee doth shine
The art, the honor, and the discipline.

LXIX.

If ten like thee of valor and of age
   Among these legions I could haply find,
I should the heat of Babel's pride assuage,
   And spread our faith from Thule to furthest Inde ;
But now I pray thee calm thy valiant rage,
   Reserve thyself till greater need us bind,
And let the rest each one write down his name,
And see whom fortune chooseth to this game ;

LXX.

Or rather see whom God's high judgment taketh,
   To whom is chance and fate and fortune slave.—
Raymond his earnest suit not yet forsaketh,
   His name writ with the res'due would he have.
Godfrey himself in his bright helmet shaketh
   The scrolls, with names of all the champions brave.
They drew, and read the first whereon they hit,
Wherein was Raymond, Earl of Tholouse, writ.

LXXI.

His name with joy and mighty shouts they bliss;
  The rest allow his choice, and fortune praise:
New vigor blushed through those looks of his,
  It seem'd he now resum'd his youthful days:
Like to a snake whose slough new changed is,
  That shines like gold against the sunny rays:
But Godfrey most approv'd his fortune high,
And wish'd him honor, conquest, victory.

LXXII.

Then from his side he took his noble brand,
  And giving it to Raymond, thus he spake:—
This is the sword wherewith, in Saxon land,
  The great Rubello battle used to make;
From him I took it, fighting hand to hand,
  And took his life with it; and many a lake
Of blood with it I have shed since that day:
With thee God grant it prove as happy may.—

LXXIII.

Of these delays meanwhile impatient,
  Argantes threat'neth loud, and sternly cries—
O glorious people of the Occident!
  Behold him here that all your host defies:
Why comes not Tancred, whose great hardiment
  With you is priz'd so dear? pardie he lies
Still on his pillow, and presumes the night
Again may shield him from my power and might.

LXXIV.

Why then some other come, by band and band
  Come all, come forth on horseback, come on foot,
If not one man dares combat hand to hand,
  In all the thousands of so great a rout:
See where the tomb of Mary's Son doth stand,
  March thither, warriors bold, what makes you doubt?
Why run you not, there for your sins to weep,
Or to what greater need these forces keep?—

LXXV.

Thus scorned by the heathen Saracine
  Were all the soldiers of Christ's sacred name.
Raymond (while others at his words repine)
  Burst forth in rage, he could not bear this shame;

For fire of courage brighter far doth shine,
   If challenges and threats augment the same;
So that upon his steed he mounted light,
Which Aquilino for his swiftness hight.

LXXVI.

This jennet was by Tagus bred; for oft
   The breeder of those beasts to war assign'd,
When first on trees bourgeon the blossoms soft,
   Prick'd forward with the sting of fertile kind,
Against the air casts up her head aloft,
   And gathereth seed so from the fruitful wind;
And thus conceiving of the gentle blast,
(A wonder strange and rare), she foals at last!

LXXVII.

And had you seen the beast you would have said
   The light and subtle wind his father was;
For if his course upon the sands he made,
   No sign was left what way the beast did pass;
Or if he manag'd were, or if he play'd,   .
   He scantly bended down the tender grass.
Thus mounted rode the Earl, and as he went,
Thus pray'd, to heaven his zealous looks up-bent :—

LXXVIII.

O Lord! that diddest save, keep, and defend
   Thy servant David from Goliah's rage,
And broughtest that huge giant to his end,
   Slain by a faithful child of tender age;
Like grace, O Lord! like mercy now extend,
   Let me this vile blasphemous pride assuage,
That all the world may to thy glory know,
Old men and babes thy foes can overthrow.—

LXXIX.

Thus pray'd the County, and his prayers dear,
   Strength'ned with zeal, with godliness and faith,
Before the throne of that great Lord appear,
   In whose sweet grace is life, death in his wrath;
Among his armies bright and legions clear,
   The Lord an angel good selected hath,
To whom the charge was given to guard the knight,
And keep him safe from that fierce Pagan's might.

LXXX.

The angel good, appointed for the guard
  Of noble Raymond from his tender eild
That kept him then, and kept him afterward,
  When spear and sword he able was to wield;
Now when his great Creator's will he heard,
  That in this fight he should him chiefly shield,
Up to a tower set on a rock did fly,
Where all the heav'nly arms and weapons lie.

LXXXI.

There stands the lance wherewith great Michael slew
  The aged dragon in a bloody fight;
There are the dreadful thunders forged new
  With storms and plagues that on poor sinners light;
The massy trident mayst thou pendent view,
  There on a golden pin hung up on height,
Wherewith sometimes he smites this solid land,
And throws down towns and towers thereon which stand.

LXXXII.

Among the blessed weapons there which stand,
  Upon a diamond shield his looks he bended,
So great that it might cover all the land
  'Twixt Caucasus and Atlas hills extended;
With it the Lord's dear flocks and faithful bands,
  The holy kings and cities are defended;
The sacred angel took this target sheen,
And by the Christian champion stood unseen.

LXXXIII.

But now the walls and turrets round about
  Both young and old with many thousands fill;
The king Clorinda sent and her brave rout
  To keep the field; she stay'd upon the hill:—
Godfrey likewise some Christian bands sent out,
  Which arm'd and rank'd in good array stood still;
And to their champions empty let remain
'Twixt either troop a large and spacious plain.

LXXXIV.

Argantes looked for Tancredie bold,
  But saw an uncouth foe at last appear;
Raymond rode on, and what he ask'd him told:—
  Better thy chance, Tancred is now elsewhere.

Yet glory not of that, myself behold
    Am come prepar'd, and bid thee battle here,
And in his place, or for myself, to fight,
Lo here I am, who scorn thy heath'nish might.—

LXXXV.

The Pagan cast a scornful smile, and said—
    But where is Tancred, is he still in bed ?
His looks late seem'd to make high heav'n afraid,
    But now for dread he is or dead or fled ;
But were earth's centre or the deep sea made
    His lurking hole, it should not save his head.—
Thou liest, he says, to say so brave a knight
Is fled from thee, who thee exceeds in might.—

LXXXVI.

The angry Pagan said—I have not spilt
    My labor then if thou his place supply ;
Go, take the field, and let 's see how thou wilt
    Maintain thy foolish words and that brave lie.—
Thus parlied they to meet in equal tilt,
    Each took his aim at other's helm on high ;
Even in the sight his foe good Raymond hit,
But shak'd him not, he did so firmly sit.

LXXXVII.

The fierce Circassian missed of his blow,
    A thing which seld befell the man before ;
The angel by unseen his force did know,
    And far awry the poignant weapon bore ;
He burst his lance against the sand below,
    And bit his lips for rage, and curst and swore ;
Against his foe return'd he swift as wind,
Half mad in arms a second match to find.

LXXXVIII.

Like to a ram that butts with horned head,
    So spurr'd he forth his horse with desp'rate race :
Raymond at his right hand let slide his steed,
    And as he pass'd struck at the Pagan's face ;
Who turn'd again ; the brave Earl nothing dread,
    Yet stepp'd aside and to his rage gave place,
And on his helm with all his strength 'gan smite,
Which was so hard his courtlax could not bite.

LXXXIX.

The Saracine employ'd his art and force
  To gripe his foe within his mighty arms;
But he avoided nimbly with his horse;
  He was no 'prentice in those fierce alarms;
About him made he many a winding course,
  No strength, no sleight the subtile warrior harms;
His nimble steed obey'd his ready hand,
And where he stept no print left in the sand.

XC.

As when a captain doth besiege some hold,
  Set in a marish or high on a hill,
And trieth ways and wiles a thousand fold
  To bring the peece subjected to his will;
So far'd the County with the Pagan bold;
  And when he did his head and breast none ill,
His weaker parts he wisely 'gan assail,
And entrance searched oft 'twixt mail and mail.

XCI.

At last he hit him on a place or twain,
  That on his arms the red blood trickled down,
And yet himself untouched did remain,
  No nail was broke, no plume cut from his crown.
Argantes raging spent his strength in vain,
  Waste were his strokes, his thrusts were idle thrown,
Yet pressed he on, and doubled still his blows,
And where he hits he neither cares nor knows.

XCII.

Among a thousand blows the Saracine
  At last struck one, when Raymond was so near
That not the swiftness of his Aquiline
  Could his dear lord from that huge danger bear:
But lo! at hand unseen was help divine,
  Which saves when worldly comforts none appear;
The angel on his targe receiv'd that stroke,
And on that shield Argantes' sword was broke:

XCIII.

The sword was broke, therein no wonder lies
  If earthly temper'd metal could not hold
Against that target forg'd above the skies.
  Down fell the blade in pieces on the mould;

The proud Circassian scant believ'd his eyes,
    Though naught were left him but the hilts of gold ;
And full of thoughts amaz'd awhile he stood,
Wond'ring the Christian's armor was so good.

XCIV.

The brittle web of that rich sword he thought
    Was broke through hardness of the County's shield ;
And so thought Raymond, who discovered naught
    What succor heav'n did for his safety yield ;
But when he saw the man 'gainst whom he fought
    Unweaponed, still stood he in the field ;
His noble heart esteem'd the glory light,
At such advantage if he slew the knight.

XCV.

Go fetch, he would have said, another blade,
    When in his heart a better thought arose,
How for Christ's glory he was champion made,
    How Godfrey had him to this combat chose,
The armies' honor on his shoulder laid ;
    To hazards new he list not that expose ;
While thus his thoughts debated on the case,
The hilt Argantes hurled at his face ;

XCVI.

And forward spurr'd his mounter fierce withal,
    Within his arms longing his foe to strain,
Upon whose helm the heavy blow did fall,
    And bent well nigh the metal to his brain :
But he, whose courage was heroical,
    Leap'd by and makes the Pagan's onset vain,
And wounds his hand, which he outstretched saw
Fiercer than eagle's talon, lion's paw.

XCVII.

Now here, now there, on every side he rode
    With nimble speed, and spurr'd now out, now in ;
And as he went and came still laid on load
    Where Lord Argantes' arms were weak and thin ;
All that huge force which in his arms abode,
    His wrath, his ire, his great desire to win,
Against his foe together all he bent,
And heav'n and fortune further'd his intent.

XCVIII.

But he, whose courage for no peril fails,
    Well arm'd and better hearted, scorns his powers;
Like a tall ship, when spent are all her sails,
    Which still resists the rage of storm and shower,
Whose mighty ribs fast bound with bands and nails,
    Withstand fierce Neptune's wrath for many an hour,
And yields not up her bruised keel to winds,
In whose stern blasts no ruth nor grace she finds:

XCIX.

Argantes such thy present danger was,
    When Satan stirr'd to aid thee at thy need,
In human shade he forg'd an airy mass,
    And made the shade a body seem indeed;
Well might the spirit for Clorinda pass,
    Like her it was in armor and in weed,
In statue, beauty, countenance, and face,
In looks, in speech, in gesture, and in pace;

C.

And for the sprite should seem the same indeed,
    From where she was whose show and shape it had,
Towards the wall it rode with feigned speed,
    Where stood the people all dismay'd and sad
To see their knight of help have so great need,
    And yet the law of arms all help forbad.
There in a turret sat a soldier stout
To watch, and at a loop-hole peeped out.

CI.

The spirit spake to him, called Oradine,
    The noblest archer then that handled bow:—
O, Oradine, quoth she, who straight as line
    Canst shoot, and hit each mark set high or low,
If yonder knight, alas! be slain in fine,
    As likest is, great ruth it were you know,
And greater shame if his victorious foe
Should with his spoils triumphant homeward go.

CII.

Now prove thy skill, thine arrow's sharp head dip
    In yonder thievish Frenchman's guilty blood;
I promise thee thy sovereign shall not slip
    To give thee large rewards for such a good;—

Thus said the sprite : the man did laugh and skip
   For hope of future gain, nor longer stood,
But from his quiver huge a shaft he hent,
And set it in his mighty bow new bent.

CIII.

Twanged the string, out flew the quarel long,
   And through the subtle air did singing pass ;
It hit the knight, the buckles rich among
   Wherewith his precious girdle fasten'd was.
It bruised them and pierc'd his hauberk strong,
   Some little blood down trickled on the grass ;
Light was the wound ; the angel by unseen
The sharp head blunted of the weapon keen.

CIV.

Raymond drew forth the shaft, as much behoved,
   And with the steel his blood out streaming came ;
With bitter words his foe he then reproved,
   For breaking faith, to his eternal shame.
Godfrey, whose careful eyes from his beloved
   Were never turned, saw and mark'd the same ;
And when he view'd the wounded County bleed,
He sigh'd, and feared more perchance than need ;

CV.

And with his words and with his threat'ning eyes
   He stirr'd his captains to revenge that wrong ;
Forthwith the spurred courser forward hies ;
   Within their rests put were their lances long ;
From either side a squadron brave out flies,
   And boldly made a fierce encounter strong ;
The raised dust to overspread begun
Their shining arms, and far more shining sun.

CVI.

Of breaking spears, of ringing helm and shield,
   A dreadful rumor roar'd on every side :
There lay a horse, another through the field
   Ran masterless, dismounted was his guide :
Here one lay dead, there did another yield,
   Some sigh'd, some sobb'd, some prayed, and some cried :
Fierce was the fight, and longer still it lasted,
Fiercer and fewer, still themselves they wasted.

CVII.

Argantes nimbly leap'd amid the throng,
　　And from a soldier wrung an iron mace,
And breaking through the ranks and ranges long,
　　Therewith he passage made himself and place ;
Raymond he sought the thickest prease among,
　　To take revenge for late receiv'd disgrace,
A greedy wolf he seem'd, and would assuage
With Raymond's blood his hunger and his rage.

CVIII.

The way he found not easy as he would,
　　But fierce encounters put him oft to pain ;
He met Ormanno and Rogero bold,
　　Of Balnavile Guy, and the Gerards twain ;
Yet nothing might his rage and haste withhold,
　　These worthies strove to stop him but in vain ;
With these strong lets increased still his ire,
Like rivers stopp'd, or closely smould'red fire.

CIX.

He slew Ormanno, wounded Guy, and laid
　　Rogero low among the people slain ;
On every side new troops the man invade,
　　Yet all their blows were waste, their onsets vain.
But while Argantes thus his prizes play'd,
　　And seem'd alone this skirmish to sustain,
The Duke his brother call'd, and thus he spake—
Go with thy troop, fight for thy Saviour's sake ;

CX.

There enter in where hottest is the fight,
　　Thy force against the left wing strongly bend.—
This said, so brave an onset gave the knight,
　　That many a Painim bold there made his end.
The Turks too weak seem'd to sustain his might,
　　And could not from his power their lines defend ;
Their ensigns rent, and broke was their array,
And men and horse on heaps together lay.

CXI.

O'erthrown likewise away the right wing ran,
　　Nor was there one again that turn'd his face
Save bold Argantes, else fled every man,
　　Fear drove them thence on heaps with headlong chace.

He stay'd alone, and battle new began ;
　　Five hundred men, weapon'd with sword and mace,
So great resistance never could have made,
As did Argantes with his single blade.

CXII.

The strokes of swords and thrusts of many a spear,
　　The shock of many a just, he long sustained ;
He seem'd of strength enough this charge to bear,
　　And time to strike now here now there he gained ;
His armors broke, his members bruised were,
　　He sweat and bled, yet courage still he feigned ;
But now his foes upon him press'd so fast,
　　That with their weight they bore him back at last.

CXIII.

His back against this storm at length he turned,
　　Whose headlong fury bore him backward still,
Not like to one that fled, but one that mourned
　　Because he did his foes no greater ill ;
His threat'ning eyes like flaming torches burned,
　　His courage thirsted yet more blood to spill ;
And every way and every mean he sought
To stay his flying mates, but all for naught.

CXIV.

This good he did, while thus he play'd his part,
　　His bands and troops at ease and safe retired ;
Yet coward dread lacks order, fear wants art,
　　Deaf to attend, commanded or desired.
But Godfrey, that perceiv'd in his wise heart
　　How his bold knights to victory aspired,
Fresh soldiers sent to make more quick pursuit,
And help to gather conquest's precious fruit.

CXV.

But this (alas !) was not th' appointed day
　　Set down by heav'n to end this mortal war ;
The Western lords this time had borne away
　　The prize for which they travell'd had so far,
Had not the devils (that saw the sure decay
　　Of their false kingdom by this bloody war)
At once made heav'n and earth with darkness blind,
And stirr'd up tempests, storms, and blust'ring wind.

CXVI.

Heav'n's glorious lamp, wrapp'd in an ugly veil
  Of shadows dark, was hid from mortal eye,
And hell's grim blackness did bright skies assail ;
  On every side the fiery light'nings fly,
The thunders roar, the streaming rain and hail
  Pour down, and make that sea which erst was dry ;
The tempests rend the oaks, and cedars brake,
And make not trees, but rocks and mountains shake.

CXVII.

The rain, the light'ning, and the raging wind,
  Beat in the Frenchmen's eyes with hideous force ;
The soldiers stay'd amaz'd in heart and mind,
  The terror such stopped both man and horse :
Surprised with this ill, no way they find
  Whither for succor to direct their course :
But wise Clorinda soon th' advantage spied,
And spurring forth, thus to her soldiers cried :—

CXVIII.

You hardy men at arms, behold (quoth she)
  How heav'n, how justice in our aid doth fight,
Our visages are from this tempest free,
  Our hands at will may wield our weapons bright ;
The fury of this friendly storm you see
  Upon the foreheads of our foes doth light,
And blinds their eyes ; then let us take the tide ;
Come, follow me, good fortune be our guide.—

CXIX.

This said, against her foes on rode the dame,
  And turn'd their backs against the wind and rain ;
Upon the French with furious rage she came,
  And scorn'd those idle blows they struck in vain ;
Argantes at the instant did the same,
  And them who chased him now chas'd again :
Naught but his fearful back each Christian shows
Against the tempest and against their blows.

CXX.

The cruel hail and deadly wounding blade
  Upon their shoulders smote them as they fled ;
The blood new spilt, while thus they slaughter made,
  The water fall'n from skies had dyed red.

Among the murder'd bodies Pyrrhus laid,
   And valiant Ralph his heart-blood there out-bled;
The first subdu'd by strong Argantes' might,
The second conquer'd by that virgin knight.

CXXI.

Thus fled the French, and them pursu'd in chase
   The wicked sprites and all the Syrian train;
But 'gainst their force, and 'gainst the fell menace
   Of hail and wind, of tempest and of rain,
Godfrey alone turn'd his audacious face,
   Blaming his barons for their fear so vain;
Himself the camp-gate boldly stood to keep,
And sav'd his men within his trenches deep;

CXXII.

And twice upon Argantes proud he flew,
   And beat him backward maugre all his might,
And twice his thirsty sword he did embrue
   In Pagans' blood where thickest was the fight.
At last himself with all his folk withdrew,
   And that day's conquest gave the virgin bright;
Which got, she home retir'd and all her men,
And thus she chas'd this lion to his den.

CXXIII.

Yet ceased not the fury and the ire
   Of these huge storms of wind, of rain, and hail;
Now was it dark, now shone the light'ning fire,
   The wind and water every place assail,
No bank was safe, no rampire left entire,
   No tent could stand when beam and cordage fail;
Wind, thunder, rain, all gave a dreadful sound,
And with that music deaf'd the trembling ground.

BOOK VIII.

~~~~~~

THE ARGUMENT.

A messenger to Godfrey sage doth tell
   The prince of Denmark's valor, death, and end.
Th' Italians, trusting signs untrue too well,
   Think their Rinaldo slain ; the wicked fiend
Breeds fury in their breasts, their bosoms swell
   With ire and hate, and war and strife forth send ;
They threaten Godfrey ; he prays to the Lord,
And calms their fury with his look and word.

~~~~~~

I.

Now were the skies of storms and tempests cleared,
   Lord Æolus shut up his winds in hold ;
The silver-mantled morning fresh appeared,
   With roses crown'd, and buskin'd high with gold :
The spirits yet which had these tempests reared
   Their malice would still more and more unfold ;
And one of them, that Astragor was named,
His speeches thus to foul Alecto framed :—

II.

Alecto, see, we could not stop nor stay
   The knight that to our foes new tidings brings,
Who from the hands escap'd with life away
   Of that great prince, chief of all Pagan kings,
He comes, the fall of his slain lord to say,
   Of death and loss he tells, and such sad things,
Great news he brings, and greatest danger is
Bertoldo's son shall be call'd home for this.

III.

Thou know'st what would befall, bestir thee then,
   Prevent with craft what force could not withstand,
Turn to their evil the speeches of the man,
   With his own weapon wound Godfredo's hand ;

Kindle debate, infect with poison wan
  The English, Switzer, and Italian band,
Great tumults move, make brawls and quarrels rife,
Set all the camp on uproar and at strife.

IV.

This act beseems thee well, and of the deed
  Much may'st thou boast before our lord and king.—
Thus said the sprite: persuasion small did need,
  The monster grants to undertake the thing.
Meanwhile the knight whose coming thus they dread,
  Before the camp his weary limbs doth bring,
And well-nigh breathless—Warriors bold, ne cried,
Who shall conduct me to your famous guide?—

V.

An hundred strove the stranger's guide to be,
  To hearken news the knights by heaps assemble;
The man fell lowly down upon his knee,
  And kiss'd the hand that made proud Babel tremble :—
Right puissant lord, whose valiant acts (quoth he)
  The sands and stars in number best resemble,
Would God some gladder news I might unfold :—
And there he paus'd and sigh'd, then thus he told :

VI.

Sweno, the King of Denmark's only heir,
  The stay and staff of his declining eild,
Longed to be among these squadrons fair,
  Who for Christ's faith here serve with spear and shield ;
No weariness, no storms of sea or air,
  No dear contents as crowns and sceptres yield,
No such entreaties of so kind a sire,
Could in his bosom quench that glorious fire ;

VII.

He thirsteth sore to learn this warlike art
  Of thee, great lord and master of the same,
And was ashamed in his noble heart
  That never act he did deserved fame ;
Besides, the news and tidings from each part
  Of young Rinaldo's worth and praises came ;
But that which most his courage stirred hath
Is zeal, religion, godliness, and faith.

VIII.

He hasted forward then without delay,
    And with him took of knights a chosen band,
Directly towards Thrace we took the way
    To Bizance old, chief fortress of that land ;
There the Greek monarch gently pray'd him stay,
    And there an herald sent from you we fand,
How Antioch was won who first declar'd,
And how defended nobly afterward ;

IX.

Defended 'gainst Corbana, valiant knight,
    That all the Persian armies had to guide,
And brought so many soldiers bold to fight
    That void of men he left that kingdom wide :
He told thine acts, thy wisdom, and thy might,
    And told the deeds of many a lord beside ;
His speech at length to young Rinaldo past,
And told his great achievements first and last ;

X.

And how this noble camp of yours of late
    Besieged had this town, and in what sort,
And how you pray'd him to participate
    Of the last conquest of this noble fort.
In hardy Sweno opened was the gate
    Of worthy anger, by this brave report ;
So that each hour seemed five years long
Till he were fighting with these Pagans strong.

XI.

And while the herald told your fights and frays,
    Himself of cowardice reprov'd he thought,
And him to stay that counsels him or prays
    He hears not, or (else heard) regardeth naught ;
He fears no perils, but (whilst he delays)
    Lest this last work without his help be wrought ;
In this his doubt, in this his danger lies,
No hazard else he fears, no peril spies.

XII.

Thus hasting on, he hasted on his death,
    Death that to him and us was fatal guide ,
The rising morn appeared yet uneath,
    When he and we were arm'd, and fit to ride ;

12

The nearest way seem'd best, o'er hoult and heath
    We went, through deserts waste, and forests wide ;
The straits and ways he openeth as he goes,
And sets each land free from intruding foes.

XIII.

Now want of food, now dang'rous ways we find,
    Now open war, now ambush closely laid ;
Yet past we forth, all perils left behind,
    Our foes or dead or run away afraid ;
Of victory so happy blew the wind,
    That careless all, and heedless too, it made ;
Until one day his tents he hapt to rear,
To Palestine when we approached near ;

XIV.

There did our scouts return, and bring us news
    That dreadful noise of horse and arms they hear,
And that they deem'd by sundry signs and shows
    There was some mighty host of Pagans near :
At these sad tidings many chang'd their hues ;
    Some looked pale for dread, some shook for fear ;
Only our noble lord was alter'd naught
In look, in face, in gesture, or in thought ;

XV.

But said—A crown prepare you to possess
    Of martyrdom, or happy victory ;
For this I hope, for that I wish no less,
    Of greater merit and of greater glory,
Brethren, this camp will shortly be, I guess,
    A temple sacred to our memory,
To which the holy men of future age
To view our graves shall come in pilgrimage.—

XVI.

This said, he set the watch in order right,
    To guard the camp, along the trenches deep ;
And as he armed was, so every knight
    He willed on his back his arms to keep.
Now had the stillness of the quiet night
    Drown'd all the world in silence and in sleep,
When suddenly we heard a dreadful sound,
Which deaft the earth and tremble made the ground.

XVII.

Arm, arm, they cry'd: Prince Sweno at the same,
    Glist'ring in shining steel, leapt foremost out;
His visage shone, his noble looks did flame,
    With kindled brand of courage bold and stout:
When, lo, the Pagans to assault us came,
    And with huge numbers hemm'd us round about;
A forest thick of spears about us grew,
And over us a cloud of arrows flew.

XVIII.

Uneven the fight, unequal was the fray,
    Our enemies were twenty men to one;
On ev'ry side the slain and wounded lay,
    Unseen, where naught but glist'ring weapons shone;
The number of the dead could no man say,
    So was the place with darkness overgone;
The night her mantle black upon us spreeds,
Hiding our losses and our valiant deeds.

XIX.

But hardy Sweno, 'midst the other train,
    By his great acts was well descried I wote,
No darkness could his valor's daylight stain,
    Such wond'rous blows on every side he smote;
A stream of blood, a bank of bodies slain,
    About him made a bulwark and a moat,
And whensoe'er he turned his fatal brand,
Dread in his looks and death sat in his hand.

XX.

Thus fought we till the morning bright appeared,
    And strewed roses on the azure sky,
But when her lamp had night's thick darkness cleared,
    Wherein the bodies dead did buried lie,
Then our sad cries to heav'n for grief we reared,
    Our loss apparent was, for we descry
How all our camp destroyed was almost,
And all our people well-nigh slain and lost.

XXI.

Of thousands twain an hundred scant survived:
    When Sweno murder'd saw each valiant knight,
I know not if his heart in sunder rived,
    For dear compassion of that woful sight:

He showed no change, but said—Since so deprived
  We are of all our friends by chance of fight,
Come, follow them, the path to heav'n their blood
Marks out, new angels made, of martyrs good,—

XXII.

This said, and glad I think of death at hand,
  The signs of heav'nly joy shone through his eyes,
Of Saracines against a mighty band
  With fearless heart and constant breast he flies :
No steel could shield them from his cutting brand,
  But whom he hits without recure he dies ;
He never struck but fell'd or kill'd his foe,
And wounded was himself from top to toe.

XXIII.

Not strength but courage now preserved on live
  This hardy champion, fortress of our faith ;
Stricken he strikes, still stronger more they strive,
  The more they hurt him, more he doth them scaith :
When towards him a furious knight 'gan drive,
  Of members huge, fierce looks, and full of wrath,
That with the aid of many a Pagan crew,
After long fight, at last Prince Sweno slew.

XXIV.

Ah, heavy chance ! down fell the valiant youth ;
  Nor 'mongst us all did one so strong appear
As to revenge his death : that this is truth,
  By this dear blood and noble bones I swear,
That of my life I had nor care nor ruth,
  No wounds I shunn'd, no blows I would off bear,
And had not heav'n my wished end denied,
Ev'n there I should, and willing should, have died.

XXV.

Alive I fell among my fellows slain,
  Yet wounded so that each one thought me dead,
Nor what our foes did since can I explain,
  So sore amazed was my heart and head ;
But when I open'd first my eyes again,
  Night's curtain black upon the earth was spread,
And through the darkness to my feeble sight
Appear'd the twinkling of a slender light.

XXVI.

Not so much force or judgment in me lies
　　As to discern things seen and not mistake,
I saw like them who ope and shut their eyes
　　By turns, now half asleep, now half awake ;
My body eke another torment tries,
　　My wounds began to smart, my hurts to ache,
For every sore each member pinched was
With night's sharp air, heav'n's frost, and earth's cold grass.

XXVII.

But still the light approached near and near,
　　And with the same a whisp'ring murmur ran,
Till at my side arrived both they were,
　　When I to spread my feeble eyes began :
Two men behold in vestures long appear,
　　With each a lamp in hand, who said—O son,
In that dear Lord who helps his servants trust,
Who, ere they ask, grants all things to the just.—

XXVIII.

This said, each one his sacred blessing flings
　　Upon my corse, with broad outstretched hand,
And mumbled hymns and psalms and holy things,
　　Which I could neither hear nor understand.—
Arise (quoth they) :—With that, as I had wings,
　　All whole and sound I leap'd up from the land.
O miracle, sweet, gentle, strange and true !
My limbs new strength receiv'd and vigor new.

XXIX.

I gaz'd on them like one whose heart denaith
　　To think that done he sees so strangely wrought ;
Till one said thus :—O thou of little faith,
　　What doubts perplex thy unbelieving thought ?
Each one of us a living body hath,
　　We are Christ's chosen servants, fear us naught,
Who to avoid the world's allurements vain,
In wilful penance hermits poor remain.—

XXX.

Us messengers to comfort thee elect
　　That Lord hath sent that rules both heav'n and hell,
Who often doth his blessed will effect
　　By such weak means as wonder is to tell ;

He will not that this body lie neglect,
　　Wherein so noble soul did lately dwell,
To which again, when it uprisen is,
It shall united be in lasting bliss;

XXXI.

I say Lord Sweno's corpse, for which prepar'd
　　A tomb there is according to his worth,
By which his honor shall be far declar'd,
　　And his just praises spread from south to north:
But lift thine eyes up to the heavens-ward,
　　Mark yonder light that like the sun shines forth,
That shall direct thee with those beams so clear,
To find the body of thy master dear.—

XXXII.

With that I saw from Cinthia's silver face,
　　Like to a falling star, a beam down slide,
That bright as golden line mark'd out the place,
　　And lighten'd with clear streams the forest wide:
So Latmos shone when Phœbe left the chace,
　　And laid her down by her Endymion's side:
Such was the light, that well discern I could
His shape, his wounds, his face (though dead) yet bold.

XXXIII.

He lay not grovelling now, but as a knight
　　That ever had to heavenly things desire,
So towards heaven the Prince lay bolt upright,
　　Like him that upward still sought to aspire;
His right hand closed held his weapon bright,
　　Ready to strike and execute his ire;
His left upon his breast was humbly laid,
That men might know that while he died he pray'd.

XXXIV.

While on his wounds with bootless tears I wept,
　　That neither helped him, nor eas'd my care,
One of those aged fathers to him stept,
　　And forc'd his hand that needless weapon spare:—
This sword (quoth he) hath yet good token kept
　　That of the Pagans' blood he drank his share,
And blushed still he could not save his lord;
Rich, strong, and sharp, was never better sword.

XXXV.

Heav'n therefore will not, though the Prince be slain
  Who used erst to wield this precious brand,
That so brave blade unused should remain,
  But that it pass from strong to stronger hand,
Who with like force can wield the same again,
  And longer shall in grace of fortune stand,
And with the same shall bitter vengeance take
On him that Sweno slew, for Sweno's sake.

XXXVI.

Great Soliman killed Sweno, Soliman
  For Sweno's sake upon this sword must die.
Here take the blade, and with it haste thee than
  Thither where Godfrey doth encamped lie,
And fear not thou that any shall or can
  Or stop thy way or lead thy steps awry,
For He that doth thee on this message send,
Thee with his hand shall guide, keep, and defend.

XXXVII.

Arrived there, it is His blessed will,
  With true report that thou declare and tell
The zeal, the strength, the courage, and the skill
  In thy beloved lord that late did dwell,
How for Christ's sake he came his blood to spill,
  And sample left to all of doing well,
That future ages may admire his deed,
And courage take when his brave end they read.

XXXVIII.

It resteth now thou know that gentle knight
  That of this sword shall be thy master's heir,
It is Rinaldo young, with whom in might
  And martial skill no champion may compare;
Give it to him, and say, the heavens bright
  Of this revenge to him commit the care.—
While thus I list'ned what this old man said,
A wonder new from further speech us stay'd;

XXXIX.

For there whereas the wounded body lay,
  A stately tomb with curious work behold,
And wond'rous art, was built out of the clay,
  Which rising round the carcass did enfold,

With words engraven in the marble grey,
    The warrior's name, his worth and praise, that told ;
On which I gazing stood, and often read
That epitaph of my dear master dead.—

XL.

Among his soldiers (quoth the hermit) here
    Must Sweno's corpse remain in marble chest,
While up to heav'n are flown their spirits dear,
    To live in endless joy for ever blest ;
His funeral thou hast with many a tear
    Accompanied, it 's now high time to rest ;
Come, be my guest until the morning ray
Shall light the world again, then take thy way.—

XLI.

This said, he led me over hoults and hags ;
    Through thorns and bushes scant my legs I drew,
Till underneath a heap of stones and crags
    At last he brought me to a secret mew ;
Amongst the bears, wild boars, the wolves, and stags,
    There dwelt he safe with his disciple true,
And fear'd no treason, force, nor hurt at all,
His guiltless conscience was his castle's wall.

XLII.

My supper, roots ; my bed was moss and leaves ;
    But weariness in little rest found ease :
But when the purple morning night bereaves
    Of late usurped rule on lands and seas,
His loathed couch each wakeful hermit leaves :
    To pray rose they ; and I, for so they please,
I congé took when ended was the same,
And hitherward as they advis'd me came.—

XLIII.

The Dane his woful tale had done, when thus
    The good Prince Godfrey answer'd him :—Sir knight,
Thou bringest tidings sad and dolorous,
    For which our heavy camp laments of right,
Since so brave troops, and so dear friends to us,
    One hour hath spent in one unlucky fight ;
And so appeared hath thy master stout,
As lightning doth, now kindled, now quench'd out :

XLIV.

But such a death and end exceedeth all
    The conquests vain of realms, or spoils of gold ;
Nor aged Rome's proud stately capital
    Did ever triumph yet like theirs behold ;
They sit in heav'n on thrones celestial,
    Crowned with glory, for their conquest bold,
Where each his hurts I think to other shows,
And glories in those bloody wounds and blows.

XLV.

But thou who hast part of thy race to run,
    With haps and hazards of this world ytoss'd,
Rejoice, for those high honors they have won,
    Which cannot be by chance or fortune cross'd :
But for thou askest for Bertoldo's son,
    Know that he wandereth, banish'd from this host,
And till of him new tidings some man tell,
Within this camp I deem it best thou dwell.

XLVI.

These words of theirs in many a soul renewed
    The sweet remembrance of fair Sophia's child,
Some with salt tears for him their cheeks bedewed,
    Lest evil tide him 'mongst the Pagans wild ;
And every one his valiant prowess showed,
    And of his battles stories long compil'd,
Telling the Dane his acts and conquests past,
Which made his ears amaz'd, his heart aghast.

XLVII.

Now when remembrance of the youth had wrought
    A tender pity in each soften'd mind,
Behold returned home with all they caught
    The bands that were to forage late assign'd,
And with them in abundance great they brought
    Both flocks and herds of every sort and kind,
And corn, although not much, and hay to feed
Their noble steeds and coursers when they need :

XLVIII.

They also brought of misadventure sad
    Tokens and signs, seem'd too apparent true ;
Rinaldo's armor frush'd and hack'd they had,
    Oft pierced through, with blood besmeared new.

About the camp (for always rumors bad
    Are farthest spread) these woful tidings flew ;
Thither assembled straight both high and low,
Longing to see what they were loth to know.

XLIX.

His heavy hauberk was both seen and known,
    And his broad shield, wherein displayed flies
The bird that proves her chickens for her own
    By looking 'gainst the sun with open eyes :
That shield was to the Pagans often shown
    In many a hard and hardy enterprise,
But now with many a gash and many a stroke
They see, and sigh to see, it frush'd and broke.

L.

While all his soldiers whisper'd under hand,
    And here and there the fault and cause do lay,
Godfrey before him called Aliprand,
    Captain of those that brought of late this prey ;
A man who did on points of virtue stand,
    Blameless in words, and true whate'er he say.—
Say (quoth the Duke) where you this armor had,
Hide not the truth, but tell it good or bad.—

LI.

He answer'd him—As far from hence, think I,
    As on two days a speedy post well rideth,
To Gaza-ward a little plain doth lie,
    Itself among the steepy hills which hideth ;
Through it, slow falling from the mountains high,
    A rolling brook 'twixt bush and bramble glideth,
Clad with thick shade of boughs of broad-leav'd treen,
Fit place for men to lie in wait unseen :

LII.

Thither to seek some flocks or herds we went,
    Perchance close hid under the greenwood shaw,
And found the springing grass with blood besprent,
    A warrior tumbled in his blood we saw ;
His arms, though dusty, bloody, hack'd and rent,
    Yet well we knew when near the corse we draw,
To which (to view his face) in vain I started,
For from his body his fair head was parted ;

LIII.

His right hand wanted eke, with many a wound
  The trunk through pierced was from back to breast;
A little by his empty helm we found
  The silver eagle shining on his crest ;
To spy at whom to ask we gazed round,
  A churle towards us his steps addrest,
But when us armed by the corse he spied,
He ran away his fearful face to hide :

LIV.

But we pursu'd him, took him, spake him fair,
  Till comforted at last he answer made,
How that the day before he saw repair
  A band of soldiers from that forest's shade,
Of whom one carried by the golden hair
  A head but late cut off with murd'ring blade ;
The face was fair and young, and on the chin
No sign of beard to bud did yet begin,

LV.

And how in sendal wrapt away he bore
  That head with him hung at his saddle-bow ;
And how the murd'rers, by the arms they wore,
  For soldiers of our camp he well did know.
The carcass I disarm'd, and weeping sore,
  Because I guess'd who should that harness owe
Away I brought it, but first order gave
That noble body should be laid in grave.

LVI.

But if it be his trunk whom I believe,
  A nobler tomb his worth deserveth well.—
This said, good Aliprando took his leave,
  Of certain truth he had no more to tell.
Sore sigh'd the Duke, so did these news him grieve,
  Fears in his heart, doubts in his bosom dwell,
He yearn'd to know, to find, and learn the truth,
And punish would them that had slain the youth.

LVII.

But now the night despread her lazy wings
  O'er the broad fields of heav'n's bright wilderness ;
Sleep, the soul's rest and ease of careful things,
  Buried in happy peace both more and less,

Thou, Argillan, alone, whom sorrow stings,
    Still wakest, musing on great deeds I guess,
Nor suff'rest in thy watchful eyes to creep
The sweet repose of mild and gentle sleep.

LVIII.

This man was strong of limbs, and all his says
    Were bold, of ready tongue and working spright,
Near Trento born, bred up in brawls and frays,
    In jars, in quarrels, and in civil fight,
For which exil'd, the hills and public ways
    He filled with blood and robb'ries day and night,
Until to Asia's wars at last he came,
And boldly there he serv'd and purchas'd fame.

LIX.

He clos'd his eyes at last when day drew near,
    Yet slept he not, but senseless lay, opprest
With strange amazedness and sudden fear,
    Which false Alecto breathed in his breast;
His working powers within deluded were;
    Stone still he quiet lay, yet took no rest,
For to his thought the fiend herself presented,
And with strange visions his weak brain tormented.

LX.

A murder'd body huge beside him stood,
    Of head and right hand both but lately spoiled,
His left hand bore the head, whose visage good
    Both pale and wan with dust and gore defoiled,
Yet spake, though dead, with whose sad words the blood
    Forth at his lips in huge abundance boiled:—
Fly, Argillan, from this false camp fly far,
Whose guide a traitor, captains murderers are.

LXI.

Godfrey hath murder'd me by treason vile,
    What favor then hope you, my trusty friends?
His villain heart is full of fraud and guile,
    To your destruction all his thoughts he bends;
Yet if thou thirst for praise of noble style,
    If in thy strength thou trust, thy strength that ends,
All hard assays, fly not, first with his blood
Appease my ghost, wandering by Lethe's flood:

LXII.

I will thy weapon whet, inflame thine ire,
    Arm thy right hand, and strengthen ev'ry part.—
This said, even while she spake she did inspire
    With fury, rage, and wrath his troubled heart.
The man awak'd, and from his eyes like fire
    The poison'd sparks of headstrong madness start,
And armed as he was, forth is he gone,
And gather'd all th' Italian bands in one.

LXIII.

He gather'd them where lay the arms that late
    Were good Rinaldo's ; then with semblance stout,
And furious words, his fore-conceived hate
    In bitter speeches thus he vomits out :
Is not this people harb'rous and ingrate,
    In whom truth finds no place, faith takes no root ;
Whose thirst unquenched is of blood and gold,
Whom no yoke boweth, bridle none can hold ?

LXIV.

So much we suffered have these seven years long
    Under this servile and unworthy yoke,
That thorough Rome and Italy our wrong
    A thousand years hereafter shall be spoke :
I count not how Cilicia's kingdom strong
    Subdued was by Prince Tancredie's stroke,
Nor how false Baldwin him that land bereaves
Of virtue's harvest, fraud there reap'd the sheaves :

LXV.

Nor speak I how each hour, at ev'ry need,
    Quick, ready, resolute at all assays,
With fire and sword we hasted forth with speed,
    And bore the brunt of all their fights and frays :
But when we had perform'd and done the deed,
    At ease and leisure they divide the preys :
We reaped naught but travail for our toil,
Theirs was the praise, the realms, the gold, the spoil.

LXVI.

Yet all this season were we willing blind,
    Offended, unreveng'd ; wrong'd, but unwroken ;
Light griefs could not provoke our quiet mind ;
    But now, alas ! the mortal blow is stroken,

Rinàldo have they slain ; and law of kind,
    Of arms, of nations, and of high heav'n broken ;
Why doth not heav'n kill them with fire and thunder ?
To swallow them why cleaves not earth asunder ?

LXVII.

They have Rinaldo slain, the sword and shield
    Of Christ's true faith, and unreveng'd he lies,
Still unrevenged lieth in the field
    His noble corpse, to feed the crows and pies.
Who murder'd him ? who shall us certain yield ?
    Who sees not that although he wanted eyes ?
Who knows not how th' Italian chivalry
Proud Godfrey and false Baldwin both envy ?

LXVIII.

What need we further proof ? Heav'n, heav'n, I swear,
    Will not consent herein we be beguiled ;
This night I saw his murder'd spright appear,
    Pale, sad, and wan with wounds and blood defiled,
A spectacle full both of grief and fear ;
    Godfrey, for murd'ring him, the ghost reviled :
I saw it was no dream before mine eyes,
Howe'er I look, still, still methinks it flies.

LXIX.

What shall we do ? Shall we be govern'd still
    By this false hand, contaminate with blood ?
Or else depart and travel forth, until
    To Euphrates we come, that sacred flood ;
Where dwells a people void of martial skill,
    Whose cities rich, whose land is fat and good,
Where kingdoms great we may at ease provide,
Far from these Frenchmen's malice, from their pride ?

LXX.

Then let us go, and no revengement take
    For this brave knight, though lie it in our power ;
No, no, that courage rather newly wake,
    Which never sleeps in fear and dread one hour,
And this pestiferous serpent, poison'd snake,
    Of all our knights that hath destroy'd the flow'r,
First let us slay, and his deserved end
Ensample make to him that kills his friend.

LXXI.

I will, I will, if your courageous force
    Dareth so much as it can well perform,
Tear out his cursed heart without remorse,
    The nest of treason false and guile enorme.—
Thus spake the angry knight; with headlong course
    The rest him follow'd like a furious storm;
Arm, arm, they cried: to arms the soldiers ran,
And as they ran, Arm, arm, cried every man.

LXXII.

'Mongst them Alecto strewed wasteful fire,
    Envenoming the hearts of most and least;
Folly, disdain, madness, strife, rancor, ire,
    Thirst to shed blood, in every breast increas'd:
This ill spread far, and till it set on fire
    With rage th' Italian lodgings, never ceas'd;
From thence unto the Switzers' camp it went,
And last infected every English tent.

LXXIII.

Not public loss of their beloved knight
    Alone stirr'd up their rage and wrath untamed,
But fore-conceived griefs and quarrels light
    Their ire still nourished and still enflamed;
Awaked was each former cause of spite
    The Frenchmen cruel and unjust they named,
And with bold threats they made their hatred known,
Hate seld kept clos'd, and oft unwisely shown:

LXXIV.

Like boiling liquor in a seething pot,
    That fumeth, swelleth high, and bubbleth fast,
Till o'er the brims among the embers hot
    Part of the broth and of the scum it cast,
Their rage and wrath those few appeased not,
    In whom of wisdom yet remain'd some taste;
Camillo, William, Tancred, were away,
And all whose greatness might their madness stay.

LXXV.

Now headlong ran to harness in this heat
    These furious people, all on heaps confused,
The roaring trumpets battle 'gan to threat,
    As it in time of mortal war is used.

The messengers ran to Godfredo great,
　　And bade him arm while on this noise he mused ;
And Baldwin first, well clad in iron hard,
Stepp'd to his side, a sure and faithful guard.

LXXVI

Their murmurs heard, to heav'n he lift his eyne,
　　As was his wont, to God for aid he fled :—
O Lord, thou knowest this right hand of mine
　　Abhorred ever civil blood to shed ;
Illumine their dark souls with light divine,
　　Repress their rage, by hellish fury bred ;
The innocency of my guiltless mind
Thou knowest, and make these know, with fury blind.—

LXXVII.

This said, he felt infused in each vein
　　A sacred heat from heav'n above distilled,
A heat in man that courage could constrain,
　　That his grave look with awful boldness filled.
Well guarded, forth he went to meet the train
　　Of those that would revenge Rinaldo killed ;
And though their threats he heard, and saw them bent
To arms on every side, yet on he went.

LXXVIII.

Above his hauberk strong a coat he ware
　　Embroidered fair with pearl and rich stone,
His hands were naked, and his face was bare,
　　Wherein a lamp of majesty bright shone ;
He shook his golden mace, wherewith he dare
　　Resist the force of his rebellious fone.
Thus he appear'd, and thus he 'gan them teach
In shape an angel, and a god in speech :—

LXXIX.

What foolish words, what threats be these I hear ?
　　What noise of arms ?　Who dares these tumults move ?
Am I so honor'd ? stand you so in fear ?
　　Where is your late obedience ? where your love ?
Of Godfrey's falsehood who can witness bear ?
　　Who dare or will these accusations prove ?
Perchance you look I should entreaties bring,
Sue for your favors, or excuse the thing :

LXXX.

Ah, God forbid these lands should hear or see
    Him so disgrac'd, at whose great name they quake:
This sceptre and my noble acts for me
    A true defence before the world can make;
Yet, for sharp justice governed shall be
    With clemency, I will no vengeance take
For this offence, but, for Rinaldo's love,
I pardon you; hereafter wiser prove:

LXXXI.

But Argillano's guilty blood shall wash
    This stain away, who kindled this debate,
And, led by hasty rage and fury rash,
    To these disorders first undid the gate.—
While thus he spoke, the lightning beams did flash
    Out of his eyes of majesty and state,
That Argillan (who would have thought it?) shook
For fear and terror, conquer'd with his look.

LXXXII.

The rest, with indiscreet and foolish wrath
    Who threaten'd late with words of shame and pride,
Whose hands so ready were to harm and scaith,
    And brandished bright swords on every side,
Now hush'd and still attend what Godfrey saith;
    With shame and fear their bashful looks they hide,
And Argillan they let in chains be bound,
Although their weapons him environ'd round.

LXXXIII.

So when a lion shakes his dreadful mane,
    And beats his tail, with courage proud and wroth,
If his commander come, who first took pain
    To tame his youth, his lofty crest down go'th,
His threats he feareth, and obeys the rein
    Of thraldom base and serviceage, though loth;
Nor can his sharp teeth nor his armed paws
Force him rebel against his ruler's laws.

LXXXIV.

Fame is, a winged warrior they beheil'd,
    With semblant fierce and furious look that stood,
And in his left hand had a splendent shield,
    Wherewith he covered safe their chieftain good;

13

His other hand a naked sword did wield,
   From which distilling fell the lukewarm blood,
The blood pardie of many a realm and town
Whereon the Lord his wrath had poured down.

LXXXV.

Thus was the tumult without bloodshed ended,
   Their arms laid down, strife into exile sent ;
Godfrey his thoughts to greater actions bended,
   And homeward to his rich pavilion went ;
For to assault the fortress he intended,
   Before the second or third day were spent :
Meanwhile his timber wrought he oft survey'd,
Whereof his rams and engines great he made.

BOOK IX.

THE ARGUMENT.

Alecto false great Soliman doth move
  By night the Christians in their tents to kill;
But God, who their intents saw from above.
  Sends Michael down from his sacred hill;
The spirits foul to hell the angel drove;
  The knights, deliver'd from the witch, at will
Destroy the Pagans, scatter all their host;
The Soldan flies when all his bands are lost.

I.

THE grisly child of Erebus the grim
  (Who saw these tumults done and tempests spent,
'Gainst stream of grace who ever strove to swim,
  And all her thoughts against heav'n's wisdom bent)
Departed now; bright Titan's beams were dim,
  And fruitful lands wax'd barren as she went;
She sought the rest of her infernal crew,
New storms to raise, new broils, and tumults new.

II.

She (that well wist her sisters had enticed,
  By their false arts, far from the Christian host,
Tancred, Rinaldo, and the rest, best prized
  For martial skill, for might esteemed most)
Said—Of these discords and these strifes advised,
  Great Soliman, when day his light hath lost,
These Christians shall assail with sudden war,
And kill them all, while thus they strive and jar.—

III.

With that, where Soliman remain'd she flew,
  And found him out with his Arabian bands;
Great Soliman, of all Christ's foes untrue,
  Boldest of courage, mightiest of his hands;

Like him was none of all that earth-bred crew
 That heaped mountains on th' Æmonian sands ;
Of Turks he sovereign was, and Nice his seat,
Where late he dwelt, and rul'd that kingdom great.

IV.

The lands forenenst the Greekish shore he held,
 From Sangar's mouth to crook'd Meander's fall,
Where they of Phrygia, Mysia, Lydia dwell'd,
 Bithynia's towns and Pontus' cities all :
But when the hearts of Christian princes swell'd,
 And rose in arms to make proud Asia thrall,
Those lands were won where he did sceptre wield,
And he twice beaten was in pitched field.

V.

When fortune oft he had in vain assay'd,
 And spent his forces, which avail'd him naught,
To Egypt's king himself he close convey'd,
 Who welcom'd him as he could best have thought,
Glad in his heart and inly well appaid
 That to his court so great a lord was brought,
For he decreed his armies huge to bring
To succor Judah's land and Judah's king.

VI.

But, ere he open war proclaim'd, he would
 That Soliman should kindle first the fire,
And with huge sums of false enticing gold,
 Th' Arabian thieves he sent him forth to hire,
While he the Asian lords and Morians bold
 Unites.—The Soldan won to his desire
Those outlaws, ready aye for gold to fight ;
The hope of gain hath such alluring might.

VII.

Thus made their captain, to destroy and burn
 In Judah land he entered is so far,
That all the ways whereby he should return,
 By Godfrey's people kept and stopped are ;
And now he 'gan his former losses mourn,
 This wound had hit him on an elder scar ;
On great adventures ran his hardy thought,
But not assur'd, he yet resolv'd on naught.

VIII.

To him Alecto came, and semblant bore
　　Of one whose age was great, whose looks were grave,
Whose cheeks were bloodless, and whose locks were hoar,
　　Mustachios strouting long, and chin close shave,
A steepled turban on her head she wore,
　　Her garments long, and by her side her glaive,
Her gilded quiver at her shoulders hung,
And in her hand a bow was stiff and strong.—

IX.

We have (quoth she) through wildernesses gone,
　　Through sterile sands, strange paths, and uncouth ways,
Yet spoil or booty have we gotten none,
　　Nor victory deserving fame or praise ;
Godfrey meanwhile, to ruin stick and stone
　　Of this fair town, with battery sore assays ;
And if awhile we rest, we shall behold
This glorious city smoking lie in mould.

X.

Are sheep-cotes burnt, or prize of sheep or kine,
　　The cause why Soliman these bands did arm ?
Canst thou that kingdom lately lost of thine
　　Recover thus, or thus redress thy harm ?
No, no ; when heav'n's small candles next shall shine,
　　Within their tents give them a bold alarm ;
Believe Araspes old, whose grave advice
Thou hast in exile prov'd, and prov'd in Nice.

XI.

He feareth naught, he doubts no sudden broil,
　　From these ill-armed and worse-hearted bands ;
He thinks this people, us'd to rob and spoil,
　　To such exploit dare not lift up their hands :
Up then, and with their courage put to foil
　　This fearless camp, while thus secure it stands.—
This said, her poison in his breast she hides,
And then to shapeless air unseen she glides.

XII.

The Soldan cried—O thou, which in my thought
　　Increased hast my rage and fury so,
Nor seem'st a wight of mortal metal wrought,
　　I follow thee whereso thou list to go ;

Mountains of men, by dint of sword down brought,
  Thou shalt behold, and seas of red blood flow,
Where'er I go ; only be thou my guide,
When sable night the azure skies shall hide.—

XIII.

When this was said, he muster'd all his crew,
  Reprov'd the coward, and allow'd the bold ;
His forward camp, inspir'd with courage new,
  Was ready dight to follow where he would :
Alecto's self the warning trumpet blew,
  And to the wind his standard great unroll'd :
Thus on they marched, and thus on they went,
Of their approach their speed the news prevent.

XIV.

Alecto left them, and her person dight
  Like one that came some tidings new to tell :
It was the time when first the rising night
  Her sparkling diamonds poureth forth to sell :
When (into Sion come) she marched right
  Where Judah's aged tyrant us'd to dwell,
To whom of Soliman's designment bold,
The place, the manner, and the time, she told.

XV.

Their mantle dark the grisly shadows spread,
  Stained with spots of deepest sanguine hue ;
Warm drops of blood on earth's black visage shed,
  Supplied the place of pure and precious dew ;
The moon and stars for fear of sprites were fled,
  The shrieking goblins eachwhere howling flew,
The furies roar, the ghosts and fairies yell,
The earth was fill'd with devils, and empty hell.

XVI.

The Soldan fierce through all this horror went
  Toward the camp of his redoubted foes ;
The night was more than half consum'd and spent,
  Now headlong down the western hill she goes,
When distant scant a mile from Godfrey's tent,
  He let his people there awhile repose,
And victualled them, and then he boldly spoke
These words, which rage and courage might provoke :

XVII.

See there a camp full stuff'd of spoils and preys,
    Not half so strong as false report recordeth ;
See there the storehouse where their captain lays
    Our treasures stolen, where Asia's wealth he hoardeth :
Now chance the ball unto our racket plays,
    Take then the 'vantage which good luck affordeth,
For all their arms, their horses, gold, and treasure,
Are ours ; ours without loss, harm, or displeasure.

XVIII.

Nor is this camp that great victorious host
    That slew the Persian lords, and Nice hath won ;
For those in this long war are spent and lost,
    These are the dregs, the wine is all outrun,
And these few left are drown'd and dead almost
    In heavy sleep, the labor half is done
To send them headlong to Avernus' deep,
For little differs death and heavy sleep.

XIX.

Come, come, this sword the passage open shall
    Into their camp, and on their bodies slain
We will pass o'er their rampire and their wall ;
    This blade, as scythes cut down the fields of grain,
Shall cut them so, Christ's kingdom now shall fall ;
    Asia her freedom, you shall praise obtain.—
Thus he inflam'd his soldiers to the fight,
And led them on through silence of the night.

XX.

The sentinels by starlight (lo !) descried
    This mighty Soldan and his host draw near,
Who found not as he hop'd the Christians' guide
    Unware, ne yet unready was his gear ;
The scouts when this huge army they descried,
    Ran back, and 'gan with shouts the larum rear :
The watch start up and draw their weapons bright,
And busk'd them bold to battle and to fight.

XXI.

Th' Arabians wist they could not come unseen,
    And therefore loud their jarring trumpets sound,
Their yelling cries to heav'n up-heaved been,
    The horses thunder'd on the solid ground,

The mountains roared, and the valleys green,
   The echo sighed from the caves around,
Alecto with her brand (kindled in hell)
Token'd to them in David's tower that dwell.

XXII.

Before the rest forth prick'd the Soldan fast
   Against the watch, not yet in order just,
As swift as hideous Boreas' hasty blast,
   From hollow rocks when first his storms out burst,
The raging floods that trees and rocks downcast,
   Thunders that towns and towers drive to dust,
Earthquakes to tear the world in twain that threat,
Are naught compared to his fury great.

XXIII.

He struck no blow but that his foe he hit,
   And never hit but made a grievous wound,
And never wounded but death followed it;
   And yet no peril, hurt, or harm he found;
No weapon on his harden'd helmet bit,
   No puissant stroke his senses once astound,
Yet like a bell his tinkling helmet rong,
And thence flew flames of fire and sparks among.

XXIV.

Himself well nigh had put the watch to flight,
   A jolly troop of Frenchmen strong and stout,
When his Arabians came by heaps to fight,
   Covering like raging floods the fields about:
The beaten Christians ran away full light;
   The Pagans, mingled with the flying rout,
Enter'd their camp, and filled as they stood
Their tents with ruin, slaughter, death, and blood.

XXV.

High on the Soldan's helm enamell'd laid
   A hideous dragon, arm'd with many a scale,
With iron paws, and leathern wings display'd,
   Which twisted in a knot her forked tail;
With triple tongue it seem'd she hiss'd and bray'd;
   About her jaws the froth and venom trail,
And as he stirr'd, and as his foes him hit,
So flames to cast and fire she seem'd to spit.

XXVI.

With this strange light the Soldan fierce appeared
  Dreadful to those that round about him been,
As to poor sailors, when huge storms are reared,
  With lightning flash the raging seas are seen ;
Some fled away because his strength they feared,
  Some bolder 'gainst him bent their weapons keen ;
And froward night, in ills and mischiefs pleased,
Their dangers hid, and dangers still increased.

XXVII.

Among the rest that strove to merit praise
  Was old Latinus, born by Tiber's bank,
To whose stout heart in fights and bloody frays,
  For all his eild, base fear yet never sank :
Five sons he had, the comforts of his days,
  That from his side in no adventure shrank,
But, long before their time, in iron strong
They clad their members, tender, soft, and young.

XXVIII.

The bold ensample of their father's might
  Their weapons whetted and their wrath increas'd.—
Come, let us go (quoth he) where yonder knight
  Upon our soldiers makes his bloody feast ;
Let not their slaughter once your hearts affright,
  Where danger most appears there fear it least ;
For honor dwells in hard attempts, my sons,
And greatest praise in greatest peril wons.—

XXIX.

Her tender brood the forest's savage queen
  (Ere on their crests their rugged manes appear,
Before their mouths by nature armed been,
  Or paws have strength a seely lamb to tear)
So leadeth forth to prey, and makes them keen,
  And learns by her ensample naught to fear
The hunter in those desert woods that takes
The lesser beasts, whereon his feast he makes.

XXX.

The noble father and his hardy crew
  Fierce Soliman on every side invade ;
At once all six upon the Soldan flew
  With lances sharp, and strong encounters made :

His broken spear the eldest boy down threw,
  And boldly (over boldly) drew his blade,
Wherewith he strove, but strove therewith in vain,
The Pagan's steed, unmarked, to have slain.

XXXI.

But as a mountain or a cape of land,
  Assail'd with storms and seas on every side,
Doth unremoved, steadfast, still withstand
  Storm, thunder, lightning, tempest, wind, and tide ;
The Soldan so withstood Latinus' band,
  And unremov'd did all their jousts abide,
And of that hapless youth, who hurt his steed,
Down to the chin he cleft in twain the head.

XXXII.

Kind Aramante, who saw his brother slain,
  To hold him up stretch'd forth his friendly arm ;
O foolish kindness, and O pity vain,
  To add our proper loss to others' harm !
The Prince let fall his sword, and cut in twain
  (About his brother twin'd) the child's weak arm :
Down from their saddles both together slide,
Together mourn'd they, and together died.

XXXIII.

That done, Sabino's lance with nimble force
  He cut in twain, and 'gainst the stripling bold
He spurr'd his steed, that underneath his horse
  The hardy infant tumbled on the mould,
Whose soul, out-squeezed from his bruised corse,
  With ugly painfulness forsook her hold,
And deeply mourn'd that of so sweet a cage
She left the bliss and joys of youthful age.

XXXIV.

But Picus yet and Laurence were alive,
  Whom at one birth their mother fair brought out,
A pair whose likeness made the parents strive
  Oft which was which, and joyed in their doubt :
But what their birth did undistinguish'd give
  The Soldan's rage made known, for Picus stout
Headless at one huge blow he laid in dust,
And through the breast his gentle brother thrust.

XXXV

Their father (but no father now, alas !),
  When all his noble sons at once were slain,
In their five deaths so often murder'd was,
  I know not how his life could him sustain,
Except his heart were forg'd of steel or brass,
  Yet still he liv'd, pardie he saw not plain
Their dying looks, although their deaths he knows ;
It is some ease not to behold our woes.

XXXVI.

He wept not, for the night her curtain spread
  Between his cause of weeping and his eyes,
But still he mourn'd, and on sharp vengeance fed,
  And thinks he conquers if reveng'd he dies ;
He thirsts the Soldan's heath'nish blood to shed,
  And yet his own at less than naught doth prize,
Nor can he tell whether he liefer would
Or die himself, or kill the Pagan bold.

XXXVII.

At last—Is this right hand (quoth he) so weak
  That thou disdain'st 'gainst me to use thy might ?
Can it naught do ? Can this tongue nothing speak
  That may provoke thine ire, thy wrath, and spite ?—
With that he struck, his anger great to wreak,
  A blow that pierc'd the mail and metal bright,
And in his flank set ope a floodgate wide,
Whereat the blood outstreamed from his side.

XXXVIII.

Provoked with his cry, and with that blow,
  The Turk upon him 'gan his blade discharge,
He cleft his breastplate, having first pierc'd thro'
  (Lined with seven bulls' hides) his mighty targe,
And sheath'd his weapon in his guts below ;
  Wretched Latinus, at that issue large,
And at his mouth, 'pour'd out his vital blood,
And sprinkled with the same his murder'd brood.

XXXIX.

On Apennine, like as a sturdy tree,
  Against the winds that makes resistance stout,
If with a storm it overturned be,
  Falls down and breaks the trees and plants about ;

So Latine fell, and with him felled he
    And slew the nearest of the Pagans' rout;
A worthy end, fit for a man of fame,
That dying slew, and conquer'd overcame.

XL.

Meanwhile the Soldan strove his rage interne
    To satisfy with blood of Christians spill'd ;
Th' Arabians, hearten'd by their captain stern,
    With murder every tent and cabin fill'd :
Henry the English knight, and Olipherne,
    O fierce Draguto ! by thy hands were kill'd ;
Gilbert and Philip were by Ariadene
Both slain, both born upon the banks of Rhene.

XLI.

Albazar with his mace Ernesto slew,
    Under Algazell Engerlan down fell ;
But the huge murder of the meaner crew,
    Or manner of their deaths, what tongue can tell ?
Godfrey, when first the heathen trumpets blew,
    Awak'd, which heard, no fear could make him dwell,
But he and his were up and arm'd ere long,
And marched forward with a squadron strong.

XLII.

He that well heard the rumor and the cry,
    And mark'd the tumult still grow more and more,
Th' Arabian thieves he judged by and by
    Against his soldiers made this battle sore ;
For that they forray'd all the countries nigh,
    And spoil'd the fields, the Duke knew well before ;
Yet thought he not they had the hardiment
So to assail him in his armed tent.

XLIII.

All suddenly he heard, while on he went,
    How to the city-ward, arm, arm, they cried,—
The noise upreared to the firmament
    With dreadful howling fill'd the valleys wide :
This was Clorinda, whom the king forth sent,
    To battle, and Argantes by her side :
The Duke (this heard) to Guelpho turn'd, and pray'd
    Him his lieutenant be, and to him said :—

XLIV.

You hear this new alarm from yonder part,
  That from the town breaks out with so much rage,
Us needeth much your valor and your art
  To calm their fury, and their heat to 'suage ;
Go thither then, and with you take some part
  Of these brave soldiers of mine equipage,
While, with the res'due of my champions bold,
I drive these wolves again out of our fold.—

XLV.

They parted (this agreed on them between)
  By divers paths, Lord Guelpho to the hill,
And Godfrey hasted where th' Arabians keen
  His men like silly sheep destroy and kill ;
But as he went his troops increased been,
  From every part the people flocked still,
That now grown strong enough, he 'proached nigh
Where the fierce Turk caus'd many a Christian die.

XLVI.

So, from the top of Vesulus the cold,
  Down to the sandy valleys tumbleth Po,
Whose streams the farther from their fountain rolled,
  Still stronger wax, and with more puissance go ;
And, horned like a bull, his forehead bold
  He lifts, and o'er his broken banks doth flow,
And with his horns to pierce the sea assays,
To which he proffereth war, not tribute pays.

XLVII.

The Duke his men fast flying did espy,
  And thither ran, and thus (displeased) spake :—
What fear is this ?   O whither do you fly ?
  See who they be that this pursuit do make,
A heartless band, that dare no battle try,
  Who wounds before dare neither give nor take ;
Against them turn your stern eyes' threat'ning sight,
An angry look will put them all to flight.—

XLVIII.

This said, he spurred forth where Soliman
  Destroy'd Christ's vineyard like a savage boar ;
Through streams of blood, through dust and dirt he ran,
  O'er heaps of bodies wallowing in their gore ;

The squadrons close his sword to ope began,
  He brake their ranks, behind, beside, before,
And where he goes under his feet he treads
The armed Saracens and barbed steeds.

XLIX.

This slaughter-house of angry Mars he past,
  Where thousands dead, half dead, and dying were :
The hardy Soldan saw him come in haste,
  Yet neither stepp'd aside nor shrunk for fear,
But busk'd him bold to fight, aloft he cast
  His blade, prepar'd to strike, and stepped near ;
These noble princes twain (so fortune wrought)
From the world's ends here met, and here they fought :

L.

With virtue fury, strength with courage strove,
  For Asia's mighty empire : who can tell
With how strange force their cruel blows they drove,
  How sore their combat was, how fierce, how fell ?
Great deeds they wrought, each other's harness clove ;
  Yet still in darkness (more the ruth) they dwell :
The night their acts her black veil covered under,
Their acts whereat the sun, the world, might wonder.

LI.

The Christians (by their guide's ensample hearted)
  Of their best armed made a squadron strong,
And to defend their chieftain forth they started :
  The Pagans also sav'd their knight from wrong,
Fortune her favors 'twixt them ev'nly parted ;
  Fierce was th' encounter, bloody, doubtful, long ;
These won, those lost ; these lost, those won again ;
The loss was equal, ev'n the numbers slain.

LII.

With equal rage as when the southern wind
  Meeteth in battle strong the northern blast,
The sea and air to neither is resign'd,
  But cloud 'gainst cloud, and wave 'gainst wave they cast ·
So from this skirmish neither part declin'd,
  But fought it out, and kept their footings fast,
And oft with furious shock together rush,
And shield 'gainst shield, and helm 'gainst helm they crush.

LIII.

The battle eke to Sion-ward grew hot,
 The soldiers slain, the hardy knights were kill'd ;
Legions of sprites from Limbo's prisons got,
 The empty air, the hills and valleys fill'd,
Hearting the Pagans that they shrinked not,
 Till where they stood their dearest blood they spill'd ;
And with new rage Argantes they inspire,
Whose heat no flames, whose burning needs no fire ;

LIV.

Where he came in he put to shameful flight
 The fearful watch, and o'er the trenches leap'd,
Even with the ground he made the rampire's height,
 And murder'd bodies in the ditch up-heap'd ;
So that his greedy mates with labor light
 Amid the tents a bloody harvest reap'd.
Clorinda went the proud Circassian by,
So from a piece two chained bullets fly.

LV.

Now fled the Frenchmen ; when in lucky hour
 Arrived Guelpho and his helping band ;
He made them turn against this stormy show'r,
 And with bold face their wicked foes withstand.
Sternly they fought, that from their wounds down pour
 The streams of blood, and ran on either hand.
The Lord of heaven meanwhile upon this fight
From his high throne bent down his gracious sight ;

LVI.

From whence, with grace and goodness compass'd round,
 He ruleth, blesseth, keepeth all he wrought,
Above the air, the fire, the sea, and ground,
 Our sense, our wit, our reason, and our thought ;
Where persons three (with power and glory crown'd)
 Are all one God, who made all things of naught,
Under whose feet (subjected to his grace)
Sit nature, fortune, motion, time and place :

LVII.

This is the place from whence, like smoke and dust,
 Of this frail world the wealth, the pomp, and pow'r,
He tosseth, tumbleth, turneth as he lust,
 And guides our life, our death, our end, and hour :

No eye (however virtuous, pure, and just)
   Can view the brightness of that glorious bow'r ;
On every side the blessed spirits be
Equal in joys, though diff'ring in degree :

LVIII.

With harmony of their celestial song
   The palace echoed from the chambers pure :
At last he Michael call'd (in harness strong
   Of never-yielding diamonds armed sure)—
Behold (quoth he) to do despite and wrong
   To that dear flock my mercy hath in cure
How Satan from hell's loathsome prison sends
His ghosts, his sprites, his furies, and his fiends :

LIX.

Go, bid them all depart, and leave the care
   Of war to soldiers, as doth best pertain ;
Bid them forbear t'infect the earth and air,
   To darken heav'n's fair light bid them refrain ;
Bid them to Acheron's black flood repair,
   Fit house for them, the house of grief and pain ;
There let their king himself and them torment ;
So I command, go tell them mine intent.—

LX.

This said, the winged warrior low inclin'd
   At his Creator's feet with rev'rence due ;
Then spread his golden feathers to the wind,
   And swift as thought away the angel flew ;
He past the light and shining fire assign'd
   The glorious seat of his selected crew,
The mover first and circle crystalline,
The firmament where fixed stars all shine :

LXI.

Unlike in working, then, in shape and show,
   At his left hand Saturn he left and Jove,
And these untruly errant called, I trow,
   Since he errs not who doth them guide and move :
The fields he passed then whence hail and snow,
   Thunder and rain, fall down from clouds above,
Where heat and cold, dryness and moisture strive,
Whose wars all creatures kill, and slain revive :

LXII.

The horrid darkness and the shadows dun
  Dispersed he with his eternal wings
The flames which from his heav'nly eyes outrun
  Begild the earth and all her sable things:
After a storm so spreadeth forth the sun
  His rays, and binds the clouds in golden strings;
Or in the stillness of a moonshine even,
A falling star so glideth down from heaven.

LXIII.

But when th' infernal troop he 'proached near,
  That still the pagans' ire and rage provoke,
The angel on his wings himself did bear,
  And shook his lance, and thus at last he spoke:—
Have you not learned yet to know and fear
  The Lord's just wrath, and thunder's dreadful stroke?
Or, in the torments of your endless ill,
Are you still fierce, still proud, rebellious still?

LXIV.

The Lord hath sworn to break the iron bands
  The brazen gates of Sion's fort which close,
Who is it that his sacred will withstands?
  Against his wrath who dares himself oppose?
Go hence, ye curs'd, to your appointed lands,
  The realms of death, of torments, and of woes,
And in the depths of that infernal lake
Your battles fight, and there your triumphs make;

LXV.

There tyrannize upon the souls you find
  Condemn'd to wo, and double still their pains,
Where some complain, where some their teeth do grind,
  Some howl and weep, some clink their iron chains.—
This said, they fled; and those that stay'd behind
  With his sharp lance he driveth and constrains;
They sighing left the lands, his silver sheep
Where Hesperus doth lead, doth feed, doth keep:

LXVI.

And towards hell their lazy wings display,
  To wreak their malice on the damned ghosts:
The birds that follow Titan's hottest ray
  Pass not by so great flocks to warmer coasts,
14

Nor leaves by so great numbers fall away
    When winter nips them with his new-come frosts:
The earth (delivered from so foul annoy)
Recall'd her beauty and resum'd her joy.

LXVII.

But not for this in fierce Argantes' breast
    Lessen'd the rancor or decay'd the ire:
Although Alecto left him to infest
    With the hot brands of her infernal fire,
His armed head with his sharp blade he blest,
    And those thick ranks which seemed most entire
He broke; the strong, the weak, the high, the low,
Were equalised by his murdering blow.

LXVIII.

Not far from him, amid the blood and dust,
    Heads, arms, and legs Clorinda strewed wide;
Her sword through Berengario's breast she thrust,
    Quite through his heart where life doth chiefly bide,
And that fell blow she struck so sure and just,
    That at his back his blood and life forth glide;
Even in the mouth she smote Albinus then,
And cut in twain the visage of the man:

LXIX.

Gernier's right hand she from his arm divided,
    Whereof but late she had receiv'd a wound;
The hand his sword still held, although not guided,
    The fingers, half alive, stirr'd on the ground;
So from a serpent slain the tail divided
    Moves in the grass, rolleth and tumbleth round:
The championess so wounded left the knight,
And 'gainst Achilles turned her weapon bright;

LXX.

Upon his neck 'light that unhappy blow,
    And cut the sinews and the throat in twain;
The head fell down upon the earth below,
    And soil'd with dust the visage on the plain;
The headless trunk (a woful thing to know!)
    Still in the saddle seated did remain,
Until his steed (that felt the reins at large)
With leaps and flings that burthen did discharge.

LXXI.

While thus this fair and fierce Bellona slew
　　The western lords, and put their troops to flight,
Gildippes raged 'mongst the Pagan crew,
　　And low in dust laid many a hardy knight:
Like was their sex, their beauty, and their hue.
　　Like was their youth, their courage, and their might;
Yet fortune would they should the battle try
Of mightier foes, for both were fram'd to die:

LXXII.

Yet wish'd they oft, and strove in vain to meet,
　　So great betwixt them was the prease and throng.
But hardy Guelpho 'gainst Clorinda sweet
　　Ventur'd his sword, to work her harm and wrong,
And with a cutting blow so did her greet
　　That from her side the blood stream'd down along;
But with a thrust an answer sharp she made,
And 'twixt his ribs color'd some-deal her blade:

LXXIII.

Lord Guelpho struck again, but hit her not,
　　For strong Osmida haply passed by,
And, not meant him, another's wound he got,
　　That cleft his front in twain above his eye.
Near Guelpho now the battle waxed hot,
　　For all the troops he led 'gan thither hie,
And thither drew eke many a Painim knight,
That fierce, stern, bloody, deadly wax'd the fight.

LXXIV.

Meanwhile the purple morning peeped o'er
　　The eastern threshold to our half of land,
And Argillano in this great uproar
　　From prison loosed was, and what he fand
Those arms he hent, and to the field them bore,
　　Resolv'd to take his chance what came to hand;
And with great acts amid the Pagan host
Would win again his reputation lost.

LXXV.

As a fierce steed 'scap'd from his stall at large,
　　Where he had long been kept for warlike need,
Runs through the fields unto the flow'ry marge
　　Of some green forest where he us'd to feed,

His curled mane his shoulders broad doth charge,
   And from his lofty crest doth spring and spread,
Thunder his feet, his nostrils fire breathe out,
   And with his neigh the world resounds about:

LXXVI.

So Argillan rush'd forth, sparkled his eyes,
   His front high lifted was, no fear therein;
Lightly he leaps and skips, it seems he flies,
   He left no sign in dust imprinted thin;
And coming near his foes, he sternly cries,
   As one that fear'd not all their strength a pin:—
You outcasts of the world, you men of naught,
What hath in you this boldness newly wrought?

LXXVII.

Too weak are you to bear an helm or shield,
   Unfit to arm your breast in iron bright,
You run half naked trembling through the field,
   Your blows are feeble, and your hope in flight,
Your feats and all the actions that you wield
   The darkness hides, your bulwark is the night,
Now she is gone, how will your fights succeed?
Now better arms and better hearts you need.—

LXXVIII.

While thus he spoke, he gave a cruel stroke
   Against Algazell's throat with might and main,
And as he would have answer'd him and spoke,
   He stopp'd his words and cut his jaws in twain;
Upon his eyes death spread his misty cloak,
   A chilling frost congealed every vein;
He fell, and with his teeth the earth he tore,
Raging in death, and full of rage before:

LXXIX.

Then by his puissance mighty Saladine,
   Proud Agricalt, and Muleasses died;
And at one wond'rous blow his weapon fine
   Did Adiazell in two parts divide;
Then through the breast he wounded Ariadine,
   Whom dying with sharp taunts he 'gan deride;
He, lifting up uneath his feeble eyes,
To his proud scorns thus answereth ere he dies:—

LXXX.

Not thou (whoe'er thou art) shall glory long
　　Thy happy conquest in my death, I trow ;
Like chance awaits thee from a hand more strong,
　　Which by my side will shortly lay thee low.—
He smil'd, and said :—Of mine hour short or long
　　Let heav'n take care ; but here meanwhile die thou,
Pasture for wolves and crows.—On him his foot
He set, and drew his sword and life both out.

LXXXI.

Among this squadron rode a gentle page,
　　The Soldan's minion, darling, and delight,
On whose fair chin the spring-time of his age
　　Yet blossom'd not her flowers small or light ;
The sweat (spread on his cheeks with heat and rage)
　　Seem'd pearls or morning dews on lilies white,
The dust therein uproll'd adorn'd his hair,
His face seem'd fierce and sweet, wrathful and fair :

LXXXII.

His steed was white, and white as purest snow
　　That falls on tops of aged Apennine,
Lightning and storm are not so swift, I trow,
　　As he, to run, to stop, to turn, and twine :
A dart his right hand shaked, prest to throw,
　　His curtlax by his thigh short hooked ; fine
And braving in his Turkish pomp he shone,
In purple robe, o'erfret with gold and stone :

LXXXIII.

The hardy boy (while thirst of warlike praise
　　Bewitched so his unadvised thought)
'Gainst every band his childish strength assays,
　　And little danger found, though much he sought ;
Till Argillan (that watch'd fit time always
　　In his swift turns to strike him as he fought)
Did unawares his snow-white courser slay,
And under him his master tumbling lay ;

LXXXIV.

And 'gainst his face (where love and pity stand
　　To pray him that rich throne of beauty spare)
The cruel man stretch'd forth his murd'ring hand,
　　To spoil those gifts, whereof he had no share :

It seem'd remorse and sense was in his brand,
    Which, lighting flat, to hurt the lad forbare ;
But all for naught, 'gainst him the point he bent,
That (what the edge had spar'd) pierced and rent.

LXXXV.

Fierce Soliman, that with Godfredo strived
    Who first should enter conquest's glorious gate,
Left off the fray, and thither headlong drived,
    When first he saw the lad in such estate ;
He brake the prease, and soon enough arrived
    To take revenge, but to his aid too late,
Because he saw his Lesbine slain and lost,
Like a sweet flower nipp'd with untimely frost :

LXXXVI.

He saw wax dim the star-light of his eyes,
    His ivory neck upon his shoulders fell,
In his pale looks kind pity's image lies,
    That death e'en mourn'd to hear his passing-bell ;
His marble heart such soft impression tries,
    That midst his wrath his manly tears outwell
(Thou weepest, Soliman ! thou that beheild
Thy kingdoms lost, and not one tear couldst yield).

LXXXVII.

But when the murd'rer's sword he happ'd to view
    Dropping with blood of his Lesbino dead,
His pity vanish'd, ire and rage renew,
    He had no leisure bootless tears to shed ;
But with his blade on Argillano flew,
    And cleft his shield, his helmet, and his head
Down to his throat ; and worthy was that blow
Of Soliman, his strength and wrath to show ;

LXXXVIII.

And not content with this, down from his horse
    He light, and that dead carcass rent and tore,
Like a fierce dog that takes his angry course
    To bite the stone which him had hit before.
O comfort vain for grief of so great force,
    To wound the senseless earth that feels no sore !
But mighty Godfrey 'gainst the Soldan's train
Spent not this while his force and blows in vain :

LXXXIX.

A thousand hardy Turks in front he had,
    In sturdy iron arm'd from head to foot,
Resolv'd in all adventures good or bad,
    In actions wise, in execution stout,
Whom Soliman into Arabia lad,
    When from his kingdom he was first cast out,
Where living wild with their exiled guide,
To him in all extremes they faithful bide:

XC.

All these in thickest order sure unite;
    From Godfrey's valor small or nothing shrank:
Corcutes first he on the face did smite,
    Then wounded strong Rosteno in the flank,
At one blow Selim's head he struck off quite,
    Then both Rossano's arms; in every rank
The boldest knights of all that chosen crew
He felled, maimed, wounded, hurt, and slew.

XCI.

While thus he killed many a Saracine,
    And all their fierce assaults unhurt sustain'd,
Ere fortune wholly from the Turks decline,
    While still they hoped much, though small they gain'd,
Behold a cloud of dust, wherein doth shine
    Lightning of war in midst thereof contain'd,
Whence unawares burst forth a storm of swords,
Which tremble made the Pagan knights and lords:

XCII.

These fifty champions were, 'mongst whom there stands
    (In silver field) the ensign of Christ's death:
If I had mouths and tongues as Briareus hands,
    If voice as iron tough, if iron breath,
What harm this troop wrought to the heathen bands,
    What knights they slew, I could recount uneath:
In vain the Turks resist, th' Arabians fly;
For if they fly, they're slain; if fight, they die.

XCIII.

Fear, cruelty, grief, horror, sorrow, pain,
    Ran through the field, disguis'd in divers shapes;
Death might you see triumphant on the plain,
    Drowning in blood him that from blows escapes.

The King meanwhile, with parcel of his train,
  Comes hastely out, and for sure conquest gapes ;
And from a bank whereon he stood beheild
The doubtful hazard of that bloody field:

XCIV.

But when he saw the Pagans shrink away,
  He sounded the retreat, and 'gan desire
His messengers in his behalf to pray
  Argantes and Clorinda to retire :
The furious couple both at once said nay,
  Ev'n drunk with shedding blood, and mad with ire.
At last they went, and to recomfort thought
And stay their troops from flight, but all for naught ;

XCV.

For who can govern cowardice or fear ?
  Their host already was begun to fly,
They cast their shields and cutting swords a-rear,
  As not defended, but made slow thereby.
A hollow dale, the city's bulwarks near,
  From west to south outstretched long doth lie,
Thither they fled, and in a mist of dust,
Towards the walls they run, they throng, they thrust.

XCVI.

While down the bank disorder'd thus they ran,
  The Christian knights huge slaughter on them made ;
But when to climb the other hill they 'gan,
  Old Aladine came fiercely to their aid :
On that steep bray Lord Guelpho would not then
  Hazard his folk, but there his soldiers stay'd ;
And safe within the city's walls the king
The reliques small of that sharp fight did bring.

XCVII.

Meanwhile the Soldan in this latest charge
  Had done as much as human force was able,
All sweat and blood appear'd his members large,
  His breath was short, his courage wax'd unstable,
His arm grew weak to bear his mighty targe,
  His hand to rule his heavy sword unable,
Which bruis'd, not cut, so blunted was the blade
It lost the use for which a sword was made.

XCVIII.

Feeling his weakness, he 'gan musing stand,
   And in his troubled thought this question tost,
If he himself should murder with his hand
   (Because none else should of his conquest boast),
Or he should save his life, when on the land
   Lay slain the pride of his subdued host:
.At last—To fortune's power (quoth he) I yield,
And on my flight let her her trophies bild.

XCIX.

Let Godfrey view my flight, and smile to see
   This mine unworthy second banishment ;
For arm'd again soon shall he hear of me,
   From his proud head the unsettled crown to rent ;
For, as my wrongs, my wrath eterne shall be,
   And every hour, the bow of war new bent,
I will arise again, a foe, fierce, bold,
Though dead, though slain, though burnt to ashes cold.

BOOK X.

THE ARGUMENT.

Ismen from sleep awakes the Soldan great,
    And into Sion brings the Prince by night,
Where the sad king sits fearful on his seat,
    Whom he embold'neth and excites to fight.
Godfredo hears his lords and knights repeat
    How they escap'd Armida's wrath and spite :
Rinaldo known to live, Peter foresays
His offspring's virtue, good deserts, and praise.

I.

A GALLANT steed (while thus the Soldan said)
    Came trotting by him, without lord or guide,
Quickly his hand upon the reins he laid,
    And, weak and weary, climbed up to ride.
The snake (that on his crest hot fire outbray'd),
    Was quite cut off, his helm had lost its pride,
His coat was rent, his harness hack'd and cleft
And of his kingly pomp no sign was left.

II.

As when a savage wolf, chas'd from the fold,
    To hide his head runs to some holt or wood,
Who (though he filled hath while it might hold
    His greedy paunch) yet hung'reth after food,

With sanguine tongue forth of his lips out roll'd,
　　About his jaws that licks up foam and blood ;
So from his bloody fray the Soldan hied,
His rage unquench'd, his wrath unsatisfied.

III.

And (as his fortune would) he 'scaped free
　　From thousand arrows which about him flew,
From swords and lances, instruments that be
　　Of certain death, himself he safe withdrew ;
Unknown, unseen, disguised, travell'd he
　　By desert paths and ways but us'd by few;
And rode, revolving in his troubled thought
What course to take, and yet resolv'd on naught.

IV.

Thither at last he meant to take his way
　　Where Egypt's king assembled all his host,
To join with him, and once again assay
　　To win by fight, by which so oft he lost :
Determin'd thus, he made no longer stay,
　　But thitherward spurr'd forth his steed in post ;
Nor need he guide, the way right well he could
That leads to sandy plains of Gaza old.

V.

Nor though his smarting wounds torment him oft,
　　His body weak and wounded back and side,
Not rested he, nor once his armor doft,
　　But all day long o'er hills and dales doth ride :
But when the night cast up her shade aloft,
　　And all earth's colors strange in sable dy'd,
He light, and as he could his wounds upbound,
And shook ripe dates down from a palm he found.

VI.

On them he supped, and amid the field
　　To rest his weary limbs awhile he sought ;
He made his pillow of his broken shield,
　　To ease the griefs of his distemper'd thought ;
But little ease could so hard lodging yield,
　　His wounds so smarted that he slept right naught,
And in his breast his proud heart rent in twain
Two inward vultures, sorrow and disdain.

VII.

At length, when midnight with her silence deep
    Did heav'n and earth hush'd, still, and quiet make,
Sore watch'd and weary, he began to steep
    His cares and sorrows in oblivion's lake,
And in a little, short, unquiet sleep,
    Some small repose his fainting spirits take ;
But (while he slept) a voice, grave and severe,
At unawares thus thunder'd in his ear :—

VIII.

O Soliman ! thou far-renowned king,
    Till better season serve, forbear thy rest ;
A stranger doth thy lands in thraldom bring ;
    Nice is a slave, by Christian yoke oppress'd ;
Sleepest thou here, forgetful of this thing,
    That here thy friends lie slain, not laid in chest,
Whose bones bear witness of thy shame and scorn,
And wilt thou idly here attend the morn ?—

IX.

The king awak'd, and saw before his eyes
    A man whose presence seemed grave and old,
A writhen staff his steps unstable guides,
    Which serv'd his feeble members to uphold.—
And what art thou ? (the prince in scorn replies)
    What sprite to vex poor passengers so bold,
To break their sleep ; or what to thee belongs
My shame, my loss, my vengeance, or my wrongs ?—

X.

I am the man, of thine intent (quoth he)
    And purpose new that sure conjecture hath,
And better than thou weenest know I thee ;
    I proffer thee my service and my faith ;
My speeches therefore sharp and biting be,
    Because quick words the whetstones are of wrath ;
Accept in gree, my lord, the words I spoke,
As spurs thine ire and courage to provoke.

XI.

But now to visit Egypt's mighty king,
    Unless my judgment fail, you are prepar'd ;
I prophesy, about a needless thing,
    You suffer shall a voyage long and hard :

For though you stay, the monarch great will bring
   His new assembled force to Judah-ward ;
No place of service there, no cause of fight,
Nor 'gainst our foes to use your force and might :

XII.

But, if you follow me, within this wall
   (With Christian arms hemm'd in on every side),
Withouten battaile, fight, or stroke at all,
   Ev'n at noon day I will you safely guide,
Where your delight, rejoice, and glory shall,
   In perils great to see your prowess tried.
That noble town you may preserve and shield,
'Till Egypt's host come to renew the field.—

XIII.

While thus he parlied, of this aged guest
   The Turk the words and looks did both admire,
And from his haughty eyes and furious breast
   He laid apart his pride, his rage, his ire ;
And humbly said—I willing am and prest
   To follow where thou leadest, reverend sire ;
And that advice best fits my angry vein,
That tells of greatest peril, greatest pain.—

XIV.

The old man prais'd his words ; and for the air
   His late received wounds to worse disposes,
A quintessence therein he poured fair,
   That stops the bleeding, and incision closes:
Beholding then before Apollo's chair
   How fresh Aurora violets strew'd and roses,—
It 's time (he says) to wend, for Titan bright
To wonted labor summons every wight.—

XV.

And to a chariot (that beside did stand)
   Ascended he, and with him Soliman :
He took the reins, and with a mastering hand
   Ruled his steeds, and whip'd them now and then :
The wheels or horses' feet upon the land
   Had left no sign or token where they ran ;
The coursers pant and smoke with lukewarm sweat,
And, foaming cream, their iron mouthfuls eat.

XVI.

The air about them round (a wond'rous thing!)
   Itself on heaps in solid thickness drew,
The chariot hiding and environing;
   The subtile mist no mortal eye could view,
And yet no stone from engine cast or sling
   Could pierce the cloud, it was of proof so true;
Yet seen it was to them within which ride,
And heaven and earth without all clear beside.

XVII

His beetle brows the Turk amazed bent,
   He wrinkled up his front, and wildly star'd
Upon the cloud and chariot as it went,
   For speed to Cinthia's car right well compar'd;
The other seeing his astonishment,
   How he bewonder'd was, and how he far'd,
All suddenly by name the prince 'gan call,
By which awaked, thus he spoke withal:—

XVIII.

Whoe'er thou art, above all worldly wit,
   That hast these high and wondrous marvels wrought,
And know'st the deep intents which hidden sit
   In secret closet of man's private thought,
If in thy skilful heart this lore be writ,
   To tell th' event of things to end unbrought,
Then say what issue and what end the stars
Allot to Asia's troubles, broils, and wars?

XIX.

But tell me first thy name, and by what art
   Thou dost these wonders strange, above our skill;
For full of marvel is my troubled heart; *
   Tell then, and leave me not amazed still.—
The wizard smil'd and answer'd:—In some part
   Easy it is to satisfy thy will;
Ismen I hight, call'd an enchanter great,
Such skill have I in magic's secret feat:

XX.

But that I should the sure events unfold
   Of things to come, or destinies foretell,
Too rash is your desire, your wish too bold,
   To mortal heart such knowledge never fell:

Our wit and strength on us bestow'd, I hold,
   To shun th' evils and harms 'mongst which we dwell ;
They make their fortune who are stout and wise,
Wit rules the heav'ns, discretion guides the skies.

XXI.

That puissant arm of thine, that well can rend
   From Godfrey's brow the new usurped crown,
And not alone protect, save and defend
   From his fierce people this besieged town,
'Gainst fire and sword with strength and courage bend,
   Adventure, suffer, trust, tread perils down ;
And to consent and to encourage thee,
Know this, which I as in a cloud foresee :

XXII.

I guess (before the over-gliding sun
   Shall many years mete out by weeks and days)
A prince (that shall in fertile Egypt won)
   Shall fill all Asia with his prosp'rous frays ;
I speak not of his acts in quiet done,
   His policy, his rule, his wisdom's praise ;
Let this suffice, by him these Christians shall
In fight subdued fly, and conquered fall ;

XXIII.

And their great empire and usurped state
   Shall overthrown in dust and ashes lie ;
Their woful remnant in an angle strait,
   Compass'd with sea, themselves shall fortify.
From thee shall spring this lord of war and fate.—
   Whereto great Soliman 'gan thus reply :—
O happy man, to so great praise ybore !—
Thus he rejoiced, but yet envied more ;

XXIV.

And said—Let chance with good or bad aspect
   Upon me look as sacred heav'ns decree,
This heart to her I never will subject,
   Nor ever conquer'd shall she look on me ;
The moon her chariot shall awry direct,
   Ere from this course I will diverted be.—
While thus he spake, it seem'd he breathed fire,
So fierce his courage was, so hot his ire.

XXV.

Thus talked they, till they arrived been
    Nigh to the place were Godfrey's tents were rear'd ;
There was a woful spectacle yseen,
    Death in a thousand ugly forms appear'd ;
The Soldan changed hue for grief and teen,
    On that sad book his shame and loss he lear'd :
Ah ! with what grief his men, his friends, he found,
And standards proud, inglorious lie on ground !

XXVI.

And saw, on visage of some well-known friend
    (In foul despite) a rascal Frenchman tread ;
And there another ragged peasant rend
    The arms and garments from some champion dead ;
And there with stately pomp by heaps they wend,
    And Christians slain roll up in webs of lead :
Lastly, the Turks and slain Arabians (brought
On heaps) he saw them burn with fire to naught.

XXVII.

Deeply he sighed, and with naked sword
    Out of the coach he leaped in the mire,
But Ismen call'd again the angry lord,
    And with grave words appeas'd his foolish ire.
The prince content remounted at his word ;
    Towards a hill on drove the aged sire,
And hasting forward up the bank they pass,
Till far behind the Christian leader was.

XXVIII.

There they alight and took their way on foot,
    The empty chariot vanish'd out of sight,
Yet still the cloud environ'd them about ;
    At their left hand down went they from the height
Of Sion's hill, till they approach'd the rout ;
    On that side where to west he looketh right,
There Ismen stayed, and his eyesight bent
Upon the bushy rocks, and thither went.

XXIX.

A hollow cave was in the craggy stone,
    Wrought out by hand a number years tofore.
And for of long that way had walked none,
    The vault was hid with plants and bushes hoar :

The wizard stooping in thereat to gone,
   The thorns aside and scratching brambles bore ;
His right hand sought the passage through the cleft,
And for his guide he gave the prince his left.—

XXX.

What ! (quoth the Soldan) by what privy mine,
   What hidden vault, behoves it me to creep ?
This sword can find a better way than thine,
   Although our foes the passage guard and keep.—
Let not (quoth he) thy princely foot repine
   To tread this secret path, though dark and deep ;
For great king Herod us'd to tread the same,
He that in arms had whilome so great fame.

XXXI.

This passage made he, when he would suppress
   His subjects' pride, and them in bondage hold ;
By this he could from that small forteress
   Antonia call'd, of Antonie the bold,
Convey his folk, unseen of more and less,
   Even to the middest of the temple old ;
Thence hither, where these privy ways begin,
And bring unseen whole armies out and in :

XXXII.

But now, save I, in all this world lives none
   That knows the secret of this darksome place ;
Come then where Aladine sits on his throne,
   With lords and princes set about his grace ;
He feareth more than fitteth such an one,
   Such signs of doubt show in his cheer and face ;
Fitly you come ; hear, see, and keep you still,
Till time and season serve, then speak your fill.

XXXIII.

This said, that narrow entrance past the knight
   (So creeps a camel through a needle's eye),
And through the ways as black as darkest night
   He followed him that did him rule and guie :
Strait was the way at first, withouten light,
   But further in did further amplify,
So that upright walked at ease the men
Ere they had passed half that secret den.

XXXIV.

A privy door Ismen unlock'd at last,
  And up they climb'd a little-used stair,
Thereat the day a feeble beam in cast,
  Dim was the light, and nothing clear the air;
Out of the hollow cave at length they pass'd,
  Into a goodly hall, high, broad, and fair,
Where crown'd with gold, and all in purple clad,
Sate the sad king among his nobles sad.

XXXV.

The Turk (close in his hollow cloud imbar'd),
  Unseen, at will did all the prease behold,
These heavy speeches of the king he heard,
  Who thus from lofty siege his pleasure told:—
My lords, last day our state was much impair'd,
  Our friends were slain, kill'd were our soldiers bold,
Great helps and greater hopes are us bereft,
Nor aught but aid from Egypt land is left:

XXXVI.

And well you see far distant is that aid;
  Upon our heels our danger treadeth still;
For your advice was this assembly made,
  Each what he thinketh speak, and what he will.—
A whisper soft arose when this was said,
  As gentle winds the groves with murmurs fill;
But with bold face, high looks, and merry cheer,
Argantes rose; the rest their talk forbear.—

XXXVII.

O worthy sovereign (thus began to say
  The hardy young man to the tyrant wise)
What words be these? what fears do you dismay?
  Who knows not this, you need not our advice?
But on our hands your hope of conquest lay,
  And, for no loss true virtue damnifies,
Make her our shield, pray her us succors give,
And without her let us not wish to live.

XXXVIII.

Nor say I this for that I aught misdeem
  That Egypt's promis'd succors fail us might;
Doubtful of my great master's words to seem,
  To me were neither lawful, just, nor right;

I speak these words, for spurs I them esteem
   To waken up each dull and fearful sprite,
And make our hearts resolv'd to all assays,
   To win with honor, or to die with praise.—

XXXIX.

Thus much Argantes said, and said no more
   (As if the case were clear of which he spoke) :
Orcano rose, of princely stem ybore,
   Whose presence 'mongst them bore a mighty stroke ;
A man esteemed well in arms of yore,
   But now was coupled new in marriage yoke ;
Young babes he had, to fight which made him loth ;
He was a husband and a father both.—

XL.

My lord (quoth he) I will not reprehend
   The earnest zeal of this audacious speech,
From courage sprung, which seld is close ypen'd
   In swelling stomach without violent breach ;
And though to you our good Circassian friend
   In terms too bold and fervent oft doth preach,
Yet hold I that for good, in warlike feat
For his great deeds respond his speeches great :

XLI.

But if it you beseem (whom graver age
   And long experience hath made wise and sly)
To rule the heat of youth and hardy rage,
   Which somewhat have misled this knight awry,
In equal balance ponder then and gage
   Your hopes far distant with your perils nigh ;
This town's old walls and rampires new compare
With Godfrey's forces, and his engines rare :

XLII.

But (if I may say what I think unblamed)
   This town is strong by nature, site, and art ;
But engines huge and instruments are framed
   'Gainst these defences by our adverse part ;
Who thinks him most secure is eathest shamed ;
   I hope the best, yet fear inconstant Mart ;
And with this siege if we be long up-pent,
Famine I doubt, our store will all be spent ;

XLIII.

For all that store of cattle and of grain
　　Which yesterday within these walls you brought,
While your proud foes triumphant through the plain
　　On naught but shedding blood and conquest thought,
Too little is this city to sustain,
　　To raise the siege unless some means be sought;
And it must last till the prefixed hour,
That it be rais'd by Egypt's aid and pow'r:

XLIV.

But what if that appointed day they miss?
　　Or else ere we expect what if they came?
The victory yet is not ours for this.
　　Oh save this town from ruin, us from shame!
With that same Godfrey still our warfare is,
　　These armies, soldiers, captains, are the same
Who have so oft, amid the dusty plain,
Turks, Persians, Syrians, and Arabians slain.

XLV.

And thou, Argantes, wottest what they be;
　　Oft hast thou fled from that victorious host,
Thy shoulders often hast thou let them see,
　　And in thy feet hath been thy safeguard most;
Clorinda bright and I fled both with thee;
　　None than his fellows had more cause to boast,
Nor blame I any, for in every fight
We showed courage, valor, strength, and might:

XLVI.

And though this hardy knight the certain threat
　　Of near approaching death to hear disdain;
Yet to this state of loss and danger great,
　　From this strong foe, I see the tokens plain;
No fort, how strong soe'er by art or seat,
　　Can hinder Godfrey why he should not reign:
This makes me say (to witness heav'n I bring)
Zeal to this state, love to my lord and king.

XLVII.

The king of Tripoli was well advis'd
　　To purchase peace and so preserve his crown;
But Soliman (who Godfrey's love despis'd)
　　Is either dead or deep in prison thrown;

Else fearful is he run away disguis'd,
  And scant his life is left him for his own ;
And yet with gifts, with tribute, and with gold,
He might in peace his empire still have hold.—

XLVIII.

Thus spake Orcanes, and some inkling gave
  In doubtful words of that he would have said ;
To sue for peace, or yield himself a slave,
  He durst not openly his king persuade :
But at these words the Soldan 'gan to rave,
  And 'gainst his will wrapt in the cloud he stay'd ;
Whom Ismen thus bespake :—How can you bear
These words, my lord, or these reproaches hear ?

XLIX

Oh let me speak (quoth he) with ire and scorn
  I burn, and 'gainst my will thus hid I stay.—
This said, the smoky cloud was cleft and torn,
  Which like a veil upon them stretched lay,
And up to open heav'n forthwith was borne,
  And left the prince in view of lightsome day ;
With princely look amid the prease he shin'd,
And on a sudden thus declar'd his mind :—

L.

Of whom you speak behold the Soldan here,
  Neither afraid, nor run away for dread ;
And that these slanders, lies, and fables were,
  This hand shall prove upon that coward's head ;
I, who have shed a sea of blood well near,
  And heap'd up mountains high of Christians dead ;
I in their camp who still maintain'd the fray
(My men all murder'd), I that ran away.

LI.

If this, or any coward vile beside,
  False to his faith and country, dares reply,
And speak of concord with yond men of pride,
  By your good leave, sir king, here shall he die ;
The lambs and wolves shall in one fold abide,
  The doves and serpents in one nest shall lie,
Before one town us and these Christians shall
In peace and love unite within one wall.—

LII.

While thus he spoke, his broad and trenchant sword
   His hand held high aloft in threat'ning guise :
Dumb stood the knights, so dreadful was his word :
   A storm was in his front, fire in his eyes ;
He turn'd at last to Sion's aged lord,
   And calm'd his visage stern in humbler wise :—
Behold (quoth he), good prince, what aid I bring,
Since Soliman is join'd with Judah's king.—

LIII.

King Aladine from his rich throne upstart,
   And said—Oh how I joy thy face to view,
My noble friend, it less'neth in some part
   My grief for slaughter of my subjects true ;
My weak estate to 'stablish come thou art,
   And may'st thine own again in time renew,
If heav'ns consent.—With that the Soldan bold
In dear embracements did he long enfold.

LIV.

Their greetings done, the king resign'd his throne
   To Soliman, and set himself beside
In a rich seat adorn'd with gold and stone,
   And Ismen sage did at his elbow bide,
Of whom he ask'd what way they two had gone,
   And he declar'd all what had them betide.
Clorinda bright to Soliman address'd
Her salutations first, then all the rest.

LV.

Among them rose Ormusses, valiant knight,
   Whom late the Soldan with a convoy sent,
And when most hot and bloody was the fight,
   By secret paths and blind bye-ways he went,
Till, aided by the silence and the night,
   Safe in the city's walls himself he pent,
And there refresh'd with corn and cattle store
The pined soldiers, famish'd nigh before.

LVI.

With surly count'nance and disdainful grace,
   Sullen and sad, sat the Circassian stout,
Like a fierce lion grumbling in his place,
   His fiery eyes that turns and rolls about :

Nor durst Orcanes view the Soldan's face,
　　But still upon the floor did pore and tout.
Thus with his lords and peers in counselling,
The Turkish monarch sat with Judah's king.

LVII.

Godfrey this while gave victory the rein,
　　And following her the straits he opened all ;
Then, for his soldiers and his captains slain,
　　He celebrates a stately funeral,
And told his camp within a day or twain
　　He would assault the city's mighty wall,
And all the heathen there inclos'd doth threat
With fire and sword, with death and danger great :

LVIII.

And, for he had that noble squadron known,
　　In the last fight which brought him so great aid,
To be the lords and princes of his own,
　　Who follow'd late the sly enticing maid,
And with them Tancred (who had late been thrown
　　In prison deep, by that false witch betray'd),
Before the hermit and some private friends,
For all those worthies, lords and knights, he sends ;

LIX.

And thus he said :——Some one of you declare
　　Your fortunes, whether good or to be blamed,
And to assist us with your valors rare
　　(In so great need) how was your coming framed ?——
They blush, and on the ground amazed stare
　　(For virtue is of little guilt ashamed) ;
At last the English prince, with count'nance bold,
The silence broke, and thus their errors told :

LX.

We (not elect to that exploit by lot)
　　With secret flight from hence ourselves withdrew,
Following false Cupid, I deny it not,
　　Enticed forth by love and beauty's hue ;
A jealous fire burnt in our stomachs hot,
　　And by close ways we passed least in view :
Her words, her looks (alas ! I know too late),
Nursed our love, our jealousy, our hate.

LXI.

At last we 'gan approach that woful clime
 Where fire and brimstone down from heav'n was sent,
To take revenge for sin and shameful crime
 'Gainst kind commit, by those who nould repent:
A loathsome lake of brimstone, pitch, and slime,
 O'ergoes that land, erst sweet and redolent;
And when it moves, thence stench and smoke up-flies
Which dim the welkin and infect the skies.

LXII.

This is the lake in which yet never might
 Aught that hath weight sink to the bottom down,
But like to cork, to leaves, or feathers light,
 Stones, iron, men, there float, and never drown:
Therein a castle stands, to which by sight
 But o'er a narrow bridge no way is known;
Hither us brought, here welcom'd us the witch;
The house within was stately, pleasant, rich.

LXIII.

The heav'ns were clear, and wholesome was the air,
 High trees, sweet meadows, waters pure and good;
For there in thickest shade of myrtles fair
 A crystal spring pour'd out a silver flood;
Amid the herbs, the grass, and flowers rare,
 The falling leaves down patter'd from the wood;
The birds sang hymns of love; yet speak I naught
Of gold and marble rich, and richly wrought.

LXIV.

Under the curtain of the green-wood shade,
 Beside the brook, upon the velvet grass,
In massy vessels of pure silver made,
 A banquet rich and costly furnish'd was.
All beasts, all birds, beguil'd by fowler's trade;
 All fish were there in floods or seas that pass;
All dainties made by art; and at the table
An hundred virgins serv'd, for husbands able.

LXV.

She, with sweet words and false enticing smiles,
 Infused love among the dainties set,
And with empoison'd cups our souls beguiles,
 And made each knight himself and God forget.

She rose, and turn'd again within short whiles,
    With changed looks where wrath and anger met ;
A charming rod, a book, with her she brings,
On which she mumbled strange and secret things.

LXVI

She read, and chang'd I felt my will and thought,
    I long'd to change my life and place of biding ;
That virtue strange in me no pleasure wrought,
    I leap'd into the flood myself there hiding ;
My legs and feet both into one were brought,
    Mine arms and hands into my shoulders sliding,
My skin was full of scales like shields of brass ;
Now made a fish, where late a knight I was.

LXVII.

The rest with me like shape, like garments wore,
    And div'd with me in that quick silver stream :
Such mind (to my remembrance) then I bore,
    As when on vain and foolish things men dream.
At last our shape it pleas'd her to restore,
    Then full of wonder and of fear we seem,
And with an ireful look the angry maid
Thus threaten'd us, and made us thus afraid :—

LXVIII.

You see (quoth she) my sacred might and skill,
    How you are subject to my rule and power ;
In endless thraldom damned, if I will,
    I can torment and keep you in this tower ;
Or make you birds, or trees on craggy hill,
    To bide the bitter blasts of storm and shower,
Or harden you to rocks on mountains old,
Or melt your flesh and bones to rivers cold.

LXIX.

Yet may you well avoid mine ire and wrath,
    If to my will your yielding hearts you bend,
You must forsake your Christendom and faith,
    And 'gainst Godfredo false my crown defend.—
We all refus'd, for speedy death each pray'th,
    Save false Rambaldo, he became her friend ;
We in a dungeon deep were helpless cast,
In misery and iron chained fast.

LXX.

Then (for alone they say falls no mishap)
  Within short while Prince Tancred thither came,
And was un'wares surprised in the trap:
  But there short while we stay'd: the wily dame
In other folds our mischiefs would upwrap;
  From Hidraort an hundred horsemen came,
Whose guide, a baron bold, to Egypt's king
Should us disarm'd, and bound in fetters bring.

LXXI.

Now on our way, the way to death, we ride:
  But Providence divine thus for us wrought;
Rinaldo (whose high virtue is his guide
  To great exploits exceeding human thought)
Met us, and all at once our guard defy'd,
  And, ere he left the fight, to earth them brought;
And in their harness arm'd us in the place,
Which late were ours before our late disgrace.

LXXII.

I and all these the hardy champion knew,
  We saw his valor and his voice we heard.
Then is the rumor of his death untrue,
  His life is safe, good fortune long it guard:
Three times the golden sun has risen new
  Since us he left and rode to Antioch-ward;
But first his armors broken, hack'd, and cleft,
Unfit for service, there he doft and left.—

LXXIII.

Thus spake the Briton prince: with humble cheer
  The hermit sage to heav'n cast up his eyne,
His color and his count'nance changed were,
  With heavenly grace his looks and visage shine;
Ravish'd with zeal, his soul approached near
  The seat of angels pure and saints divine;
And there he learn'd of things and haps to come,
To give foreknowledge true, and certain doom.

LXXIV.

At last he spoke (in more than human sound),
  And told what things his wisdom great foresaw;
And at his thund'ring voice the folk around
  Attentive stood, with trembling and with awe:—

Rinaldo lives, he said ; the tokens found
    From women's craft their false beginnings draw ;
He lives, and heav'n will long preserve his days,
To greater glory and to greater praise.

LXXV.

These are but trifles yet, though Asia's kings
    Shrink at his name and tremble at his view ;
I well foresee he shall do greater things,
    And wicked emperors conquer and subdue ;
Under the shadow of his eagle's wings
    Shall holy church preserve her sacred crew ;
From Cæsar's bird he shall the sable train
Pluck off, and break her talons sharp in twain.:

LXXVI.

His children's children at his hardiness
    And great attempts shall take ensample fair,
From emperors unjust in all distress
    They shall defend the state of Peter's chair ;
To raise the humble up, pride to suppress,
    To help the innocents, shall be their care :
This bird of east shall fly with conquest great
As far as moon gives light or sun gives heat :

LXXVII.

Her eyes behold the truth and purest light,
    And thunders down in Peter's aid she brings,
And where for Christ and Christian faith men fight,
    There forth she spreadeth her victorious wings ;
This virtue Nature gives her and this might.
    Then lure her home, for on her presence hings
The happy end of this great enterprise ;
So heav'n decrees, and so command the skies.—

LXXVIII.

These words of his, of Prince Rinaldo's death
    Out of their troubled hearts the fear had rased :
In all this joy yet Godfrey smil'd uneath,
    In his wise thought such care and heed was placed.
But now from deeps of regions underneath
    Night's veil arose, and sun's bright lustre chased ;
When all full sweetly in their cabins slept,
Save he whose thoughts his eyes still open kept.

BOOK XI.

I.

THE Christian armies' great and puissant guide,
   T' assault the town that all his thoughts had bent,
Did ladders, rams, and engines huge provide,
   When reverend Peter to him gravely went,
And drawing him with sober grace aside,
   With words severe thus told his high intent :—
Right well, my lord, these earthly strengths you move,
But let us first begin from heav'n above ;

II.

With public prayer, zeal, and faith devout,
   The aid, assistance, and the help obtain,
Of all the blessed of the heav'nly rout,
   With whose support you conquest sure may gain.
First let the priests, before thine armies stout,
   With sacred hymns their holy voices strain ;
And thou, and all thy lords and peers with thee,
Of godliness and faith ensamples be.—

III.

Thus spake the hermit grave in words severe ;
   Godfrey allow'd his counsel sage and wise :—
Of Christ the lord (quoth he) thou servant dear,
   I yield to follow thy divine advice ;

And while the princes I assemble here,
    The great procession, songs, and sacrifice,
With Bishop William, thou and Ademare
With sacred and with solemn pomp prepare.—

IV.

Next morn the bishops twain, the heremite,
    And all the clerks and priests of less estate,
Did in the middest of the camp unite
    Within a place for prayer consecrate :
Each priest adorn'd was in a surplice white,
    The bishops don'd their albes and copes of state,
Above their rochets button'd fair before,
And mitres on their heads like crowns they wore.

V.

Peter alone, before, spread to the wind
    The glorious sign of our salvation great ;
With easy pace the choir came all behind,
    And hymns and psalms in order true repeat ;
With sweet respondence in harmonious kind,
    Their humble song the yielding air doth beat ;
Lastly, together went the reverend pair
Of prelates sage, William and Ademare :

VI.

The mighty Duke came next, as princes do,
    Without companion, marching all alone ;
The lords and captains came by two and two ;
    The soldiers for their guard were arm'd each one.
With easy pace thus order'd, passing through
    The trench and rampire, to the fields they gone ;
No thund'ring drum, no trumpet shrill they hear,
Their godly music psalms and prayers were.

VII.

To thee, O Father, Son, and sacred Spright,
    One true, eternal, everlasting King,
To Christ's dear mother Mary, virgin bright,
    Psalms of thanksgiving and of praise they sing ;
To them that angels down from heav'n to fight,
    'Gainst the blasphemous beast and dragon bring ;
To him also that of our Saviour good
Washed the sacred front in Jordan's flood ;

VIII.

Him likewise they invoke, called the rock
    Whereon the Lord, they say, his church did rear,
Whose true successors close or else unlock
    The blessed gates of grace and mercy dear;
And all th' elected twelve, the chosen flock,
    Of his triumphant death who witness bear;
And them by torment, slaughter, fire and sword,
Who martyrs died to confirm his word;

IX.

And them also whose books and writings tell
    What certain path to heav'nly bliss us leads;
And hermits good and anchresses, that dwell
    Mew'd up in walls, and mumble on their beads;
And virgin nuns in close and private cell,
    Where (but shrift fathers) never mankind treads:
On these they called, and on all the rout
Of angels, martyrs, and of saints devout.

X.

Singing and saying thus the camp devout
    Spread forth her zealous squadrons broad and wide,
Towards mount Olivet went all this rout,
    So call'd of olive trees the hill which hide;
A mountain known by fame the world throughout,
    Which riseth on the city's eastern side,
From it divided by the valley green
Of Josaphat, that fills the space between.

XI.

Hither the armies went, and chaunted shrill,
    That all the deep and hollow dales resound;
From hollow mounts and caves in every hill
    A thousand echoes also sung around;
It seem'd some choir that sung with art and skill
    Dwelt in those savage dens and shady ground,
For oft resounded from the banks they hear
The name of Christ and of his mother dear.

XII.

Upon the walls the pagans old and young
    Stood hush'd and still, amated and amazed
At their grave order and their humble song,
    At their strange pomp and customs new they gazed;

But when the show they had beholden long,
  An hideous yell the wicked miscreants raised,
That with vile blasphemies the mountains hoar,
The woods, the waters, and the valleys roar.

XIII.

But yet with sacred notes the hosts proceed,
  Though blasphemies they hear and cursed things:
So with Apollo's harp Pan tunes his reed,
  So adders hiss where Philomela sings.
Nor flying darts nor stones the Christians dread,
  Nor arrows shot, nor quarries cast from slings;
But with assured faith, as dreading naught,
The holy work begun to end they brought.

XIV.

A table set they on the mountain's height,
  To minister thereon the sacrament;
In golden candlesticks a hallowed light
  At either end of virgin wax there brent;
In costly vestments sacred William dight,
  With fear and trembling to the altar went,
And prayer there and service loud begins,
Both for his own and all his armies' sins.

XV.

Humbly they heard his words that stood him nigh,
  The rest far off upon him bent their eyes;
But when he ended had the service high,—
  You servants of the Lord depart—he cries:
His hands he lifted then up to the sky,
  And blessed all those warlike companies;
And they dismiss'd return'd the way they came,
Their order as before, their pomp the same.

XVI.

Within their camp arriv'd, this voyage ended,
  Towards his tent the Duke himself withdrew;
Upon their guide by heaps the bands attended,
  Till his pavilion's stately door they view;
There to the Lord his welfare they commended,
  And with him left the worthies of the crew,
Whom at a costly and rich feast he placed,
And with the highest room old Raimond graced.

XVII.

Now when the hungry knights sufficed are
  With meat, with drink, with spices of the best,
Quoth he—When next you see the morning star,
  T' assault the town be ready all and prest:
To-morrow is a day of pains and war,
  This of repose, of quiet, peace, and rest;
Go, take your ease this evening and this night,
And make you strong against to-morrow's fight.—

XVIII.

They took their leave, and Godfrey's heralds rode
  To intimate his will on every side,
And publish'd it through all the lodgings broad,
  That 'gainst the morn each should himself provide;
Meanwhile they might their hearts of cares unload,
  And rest their tired limbs that evening tide.
Thus fared they till night their eyes did close,
Night, friend to gentle rest and sweet repose.

XIX.

With little sign as yet of springing day
  Out peep'd, not well appear'd, the rising morn,
The plough yet tore not up the fertile lay,
  Nor to their feed the sheep from folds return,
The birds sat silent on the green-wood spray,
  Amid the groves unheard was hound and horn;
When trumpets shrill, true signs of hardy fights,
Call'd up to arms the soldiers, call'd the knights.

XX.

Arm! arm! at once an hundred squadrons cried,
  And with their cry to arm them all begin;
Godfrey arose; that day he laid aside
  His hawberk strong he wont to combat in,
And don'd a breast-plate fair, of proof untried,
  Such one as footmen use, light, easy, thin:
Scantly their lord thus clothed had his grooms,
When aged Raimond to his presence comes;

XXI.

And furnish'd thus when he the man beheld,
  By his attire his secret thought he guess'd:
Where is (quoth he) your sure and trusty shield,
  Your helm, your hawberk strong, where all the rest?

Why be you half-disarm'd ? why to the field
    Approach you in these weak defences drest ?
I see this day you mean a course to run,
Wherein may peril much, small praise be won :

XXII.

Alas ! do you that idle praise expect,
    To set first foot this conquer'd wall above ?
Of less account some knight thereto object,
    Whose loss so great and harmful cannot prove :
My lord, your life with greater care protect,
    And love yourself because all us you love ;
Your happy life is spirit, soul, and breath,
Of all this camp, preserve it then from death.—

XXIII.

To this he answered thus :—You know (he said)
    In Clarimont, by mighty Urban's hand
When I was girded with this noble blade,
    For Christ's true faith to fight in every land,
To God ev'n then a secret vow I made,
    Not as a captain here this day to stand
And give directions, but with shield and sword
To fight, to win, or die for Christ my Lord.

XXIV.

When all this camp in battle strong shall be
    Ordain'd and order'd, well disposed all,
And all things done which to the high degree
    And sacred place I hold belongen shall ;
Then reason is it, nor dissuade thou me,
    That I likewise assault this sacred wall,
Lest from my vow to God late made I swerve ;
He shall this life defend, keep, and preserve.

XXV.

Thus he concludes ; and every hardy knight
    His sample follow'd, and his brethren twain :
The other princes put on harness light
    As footmen use ; but all the Pagan train
Towards that side bent their defensive might
    That lies expos'd to view of Charles-wain
And Zephyrus' sweet blasts ; for on that part
The town was weakest both by site and art.

XXVI.

On all parts else the fort was strong by site,
    With mighty hills defenc'd from foreign rage ;
And to this part the tyrant 'gan unite
    His subjects born, and bands that serve for wage ;
From this exploit he spar'd nor great nor lite :
    The aged men and boys of tender age
To fire of angry war still brought new fuel,
Stones, darts, lime, brimstone, and bitumen cruel.

XXVII.

All full of arms and weapons was the wall
    Under whose basis that fair plain doth run ;
There stood the Soldan like a giant tall
    (So stood at Rhodes the coloss of the sun) ;
Waist-high Argantes show'd himself withall,
    At whose stern looks the French to quake begun ;
Clorinda on the corner tower alone,
In silver arms, like rising Cinthia shone ;

XXVIII.

Her rattling quiver at her shoulders hung,
    Therein a flash of arrows feathered weel ;
In her left hand her bow was bended strung,
    Therein a shaft headed with mortal steel ;
So fit to shoot, she singled forth among
    Her foes who first her quarry's strength should feel ;
So fit to shoot Latona's daughter stood,
When Niobe she kill'd and all her brood.

XXIX.

The aged tyrant trotted on his feet
    From gate to gate, from wall to wall he flew ;
He comforts all his bands with speeches sweet,
    And every fort and bastion doth review ;
For every need prepar'd, in every street
    New regiments he plac'd, and weapons new.
The matrons grave within their temples hie,
To idols false for succors call, and cry :—

XXX.

O Macon ! break in twain the steeled lance
    Of wicked Godfrey with thy righteous hands,
Against thy name he doth his arm advance ;
    His rebel blood pour out upon these sands.—

These cries within his ears no enterance
   Could find ; for naught he hears, naught understands
While thus the town for her defence ordains,
His armies Godfrey ordereth on the plains.

XXXI.

His forces first on foot he forward brought,
   With goodly order, providence, and art ;
And 'gainst those towers which t' assail he thought,
   In battles twain his strength he doth depart ;
Between them cross-bows stood, and engines wrought
   To cast a stone, a quarry, or a dart,
From whence, like thunder's dint, or lightnings new,
Against the bulwarks stones and lances flew :

XXXII.

His men-at-arms did back his bands on foot:
   The light-horse ride far off, and serve for wings.
He gave the sign ; so mighty was the rout
   Of those that shot with bows and cast with slings,
Such storms of shafts and stones flew all about,
   That many a Pagan proud to death it brings :
Some died, some at the loops durst scarce out peep,
Some fled and left the place they took to keep.

XXXIII.

The hardy Frenchmen, full of heat and haste,
   Ran boldly forward to the ditches large,
And o'er their heads an iron penthouse vast
   They built, by joining many a shield and targe :
Some with their engines ceaseless shot and cast,
   And volleys huge of arrows sharp discharge ;
Upon the ditches some employ'd their pain,
To fill the moat and even it with the plain.

XXXIV.

With slime or mud the ditches were not soft,
   But dry and sandy, void of waters clear ;
Though large and deep, the Christians fill them oft
   With rubbish, fagots, stones, and trees they bear.
Adrastus first advanc'd his crest aloft,
   And boldly 'gan a strong scalado rear,
And through the falling storm did upward climb
Of stones, darts, arrows, fire, pitch, and lime.

XXXV.

The hardy Switzer now so far was gone,
  That half-way-up with mickle pain he got,
A thousand weapons he sustain'd alone,
  And his audacious climbing ceased not ;
At last upon him fell a mighty stone,
  As from some engine great it had been shot,
It broke his helm, he tumbled from the height ;
The strong Circassian cast that wond'rous weight.

XXXVI.

Not mortal was the blow, yet with the fall
  On earth sore bruis'd the man lay in a swoon.
Argantes 'gan with boasting words to call,—
  Who cometh next ? this first is tumbled down :
Come, hardy soldiers, come, assault this wall ;
  I will not shrink, nor fly, nor hide my crown ;
If in your trench yourselves for dread you hold,
There shall you die, like sheep kill'd in their fold.—

XXXVII.

Thus boasted he ; but in their trenches deep
  The hidden squadrons kept themselves from scath ;
The curtain made of shields did well off keep
  Both darts and shot, and scorned all their wrath.
But now the ram, upon the rampire's steep,
  On mighty beams his head advanced hath,
With dreadful horns of iron tough tree-great ;
The walls and bulwarks trembled at his threat.

XXXVIII.

An hundred able men meanwhile let fall
  The weights behind, the engine tumbled down,
And batter'd flat the battlements and wall
  (So fell Taigetus' hill on Sparta town) ;
It crush'd the steeled shield in pieces small,
  And beat the helmet to the wearer's crown,
And on the ruins of the walls and stones
Dispersed left their blood, their brains, and bones.

XXXIX.

The fierce assailants kept no longer close
  Under the shelter of their targets fine,
But their bold fronts to chance of war expose,
  And 'gainst those towers let their virtue shine :

The scaling ladders up to skies arose ;
   The ground-works deep some closely undermine ;
The walls before the Frenchmen shrink and shake,
And gaping sign of headlong falling make :

XL.

And fall'n they had (so far the strength extends
   Of that fierce ram, and his redoubted stroke),
But that the Pagans' care the place defends,
   And sav'd by warlike skill the wall nigh broke ;
For to what part soe'er the engine bends,
   There sacks of wool they place, the blow to choke,
Whose yielding breaks the strokes thereon which light ;
So weakness oft subdues the greatest might.

XLI.

While thus the worthies of the western crew
   Maintain'd their brave assault and skirmish hot,
Her mighty bow Clorinda often drew,
   And many a sharp and deadly arrow shot ;
And from her bow no steeled shaft there flew,
   But that some blood the cursed engine got,
Blood of some valiant knight or man of fame,
For that proud shootress scorned weaker game.

XLII.

The first she hit among the Christian peers
   Was the bold son of England's noble king ;
Above the trench himself he scantly rears,
   But she an arrow loosed from the string ;
The wicked steel his gauntlet breaks and tears,
   And through his right hand thrust the piercing sting :
Disabled thus from fight, he 'gan retire,
Groaning for pain, but fretting more for ire.

XLIII.

Lord Stephen of Amboise on the ditch's brim,
   And on a ladder high Clotharius, died ;
From back to breast an arrow pierced him,
   The other was shot through from side to side.
Then, as he manag'd brave his courser trim,
   On his left arm she hit the Flemings' guide ;
He stopt, and from the wound the reed out-twin'd,
But left the iron in his flesh behind.

XLIV.

As Ademare stood to behold the fight,
  High on a bank withdrawn to breathe a space,
A fatal shaft upon his forehead light,
  His hand he lifted up to feel the place,
Whereon a second arrow chanced right,
  And nail'd his hand unto his wounded face:
He fell, and with his blood distain'd the land,
His holy blood shed by a virgin's hand.

XLV.

While Palamede stood near the battlement,
  Despising perils all and all mishap,
And upward still his hardy footings bent,
  On his right eye he caught a deadly clap,
Through his right eye Clorinda's seventh shaft went,
  And in his neck broke forth a bloody gap;
He underneath that bulwark dying fell,
Which late to scale and win he trusted well.

XLVI.

Thus shot the maid.   The Duke with hard assay
  And sharp assault meanwhile the town oppress'd:
Against that part which to his camp-ward lay,
  An engine huge and wondrous he address'd,
A tower of wood, built for the town's decay,
  As high as were the walls and bulwarks best;
A turret full of men and weapons pent,
And yet on wheels it rolled, mov'd, and went.

XLVII.

This rolling fort his nigh approaches made,
  And darts and arrows spit against his foes,
As ships are wont in fight; so it assay'd
  With the strong wall to grapple and to close.
The Pagans on each side the peece invade,
  And all their force against this mass oppose;
Sometimes the wheels, sometimes the battlement,
With timber, logs, and stones, they broke and rent.

XLVIII.

So thick flew stones and darts, that no man sees
  The azure heavens, the sun his brightness lost,
The clouds of weapons, like two swarms of bees,
  Met in the air, and there each other cross'd.

And look how falling leaves drop down from trees,
  When the moist sap is nipp'd with timely frost,
Or apples in strong winds from branches fall,
The Saracines so tumbled from the wall;

XLIX.

For on their part the greatest slaughter light,
  They had no shelter 'gainst so sharp a shower;
Some left alive betook themselves to flight,
  So feared they this deadly thund'ring tower:
But Soliman stay'd like a valiant knight,
  And some with him that trusted in his power;
Argantes, with a long beech tree in hand,
Ran thither, this huge engine to withstand:

L.

With this he push'd the tower, and back it drives
  The length of all his tree, a wond'rous way:
The hardy virgin by his side arrives,
  To help Argantes in this hard assay.
The band that us'd the ram, this season, strives
  To cut the cords wherein the woolpacks lay;
Which done, the sacks down in the trenches fall,
And to the battery naked left the wall.

LI.

The tower above, the ram beneath, doth thunder;
  What lime and stone such puissance could abide?
The wall began (now bruis'd and crush'd asunder)
  Her wounded lap to open broad and wide:
Godfrey himself and his brought safely under
  The shatter'd wall, where greatest breach he spied;
Himself he saves behind his mighty targe,
A shield not us'd but in some desp'rate charge.

LII.

From hence he sees where Soliman descends
  Down to the threshold of the gaping breach,
And there it seems the mighty prince intends,
  Godfredo's hoped entrance to impeach;
Argantes (and with him the maid) defends
  The walls above, to which the tower doth reach:
His noble heart, when Godfrey this beheld,
With courage new, with wrath and valor swell'd:

LIII.

He turn'd about and to good Sigiere spake,
  Who bare his greatest shield and mighty bow :—
That sure and trusty target let me take,
  Impenetrable is that shield I know ;
Over these ruins will I passage make,
  And enter first, the way is eath and low ;
And time requires that by some noble feat
I should make known my strength and puissance great.

LIV.

He scant had spoken, scant receiv'd the targe,
  When on his leg a sudden shaft him hit,
And through that part a hole made wide and large,
  Where his strong sinews fasten'd were and knit.
Clorinda, thou this arrow did'st discharge,
  And let the Pagans bless thy hand for it,
For by that shot thou saved'st them that day
From bondage vile, from death and sure decay.

LV.

The wounded Duke, as though he felt no pain,
  Still forward went and mounted up the breach ;
His high attempt at first he nould refrain,
  And after call'd his lords with cheerful speech :
But when his leg could not his weight sustain,
  He saw his will did far his power outreach,
And more he strove his grief increas'd the more,
The bold assault he left at length therefore ;

LVI.

And with his hand he beckon'd Guelpho near,
  And said—I must withdraw me to my tent,
My place and person in mine absence bear,
  Supply my want ; let not the fight relent ;
I go, and will ere long again be here,
  I go, and straight return.—This said, he went ;
On a light steed he leap'd, and o'er the green
He rode, but rode not (as he thought) unseen.

LVII.

When Godfrey parted, parted eke the heart,
  The strength and fortune of the Christian bands ;
Courage increased in their adverse part,
  Wrath in their hearts, and vigor in their hands :

Valor, success, strength, hardiness, and art,
    Fail'd in the princes of the western lands;
Their swords were blunt, faint was their trumpet's blast,
Their sun was set, or else with clouds o'ercast.

LVIII.

Upon the bulwarks now appeared bold
    That fearful band that late for dread was fled;
The women that Clorinda's strength behold,
    Their country's love to war encouraged;
They weapons got, and fight like men they would,
    Their gowns tuck'd up, their locks were loose and spread,
Sharp darts they cast, and without dread or fear,
Expos'd their breasts to save their fortress dear.

LIX.

But that which most dismay'd the Christian knights,
    And added courage to the Pagans most,
Was Guelpho's sudden fall, in all men's sights,
    Who tumbled headlong down, his footing lost;
A mighty stone upon the worthy lights,
    But whence it came none wist, nor from what coast;
And with like blow, which more their hearts dismay'd,
Beside him low in dust old Raimond laid,

LX.

And Eustace eke: within the ditches large,
    To narrow shifts and last extremes they drive,
Upon their foes so fierce the Pagans charge,
    And with good fortune so their blows they give,
That whom they hit, in spite of helm or targe.
    They deeply wound, or else of life deprive.
At this their good success Argantes proud,
Waxing more fell, thus roar'd and cried aloud :—

LXI.

This is not Antioch, nor the evening dark
    Can help your privy sleights with friendly shade;
The sun yet shines, your falsehood can we mark,
    In other ways this bold assault is made;
Of praise and glory quenched is the spark
    That made you first these eastern lands invade:
Why cease you now? why take you not this fort?
What, are you weary for a charge so short?—

LXII.

Thus raged he, and in such hellish sort
  Increas'd the fury in the brain-sick knight,
That he esteem'd that large and ample fort
  Too strait a field wherein to prove his might ,
There where the breach had fram'd a new-made port
  Himself he plac'd, with nimble skips and light ;
He clear'd the passage out, and thus he cried
To Soliman, that fought close by his side :—

LXIII.

Come, Soliman, the time and place behold
  That of our valors well may judge the doubt ;
What stayest thou ? among these Christians bold
  First leap he forth that holds himself most stout.—
While thus his will the mighty champion told,
  Both Soliman and he at once leap'd out :
Fury the first provok'd, disdain the last,
Who scorn'd the challenge ere his lips it past.

LXIV.

Upon their foes unlooked for they flew,
  Each spited other for his virtue's sake ;
So many soldiers this fierce couple slew,
  So many shields they cleft and helms they brake,
So many ladders to the earth they threw,
  That well they seem'd a mount thereof to make,
Or else some vamure fit to save the town,
Instead of that the Christians late beat down.

LXV.

The folk that strove with rage and haste before
  Who first the wall and rampire should ascend,
Retire, and for that honor strive no more,
  Scantly they could their limbs and lives defend ;
They fled ; their engines lost the Pagans tore
  In pieces small, their rams to naught they rend,
And all unfit for further service make,
With so great force and rage their beams they brake.

LXVI.

The Pagans ran, transported with their ire,
  Now here, now there, and woful slaughters wrought,
At last they called for devouring fire,
  Two burning pines against the tower they brought :

So from the palace of their hellish sire
  (When all this world they would consume to naught)
The fury sisters come with fire in hands,
Shaking their snaky locks and sparkling brands.

LXVII.

But noble Tancred, who this while applied,
  Gave exhortations to his bold Latines ;
When of these knights the wond'rous acts he spied,
  And saw the champions with their burning pines,
He left his talk and thither forthwith hied,
  To stop the rage of those fell Saracines,
And with such force the fight he there renewed,
That now they fled and lost who late pursued.

LXVIII.

Thus chang'd the state and fortune of the fray.
  Meanwhile the wounded Duke, in grief and teen,
Within his great pavilion rich and gay,
  Good Sigiere and Baldwin stood between :
His other friends, whom his mishap dismay,
  With grief and tears about assembled been :
He strove in haste the weapon out to wind,
And broke the reed, but left the head behind.

LXIX.

He bade them take the speediest way they might,
  Of that unlucky hurt to make him sound,
And to lay ope the depth thereof to sight ;
  He will'd them open, search, and lance the wound.—
Send me again (quoth he) to end this fight,
  Before the sun be sunken under ground.—
And leaning on a broken spear, he thrust
His leg straight out to him that cure it must.

LXX.

Erotimus, born on the banks of Po,
  Was he that undertook to cure the knight ;
All what green herbs or waters pure could do,
  He knew their power, their virtue, and their might ;
A noble poet was the man also ;
  But in this science he had more delight ;
He could restore to health death-wounded men,
And make their names immortal with his pen.

LXXI.

The mighty Duke yet never changed cheer,
    But griev'd to see his friends lamenting stand :
The leach prepar'd his cloths and cleansing gear,
    And with a belt his gown about him band ;
Now with his herbs the steely head to tear
    Out of the flesh he prov'd, now with his hand ;
Now with his hand, now with his instrument,
He shak'd and pluck'd it, yet not forth it went :

LXXII.

His labor vain, his art prevailed naught,
    His luck was ill although his skill was good :
To such extremes the wounded Prince he brought,
    That with fell pain he swooned as he stood.
But th' angel pure (that kept him) went and sought
    Divine dictamnum out of Ida wood ;
This herb is rough and bears a purple flower,
And in his budding leaves lies all his power :

LXXIII.

Kind nature first upon the craggy clift,
    Bewray'd this herb unto the mountain goat,
That when her sides a cruel shaft hath rift,
    With it she shakes the reed out of her coat.
This in a moment fetch'd the angel swift,
    And brought from Ida hill, though far remote ;
The juice whereof in a prepared bath,
Unseen the blessed spirit poured hath :

LXXIV.

Pure nectar from that spring of Lydia then,
    And panaces divine, therein he threw :
The cunning leach to bathe the wound began,
    And of itself the steely head out flew ;
The bleeding staunch'd, no vermile drop out-ran ;
    The leg again wax'd strong, with vigor new :
Erotimus cried out—This hurt and wound
No human art or hand so soon makes sound ;

LXXV.

Some angel good I think, come down from skies,
    Thy surgeon is, for here plain tokens are
Of grace divine, to which thy help applies :
    Thy weapon take, and haste again to war.—

In pretious cloths his leg the chieftain ties,
　　Naught could the man from blood and fight debar ;
A sturdy lance in his right hand he braced,
His shield he took, and on his helmet laced ;

LXXVI.

And with a thousand knights and barons bold
　　Towards the town he hasted from his camp ;
In clouds of dust was Titan's face enroll'd
　　Trembled the earth whereon the worthies stamp ;
His foes far off his dreadful looks behold,
　　Which in their hearts of courage quench'd the lamp,
A chilling fear ran cold through every vein.
Lord Godfrey shouted thrice and all his train :

LXXVII.

The sovereign's voice his hardy people knew,
　　And his loud cries that cheer'd each fearful heart ;
Thereat new strength they took and courage new,
　　And to the fierce assault again they start.
The Pagans twain this while themselves withdrew
　　Within the breach, to save that batter'd part,
And with great loss a skirmish hot they hold
Against Tancredie and his squadron bold.

LXXVIII.

Thither came Godfrey, armed round about
　　In trusty plate, with fierce and dreadful look :
At first approach against Argantes stout,
　　Headed with poignant steel, a lance he shook ;
No casting engine with such force throws out
　　A knotty spear, and as the way it took
It whistled in the air : the fearless knight
Oppos'd his shield against that weapon's might :

LXXIX.

The dreadful blow quite through his target drove,
　　And bored through his breast-plate strong and thick,
The tender skin it in his bosom rove,
　　The purple blood outstreamed from the quick.
To wrest it out the wounded Pagan strove,
　　And little leisure gave it there to stick ;
At Godfrey's head the lance again he cast,
And said—Lo, there again thy dart thou hast.—

LXXX.

The spear flew back the way it lately came,
  And would revenge the harm itself had done,
But miss'd the mark whereat the man did aim,
  He stepp'd aside the furious blow to shun :
But Sigiere in his throat receiv'd the same,
  The murdering weapon at his neck out-run ;
Nor aught it griev'd the man to lose his breath,
Since in his Prince's stead he suffer'd death.

LXXXI.

Ev'n then the Soldan struck, with monstrous main,
  The noble leader of the Norman band ;
He reel'd awhile and stagger'd with the pain,
  And wheeling round fell grov'ling on the sand.
Godfrey no longer could the grief sustain
  Of these displeasures, but with flaming brand
Up to the breach in heat and haste he goes,
And hand to hand there combats with his foes :

LXXXII.

And there great wonders surely wrought he had,
  Mortal the fight, and fierce had been the fray,
But that dark night, from her pavilion sad,
  Her cloudy wings did on the earth display,
Her quiet shades she interposed, glad
  To cause the knights their arms aside to lay.
Godfrey withdrew, and to their tents they wend,
And thus this bloody day was brought to end.

LXXXIII.

The weak and wounded, ere he left the field,
  The godly Duke to safety thence convey'd,
Nor to his foes his engines would he yield,
  In them his hope to win the fortress laid ;
Then to the tower he went and it behield,
  The tower that late the Pagan lords dismay'd,
But now stood bruised, broken, crack'd, and shivered,
From some sharp storm as it were late delivered ;

LXXXIV.

From dangers great escap'd but late it was,
  And now to safety brought well nigh it seems ;
But as a ship that under sail doth pass
  The roaring billows and the raging streams,

And drawing nigh the wished port, alas!
   Breaks on some hidden rock her ribs and beams;
Or as a steed rough ways that well hath past,
Before his inn stumbleth and falls at last;

LXXXV.

Such hap befel that tower; for on that side
   'Gainst which the Pagans' force and batt'ry bend,
Two wheels were broke whereon the peece should ride,
   The maimed engine could no farther wend:
The troop that guarded it that part provide
   To underprop with posts, and it defend,
Till carpenters and cunning workmen came,
Whose skill should help and rear again the same.

LXXXVI.

Thus Godfrey bids, and that ere springing day
   The cracks and bruises all amend they should;
Each open passage and each privy way
   About the peece he kept with soldiers bold:
But the loud rumor both of that they say
   And that they do is heard within the hold;
A thousand lights about the tower they view,
And what they wrought all night both saw and knew.

BOOK XII.

I.

Now in dark night was all the world imbar'd,
   But yet the tired armies took no rest,
The careful French kept heedful watch and ward,
   While their high tower the workmen newly dress'd :
The Pagan crew to reinforce prepar'd
   The weaken'd bulwarks, late to earth down kest,
Their rampires broke and bruised walls to mend :
Lastly their hurts the wounded knights attend :

II.

Their wounds were dress'd ; part of the work was brought
   To wished end, part left to other days.
A dull desire to rest deep midnight wrought,
   His heavy rod sleep on their eye-lids lays :
Yet rested not Clorinda's working thought,
   Which thirsted still for fame and warlike praise ;
Argantes eke accompanied the maid
From place to place, who to herself thus said :—

III.

This day Argantes strong and Soliman
   Strange things have done, and purchas'd great renown,
Among our foes out of the walls they ran,
   Their rams they broke and rent their engines down :

I us'd my bow, of naught else boast I can ;
   Myself stood safe meanwhile within this town,
And happy was my shot and prosp'rous too,
But that was all a woman's hand could do.

IV.

On birds and beasts in forests wild that feed
   It were more fit mine arrows to bestow,
Than for a feeble maid in warlike deed
   With strong and hardy knights herself to show :
Why take I not again my virgin weeds,
   And spend my days in secret cell unknow ?—
Thus thought, thus mused, thus devis'd the maid,
And turning to the knight, at last thus said ;—

V.

My thoughts are full, my lord, of strange desire
   Some high attempt of war to undertake ;
Whether high God my mind therewith inspire,
   Or of his will his god mankind doth make ;
Among our foes behold the light and fire ;
   I will among them wend, and burn or break
The tower ; God grant therein I have my will,
And that perform'd, betide me good or ill.

VI.

But if it fortune such my chance should be,
   That to this town I never turn again,
Mine eunuch (whom I dearly love) with thee
   I leave ; my faithful maids, and all my train ;
To Egypt then conducted safely see
   Those woful damsels, and that aged swain ;
Help them, my lord, in that distressed case,
Their feeble sex, his age, deserveth grace.

VII.

Argantes wond'ring stood, and felt th' effect
   Of true renown pierce through his glorious mind ;—
And wilt thou go (quoth he) and me neglect,
   Disgrac'd, despis'd, leave in this fort behind ?
Shall I, while these strong walls my life protect,
   Behold thy flames and fires toss'd in the wind ?
No, no, thy fellow have I been in arms,
And will be still, in praise, in death, in harms.

VIII.

This heart of mine death's bitter stroke despiseth,
    For praise this life, for glory take this breath.—
My soul the more (quoth she) thy friendship prizeth,
    For this thy proffer'd aid requir'd uneath ;
I but a woman am, no loss ariseth
    To this besieged city by my death ;
But if (as God forbid) this night thou fall,
Ah ! who shall then, who can, defend this wall ?

IX.

Too late these 'scuses vain (the knight replied)
    You bring, my will is firm, my mind is set ;
I follow you whereso you list me guide,
    Or go before if you my purpose let.—
This said, they hasted to the palace wide,
    About their prince where all his lords were met ;
Clorinda spoke for both, and said—Sir King,
Attend my words, hear, and allow the thing :

X.

Argantes here, this bold and hardy knight,
    Will undertake to burn the wond'rous tow'r,
And I with him ; only we stay till night
    Bury in sleep our foes at deadest hour.—
The King with that cast up his hands on hight,
    The tears for joy upon his cheeks down pour ;
Praised (quoth he) be Macon whom we serve !
This land I see he keeps, and will preserve :

XI.

Nor shall so soon this shaken kingdom fall,
    While such unconquer'd hearts my state defend :
But for this act what praise or guerdon shall
    I give your virtues, which so far extend ?
Let fame your praises sound through nations all,
    And fill the world therewith to either end ;
Take half my wealth and kingdom for your meed,
You are rewarded half ev'n with the deed.—

XII.

Thus spake the Prince, and gently 'gan distrain
    Now him, now her, between his friendly arms.
The Soldan by, no longer could refrain
    That noble envy which his bosom warms :

Nor I (quoth he) bear this broad sword in vain,
  Nor yet am unexpert in night alarms ;
Take me with you.—Ah (quoth Clorinda) no !
Whom leave we here of prowess if you go ?—

XIII.

This spoken, ready with a proud refuse
  Argantes was his proffer'd aid to scorn,
Whom Aladine prevents, and with excuse
  To Soliman thus 'gan his speeches turn :—
Right, noble Prince, as aye hath been your use,
  Yourself so still you bear, and long have borne,
Bold in all acts, no danger can affright
Your heart, nor tired is your strength with fight :

XIV.

If you went forth, great things perform you would
  In my conceit, yet far unfit it seems
That you (who most excel in courage bold)
  At once should leave this town in these extremes ;
Nor would I that these twain should leave this hold ;
  My heart their noble lives far worthier deems,
If this attempt of less importance were,
Or weaker posts so great a weight could bear :

XV.

But, for well guarded is the mighty tower,
  With hardy troops and squadrons round about,
And cannot harmed be with little power,
  Nor fits the time to send whole armies out ;
This pair, who past have many a dreadful stour,
  And proffer now to prove this venture stout,
Alone to this attempt let them go forth,
Alone than thousands of more price and worth.

XVI.

Thou (as it best beseems a mighty king)
  With ready bands beside the gate attend,
That when this couple have perform'd the thing,
  And shall again their footsteps homeward bend,
From their strong foes upon them following
  Thou mayst them keep, preserve, save, and defend.—
Thus said the King ; the Soldan must consent ;
Silent remain'd the Turk, and discontent.

XVII.

Then Ismen said :—You twain that undertake
  This hard attempt, awhile I pray you stay,
Till I a wild-fire of fine temper make,
  That this great engine burn to ashes may ;
Haply the guard, that now doth watch and wake,
  Will then lie tumbled sleeping on the lay.—
Thus they conclude, and in their chambers sit
To wait the time for this adventure fit.

XVIII.

Clorinda there her silver arms off rent,
  Her helm, her shield, her hawberk shining bright ;
An armor black as jet or coal she hent,
  Wherein without a plume herself she dight ;
For thus disguis'd amid her foes she meant
  To pass unseen, by help of friendly night ;
To whom her eunuch, old Arsetes, came,
That from her cradle nurs'd and kept the dame.

XIX.

This aged sire had follow'd far and near,
  Through lands and seas, the strong and hardy maid,
He saw her leave her arms and wonted gear,
  Her danger nigh that sudden change foresaid :
By his white locks, from black that changed were
  In following her, the woful man her pray'd,
By all his service and his taken pain,
To leave that fond attempt ; but pray'd in vain.

XX.

At last quoth he—Since, harden'd to thine ill,
  Thy cruel heart is to thy loss prepar'd,
That my weak age, nor tears that down distil,
  Nor humble suit, nor plaint, thou list regard ;
Attend awhile, strange things unfold I will,
  Hear both thy birth and high estate declar'd ;
Follow my counsel, or thy will, that done.—
She fit to hear, the eunuch thus begun :—

XXI.

Senapus rul'd, and yet perchance doth reign,
  In mighty Ethiope and her deserts waste ;
The lore of Christ both he and all his train
  Of people black hath kept and long embrac'd :

To him a Pagan was I sold for gain,
    And with his queen (as her chief eunuch) plac'd.
Black was this queen as jet, yet on her eyes
    Sweet loveliness in black attired lies.

XXII.

The fire of love and frost of jealousy
    Her husband's troubled soul alike torment ;
The tide of fond suspicion flowed high,
    The foe to love, and plague to sweet content ;
He mew'd her up from sight of mortal eye,
    Nor day he would his beams on her had bent :
She, wise and lowly, by her husband's pleasure
Her joy, her peace, her will, her wish, did measure.

XXIII.

Her prison was a chamber, painted round
    With goodly portraits and with stories old :
As white as snow there stood a virgin bound
    Beside a dragon fierce ; a champion bold
The monster did with poignant spear through wound ;
    The gored beast lay dead upon the mould.
The gentle queen before this image laid,
She plain'd, she mourn'd, she wept, she sigh'd, she play'd.

XXIV.

At last with child she prov'd, and forth she brought
    (And thou art she) a daughter fair and bright ;
In her thy color white new terror wrought,
    She wonder'd on thy face with strange affright ;
But yet she purpos'd in her fearful thought
    To hide thee from the king thy father's sight,
Lest thy bright hue should his suspect approve,
For seld a crow begets a silver dove.

XXV.

And to her spouse to show she was dispos'd
    A negro's babe, late born, in room of thee ;
And for the tower wherein she lay enclos'd
    Was with her damsels only wond and me,
To me, on whose true faith she most repos'd,
    She gave thee, ere thou couldest christen'd be ;
Nor could I since find means thee to baptize,
In Pagan lands thou know'st it's not the guise.

XXVI.

To me she gave thee, and she wept withal,
    To foster thee in some far distant place :
Who can her griefs and plaints to reck'ning call,
    How oft she swooned at the last embrace ?
Her streaming tears amid her kisses fall,
    Her sighs her dire complaints did interlace :
And looking up at last—O God ! quoth she,
Who dost my heart and inward mourning see,

XXVII.

If mind and body spotless to this day,
    If I have kept my bed still undefil'd
(Not for myself, a sinful wretch, I pray,
    That in thy presence am an abject vilde),
Preserve this babe, whose mother must denay
    To nourish it, preserve this harmless child ;
Oh let it live, and chaste like me it make,
But for good fortune elsewhere sample take.

XXVIII.

Thou heav'nly soldier, which deliver'd hast
    That sacred virgin from the serpent old,
If on thine altars I have offerings plac'd,
    And sacrific'd myrrh, frankincense, and gold,
On this poor child thy heav'nly looks down cast,
    With gracious eye this seely babe behold.—
This said, her strength and living sprite was fled,
She sigh'd, she groan'd, she swooned in her bed.

XXIX.

Weeping I took thee ; in a little chest,
    Cover'd with herbs and leaves, I brought thee out
So secretly, that none of all the rest
    Of such an act suspicion had or doubt ;
To wilderness my steps I first address'd,
    Where horrid shades inclos'd me round about :
A tigress there I met, in whose fierce eyes
Fury and wrath, rage, death, and terror lies.

XXX.

Up to a tree I leapt, and on the grass
    (Such was my sudden fear) I left thee lying :
To thee the beast with furious course did pass,
    With curious looks upon thy visage prying,

All suddenly both meek and mild she was,
   With friendly cheer thy tender body eyeing ;
At last she lick'd thee, and with gesture mild
About thee play'd, and thou upon her smil'd.

XXXI.

Her fearful muzzle, full of dreadful threat,
   In thy weak hand thou took'st, withouten dread ;
The gentle beast with milk-outstretched teat
   (As nurses custom) proffer'd thee to feed.
As one that wond'reth on some marvel great,
   I stood this while amazed at the deed.
When thee she saw were fill'd and satisfied,
Unto the woods again the tigress hied.

XXXII.

She gone, down from the tree I came in haste,
   And took thee up, and on my journey wend.
Within a little thorpe I stay'd at last,
   And to a nurse the charge of thee commend ;
And sporting with thee there long time I past,
   Till term of sixteen months were brought to end,
And thou began (as little children do)
With half-clipt words to prattle, and to go.

XXXIII.

But having past the August of mine age,
   When more than half my tap of life was run,
Rich by rewards given by your mother sage,
   For merits past and service yet undone,
I long'd to leave this wand'ring pilgrimage,
   And in my native soil again to won ;
To get some seely home I had desire,
Loth still to warm me at another's fire.

XXXIV.

To Egypt-ward, where I was born, I went,
   And bore thee with me by a rolling flood,
Till I with savage thieves well nigh was hent ;
   Before the brook, the thieves behind me stood :
Thee to forsake I never could consent,
   And gladly would I 'scape those outlaws wood : .
Into the flood I leapt far from the brim,
My left hand bore thee, with the right I swim.

XXXV.

Swift was the current; in the middle stream
  A whirlpool gaped with devouring jaws,
The gulf (on such mishap ere I could dream)
  Into his deep abyss my carcass draws:
There I forsook thee; the wild waters seem
  To pity thee; a gentle wind there blows,
Whose friendly puffs safe to the shore thee drive,
Where wet and weary I at last arrive.

XXXVI.

I took thee up, and in my dream that night
  (When buried was the world in sleep and shade)
I saw a champion clad in armor bright,
  That o'er my head shaked a flaming blade:
He saw—I charge thee execute aright
  That charge this infant's mother on thee laid;
Baptize the child, high Heav'n esteems her dear,
And I her keeper will attend her near:

XXXVII.

I will her keep, defend, save, and protect;
  I made the waters mild, the tigress tame:
O wretch, that heav'nly warnings doth reject:—
  The warrior vanish'd having said the same.
I rose and journey'd on my way direct,
  When blushing morn from Titan's bed forth came;
But, for my faith is true and sure I ween,
And dreams are false, you still unchristened been.

XXXVIII.

A Pagan, therefore, thee I fostered have,
  Nor of thy birth the truth did ever tell.
Since you increased are in courage brave,
  Your sex and nature's self you both excel;
Full many a realm have you made bond and slave,
  Your fortunes last yourself remember well,
And how in peace and war, in joy and teen,
I have your servant and your tutor been.

XXXIX.

Last morn, from skies ere stars exiled were,
  In deep and death-like sleep my senses drown'd,
The self-same vision did again appear,
  With stormy wrathful looks and thund'ring sound:—

Villain, quoth he, within short while thy dear
 Must change her life and leave this sinful ground;
Thine be the loss, the torment, and the care—
This said, he fled through skies, through clouds, and air.

XL.

Hear then, my joy, my hope, my darling, hear!
 High heav'n some dire misfortune threatened hath,
Displeas'd, pardie, because I did thee lear
 A lore repugnant to thy parents' faith.
Ah! for my sake this bold attempt forbear;
 Put off these sable arms, appease thy wrath.—
This said, he wept: she pensive stood and sad,
Because like dream herself but lately had.

XLI.

With cheerful smile she answered him at last—
 I will this faith observe, it seems me true,
Which from my cradle age thou taught me hast;
 I will not change it for religion new,
Nor with vain shows of fear and dread aghast,
 This enterprise forbear I to pursue;
No, not if death, in his most dreadful face
Wherewith he scareth mankind, kept the place.—

XLII.

Approaching 'gan the time (while thus she spake)
 Wherein they ought that dreadful hazard try.
She to Argantes went, who should partake
 Of her renown and praise, or with her die.
Ismen, with words more hasty, still did make
 Their virtue great, which by itself did fly;
Two balls he gave them made of hollow brass,
Wherein inclos'd fire, pitch, and brimstone was.

XLIII.

And forth they went, and over dale and hill
 They hasted forward with a speedy pace,
Unseen, unmarked, undescried, until
 Beside the engine close themselves they place:
New courage there their swelling hearts did fill,
 Rage in their breasts, fury shone in their face,
They yearn'd to blow the fire, and draw the sword;
The watch descried them both, and gave the word.

XLIV.

Silent they passed on ; the watch begun
   To rear a huge alarm with hideous cries ;
Therewith the hardy couple forward run
   To execute their valiant enterprise :
So from a cannon or a roaring gun
   At once the noise, the flame and bullet flies.
They run, they give the charge, begin the fray,
And all at once their foes break, spoil, and slay.

XLV.

They passed first through thousand thousand blows,
   And then performed their designments bold ;
A fiery ball each on the engine throws ;
   The stuff was dry, the fire took quickly hold ;
Furious upon the timber work it grows ;
   How it increased cannot well be told,
How it crept up the peece, and how to skies
The burning sparks and tow'ring smoke upflies.

XLVI.

A mass of solid fire, burning bright,
   Roll'd up in smould'ring fumes there bursteth out ;
And there the blust'ring winds add strength and might,
   And gather close the 'spersed flames about.
The Frenchmen trembled at the dreadful sight,
   To arms in haste and fear ran all the rout :
Down fell the peece, dreaded so much in war ;
Thus, what long days doth make one hour doth mar.

XLVII.

Two Christian bands this while came to the place
   With speedy haste, where they beheld the fire ;
Argantes to them cried with scornful grace,—
   Your blood shall quench these flames and quench mine ire ;
This said, the maid and he with sober pace
   Drew back, and to the bank themselves retire.
Faster than brooks which falling showers increase
Their foes augment, and faster on them prease.

XLVIII.

The golden port was open'd, and forth stept,
   With all his soldiers bold, the Turkish king,
Ready to aid them two his force he kept,
   When fortune should them home with conquest bring.

Over the bars the hardy couple leapt,
   And after them a band of Christians fling,
Whom Soliman drove back with courage stout,
And shut the gate, but shut Clorinda out.

XLIX.

Alone was she shut forth, for in that hour
   Wherein they clos'd the port, the virgin went,
And, full of heat and wrath, her strength and power
   'Gainst Arimon (that struck her erst) she bent.
She slew the knight ; nor Argant, in that stower,
   Wist of her parting or her fierce intent :
The fight, the prease, the night, and darksome skies,
Care from his heart had ta'en, sight from his eyes.

L.

But when appeased was her angry mood,
   Her fury calm'd, and settled was her head,
She saw the gates were shut, and how she stood
   Amid her foes, she held herself for dead.
While none her mark'd, at last she thought it good
   To save her life some other path to tread ;
She feigned her one of them, and close she drew
Amid the prease, that none her saw nor knew.

LI.

Then as a wolf, guilty of some misdeed,
   Flies to some grove to hide himself from view,
So, favor'd with the night, with secret speed,
   Dissever'd from the prease, the damsel flew.
Tancred alone of her escape took heed ;
   He on that quarter was arrived new ;
When Arimon she kill'd he thither came,
He saw it, mark'd it, and pursued the dame :

LII.

He deem'd she was some man of mickle might,
   And on her person would he worship win,
Over the hills the nymph her journey dight,
   Towards another port, there to get in.
With hideous noise fast after spurr'd the knight.
   She heard and stay'd, and thus her words begin :
What haste hast thou ? ride softly ; take thy breath ;
What bringest thou ?—He answer'd, War and death.—

LIII.

And war and death (quoth she) here mayst thou get,
  If thou for battle come :—with that she stay'd.
Tancred to ground his foot in haste down set,
  And left his steed ; on foot he saw the maid.
Their courage hot, their ire and wrath they whet,
  And either champion drew a trenchant blade :
Together ran they and together struck,
Like two fierce bulls whom rage and love provoke.

LIV.

Worthy of royal lists and brightest day,
  Worthy a golden trump and laurel crown,
The actions were and wonders of that fray,
  Which sable night did in dark bosom drown.
Yet, night, consent that I their acts display,
  And make their deeds to future ages known,
And in records of long enduring story,
Enrol their praise, their fame, their worth, and glory.

LV.

They neither shrunk nor 'vantage sought of ground,
  They travers'd not, nor skipt from part to part,
Their blows were neither false nor feigned found ;
  The night, their rage, would let them use no art ;
Their swords together clash with dreadful sound,
  Their feet stand fast, and neither stir nor start ;
They move their hands, steadfast their feet remain,
Nor blow nor foin they struck or thrust in vain.

LVI.

Shame bred desire a sharp revenge to take,
  And veng'ance taken gave new cause of shame ;
So that with haste and little heed they strake,
  Fuel enough they had to feed the flame.
At last so close their battle fierce they make,
  They could not wield their swords, so nigh they came ;
They us'd the hilts, and each on other rush'd,
And helm to helm and shield to shield they crush'd.

LVII.

Thrice his strong arms he folds about her waist,
  And thrice was forc'd to let the virgin go,
For she disdained to be so embrac'd,
  No lover would have strain'd his mistress so :

They took their swords again, and each enchas'd
　　Deep wounds in the soft flesh of his strong foe ;
Till weak and weary, faint, alive, uneath
They both retired at once, at once took breath :

LVIII.

Each other long beheld, and leaning stood
　　Upon their swords, whose points in earth were pight,
When daybreak rising from the eastern flood,
　　Put forth the thousand eyes of blindfold night :
Tancred beheld his foe's out-streaming blood
　　And gaping wounds, and wax'd proud was the sight.
O vanity of man's unstable mind,
Puft up with every blast of friendly wind !

LIX.

Why joy'st thou, wretch ? O what shall be thy gain ?
　　What trophy for this conquest is 't thou rears ?
Thine eyes shall shed (in case thou be not slain)
　　For every drop of blood a sea of tears,
The bleeding warriors leaning thus remain,
　　Each one to speak one word long time forbears ;
Tancred the silence broke at last, and said,
(For he would know with whom this fight he made :)—

LX.

Ill is our chance, and hard our fortune is,
　　Who here in silence and in shade debate,
Where light of sun and witness all we miss,
　　That should our prowess and our praise dilate :
If words in arms find place, yet grant me this,
　　Tell me thy name, thy country, and estate,
That I may know (this dang'rous combat done)
Whom I have conquer'd, or who hath me won.—

LXI.

What I nill tell you ask (quoth she) in vain,
　　Nor mov'd by prayer, nor constrain'd by power ;
But this much know, I am one of those twain
　　Who late with kindled fire destroy'd the tower.—
Tancred, at her proud words, swell'd with disdain :
　　That hast thou said (quoth he) in evil hour ;
Thy vaunting speeches, and thy silence both,
Uncivil wretch, hath made my heart more wroth.—

LXII.

Ire in their chafed breasts renew'd the fray ;
  Fierce was the fight, though feeble was their might ;
Their strength was gone, their cunning was away,
  And fury in their stead maintain'd the fight :
Their swords both points and edges sharp embay
  In purple blood whereso they hit or light ;
And if weak life yet in their bosoms lie,
They liv'd because they both disdain'd to die.

LXIII.

As Ægean's seas, when storms be calm'd again
  That roll'd their tumbling waves with troublous blast,
Do yet of tempests past some show retain,
  And here and there their swelling billows cast ;
So, though their strength were gone, and might were vain,
  Of their first fierceness still the fury lasts ;
Wherewith sustain'd, they to their tackling stood,
And heaped wound on wound, and blood on blood.

LXIV.

But now, alas ! the fatal hour arrives
  That her sweet life must leave that tender hold ;
His sword into her bosom deep he drives,
  And bath'd in lukewarm blood his iron cold ;
Between her breasts the cruel weapon rives
  Her curious square embost with swelling gold ;
Her knees grow weak, the pains of death she feels,
And, like a falling cedar, bends and reels.

LXV.

The Prince his hand upon her shield doth stretch,
  And low on earth the wounded damsel laith,
And while she fell, with weak and woful speech
  Her prayers last and last complaints she saith :
A spirit new did her those prayers teach,
  Spirit of hope, of charity, and faith ;
And though her life to Christ rebellious were,
Yet died she his child and handmaid dear.—

LXVI.

Friend, thou hast won ; I pardon thee ; nor save
  This body, that all torments can endure,
But save my soul ; baptism I dying crave,
  Come, wash away my sins with waters pure.—

His heart relenting nigh in sunder rave,
    With woful speech of that sweet creature ;
So that his rage, his wrath, and anger died,
And on his cheeks salt tears for ruth down slide.

LXVII.

With murmur loud down from the mountain's side
    A little runnel tumbled near the place,
Thither he ran and filled his helmet wide,
    And quick return'd to do that work of grace :
With trembling hands her beaver he untied,
    Which done, he saw, and seeing knew her face,
And lost therewith his speech and moving quite ;
O woful knowledge ! ah unhappy sight !

LXVIII.

He died not, but all his strength unites,
    And to his virtues gave his heart in guard ;
Bridling his grief, with water he requites
    The life that he bereft with iron hard :
And while the sacred words the knight recites,
    The nymph to heav'n with joy herself prepar'd ;
And as her life decays her joys increase ;
She smil'd and said—Farewell ! I die in peace.—

LXIX.

As violets blue 'mongst lilies pure men throw,
    So paleness 'midst her native white begun.
Her looks to heav'n she cast ; their eyes, I trow,
    Downward for pity bent both heav'n and sun.
Her naked hand she gave the knight, in show
    Of love and peace ; her speech, alas ! was done.
And thus the virgin fell on endless sleep.
Love, beauty, virtue, for your darling weep !

LXX.

But when he saw her gentle soul was went,
    His manly courage to relent began ;
Grief, sorrow, anguish, sadness, discontent,
    Free empire got and lordship on the man,
His life within his heart they close up pent,
    Death through his senses and his visage ran ;
Like his dead lady dead seem'd Tancred good,
In paleness, stillness, wounds, and streams of blood :

LXXI.

And his weak sprite (to be unbodied
   From fleshly prison free that ceaseless strived)
Had followed her fair soul but lately fled,
   Had not a Christian squadron there arrived,
To seek fresh water thither haply led,
   And found the Princess dead, and him deprived
Of signs of life ; yet did the knight remain
On live, nigh dead, for her himself had slain.

LXXII.

Their guide far off the Prince knew by his shield,
   And thither hasted full of grief and fear,
Her dead, him seeming so, he there beheld,
   And for that strange mishap shed many a tear :
He would not leave the corses fair in field
   For food to wolves, though she a Pagan were,
But in their arms the soldiers both uphent,
And both lamenting brought to Tancred's tent.

LXXIII.

With these dear burdens to their camp they pass,
   Yet would not that dead-seeming knight awake ;
At last he deeply groan'd, which token was
   His feeble soul had not her flight yet take :
The other lay a still and heavy mass,
   Her spirit had that earthen cage forsake.
Thus were they brought, and thus they placed were
In sundry rooms, yet both adjoining near.

LXXIV.

All skill and art his careful servants used
   To life again their dying lord to bring ;
At last his eyes unclos'd, with tears suffused,
   He felt their hands and heard their whispering ;
But how he thither came long time he mused,
   His mind astonish'd was with everything :
He gaz'd about, his squires in fine he knew,
Then weak and woful thus his plaints out threw :—

LXXV.

What ! live I yet ? and do I breathe and see
   Of this accursed day the hateful light,
This spiteful ray which still upbraideth me
   With that accursed deed I did this night ?

Ah, coward hand ! afraid why should'st thou be ?
   (Thou instrument of death, shame, and despite !)
Why should'st thou fear, with sharp and trenchant knife
To cut the thread of this blood-guilty life !

LXXVI.

Pierce through this bosom, and my cruel heart
   In pieces cleave, break every string and vein !
But thou, to slaughters vile which used art,
   Think'st it were pity so to ease my pain :
Of luckless love therefore in torments smart
   A sad example must I still remain ;
A woful monster of unhappy love,
Who still must live, lest death his comfort prove :

LXXVII.

Still must I live in anguish, grief, and care ;
   Furies my guilty conscience that torment,
The ugly shades, dark night, and troubled air,
   In grisly forms her slaughter still present ;
Madness and death about my bed repair,
   Hell gapeth wide to swallow up his tent ;
Swift from myself I run, myself I fear,
Yet still my hell within myself I bear.

LXXVIII.

But where, alas ! where be those relics sweet,
   Wherein dwelt late all love, all joy, all good ?
My fury left them cast in open street ;
   Some beast hath torn her flesh and lick'd her blood,
Ah ! noble prey for savage beast unmeet !
   Ah ! sweet, too sweet, and far too precious food,
Ah ! seely nymph ! whom night and darksome shade
To beasts and me (far worse than beasts) betray'd.

LXXIX.

But where you be, if still you be, I wend
   To gather up those relics dear at least :
But if some beast hath from the hills descend,
   And on her tender bowels made his feast,
Let that self monster me in pieces rend,
   And deep entomb me in his hollow chest ;
For where she buried is there shall I have
A stately tomb, a rich and costly grave.—

Thus mourn'd the knight : his squires him told at last
  They had her there for whom these tears he shed :
A beam of comfort his dim eyes outcast,
  Like lightning through thick clouds of darkness spread ;
The heavy burden of his limbs in haste,
  With mickle pain, he drew forth of his bed,
And scant of strength to stand, to move, or go,
Thither he stagger'd, reeling to and fro.

LXXXI

When he came there, and in her breast espied
  (His handiwork) that deep and cruel wound,
And her sweet face with leaden paleness dyed,
  Where beauty late spread forth her beams around,
He trembled so, that near his squires beside
  To hold him up, he had sunk down to ground ;
And said—O face ! in death still sweet and fair,
Thou canst not sweeten yet my grief and care.

O fair right hand ! the pledge of faith and love,
  Given me but late, too late, in sign of peace,
How haps it now thou canst not stir nor move ?
  And you, dear limbs ! now laid in rest and ease,
Through which my cruel blade this flood-gate rove,
  Your pains have end, my torments never cease :
O hands ! O cruel eyes ! accurs'd alike,
You gave the wound, you gave them light to strike :

LXXXIII

But thither now run forth my guilty blood,
  Whither my plaints, my sorrows cannot wend.—
He said no more ; but, as his passion wood
  Enforced him, he 'gan to tear and rend
His hair, his face, his wounds ; a purple flood
  Did from each side in rolling streams descend :
He had been slain, but that his pain and wo
Bereft his senses, and preserv'd him so.

Cast on his bed, his squires recall'd his sprite
  To execute again her hateful charge :
But tattling fame the sorrows of the knight,
  And hard mischance, had told this while at large.

Godfrey and all his lords of worth and might
   Ran thither, and the duty would discharge
Of friendship true, and with sweet words the rage
Of bitter grief and wo they would assuage.

LXXXV.

But as a mortal wound the more doth smart
   The more it searched is, handled, or sought,
So their sweet words to his afflicted heart
   More grief, more anguish, pain, and torment brought:
But reverend Peter, that nould set apart
   Care of his sheep, as a good shepherd ought,
His vanity with grave advice reproved,
And told what mourning Christian knights behoved.—

LXXXVI.

O Tancred! Tancred! how far different
   From thy beginnings good these follies be!
What makes thee deaf? what hath thy eyesight blent?
   What mist, what cloud thus overshadeth thee?
This is a warning good from heaven down sent,
   Yet His advice thou can'st not hear nor see,
Who calleth and conducts thee to the way
From which thou willing dost and witting stray:

LXXXVII.

To worthy actions and achievements fit
   For Christian knights He would thee home recall,
But thou hast left that course, and changed it
   To make thyself a heathen damsel's thrall:
But see, thy grief and sorrows' painful fit
   Is made the rod to scourge thy sins withal;
Of thine own good thyself the means He makes,
But thou His mercy, goodness, grace forsakes:

LXXXVIII.

Thou dost refuse of Heav'n the proffer'd grace,
   And 'gainst it still rebel with sinful ire;
O wretch! O whither doth thy rage thee chase?
   Refrain thy grief, bridle thy fond desire;
At hell's wide gate vain sorrow doth thee place,
   Sorrow, misfortune's son, despair's foul sire:
O see thine ill, thy plaint and wo refrain,
The guides to death, to hell, and endless pain.—

LXXXIX.

This said, his will to die the patient
  Abandoned, that second death he feared;
These words of comfort to his heart down went,
  And that dark night of sorrow somewhat cleared;
Yet now and then his grief deep sighs forth sent,
  His voice shrill plaints and sad laments oft reared;
Now to himself, now to his murder'd love,
He spoke, who heard perchance from heav'n above.

XC.

Till Phœbus' rising, from his evening fall,
  To her, for her, he mourns, he calls, he cries.
The nightingale so, when her children small
  Some churle takes before their parents' eyes,
Alone, dismay'd, quite bare of comforts all,
  Tires with complaints the seas, the shores, the skies,
Till in sweet sleep against the morning bright
  She fall at last; so mourn'd, so slept the knight:

XCI.

And clad in starry veil, amid his dream
  (For whose sweet sake he mourn'd) appear'd the maid,
Fairer than erst, yet with that heav'nly beam,
  Not out of knowledge was her lovely shade;
With looks of ruth her eyes celestial seem
  To pity his sad plight, and thus she said:—
Behold how fair, how glad thy love appears,
And for my sake, my dear, forbear these tears:

XCII.

Thine be the thanks, my soul thou madest flit
  At unawares out of her earthly nest;
Thine be the thanks, thou hast advanced it
  In Abraham's dear bosom long to rest;
There still I love thee, there for Tancred fit
  A seat prepared is among the bless'd;
There in eternal joy, eternal light,
Thou shalt thy love enjoy, and she her knight;

XCIII.

Unless thyself thyself heav'n's joys envy,
  And thy vain sorrow thee of bliss deprive:
Live; know I love thee, that I nill deny,
  As angels men, as saints may wights alive.—

This said, of zeal and love forth of her eye
    A hundred glorious beams bright shining drive,
Amid which rays herself she clos'd from sight,
And with new joy, new comfort, left her knight.

XCIV.

Thus comforted he wak'd, and men discreet
    In surgery to cure his wounds were sought.
Meanwhile of his dear love the relics sweet
    (As best he could) to grave with pomp he brought.
Her tomb was not of varied Spartan grit,
    Nor yet by cunning hand of Scopas wrought,
But built of polish'd stone, and thereon laid
The lively shape and portrait of the maid.

XCV.

With sacred burning lamps in order long
    And mournful pomp the corpse was brought to ground ;
Her arms upon a leafless pine were hong,
    The hearse with cypress, arms with laurel crown'd.
Next day the Prince (whose love and courage strong
    Drew forth his limbs, weak, feeble, and unsound)
To visit went, with care and rev'rence meet,
The buried ashes of his mistress sweet.

XCVI.

Before her new-made tomb at last arrived,
    The woful prison of his living spright,
Pale, cold, sad, comfortless, of sense deprived,
    Upon the marble grey he fix'd his sight ;
Two streams of tears were from his eyes derived :
    Thus, with a sad alas, began the knight :—
Oh, marble dear ! on my dear mistress plac'd,
My flames within, without my tears thou hast.

XCVII.

Not of dead bones art thou the mournful grave,
    But of quick love the fortress and the hold ;
Still in my heart thy wonted brand I have,
    More bitter far, alas ! but not more cold.
Receive these sighs, these kisses sweet receive,
    In liquid drops of melting tears enroll'd,
And give them to that body pure and chaste
Which in thy bosom cold entomb'd thou hast :

XCVIII.

For if her happy soul her eye doth bend
  On that sweet body which it lately dress'd,
My love, thy pity, cannot her offend,
  Anger and wrath is not in angels bless'd ;
She pardon will the trespass of her friend ;
  That hope relieves me with these griefs oppress'd.
This hand she knows hath only sinn'd, not I,
Who living lov'd her, and for love now die ;

XCIX.

And loving will I die ; O happy day
  Whene'er it chanceth ! but O far more blest,
If as about thy polish'd sides I stray,
  My bones within thy hollow grave might rest ;
Together should in heav'n our spirits stay,
  Together should our bodies lie in chest ;
So happy death should join what life doth sever :
O death ! O life ! sweet both, both blessed ever.—

C.

Meanwhile the news in that besieged town
  Of this mishap was whisper'd here and there ;
Forthwith it spread, and for too true was known,
  Her woful loss was talked everywhere,
Mingled with cries and plaints to heaven up thrown,
  As if the city's self new taken were
With conqu'ring foes, or as if flame and fire
Nor house, nor church, nor street had left entire.

CI.

But all men's eyes were on Arsetes bent ;
  His sighs were deep, his looks full of despair ;
Out of his woful eyes no tears there went,
  His heart was harden'd with his too much care ;
His silver locks with dust he foul besprent,
  He knock'd his breast, his face he rent and tare ;
And while the prease flock'd to the eunuch old,
Thus to the people spake Argantes bold :—

CII.

I would, when first I knew the hardy maid
  Excluded was among her Christian foes,
Have follow'd her to give her timely aid,
  Or by her side this breath and life to lose.

What did I not, or what left I unsaid,
  To make the king the gates again unclose?
But he denied; his power did aye restrain
My will; my suit was waste, my speech was vain.

CIII.

Ah! had I gone, I would from danger free
  Have brought to Sion that sweet nymph again,
Or in the bloody fight, where kill'd was she,
  In her defence there nobly have been slain.
But what could I do more?   The counsels be
  Of God and man 'gainst my designments plain.
Dead is Clorinda fair, laid in cold grave;
Let me revenge her whom I could not save.

CIV.

Hierusalem! hear what Argantes saith;
  Hear heav'n! and if he break his oath and word,
Upon this head cast thunder in thy wrath;
  I will destroy and kill that Christian lord,
Who this fair dame by night thus murder'd hath;
  Nor from my side I will ungird this sword,
Till Tancred's heart it cleave and shed his blood,
And leave his corse to wolves and crows for food.—

CV.

This said, the people with a joyful shout
  Applaud his speeches and his words approve,
And calm'd their grief, in hope the boaster stout
  Would kill the Prince who late had slain his love.
O promise vain! it otherwise fell out.
  Men purpose, but high Gods dispose above;
For underneath his sword this boaster died,
Whom thus he scorn'd and threaten'd in his pride.

BOOK XIII.

THE ARGUMENT.

Ismeno sets, to guard the forest old,
  The wicked sprites, whose ugly shapes affray
And put to flight the men, whose labor would
  To their dark shades let in heav'n's golden ray.
Thither goes Tancred, hardy, faithful, bold;
  But foolish pity lets him not assay
His strength and courage.—Heat the Christian power
Annoys, whom to refresh God sends a shower.

I.

But scant dissolved into ashes cold
  The smoking tower fell on the scorched grass,
When new device found out th' enchanter old,
  By which the town besieg'd secured was.
Of timber fit his foes deprive he would;
  Such terror bred that late-consumed mass;
So that, the strength of Sion's walls to shake,
They should no turrets, rams, nor engines make.

II.

From Godfrey's camp a grove a little way,
  Amid the valleys deep, grows out of sight,
Thick with old trees, whose horrid arms display
  An ugly shade, like everlasting night:
There, when the sun spreads forth his clearest ray,
  Dim, thick, uncertain, gloomy seems the light;
As when, in ev'ning, day and darkness strive
Which should his foe from our horizon drive.

III.

But when the sun his chair in seas doth steep,
  Night, horror, darkness thick, the place invade,
Which veil the mortal eyes with blindness deep,
  And with sad terror make weak hearts afraid.

Thither no groom drives forth his tender sheep
    To browse, or ease their faint in cooling shade;
Nor traveller nor pilgrim there to enter
    (So awful seems that forest old) dare venture.

IV.

United there the ghosts and goblins meet
    To frolic with their mates in silent night;
With dragon wings some cleave the welkin fleet,
    Some nimbly run o'er hills and valleys light;
A wicked troop that with allurement sweet
    Draws sinful man from what is good and right;
And there with hellish pomp their banquets brought,
They solemnise: thus the vain pagans thought.

V.

No twist, no twig, no bough, nor branch, therefore,
    The Saracines cut from that sacred spring;
But yet the Christians spared ne'er the more
    The trees to earth with cutting steel to bring.
Thither went Ismen old with tresses hoar,
    When night on all this earth spread forth her wing;
And there, in silence deaf and mirksome shade,
His characters and circles vain he made.

VI.

He in the circle set one foot unshod,
    And whisper'd dreadful charms in ghastly wise;
Three times (for witchcraft loveth numbers odd)
    Toward the east he gaped, westward thrice:
He struck the earth thrice with his charmed rod,
    Wherewith dead bones he makes from graves to rise:
And thrice the ground with naked foot he smote,
And thus he cried loud with thund'ring note:—

VII.

Hear! hear! ye spirits all that whilome fell,
    Cast down from heav'n with dint of roaring thunder;
Hear! ye amid the empty air that dwell,
    And storms and show'rs pour on these kingdoms under;
Hear! all ye devils that lie in deepest hell,
    And rend with torments damned ghosts asunder;
And of those lands of death, of pain and fear,
Thou monarch great, great Dis, great Pluto hear!

VIII.

Keep ye this forest well, keep every tree;
  Number'd I give you them, and truly told:
As souls of men in bodies clothed be,
  So every plant a sprite shall hide and hold:
With trembling fear make all the Christians flee,
  When they presume to cut these cedars old,—
This said, his charms he 'gan again repeat,
Which none can say but they that use like feat.

IX.

At those strange speeches, still night's splendent fires
  Quenched their lights, and shrunk away for doubt;
The feeble moon her silver beams retires,
  And wraps her horns with folding clouds about.
Ismen his sprites to come with speed requires:—
  Why come ye not, ye ever damned rout?
Why tarry ye so long? pardie ye stay
Till stronger charms and greater words I say.

X.

I have not yet forgot for want of use
  What dreadful terms belong this sacred feat;
My tongue (if still your stubborn hearts refuse)
  That so much dreaded name can well repeat,
Which heard, great Dis cannot himself excuse,
  But hither run from his eternal seat;
O great and fearful!—More he would have said,
But that he saw the sturdy sprites obey'd.

XI.

Legions of devils by thousands thither come;
  Such as in sparsed air their biding make;
And thousands also which by heavenly doom
  Condemned lie in deep Avernus' lake:
But slow they come, displeased all and some
  Because those woods they should in keeping take;
Yet they obey'd, and took the charge in hand,
And under every branch and leaf they stand.

XII.

When thus his cursed work performed was,
  The wizard to his king declar'd the feat:—
My lord, let fear, let doubt and sorrow pass,
  Henceforth in safety stands your regal seat:

Your foe (as he supposed) no mean now has
    To build again his rams and engines great.—
And then he told at large from part to part
All what he late perform'd by wondrous art.

XIII.

Besides this help, another hap (quoth he)
    Will shortly chance that brings not profit small ;
Within few days Mars and the Sun I see
    Their fiery beams unite in Leo shall ;
And then extreme the scorching heat will be,
    Which neither rain can quench nor dews that fall ;
So placed are the planets high and low,
That heat, fire, burning, all the heav'ns foreshow :

XIV.

So great with us will be the warmth therefore,
    As with the Garamantes or those of Inde ;
Yet nill it grieve us in this town so sore ;
    We have sweet shade and waters cold by kind ;
Our foes abroad will be tormented more ;
    What shield can they or what refreshing find ?
Heav'n will them vanquish first, then Egypt's crew
Destroy them quite, weak, weary, faint, and few.

XV.

Thou shalt sit still and conquer ; prove no more
    The doubtful hazard of uncertain fight ;
But if Argantes bold (that hates so sore
    All cause of quiet peace, though just and right)
Provoke thee forth to battle as before,
    Find means to calm the rage of that fierce knight ;
For shortly heav'n will send thee ease and peace,
And war and trouble 'mongst thy foes increase.—

XVI.

The king, assured by these speeches fair,
    Held Godfrey's power, his might, and strength, in scorn ;
And now the walls he 'gan in part repair,
    Which late the ram had bruis'd with iron horn :
With wise foresight and well-advised care
    He fortified each breach and bulwark torn ;
And all his folk, men, women, children small,
    With endless toil again repair'd the wall.

XVII.

But Godfrey nould this while bring forth his power
  To give assault against that fort in vain,
Till he had builded new his dreadful tower,
  And reared high his downfall'n rams again.
His workmen therefore he dispatch'd that hour,
  To hew the trees out of the forest main.
They went, and scant the wood appear'd in sight,
When wonders new their fearful hearts affright.

XVIII.

As seely children dare not bend their eye
  Where they are told strange bugbears haunt the place ;
Or as new monsters, while in bed they lie,
  Their fearful thoughts present before their face ;
So feared they and fled, yet wist not why,
  Nor what pursu'd them in that fearful chace ;
Except their fear perchance, while thus they fled,
New chimeres, sphinxes, or like monsters bred.

XIX.

Swift to the camp they turned back dismay'd ;
  With words confus'd uncertain tales they told,
That all which heard them scorned what they said,
  And these reports for lies and fables hold.
A chosen crew, in shining arms array'd,
  Duke Godfrey thither sent of soldiers bold,
To guard the men, and their faint arms provoke,
To cut the dreadful trees with hardy stroke.

XX.

These drawing near the wood, where close ypent
  The wicked sprites in sylvan pinfolds were,
Their eyes upon those shades no sooner bent,
  But frozen dread pierc'd through their entrails dear.
Yet on they stalked still, and on they went,
  Under bold semblance hiding coward fear,
And so far wander'd forth with trembling pace
Till they approach'd nigh that enchanted place :

XXI.

When from the grove a fearful sound out breaks,
  As if some earthquake hill and mountain tore,
Wherein the southern wind a rumbling makes,
  Or like sea-waves against the craggy shore :

There lions grumble, there hiss scaly snakes,
   There howl the wolves, the rugged bears there roar,
There trumpets shrill are heard and thunders fell,
And all these sounds one sound expressed well.

XXII.

Upon their faces pale well might you note
   A thousand signs of heart-amating fear ;
Their reason gone, by no device they wote
   How to prease nigh or stay still where they were ;
Against that sudden dread their breasts which smote,
   Their courage weak no shield of proof could bear :
At last they fled, and one, than all more bold,
Excus'd their flight, and thus the wonders told :—

XXIII.

My lord, not one of us there is, I grant,
   ·That dares cut down one branch in yonder spring ;
I think there dwells a sprite in every plant,
   There keeps his court great Dis, infernal king :
He hath a heart of harden'd adamant
   That without trembling dares attempt the thing ;
And sense he wanteth who so hardy is
To hear the forest thunder, roar, and hiss.—

XXIV.

This said, Alcasto to his words gave heed,
   Alcasto, leader of the Switzers grim ;
A man both void of wit and void of dread,
   Who fear'd not loss of life nor loss of limb ;
No savage beasts in deserts wild that feed,
   Nor ugly monster, could dishearten him ;
Nor whirlwind, thunder, earthquake, storm, or aught
That in this world is strange or fearful thought.

XXV.

He shook his head, and smiling thus 'gan say :—
   The hardiness have I that wood to fell,
And those proud trees low in the dust to lay,
   Wherein such grisly fiends and monsters dwell ;
No roaring ghost my courage can dismay,
   No shriek of birds, beasts' roar, or dragon's yell ;
But through and through that forest will I wend,
Although to deepest hell the paths descend.—

XXVI.

Thus boasted he, and leave to go desired,
  And forward went with joyful cheer and will:
He view'd the wood and those thick shades admired;
  He heard the wond'rous noise and rumbling shrill;
Yet not one foot th' audacious man retired;
  He scorn'd the peril, preasing forward still,
Till on the forest's outmost marge he stept;
A flaming fire from entrance there him kept.

XXVII.

The fire increas'd, and built a stately wall
  Of burning coals, quick sparks, and embers hot;
And with bright flames the wood environ'd all,
  That there no tree nor twist Alcasto got:
The higher stretched flames seem'd bulwarks tall,
  Castles and turrets full of fiery shot,
With slings and engines strong of every sort;
What mortal wight durst scale so strange a fort?

XXVIII.

O what strange monsters on the battlément
  In loathsome forms stood to defend the place!
Their frowning looks upon the knight they bent,
  And threaten'd death with shot, with sword, and mace.
At last he fled, and though but slow he went,
  As lions do whom jolly hunters chase,
Yet fled the man, and with sad fear withdrew,
Though fear till then he never felt nor knew.

XXIX.

That he had fled long time he never wist,
  But when far run he had discover'd it,
Himself for wonder with his hand he blist,
  A bitter sorrow by the heart him bit;
Amaz'd, asham'd, disgrac'd, sad, silent, trist,
  Alone he would all day in darkness sit;
Nor durst he look on man of worth or fame,
His pride late great now greater made his shame.

XXX.

Godfredo call'd him, but he found delays
  And causes why he should his cabin keep:
At length perforce he comes, but naught he says,
  Or talks like those that babble in their sleep.

His shamefac'dness to Godfrey plain bewrays
    His flight, so doth his sighs and sadness deep.
Whereat amaz'd—What chance is this? (quoth he)
These witchcrafts strange or nature's wonders be;

XXXI.

But if his courage any champion move
    To try the hazard of this dreadful spring,
I give him leave th' adventure great to prove,
    Some news he may report us of the thing.—
This said, his lords attempt the charmed grove,
    Yet nothing back but fear and flight they bring;
For them enforc'd with trembling to retire,
The sight, the sound, the monsters, and the fire.

XXXII.

This hapt when woful Tancred left his bed,
    To lay in marble cold his mistress dear;
The lively color from his cheek was fled,
    His limbs were weak his helm or targe to bear:
Nathless, when need to high attempts him led,
    No labor would he shun, no danger fear;
His valor, boldness, heart, and courage brave,
To his faint body strength and vigor gave.

XXXIII.

To this exploit forth went the vent'rous knight,
    Fearless, yet heedful; silent, well advised;
The terrors of that forest's dreadful sight,
    Storms, earthquakes, thunders, cries, he all despised.
He feared nothing; yet a motion light
    (That quickly vanish'd) in his heart arised;
When, lo! between him and the charmed wood
A fiery city high as heav'n up stood.

XXXIV.

The knight stept back and took a sudden pause,
    And to himself—What help these arms (quoth he),
If in this fire, or monsters' gaping jaws,
    I headlong cast myself, what boots it me?
For common profit, or my country's cause,
    To hazard life before me none should be;
But this exploit of no such weight I hold,
For it to lose a prince or champion bold.

xxxv.

But if I fly, what will the pagans say ?
　　If I retire, who shall cut down this spring ?
Godfredo will attempt it every day ;
　　What if some other knight perform the thing ?
These flames uprisen to forestall my way,
　　Perchance more terror far than danger bring :
But hap what shall.—This said, he forward stept,
And through the fire (O wondrous boldness !) leapt.

xxxvi.

He bolted through, but neither warmth nor heat
　　He felt, nor sign of fire or scorching flame ;
Yet wist he not, in his dismay'd conceit,
　　If that were fire or no through which he came ;
For at first touch vanish'd those monsters great,
　　And in their stead the clouds black night did frame,
And hideous storms and showers of hail and rain ;
Yet storms and tempests vanished straight again.

xxxvii.

Amaz'd, but not afraid, the champion good
　　Stood still ; but when the tempest past he spied,
He enter'd boldly that forbidden wood,
　　And of the forest all the secrets eyed :
In all his walk no spright or fantasme stood,
　　That stopt his way or passage free denied ;
Save that the growing trees so thick were set,
That oft his sight and passage oft they let.

xxxviii.

At length a fair and spacious green he spied,
　　Like calmest waters plain, like velvet soft,
Wherein a cypress, clad in summer's pride,
　　Pyramid-wise, lift up its tops aloft ;
In whose smooth bark, upon the evenest side,
　　Strange characters he found, and view'd them oft ;
Like those which priests of Egypt erst in stead
Of letters us'd, which none but they could read :

xxxix.

'Mongst them he picked out these words at last,
　　Writ in the Syriac tongue, which well he could :—
O hardy knight ! who through these woods hath pass'd,
　　Where death his palace and his court doth hold,

O trouble not these souls in quiet plac'd !
  O be not cruel as thy heart is bold !
Pardon these ghosts depriv'd of heav'nly light ;
With spirits dead why should men living fight ?—

XL.

This found he graven in the tender rind ;
  And while he mused on this uncouth writ,
Him thought he heard the softly whistling wind,
  His blasts amid the leaves and branches knit,
And frame a sound like speech of human kind,
  But full of sorrow, grief, and wo was it ;
Whereby his gentle thoughts all filled were
With pity, sadness, grief, compassion, fear.

XLI.

He drew his sword at last, and gave the tree
  A mighty blow that made a gaping wound ;
Out of the rift red streams he trickling see
  That all bebled the verdant plain around ;
His hair start up ; yet once again struck he,
  (He nould give over till the end he found
Of this adventure), when with plaint and moan,
As from some hollow grave, he heard one groan.—

XLII.

Enough, enough (the voice lamenting said),
  Tancred, thou hast me hurt ; thou didst me drive
Out of the body of a noble maid,
  Who with me liv'd, whom late I kept alive ;
And now, within this woful cypress laid,
  My tender rind thy weapon sharp doth rive.
Cruel ! is 't not enough thy foes to kill,
But in their graves wilt thou torment them still ?

XLIII.

I was Clorinda ; now imprison'd here
  (Yet not alone) within this plant I dwell ;
For every Pagan lord and Christian peer,
  Before the city's walls last day that fell
(In bodies new or graves, I wot not clear),
  But here they are confin'd by magic's spell,
So that each tree hath life, and sense each bough ;
A murd'rer if thou cut one twist art thou.—

XLIV.

As the sick man that in his sleep doth see
  Some ugly dragon or some chimere new,
Though he suspect or half persuaded be
  It is an idle dream, no monster new,
Yet still he fears, he quakes, and strives to flee,
  So fearful is that wond'rous form to view:
So fear'd the knight, yet he both knew and thought
All were illusions false by witchcraft wrought.

XLV.

But cold and trembling wax'd his frozen heart,
  Such strange affects, such passions it torment;
Out of his feeble hand his weapon start,
  Himself out of his wits nigh after went.
Wounded he saw (he thought) for pain and smart
  His lady weep, complain, mourn, and lament;
Nor could he suffer her dear blood to see,
Or hear her sighs that deep far fetched be.

XLVI.

Thus his fierce heart, which death had scorned oft,
  Whom no strange shape or monster could dismay,
With feigned shows of tender love made soft,
  A spirit false did with vain plaints betray.
A whirling wind his sword heav'd up aloft,
  And through the forest bare it quite away.
O'ercome retir'd the prince, and as he came
His sword he found, and repossess'd the same:

XLVII.

Yet nould return; he had no mind to try
  His courage further in those forests green;
But when to Godfrey's tent he 'proached nigh,
  His spirit wak'd, his thoughts composed been.—
My lord (quoth he), a witness true am I
  Of wonders strange, believed scant though seen;
What of the fire, the shades, the dreadful sound,
You heard, all true by proof myself have found:

XLVIII.

A burning fire (so are those deserts charm'd)
  Built like a battled wall to heav'n was rear'd,
Whereon, with darts and dreadful weapons armed,
  Of monsters foul misshap'd whole bands appeared;

But through them all I past, unhurt, unharmed,
    No flame or threaten'd blow I felt or feared ;
Then rain and night I found, but straight again
To day the night, to sunshine turn'd the rain.

XLIX.

What would you more ?   Each tree through all that wood
    Hath sense, hath life, hath speech, like human kind :
I heard their words as in that grove I stood ;
    That mournful voice still, still I bear in mind ;
And (as they were of flesh) the purple blood
    At every blow streams from the wounded rind.
No, no ! not I, nor any else (I trow),
Hath power to cut one leaf, one branch, one bough.—

L.

While thus he said, the Christians' noble Guide
    Felt uncouth strife in his contentious thought ;
He thought, what if himself in person tried
    Those witchcrafts strange, and bring those charms to naught ;
For such he deem'd them ; or elsewhere provide
    For timber easier got, though farther sought :
But from his study he at last abray'd,
Call'd by the hermit old, that to him said :—

LI.

Leave off thy hardy thought ; another's hands
    Of these her plants the wood dispoilen shall :
Now, now the fatal ship of conquest lands,
    Her sails are struck, her silver anchors fall ;
Our champion broken hath his worthless bands,
    And looseth from the soil which held him thrall :
The time draws nigh when our proud foes in field
Shall slaughter'd lie, and Sion's fort shall yield.—

LII.

This said, his visage shone with beams divine,
    And more than mortal was his voice's sound.
Godfredo's thoughts to other acts incline,
    His working brain was never idle found.
But in the Crab now did bright Titan shine,
    And scorch'd with scalding beams the parched ground ;
And, made unfit for toil or warlike feat,
His soldiers, weak with labor, faint with sweat.

LIII.

The planets mild their lamps benign quench'd out,
  And cruel stars in heav'n did signorise,
Whose influence cast fiery flames about,
  And hot impressions through the earth and skies:
The growing heat still gather'd deeper root,
  The noisome warmth through lands and kingdoms flies;
A harmful night a hurtful day succeeds,
And worse than both next morn her light outspreads.

LIV.

When Phœbus rose, he left his golden weed,
  And don'd a gite in deepest purple dy'd;
His sanguine beams about his forehead spread,
  A sad presage of ill that should betide;
With vermeil drops at even his tresses bleed,
  Foreshows of future heat, from th' ocean wide
When next he rose; and thus increased still
Their present harms with dread of future ill.

LV.

While thus he bent 'gainst earth his scorching rays,
  He burnt the flow'rets, burnt his Clitie dear;
The leaves grew wan upon the wither'd sprays,
  The grass and growing herbs all parched were;
Earth cleft in rifts, in floods each stream decays;
  The barren clouds with lightning bright appear;
And mankind fear'd lest Climene's child again
Had driven awry his sire's ill-guided wain.

LVI.

As from a furnace flew the smoke to skies,
  Such smoke as that when damned Sodom brent;
Within his caves sweet Zephyr silent lies;
  Still was the air, the rack nor came nor went,
But o'er the lands with lukewarm breathing flies
  The southern wind, from sunburnt Afric sent,
Which, thick and warm, his interrupted blasts
Upon their bosoms, throats, and faces casts.

LVII.

Nor yet more comfort brought the gloomy night,
  In her thick shades was burning heat uproll'd,
Her sable mantle was embroider'd bright
  With blazing stars, and gliding fires for gold;

Nor to refresh (sad earth !) thy thirsty sprite,
    The niggard moon let fall her May-dews cold ;
And dried up the vital moisture was
In trees, in plants, in herbs, in flowers, in grass.

LVIII.

Sleep to his quiet dales exiled fled
    From these unquiet nights, and oft in vain
The soldiers restless sought the god in bed ;
    But most for thirst they mourn'd and most complain ;
For Judah's tyrant had strong poison shed
    (Poison that breeds more wo and deadly pain
Than Acheron or Stygian waters bring)
In every fountain, cistern, well, and spring ;

LIX.

And little Siloe, that his store bestows
    Of purest crystal on the Christian bands,
The pebbles naked in his channel shows,
    And scantly glides above the scorched sands
Nor Po in May, when o'er his bank he flows,
    Nor Ganges, waterer of the Indian lands,
Nor seven-mouth'd Nile, that yields all Egypt drink,
To quench their thirst the men sufficient think.

LX.

He that the gliding rivers erst had seen
    Adown their verdant channels gently roll'd,
Or falling streams which to the valleys green,
    Distill'd from tops of Alpine mountains cold,
Those he desir'd in vain, new torments been
    Augmented thus with wish of comforts old ;
Those waters cool he drank in vain conceit,
Which more increas'd his thirst, increas'd his heat.

LXI.

The sturdy bodies of the warriors strong,
    Whom neither marching far, nor tedious way,
Nor weighty arms which on their shoulders hong
    Could weary make, nor death itself dismay,
Now weak and feeble, cast their limbs along,
    Unwieldy burthens, on the burned clay ;
And in each vein a smould'ring fire there dwelt,
Which dried their flesh, and solid bones did melt.

LXII.

Languish'd the steed late fierce, and proffer'd grass,
  His fodder erst despis'd, and from him kest ;
Each step he stumbled, and, which lofty was
  And high advanc'd before, now fell his crest ;
His conquests gotten all forgotten pass,
  Nor with desire of glory swell'd his breast ;
The spoils won from his foe, his late rewards,
He now neglects, despises, naught regards.

LXIII.

Languish'd the faithful dog, and wonted care
  Of his dear lord and cabin both forgot ;
Panting he laid, and gather'd fresher air
  To cool the burning in his entrails hot ;
But breathing (which wise Nature did prepare
  To 'suage the stomach's heat) now booted not,
For little ease (alas!) small help they win,
That breathe forth air and scalding fire suck in.

LXIV.

Thus languished the earth ; in this estate
  Lay woful thousands of the Christians stout ;
The faithful people grew nigh desperate
  Of hoped conquest, shameful death they doubt ;
Of their distress they talk and oft debate ;
  These sad complaints were heard the camp throughout :
What hope hath Godfrey ?   Shall we still here lie,
  Till all his soldiers, all our armies die ?

LXV.

Alas ! with what device, what strength, thinks he
  To scale these walls, or this strong fort to get ?
Whence hath he engines new ? doth he not see
  How wrathful heav'n 'gainst us his sword doth whet ?
These tokens shown true signs and witness be
  Our angry God our proud attempts doth let,
And scorching sun so hot his beams outspreads,
That not more cooling Inde nor Æthiope needs :

LXVI.

Or thinks he it an eath or little thing
  That us despis'd, neglected, and disdain'd,
Like abjects vile to death he thus should bring,
  That so his empire may be still maintain'd ?

Is it so great a bliss to be a king,
    When he that wears the crown with blood is stain'd,
And buys his sceptre with his people's lives ?
See whither glory vain fond mankind drives !

LXVII.

See, see the man, call'd holy, just, and good,
    That courteous, meek, and humble would be thought,
Yet never car'd in what distress we stood,
    If his vain honor were diminish'd naught ;
When dried up from us is spring and flood,
    His water must from Jordan streams be brought ;
And now he sits at feasts and banquets sweet,
And mingleth waters fresh with wines of Crete !—

LXVIII.

The French thus murmur'd, but the Greekish knight,
    Tatine, that of this war was weary grown—
Why die we here (quoth he), slain without fight ;
    Kill'd, not subdu'd ; murder'd, not overthrown ?
Upon the Frenchmen let the penance light
    Of Godfrey's folly, let me save mine own.—
And as he said, without farewell, the knight
And all his cornet stole away by night.

LXIX.

His bad example many a troop prepares
    To imitate, when his escape they know ;
Clotharius his band, and Ademare's,
    And all whose guides in dust were buried low,
Discharg'd of duty's chains and bondage snares,
    Free from their oath, to none they service owe,
But now concluded all on secret flight,
And shrunk away by thousands every night.

LXX.

Godfredo this both heard, and saw, and knew,
    Yet nould with death them chastise, tho' he mought,
But with that faith wherewith he could remew
    The steadfast hills, and seas dry up to naught,
He pray'd the Lord upon his flock to rew,
    To ope the springs of grace, and ease this drought ;
Out of his looks shone zeal, devotion, faith,
His hands and eyes to heav'n he heaves, and saith :

LXXI.

Father and Lord! if in the deserts waste
   Thou hadst compassion on thy children dear,
The craggy rock when Moses cleft and brast,
   And drew forth flowing streams of waters clear,
Like mercy, Lord, like grace, on us down cast;
   And though our merits less than theirs appear,
Thy grace supply that want, for though they be
Thy first-born sons, thy children yet are we.—

LXXII.

These prayers just, from humble heart forth sent,
   Were nothing slow to climb the starry sky,
But swift as winged birds themselves present
   Before the Father of the heavens high :
The Lord accepteth them, and gently bent
   Upon the faithful host his gracious eye,
And in what pain and what distress it laid
He saw, and griev'd to see, and thus he said :—

LXXIII.

Mine armies dear till now have suffer'd wo,
   Distress and danger, hell's infernal pow'r
Their enemy hath been, the world their foe ;
   But happy be their actions from this hour,
What they begin to blessed end shall go ;
   I will refresh them with a gentle show'r ;
Rinaldo shall return ; th' Egyptian crew
They shall encounter, conquer, and subdue.—

LXXIV.

At these high words great heav'n began to shake,
   The fixed stars, the planets wand'ring still,
Trembled the air, the earth and ocean quake,
   Spring, fountain, river, forest, dale and hill ;
From north to east, a lightning flash out brake,
   And coming drops presag'd with thunder shrill.
With joyful shouts the soldiers on the plain
These tokens bless of long-desired rain.

LXXV.

A sudden cloud, as when Elias pray'd
   (Not from dry earth exhal'd by Phœbus' beams),
Arose, moist heav'n his windows open laid,
   Whence clouds by heaps out-rush, and wat'ry streams ;

The world o'erspread was with a gloomy shade,
　　That like a dark and mirksome even it seems;
The dashing rain from molten skies down fell,
And o'er their banks the brooks and fountains swell.

LXXVI.

In summer season, when the cloudy sky
　　Upon the parched ground doth rain down send,
As duck and mallard in the furrows dry
　　With merry noise the promis'd showers attend,
And spreading broad their wings displayed lie
　　To keep the drops that on their plumes descend;
And where the streams swell to a gather'd lake,
Therein they dive, and sweet refreshing take;

LXXVII.

So they the streaming showers with shouts and cries
　　Salute, which heav'n shed on the thirsty lands:
The falling liquor from the dropping skies
　　He catcheth in his lap; he bare-head stands,
And his bright helm to drink therein unties;
　　In the fresh streams he dives his sweaty hands;
Their faces some, and some their temples wet,
And some to keep the drops large vessels set.

LXXVIII.

Nor man alone, to ease his burning sore,
　　Herein doth dive and wash, and hereof drinks;
But earth itself, weak, feeble, faint before,
　　Whose solid limbs were cleft with rifts and chinks,
Receiv'd the falling showers, and gather'd store
　　Of liquor sweet, that through her veins down sinks;
And moisture new infused largely was
In trees, in plants, in herbs, in flowers, in grass.

LXXIX.

Earth like the patient was whose lively blood
　　Hath overcome at last some sickness strong,
Whose feeble limbs had been the bait and food
　　Whereon his strange disease depastur'd long;
But now restor'd, in health and welfare stood,
　　As sound as erst, as fresh, as fair, as young;
So that, forgetting all his grief and pain,
His pleasant robes and crowns he takes again.

LXXX.

Ceased the rain ; the sun began to shine,
  With fruitful, sweet, benign, and gentle ray,
Full of strong power and vigor masculine,
  As be his beams in April or in May.
O happy zeal ! who trusts in help divine
  The world's afflictions thus can drive away,
Can storms appease, and times and seasons change,
And conquer fortune, fate, and dest'ny strange.

BOOK XIV.

I.

Now from the fresh, the soft, and tender bed
    Of her still mother, gentle night out flew,
The fleeting balm on hills and dales she shed,
    With honey drops of pure and precious dew,
And on the verdure of green forests spread
    The virgin primrose and the violet blue ;
And sweet-breath'd Zephyr on his spreading wings
Sleep, ease, repose, rest, peace and quiet brings.

II.

The thoughts and troubles of broad-waking day
    They softly dipt in mild oblivion's lake ;
But He, whose Godhead heav'n and earth doth sway,
    In his eternal light did watch and wake,
And bent on Godfrey down the gracious ray
    Of his bright eye, still ope for Godfrey's sake,
To whom a silent dream the Lord down sent,
Which told his will, his pleasure, and intent.

III.

Far in the east (the golden gate beside
    Whence Phœbus comes) a crystal port there is,
And ere the sun his broad doors open wide,
    The beam of springing day uncloseth this ;

Hence come the dreams, by which heav'n's sacred Guide
  Reveals to man those high decrees of his :
Hence towards Godfrey, ere he left his bed,
A vision strange his golden plumes bespread :

IV.

Such semblances, such shapes, such portraits fair
  Did never yet in dream or sleep appear,
For all the forms in sea, in earth, or air,
  The signs in heav'n, the stars in every sphere,
All what was wond'rous, uncouth, strange, and rare,
  All in that vision well presented were ;
His dream had plac'd him in a crystal wide,
Beset with golden fires, top, bottom, side :

V.

There while he wond'reth on the circles vast,
  The stars, their motions, course, and harmony,
A knight (with shining rays and fire embrac'd)
  Presents himself unwares before his eye,
Who with a voice that far for sweetness past
  All human speech, thus said, approaching nigh :—
What, Godfrey ! know'st thou not thy Hugo here ?
Come and embrace thy friend and fellow dear.—

VI.

He answer'd him :—That glorious shining light
  Which in thine eyes his glist'ring beams doth place,
Estranged hath from my foreknowledge quite
  Thy countenance, thy favor, and thy face.—
This said, three times he stretch'd his hands outright,
  And would in friendly arms the knight embrace ;
And thrice the spirit fled, and thrice he twin'd
Naught in his folded arms but air and wind.

VII.

Lord Hugo smil'd :—Not as you think (quoth he)
  I clothed am in flesh and earthly mould,
My spirit pure and naked soul you see,
  A citizen of this celestial hold ;
This place is heav'n, and here a room for thee
  Prepared is, among Christ's champions bold.—
Ah when (quoth he), these mortal bonds unknit,
Shall I in peace, in ease, and rest there sit ?—

VIII.

Hugo replied—Ere many years shall run,
    Amid the saints in bliss here shalt thou reign ;
But first great wars must by thy hand be done,
    Much blood be shed, and many pagans slain ;
The holy city by assault be won,
    The land set free from servile yoke again ;
Wherein thou shalt a Christian empire frame,
And after thee shall Baldwin rule the same.

IX.

But, to increase thy love and great desire
    To heaven-ward, this blessed place behold ;
These shining lamps, these globes of living fire,
    How they are turned, guided, mov'd, and roll'd,
The angels singing here and all their quire :
    Then bend thine eyes on yonder earth and mould,
All in that mass, that globe, and compass see,
Land, sea, spring, fountain, man, beast, grass, and tree :

X.

How vile, how small, and of how slender price,
    Is there reward of goodness, virtue's gain ;
A narrow room our glory vain up-ties,
    A little circle doth our pride contain ;
Earth like an isle amid the water lies,
    Which sea sometime is call'd, sometime the main ;
Yet naught therein responds a name so great,
It's but a lake, a pond, a marish strait.—

XI.

Thus said the one ; the other bended down
    His looks to ground, and half in scorn he smil'd ;
He saw at once earth, sea, flood, castle, town,
    Strangely divided, strangely all compil'd,
And wonder'd folly man so far should drown,
    To set his heart on things so base and vilde,
That servile empire searcheth and dumb fame,
And scorns heav'n's bliss ; yet proff'reth heav'n the same.

XII.

Wherefore he answer'd—Since the Lord not yet
    Will free my spirit from this cage of clay,
Lest worldly error vain my voyage let,
    Teach me to heav'n the best and surest way.—

Hugo replied—Thy happy foot is set
  In the true path, nor from this passage stray ;
Only from exile young Rinaldo call ;
This give I thee in charge, else naught at all :

XIII.

For as the Lord of hosts, the King of bliss,
  Hath chosen thee to rule the faithful band,
So he thy stratagems appointed is
  To execute, so both shall win this land ;
The first is thine, the second place is his,
  Thou art this army's head, and he the hand :
No other champion can his place supply,
And that thou do it doth thy state deny.

XIV.

Th' enchanted forest, and her charmed treen
  With cutting steel shall he to earth down hew ;
And thy weak armies, which too feeble been
  To scale again these walls re'nforced new,
And fainting lie dispersed on the green,
  Shall take new strength, new courage, at his view ;
The high-built towers, the eastern squadrons, all
Shall conquer'd be, shall fly, shall die, shall fall.—

XV.

He held his peace ; and Godfrey answer'd so :—
  O how his presence would recomfort me,
You that man's hidden thoughts perceive and know,
  (If I say truth, or if I love him) see :
But say, what messengers shall for him go ?
  What shall their speeches, what their errand be ?
Shall I entreat, or else command the man ?
With credit neither well perform I can.—

XVI.

Th' eternal Lord (the other knight replied)
  That with so many graces hath thee blest,
Wills, that among the troops thou hast to guide
  Thou honor'd be and fear'd of most and least :
Then speak not thou, lest blemish some betide
  Thy sacred empire if thou make request ;
But when by suit thou moved are to ruth,
Then yield, forgive, and home recall the youth.

XVII.

Guelpho shall pray thee (God shall him inspire)
    To pardon this offence, this fault commit
By hasty wrath, by rash and headstrong ire,
    To call the knight again ; yield thou to it :
And though the youth (enwrapt in fond desire,
    Far hence in love and looseness idle sit,
Yet fear it not he shall return with speed,
When most you wish him, and when most you need.

XVIII.

Your hermit Peter (to whose sapient heart
    High Heav'n his secrets open, tells, and shows)
Your messengers direct can to that part
    Where of the prince they shall hear certain news,
And learn the way, the manner, and the art
    To bring him back to these thy warlike crews ;
That all thy soldiers, wandered and misgone,
Heav'n may unite again and join in one.

XIX.

But this conclusion shall my speeches end,
    Know that his blood shall mixed be with thine,
Whence barons bold and worthies shall descend,
    That many great exploits shall bring to fine.—
This said, he vanish'd from his sleeping friend,
    Like smoke in wind, or mist in Titan's shine ;
Sleep fled likewise, and in his troubled thought,
With wonder pleasure, joy with marvel fought.

XX.

The Duke look'd up, and saw the azure sky
    With orient beams of silver morning spread,
And started up ; for praise and virtue lie
    In toil and travail, sin and shame in bed :
His arms he took, his sword girt to his thigh ;
    To his pavilion all his lords them sped,
And there in council grave the princes sit :
For strength by wisdom, war is ruled by wit.

XXI.

Lord Guelpho there (within whose gentle breast
    Heav'n had infus'd that new and sudden thought)
His pleasing words thus to the Duke address'd :—
    Good prince, mild, though unask'd, kind, unbesought,

O let thy mercy grant my just request;
　　Pardon this fault, by rage, not malice, wrought;
For great offence, I grant, so late commit,
My suit too hasty is, perchance unfit:

XXII.

But since to Godfrey meek, benign, and kind,
　　For Prince Rinaldo bold I humbly sue,
And that the suitor's self is not behind
　　Thy greatest friends, in state or friendship true;
I trust I shall thy grace and mercy find
　　Acceptable to me and all this crew:
O call him home, this trespass to amend
He shall his blood in Godfrey's service spend:

XXIII.

And if not he, who else dares undertake
　　Of this enchanted wood to cut one tree?
'Gainst death and danger who dares battle make
　　With so bold face, so fearless heart, as he?
Beat down these walls, these gates in pieces break,
　　Leap o'er these rampires high, thou shalt him see.
Restore therefore to this desirous band
Their wish, their hope, their strength, their shield, their hand;

XXIV.

To me my nephew, to thyself restore
　　A trusty help when strength of hand thou needs;
In idleness let him consume no more,
　　Recall him to his noble acts and deeds;
Known be his worth as was his strength of yore;
　　Where'er thy standard broad her cross outspreads,
O let his fame and praise spread far and wide;
Be thou his lord, his teacher, and his guide.—

XXV.

Thus he entreated, and the rest approve
　　His words, with friendly murmurs whisper'd low.
Godfrey, as though their suit his mind did move
　　To that whereon he never thought till now—
How can my heart (quoth he), if you I love,
　　To your request and suit but bend and bow?
Let rigor go, that right and justice be
Wherein you all consent and all agree.

XXVI.

Rinaldo shall return ; let him restrain
   Henceforth his headstrong wrath and hasty ire,
And with his hardy deeds let him take pain
   To correspond your hope and my desire.
Guelpho, thou must call home the knight again ;
   See that with speed he to these tents retire ;
The messengers appoint as likes thy mind,
And teach them where they should the young man find.—

XXVII.

Up starts the Dane that bore Prince Sweno's brand :—
   I will (quoth he) that message undertake ;
I will refuse no pains by sea or land
   To give the knight this sword, kept for his sake.—
This man was bold of courage, strong of hand ;
   Guelpho was glad he did the proffer make.—
Thou shalt (quoth he) ; Ubaldo shalt thou have
To go with thee, a knight, stout, wise, and grave.—

XXVIII.

Ubaldo in his youth had known and seen
   The fashion strange of many an uncouth land,
And travell'd over all the realms between
   The Arctic circle and hot Meroe's strand ;
And as a man whose wit his guide had been,
   Their customs use he could, tongues understand ;
For this, when spent his youthful seasons were,
Lord Guelpho entertain'd and held him dear.

XXIX.

To these committed was the charge and care
   To find and bring again the champion bold.
Guelpho commands them to the fort repair
   Where Boemond doth his seat and sceptre hold,
For public fame said that Bertoldo's heir
   There liv'd, there dwelt, there stay'd.   The hermit old
(That knew they were misled by false report)
Among them came, and parled in this sort :—

XXX.

Sir knights (quoth he), if you intend to ride
   And follow each report fond people say,
You follow but a rash and trothless guide,
   That leads vain men amiss and makes them stray.

Near Ascalon go to the salt sea side,
  Where a swift brook falls in with hideous sway,
An aged sire, our friend, there shall you find,
All what he saith that do, that keep in mind :

XXXI.

Of this great voyage which you undertake,
  Much by his skill, and much by mine advice,
Hath he foreknown, and welcome for my sake
  You both shall be, the man is kind and wise.—
Instructed thus no further question make
  The twain elected for this enterprise,
But humbly yielded to obey his word,
For what the hermit said, that said the Lord.

XXXII.

They took their leave and on their journey went,
  Their will could brook no stay, their zeal no let :
To Ascalon their voyage straight they bent,
  Whose broken shores with brackish waves are wet ;
And there they heard how 'gainst the clifts (besprent
  With bitter foam) the roaring surges beat ;
A tumbling brook their passage stopp'd and stay'd,
Which late-fall'n rain had proud and puissant made ;

XXXIII.

So proud that over all his banks he grew,
  And through the fields ran swift as shaft from bow.
While here they stopt and stood, before them drew
  An aged sire, grave and benign in show,
Crown'd with a beechen garland gather'd new,
  Clad in a linen robe that raught down low,
In his right hand a rod, and on the flood,
Against the stream, he march'd, and dry-shod yode :

XXXIV.

As on the Rhine (when winter's freezing cold
  Congeals the streams to thick and harden'd glass)
The beauties fair of shepherds' daughters bold,
  With wanton windlays, run, turn, play, and pass ;
So on this river pass'd the wizard old,
  Although unfrozen, soft, and swift it was ;
And thither stalked where the warriors stood,
To whom (their greetings done) he spoke and said :—

XXXV.

Great pains, great travail, lords, you have begun,
　　And of a cunning guide great need you stand ;
Far off, alas ! is great Bertoldo's son,
　　Imprison'd in a waste and desert land ;
What soil remains by which you must not run,
What promontory, rock, sea, shore, or sand ?
Your search must stretch, before the prince be found,
Beyond our world, beyond our half of ground :

XXXVI.

But yet vouchsafe to see my cell, I pray,
　　In hidden caves and vaults though builded low,
Great wonders there, strange things I will bewray,
　　Things good for you to hear, and fit to know.—
This said, he bids the river make them way ;
　　The flood retir'd, and backward 'gan to flow,
And here and there two crystal mountains rise ;
So fled the Red Sea once, and Jordan thrice.

XXXVII.

He took their hands, and led them headlong down
　　Under the flood, through vast and hollow deeps ;
Such light they had as when through shadows brown
　　Of thickest deserts feeble Cynthia peeps.
There spacious caves they saw all overflown,
　　There all his waters pure great Neptune keeps ;
And thence, to moisten all the earth, he brings
Seas, rivers, floods, lakes, fountains, wells, and springs :

XXXVIII.

Whence Ganges, Indus, Volga, Ister, Po,
　　Whence Euphrates, whence Tigris spring, they view :
Whence Tanais, whence Nilus comes also
　　(Although his head till then no creature knew) ;
But under these a wealthy stream doth go
　　That sulphur yields and ore, rich, quick, and new,
Which the sunbeam doth polish, purge, and fine,
And makes it silver pure, and gold divine ;

XXXIX.

And all his banks the rich and wealthy stream
　　Hath fair beset with pearl and precious stone,
Like stars in sky or lamps on stage that seem,
　　The darkness there was day the night was gone :

There sparkled (clothed in his azure beam)
  The heav'nly sapphire, there the hyacinth shone,
The carbuncle there flam'd, the diamond sheen
There glister'd bright, there smil'd the emerald green.

XL.

Amaz'd the knights amid these wonders pass'd,
  And fix'd so deep the marvails in their thought,
That not one word they utter'd, till at last
  Ubaldo spake, and thus his guide besought :—
O father, tell me, by what skill thou hast
  These wonders done, and to what place us brought ?
For well I know not if I wake or sleep,
My heart is drown'd in such amazement deep.—

XLI.

You are within the hollow womb (quoth he)
  Of fertile earth, the nurse of all things made ;
And but you brought and guided are by me,
  Her sacred entrails could no wight invade ;
My palace shortly shall you splendent see
  With glorious light, though built in night and shade.
A pagan was I born, but yet the Lord
To grace (by baptism) hath my soul restor'd :

XLII.

Nor yet by help of devil or aid from hell
  I do this uncouth work and wond'rous feat ;
The Lord forbid I use or charm or spell
  To raise foul Dis from his infernal seat ;
But of all herbs, of every spring and well,
  The hidden power I know and virtue great,
And all that kind hath hid from mortal sight,
And all the stars, their motions and their might ;

XLIII.

For in these caves I dwell not buried still
  From sight of heav'n, but often I resort
To tops of Lebanon or Carmel hill,
  And there in liquid air myself disport ;
There Mars and Venus I behold at will,
  As bare as erst when Vulcan took them short,
And how the rest roll, glide, and move, I see,
How their aspects benign or froward be ;

XLIV.

And underneath my feet the clouds I view,
    Now thick, now thin, now bright with Iris' bow ;
The frost and snow, the rain, the hail, the dew,
    The winds from whence they come and whence they blow ;
How Jove his thunder makes and lightning new,
    How with the bolt he strikes the earth below ;
How comate, crinite, caudate stars are fram'd,
I knew ; my skill with pride my heart inflam'd :

XLV.

So learned, cunning, wise, myself I thought,
    That I suppos'd my wit so high might climb
To know all things that God had fram'd or wrought,
    Fire, air, sea, earth, man, beast, sprite, place, and time :
But when your hermit me to baptism brought,
    And from my soul had wash'd the sin and crime,
Then I perceiv'd my sight was blindness still :
My wit was folly, ignorance my skill.

XLVI.

Then saw I that, like owls in shining sun,
    So 'gainst the beams of truth our souls are blind,
And at myself to smile I then begun,
    And at my heart puff'd up with folly's wind :
Yet still these arts as I before had done
    I practised ; such was the hermit's mind ;
Thus hath he chang'd my thoughts, my heart, my will,
And rules mine art, my knowledge, and my skill :

XLVII.

In him I rest, on him my thoughts depend,
    My lord, my teacher, and my guide is he,
This noble work he strives to bring to end,
    He is the architect, the workmen we.
The hardy youth home to this camp to send
    From prison strong, my care, my charge shall be :
So he commands, and me ere this foretold
Your coming oft to seek the champion bold.—

XLVIII.

While thus he said, he brought the champions twain
    Down to a vault wherein he dwells and lies.
It was a cave, high, wide, large, ample, plain,
    With goodly rooms, halls, chambers, galleries ;

All what is bred in rich and precious vein
  Of wealthy earth, and hid from mortal eyes,
There shines ; and fair adorn'd was every part
With riches grown by kind, not fram'd by art ;

XLIX.

A hundred grooms, quick, diligent and neat,
  Attendance gave about these strangers bold ;
Against the wall there stood a cupboard great
  Of massy plate, of silver, crystal, gold :
But when with precious wines and costly meat
  They filled were, thus spake the wizard old :
Now fits the time, Sir Knights, I tell and show
What you desire to hear and long to know.

L.

Armida's craft, her sleight, and hidden guile,
  You partly wot, her acts and arts untrue,
How to your camp she came, and by what wile
  The greatest lords and princes thence she drew :
You know she turn'd them first to monsters vile,
  And kept them since clos'd up in secret mew ;
Lastly to Gaza-ward in bonds them sent,
Whom young Rinaldo rescu'd as they went.

LI.

What chanced since I will at large declare
  (To you unknown), a story strange and true :
When first her prey, got with such pain and care,
  Escap'd and gone the witch perceiv'd and knew,
Her hands she wrung for grief, her clothes she tare,
  And full of wo these heavy words out threw :
Alas ! my knights are slain, my pris'ners free,
Yet of that conquest never boast shall he :

LII.

He in their place shall serve me, and sustain
  Their plagues, their torments suffer, sorrows bear,
And they his absence shall lament in vain,
  And wail his loss and theirs with many a tear.—
Thus talking to herself she did ordain
  A false and wicked guile, as you shall hear :
Thither she hasted where that valiant knight
Had overcome and slain her men in fight.

LIII.

Rinaldo there had doft and left his own,
    And on his back a pagan harness tied ;
Perchance he deemed so to pass unknown,
    And in those arms less noted safe to ride :
A headless corse, in fight late overthrown,
    The witch in his forsaken arms did hide,
And by a brook expos'd it on the sand,
Whither she wis'd would come a Christian band.

LIV.

Their coming might the dame foreknow right well,
    For secret spies she sent forth thousand ways,
Which every day news from the camp might tell,
    Who parted thence booties to search, or preys :
Beside, the sprites, conjur'd by secret spell,
    All what she asks or doubts reveals and says :
The body therefore plac'd she in that part
That further'd best her sleight, her craft, and art :

LV.

And near the corpse a varlet false and sly
    She left, attir'd in shepherd's homely weed,
And taught him how to counterfeit and lie
    As time requir'd, and he perform'd the deed :
With him your soldiers spoke, of jealousy
    And false suspect 'mongst them he strew'd the seed,
That since brought forth the fruit of strife and jar,
Of civil brawls, contention, discord, war :

LVI.

And as she wished, so the soldiers thought
    By Godfrey's practice that the prince was slain ;
Yet vanish'd that suspicion false to naught,
    When truth spread forth her silver wings again.
Her false devices thus Armida wrought,
    This was her first deceit, her foremost train ;
What next she practis'd shall you hear me tell,
Against our knight, and what thereof befell.

LVII.

Armida hunted him through wood and plain,
    Till on Orontes' flowery bank he stay'd ;
There, where the stream did part and meet again,
    And in the midst a gentle island made,

A pillar fair was pight beside the main,
  Near which a little frigate floating laid ;
The marble white the prince did long behold,
And this inscription read there writ in gold :—

LVIII.

Whoso thou art whom will or chance doth bring
  With happy steps to flood Orontes' sides,
Know that the world hath not so strange a thing
  'Twixt east and west as this small island hides ;
Then pass and see without more tarrying—
  The hasty youth to pass the stream provides ;
And, for the cog was narrow, small, and strait,
Alone he row'd, and bade his squires there wait.

LIX.

Landed, he stalks about, yet naught he sees
  But verdant groves, sweet shades, and mossy rocks,
With caves and fountains, flowers, herbs, and trees ;
  So that the words he read he takes for mocks :
But that green isle was sweet at all degrees,
  Wherewith entic'd, down sits he and unlocks
His closed helm, and bares his visage fair,
To take sweet breath from cool and gentle air.

LX.

A rumbling sound amid the waters deep
  Meanwhile he heard, and thither turn'd his sight,
And tumbling in the troubled stream took keep
  How the strong waves together rush and fight,
Whence first he saw, with golden tresses, peep
  The rising visage of a virgin bright,
And then her neck, her breasts, and all as low
As he for shame could see or she could show :

LXI.

So in the twilight doth sometimes appear
  A nymph, a goddess, or a fairy queen ;
And though no syren but a sprite this were,
  Yet by her beauty seem'd it she had been
One of those sisters false which haunted near
  The Tyrrhene shores, and kept those waters sheen ;
Like theirs her face, her voice was, and her sound,
And thus she sung and pleas'd both skies and ground :—

LXII.

Ye happy youths, whom April fresh and May
    Attire in flow'ring green of lusty age,
For glory vain or virtue's idle ray
    Do not your tender limbs to toil engage ;
In calm streams fishes, birds in sunshine play,
    Who followeth pleasure he is only sage ;
So nature saith, yet 'gainst her sacred will
Why still rebel you, and why strive you still ?

LXIII.

O fools, who youth possess yet scorn the same,
    A precious but a short-abiding treasure ;
Virtue itself is but an idle name,
    Priz'd by the world 'bove reason all and measure ;
And honor, glory, praise, renown, and fame,
    That men's proud hearts bewitch with tickling pleasure,
An echo is, a shade, a dream, a flower,
With each wind blasted, spoil'd with every shower :

LXIV.

But let your happy souls in joy possess
    The ivory castles of your bodies fair,
Your passed harms salve with forgetfulness,
    Haste not your coming ills with thought and care,
Regard no blazing star with burning tress,
    Nor storm, nor threat'ning sky, nor thund'ring air :
This wisdom is, good life, and worldly bliss,
Kind teacheth us, nature commands us this.—

LXV.

Thus sung the spirit false, and stealing sleep
    (To which her tunes entic'd his heavy eyes)
By step and step did on his senses creep,
    Till every limb therein unmoved lies ;
Not thunders loud could from this slumber deep
    (Of quiet death true image) make him rise :
Then from her ambush forth Armida start,
Swearing revenge, and threat'ning torments smart ;

LXVI.

But when she looked on his face awhile,
    And saw how sweet he breath'd, how still he lay,
How his fair eyes though closed seem to smile,
    At first she stay'd, astound with great dismay ;

Then sat her down (so love can art beguile),
　And as she sat and look'd, fled fast away
Her wrath.　Thus on his forehead gaz'd the maid,
As in his spring Narcissus tooting laid :

LXVII.

And with a veil she wiped now and then
　From his fair cheek the globes of silver sweat,
And cool air gather'd with a trembling fan
　To mitigate the rage of melting heat :
Thus (who would think it ?) his hot eye-glance can
　Of that cold frost dissolve the ·hardness great
Which late congeal'd the heart of that fair dame,
Who, late a· foe, a lover now became.

LXVIII.

Of woodbines, lilies, and of roses sweet,
　Which proudly flower'd through that wanton plain,
All platted fast, well knit, and joined meet,
　She fram'd a soft but surely holding chain,
Wherewith she bound his neck, his hands, and feet.
　Thus bound, thus taken, did the prince remain,
And in a coach, which two old dragons drew,
She laid the sleeping knight, and thence she flew :

LXIX.

Nor turn'd she to Damascus' kingdom large,
　Nor to the fort built in Asphalte's lake,
But jealous of her dear and precious charge,
　And of her love asham'd, the way did take
To the wide ocean, whither skiff or barge
　From us both seld or never voyage make,
And there, to frolic with her love awhile,
She chose a waste, a sole and desert isle ;

LXX.

An isle that with her fellows bears the name
　Of Fortunate, for temperate air and mould ;
There on a mountain high alight the dame,
　A hill obscur'd with shades of forests old,
Upon whose sides the witch by art did frame
　Continual snow, sharp frost, and winter cold ;
But on the top, fresh, pleasant, sweet, and green,
Beside a lake a palace built this queen :

LXXI.

There in perpetual, sweet, and flow'ring spring,
    She lives at ease, and 'joys her lord at will.
The hardy youth from this strange prison bring
    Your valors must, directed by my skill;
And overcome each monster and each thing
    That guards the palace. or that keeps the hill;
Nor shall you want a guide or engines fit
To bring you to the mount, or conquer it.

LXXII.

Beside the stream yparted shall you find
    A dame, in visage young, but old in years;
Her curled locks about her front are twin'd,
    A party-color'd robe of silk she wears;
She shall conduct you swift as air or wind,
    Or that flit bird that Jove's hot weapon bears;
A faithful pilot, cunning, trusty, sure,
As Typhis was, or skilful Palinure.

LXXIII.

At the hill's foot, whereon the witch doth dwell,
    The serpents hiss and cast their poison vile;
The ugly boars do rear their bristles fell;
    There gape the bears, and roar the lions wild:
But yet a rod I have can eas'ly quell
    Their rage and wrath, and make them meek and mild:
Yet on the top and height of all the hill
The greatest danger lies and greatest ill:

LXXIV.

There welleth out a fair, clear, bubbling spring,
    Whose waters pure the thirsty guests entice:
But in whose liquors cold the secret sting
    Of strange and deadly poison closed lies;
One sup thereof the drinker's heart doth bring
    To sudden joy, whence laughter vain doth rise;
Nor that strange merriment once stops or stays,
Till with his laughter's end he end his days.

LXXV.

Then from those deadly wicked streams refrain
    Your thirsty lips; despise the dainty cheer
You find expos'd upon the grassy plain;
    Nor those false damsels once vouchsafe to hear,

That in melodious tunes their voices strain,
  Whose faces lovely, smiling, sweet, appear ;
But you their looks, their voice, their songs despise,
And enter fair Armida's paradise :

LXXVI.

The house is builded like a maze within,
  With turning stairs, false doors, and winding ways ;
The shape whereof, plotted in vellum thin,
  I will you give, that all those sleights bewrays :
In 'midst a garden lies, where many a gin
  And net to catch frail hearts false Cupid lays ;
There, in the verdure of the arbors green,
With your brave champion lies the wanton queen.

LXXVII.

But when she haply riseth from the knight,
  And hath withdrawn her presence from the place,
Then take a shield I have of diamonds bright,
  And hold the same before the young man's face,
That he may glass therein his garments light,
  And wanton soft attire, and view his case ;
That with the sight, shame and disdain may move
His heart to leave that base and servile love.

LXXVIII.

Now resteth naught that needful is to tell,
  But that you go secure, safe, sure and bold ;
Unseen the palace may you enter well,
  And pass the dangers all I have foretold ;
For neither art, nor charm, nor magic spell,
  Can stop your passage or your steps withhold ;
Nor shall Armida (so you guarded be)
Your coming aught foreknow or once foresee :

LXXIX.

And eke as safe from that enchanted fort
  You shall return and 'scape unhurt away.
But now the time doth us to rest exhort,
  And you must rise by peep of springing day.—
This said, he led them through a narrow port,
  Into a lodging fair wherein they lay ;
There glad and full of thoughts he left his guests,
And in his wonted bed the old man rests.

BOOK XV.

I.

THE rosy-finger'd morn with gladsome ray
  Rose to her task from old Tithonus' lap,
When their grave host came where the warriors lay,
  And with him brought the shield, the rod, the map.—
Arise (quoth he), ere lately-broken day
  In his bright arms the round world fold or wrap ;
All what I promis'd here I have them brought,
Enough to bring Armida's charms to naught.—

II.

They started up, and every tender limb
  In sturdy steel and stubborn plate they dight,
Before the old man stalk'd ; they follow'd him
  Through gloomy shades of sad and sable night,
Through vaults obscure again and entries dim,
  The way they came their steps remeasur'd right ;
But at the flood arriv'd—Farewell (quoth he),
Good luck your aid, your guide good fortune be.—

III.

The flood receiv'd them in his bottom low,
  And lift them up above his billows thin ;
The waters so cast up a branch or bough,
  By violence first plung'd and div'd therein.

But when upon the shore the waves them throw,
  The knights for their fair guide to look begin ;
And gazing round, a little bark they spy'd,
Wherein a damsel sat the stern to guide ;

IV.

Upon her front her locks were curled new,
  Her eyes were courteous, full of peace and love ;
In look a saint, an angel bright in show,
  So in her visage grace and virtue strove ;
Her robe seem'd sometimes red and sometimes blue,
  And changed still as she did stir or move ;
That look how oft man's eye beheld the same,
So oft the colors changed, went and came :

V.

The feathers so, that tender, soft and plain,
  About the dove's smooth neck close couched been,
Do in one color never long remain,
  But change their hue 'gainst glimpse of Phœbus sheen ;
And now of rubies bright a vermeil chain,
  Now make a carknet rich of emeralds green ;
Now mingle both, now alter, turn, and change
To thousand colors, rich, pure, fair, and strange.—

VI.

Enter this boat, you happy men (she says),
  Wherein through raging waves secure I ride ;
To which all tempest, storm, and wind obeys,
  All burdens light, benign is stream and tide.
My Lord, that rules your journeys and your ways,
  Hath sent me here, your servant and your guide.—
This said, her shallop drove she 'gainst the sand,
And anchor cast amid the steadfast land.

VII.

They enter'd in ; her anchor she up-wound,
  And launched forth to sea her pinnace flit ;
Spread to the wind her sails she broad unbound,
  And at the helm sat down to govern it ;
Swelled the flood that all his banks he drown'd,
  To bear the greatest ship of burden fit ;
Yet was her frigate little, swift and light,
That at his lowest ebb bear it he might.

VIII.

Swifter than thought the friendly wind forth bore
    The sliding boat upon the rolling wave ;
With curded foam and froth the billows hoar
    About the cable murmur, roar and rave :
At last they came where all his watery store
    The flood in one deep channel did engrave,
And forth to greedy seas his streams he sent,
And so his waves, his name, himself, he spent.

IX.

The wond'rous boat scant touch'd the troubled main,
    But all the sea still, hush'd, and quiet was ;
Vanish'd the clouds, ceased the wind and rain,
    The tempests threaten'd over-blow and pass ;
A gentle breathing air made even and plain
    The azure face of heav'n's smooth looking-glass ;
And heav'n itself smil'd from the skies above,
With a calm clearness, on the earth his love.

X.

By Ascalon they sailed, and forth drived
    Toward the west their speedy course they frame,
In sight of Gaza till the bark arrived
    (A little port when first it took that name,
But since by others' loss so well it thrived
    A city great and rich that it became),
And there the shores and borders of the land
They found as full of armed men as sand.

XI.

The passengers to land-ward turn'd their sight,
    And there saw pitched many a stately tent ;
Soldier and footman, captain, lord, and knight ;
    Between the shore and city came and went :
Huge elephants, strong camels, coursers light,
    With horned hoofs the sandy ways out rent ;
And in the haven many a ship and boat
(With mighty anchors fasten'd) swim and float :

XII.

Some spread their sails, and some with strong oars sweep
    The waters smooth, and brush the buxom wave ;
Their breasts in sunder cleave the yielding deep,
    The broken seas for anger foam and rave.

When thus their guide began—Sir knights, take keep
    How all these shores are spread with squadrons brave,
And troops of hardy knights ; yet on these sands
The monarch scant hath gather'd half his bands.

XIII.

Of Egypt only these the forces are,
    And aid from other lands they here attend,
For 'twixt the noon-day sun and morning star,
    All realms at his command do bow and bend ;
So that I trust we shall return from far,
    And bring our journey long to wished end,
Before this king or his lieutenant shall
These armies bring to Sion's conquer'd wall.—

XIV.

While thus she said, as soaring eagles fly
    'Mongst other birds securely through the air,
And mounting up behold with wakeful eye
    The radiant beams of old Hyperion's hair ;
Her gondola so passed swiftly by
    'Twixt ship and ship, withouten fear or care
Who should her follow, trouble, stop or stay,
And forth to sea made lucky speed and way.

XV.

Themselves forenenst old Raphia's town they fand,
    A town that first to sailors doth appear
As they from Syria pass to Egypt land :
    The sterile coasts of barren Rinoceere
They pass'd ; and seas where Casius' hill doth stand,
    That with his trees o'erspreads the waters near,
Against whose roots breaketh the brackish wave,
Where Jove his temple, Pompey hath his grave :

XVI.

Then Damietta next, where they behold
    How to the sea his tribute Nilus pays,
By his seven mouths, renown'd in stories old,
    And by a hundred more ignoble ways :
They pass'd the town built by the Grecian bold,
    Of him call'd Alexandria till our days ;
And Pharos' tower and isle, remov'd of yore
Far from the land, now joined to the shore.

XVII.

Both Crete and Rhodes they left by north unseen,
    And sail'd along the coasts of Afric lands,
Whose sea towns fair, but realms more inward been
    All full of monsters and of desert sands :
With her five cities then they left Cyrene,
    Where that old temple of false Ammon stands :
Next Ptolemais, and that sacred wood
Whence spring the silent streams of Lethe flood.

XVIII.

The greater Sirtes (that sailors often cast
    In peril great of death and loss extreme)
They compass'd round about and safely pass'd ;
    Then Cape Judeca and flood Magras' stream ;
Then Tripoli, 'gainst which is Malta plac'd,
    That low and hid, to lurk in seas doth seem ;
The little Sirtes then, and Alzerbe's isle,
Where dwelt the folk that lotos eat erewhile :

XIX.

Next Tunis on the crooked shore they spy'd,
    Whose bay a rock on either side defends ;
Tunis, all towns in beauty, wealth and pride
    Above, as far as Lybia's bounds extends ;
'Gainst which (from fair Sicilia's fertile side)
    His ragged front great Lilibenni bends.
The dame there pointed out where sometimes stood
Rome's stately rival whilome, Carthage proud :

XX.

Great Carthage low in ashes cold doth lie,
    Her ruins poor the herbs in height scant pass ;
So cities fall, so perish kingdoms high,
    Their pride and pomp lie hid in sand and grass :
Then why should mortal man repine to die,
    Whose life is air, breath wind, and body glass ?
From thence the seas next Bisert's walls they cleft,
And far Sardinia on their right hand left.

XXI.

Numidia's mighty plains they coasted then,
    Where wandering shepherds us'd their flocks to feed ;
Then Bugia and Algiers, th' infamous den
    Of pirates false ; Oran they left with speed ;

All Tingitan they swiftly over-ren,
　　Where elephants and angry lions breed ;
Where now the realms of Fez and Moroc be,
'Gainst which Granada's shores and coasts they see.

XXII.

Now are they there where first the sea brake in
　　By great Alcides' help (as stories feign) ;
True may it be that where those floods begin
　　It whilome was a firm and solid main,
Before the sea there through did passage win,
　　And parted Afric from the land of Spain ;
Abila hence, thence Calpe great up springs,
Such power hath time to change the face of things.

XXIII.

Four times the sun had spread his morning ray
　　Since first the dame launch'd forth her wond'rous barge,
And never yet took port in creek or bay,
　　But fairly forward bore the knights her charge ;
Now through the strait her jolly ship made way,
　　And boldly sail'd upon the ocean large ;
But if the sea in midst of earth was great,
O what was this wherein earth hath her seat !

XXIV.

Now deep engulphed in the mighty flood,
　　They saw not Gades nor the mountains near ;
Fled was the land and towns on land that stood,
　　Heav'n cover'd sea, sea seem'd the heav'ns to bear,
At last—Fair lady (quoth Ubaldo good),
　　That in this endless main doth guide us here,
If ever man before here sailed tell,
Or other lands here be wherein men dwell ?—

XXV.

Great Hercules (quoth she) when he had quell'd
　　The monsters fierce in Afric and in Spain,
And all along your coasts and countries sail'd,
　　Yet durst he not assay the ocean main ;
Within his pillars would he have impal'd
　　The over-daring wit of mankind vain ;
Till Lord Ulysses did those bounders pass,
To see and know he so desirous was :

XXVI.

He pass'd those pillars, and in open wave
    Of the broad sea first his bold sails untwin'd ;
But yet the greedy ocean was his grave,
    Naught helped him his skill 'gainst tide and wind ;
With him all witness of his voyage brave
    Lies buried there, no truth thereof we find ;
And they whom storm hath forced that way since
Are drowned all, or unreturn'd from thence :

XXVII.

So that this mighty sea is yet unsought,
    Where thousand isles and kingdoms lie unknown ;
Not void of men as some have vainly thought,
    But peopled well and wonned like your own :
The land is fertile ground, but scant well wrought,
    Air wholesome, temp'rate sun, grass proudly grown.—
But (quoth Ubaldo) dame, I pray thee teach,
Of that hid world what be the laws and speech.—

XXVIII.

As divers be their nations (answer'd she),
    Their tongues, their rites, their laws so diff'rent are ;
Some pray to beasts, some to a stone or tree,
    Some to the earth, the sun, or morning star :
Their meats unwholesome, vile, and hateful be,
    Some eat man's flesh and captives ta'en in war ;
And all from Calpe's mountain west that dwell,
In faith profane, in life are rude and fell.—

XXIX.

But will our gracious God (the knight reply'd)
    That with his blood all sinful men hath bought,
His truth for ever and his gospel hide
    From all those lands, as yet unknown, unsought ?—
O no (quoth she), his name both far and wide
    Shall there be known, all learning thither brought ;
Nor shall these long and tedious ways for ever,
Your world and theirs, their lands your kingdoms sever.

XXX.

The time shall come that sailors shall disdain
    To talk or argue of Alcides' strait ;
And lands and seas that nameless yet remain,
    Shall well be known, their bounders, site, and seat.

The ships encompass shall the solid main,
  As far as seas outstretch their waters great,
And measure all the world; and with the sun,
About this earth, this globe, this compass run.

XXXI.

A knight of Genes shall have the hardiment
  Upon this wond'rous voyage first to wend;
Nor winds nor waves that ships in sunder rent,
  Nor seas unus'd, strange clime, or pool unken'd,
Nor other peril nor astonishment,
  That makes frail hearts of men to bow and bend,
Within Abila's strait shall keep and hold
The noble spirit of this sailor bold:

XXXII.

Thy ship, Columbus, shall her canvas wing
  Spread o'er that world that yet concealed lies;
That scant swift Fame her looks shall after bring,
  Though thousand plumes she have and thousand eyes:
Let her of Bacchus and Alcides sing,
  Of thee to future age let this suffice,
That of thine acts she some forewarning give,
Which shall in verse and noble story live.—

XXXIII.

Thus talking, swift 'twixt south and west they run,
  And sliced out 'twixt froth and foam their way;
At once they saw before the setting sun,
  Behind the rising beam of springing day;
And when the morn her drops and dews begun
  To scatter broad upon the flow'ring lay,
Far off a hill and mountain high they spy'd,
Whose top the clouds environ, clothe, and hide.

XXXIV.

And drawing near, the hill at ease they view,
  When all the clouds were molten, fallen, and fled;
Whose top, pyramid-wise, did pointed show,
  High, narrow, sharp, the sides yet more outspread;
Thence now and then fire, flame, and smoke out flew,
  As from that hill where under lies in bed
Enceladus, whence with imperious sway
Bright fire breaks out by night, black smoke by day.

XXXV.

About the hill lay other islands small,
  Where other rocks, crags, clifts, and mountains stood ;
The Isles Fortunate those elder times did call,
  To which high heav'n they feign'd so kind and good,
And of his blessings rich so liberal,
  That without tillage earth gives corn for food ;
And grapes, that swell with sweet and precious wine,
There, without pruning, yields the fertile vine ;

XXXVI.

The olive fat there ever buds and flow'rs,
  The honey drops from hollow oaks distil,
The falling brook her silver streams down pours,
  With gentle murmur from their native hill ;
The western blast temp'reth with dews and show'rs
  The sunny rays, lest heat the blossoms kill ;
The Fields Elysian (as fond heathens feign)
Were there, where souls of men in bliss remain.

XXXVII.

To these their pilot steer'd—And now (quoth she)
  Your voyage long to end is brought well near ;
The happy Isles of Fortune now you see,
  Of which great fame, and little truth, you hear ;
Sweet, wholesome, pleasant, fertile, fat they be,
  Yet not so rich as fame reports they were.—
This said, towards an island fresh she bore,
The first of ten that lie next Afric's shore.

XXXVIII.

When Charles thus—If, worthy governess,
  To our good speed such tarryance be not let,
Upon this isle that heav'n so fair doth bless,
  To view the place, on land awhile us set ;
To know the folk, and what God they confess,
  And all whereby man's heart may knowledge get,
That I may tell the wonders therein seen,
Another day, and say there have I been.—

XXXIX.

She answer'd him—Well fits this high desire
  Thy noble heart, yet cannot I consent,
For heav'n's decree, firm, stable, and entire,
  Thy wish repugns, and 'gainst thy will is bent ;

Nor yet the time hath Titan's gliding fire
   Mete forth, prefix'd for this discoverment,
Nor is it lawful of the ocean main
That you the secrets know, or known explain.

XL.

To you, withouten needle, map, or card,
   It's given to pass these seas, and there arrive
Where in strong prison lies your knight imbarr'd,
   And of her prey you must the witch deprive :
If further to aspire you be prepar'd,
   In vain 'gainst fate and heav'n's decree you strive.—
While thus she said, the first-seen isle gave place,
And high and rough the second show'd his face.

XLI.

They saw how eastward stretch'd in order long,
   The happy islands sweetly flow'ring lay ;
And how the seas betwixt those isles inthrong,
   And how they shoulder'd land from land away.
In seven of them the people rude among
   The shady trees their sheds had built of clay ;
The rest lay waste, unless wild beasts unseen,
Or wanton nymphs, roam'd on the mountains green.

XLII.

A secret place they found in one of those,
   Where the cleft shore sea in his bosom takes,
And 'twixt his stretched arms doth fold and close
   An ample bay ; a rock the haven makes,
Which to the main doth his broad back oppose,
   Whereon the roaring billow cleaves and breaks ;
And here and there two crags, like turrets high,
Point forth a port to all that sail thereby.

XLIII.

The quiet seas below lie safe and still,
   The greenwood like a garland grows aloft ;
Sweet caves within, cool shades, and waters shrill,
   Where lie the nymphs on moss and ivy soft :
No anchor there needs hold her frigate still,
   Nor cable twisted sure, though breaking oft.
Into this desert, silent, quiet glade,
Enter'd the dame, and there her haven made.—

XLIV.

The palace proudly built (quoth she) behold,
   That sits on top of yonder mountain's height,
Of Christ's true faith there lies the champion bold,
   In idleness, love, fancy, folly light.
When Phœbus shall his rising beams unfold,
   Prepare you 'gainst the hill to mount upright;
Nor let this stay in your bold hearts breed care,
For, save that one, all hours unlucky are:

XLV.

But yet this evening (if you make good speed)
   To that hill's foot with day-light might you pass.—
This said, the dame, their guide and they agreed,
   And took their leave, and leap'd forth on the grass:
They found the way that to the hill doth lead,
   And softly went that neither tired was;
But at the mountain's foot they both arrived
Before the sun his team in waters dived.

XLVI.

They saw how from the crags and clifts below
   His proud and stately pleasant top grew out,
And how his sides were clad with frost and snow;
   The height was green with herbs and flow'rets stout,
Like hairy locks the trees about him grow,
   The rocks of ice keep watch and ward about
The tender roses and the lilies new;
Thus art can nature change, and kind subdue.

XLVII.

Within a thick, a dark, and shady plot,
   At the hill's foot that night the warriors dwell;
But when the sun his rays, bright shining, hot,
   Dispred, of golden light th' eternal well,
Up, up! they cried, and fiercely up they got,
   And climbed boldly 'gainst the mountain fell;
But forth there crept (from whence I cannot say)
An ugly serpent which forestall'd their way;

XLVIII.

Armed with golden scales, his head and crest
   He lifted high, his neck swell'd great with ire,
Flamed his eyes, and hiding with his breast
   All the broad path, he poison breath'd and fire;

Now reach'd he forth in folds and forward press'd ;
　　Now would he back in rolls and heaps retire ;
Thus he presents himself to guard the place ;
The knights press'd forward with assured pace.

XLIX.

Charles drew forth his brand to strike the snake :
　　Ubaldo cried—Stay, my companion dear,
Will you with sword or weapon battaile make
　　Against this monster that affronts us here ?—
This said, he 'gan his charmed rod to shake,
　　So that the serpent durst not hiss for fear,
But fled, and dead for dread fell on the grass,
And so the passage plain, eath, open was.

L.

A little higher on the way they met
　　A lion fierce, that hugely roar'd and cry'd ;
His crest he reared high, and open set
　　Of his broad gaping jaws the furnace wide,
His stern his back oft smote his rage to whet :
　　But when the sacred staff he once espy'd,
A trembling fear through his bold heart was spread,
His native wrath was gone, and swift he fled.

LI.

The hardy couple on their way forth wend,
　　And met a host, that on them roar and gape,
Of savage beasts, tofore unseen, unken'd,
　　Diff'ring in voice, in semblance, and in shape :
All monsters which hot Afric doth forth send,
　　'Twixt Nilus, Atlas, and the southern cape,
Were all there met, and all wild beasts besides
Hyrcania breeds or Hyrcane forests hides.

LII.

But yet that fierce, that strange, and savage host,
　　Could not in presence of those worthies stand,
But fled away, their heart and courage lost,
　　When Lord Ubaldo shook his charming wand.
No other let their passage stopp'd or crost,
　　Till on the mountain's top themselves they fand,
Save that the ice, the frost, and drifted snow,
Oft made them feeble, weary, faint, and slow :

LIII.

But having passed all that frozen ground,
　　And overgone that winter sharp and keen,
A warm, mild, pleasant, gentle sky they found,
　　That overspread a large and ample green ;
The winds breath'd spikenard, myrrh, and balm around,
　　The blasts there firm, unchanged, stable been ;
Nor as elsewhere the winds now rise now fall,
And Phœbus there aye shines, sets not at all :

LIV.

Not as elsewhere, now sunshine bright, now show'rs,
　　Now heat, now cold, there interchanged were,
But everlasting spring mild heav'n down pours,
　　In which nor rain, nor storm, nor clouds appear ;
Nursing to fields their grass, to grass his flowers,
　　To flowers their smell, to trees the leaves they bear.
There by a lake a stately palace stands,
That overlooks all mountains, seas, and lands.

LV.

The passage hard against the mountain steep
　　These travellers had faint and weary made,
That through those grassy plains they scantly creep,
　　They walk'd, they rested oft, they went, they stay'd ;
When from the rocks that seem'd for joy to weep,
　　Before their feet a dropping crystal play'd,
Enticing them to drink, and on the flow'rs
The plenteous spring a thousand streams down pours.

LVI.

All which united, in the springing grass
　　Eat forth a channel through the tender green,
And underneath eternal shade did pass,
　　With murmur shrill, cold, pure, and scantly seen ;
Yet so transparent that perceived was
　　The bottom rich, and sands that golden been ;
And on the brims the silken grass aloft
Proffer'd them seats, sweet, easy, fresh, and soft.—

LVII.

See here the stream of laughter, see the spring
　　(Quoth they) of danger and of deadly pain ;
Here fond desire must by fair governing
　　Be rul'd, our lust bridled with wisdom's rein ;

Our ears be stopped while these syrens sing,
　　Their notes enticing man to pleasure vain.
Thus past they forward where the stream did make
An ample pond, a large and spacious lake:

LVIII.

There on the table was all dainty food
　　That sea, that earth, or liquid air could give;
And in the crystal of the laughing flood
　　They saw two naked virgins bathe and dive,
That sometimes toying, sometimes wrestling stood,
　　Sometimes for speed and skill in swimming strive;
Now underneath they div'd, now rose above,
And 'ticing baits laid forth of lust and love:

LIX.

These naked wantons, tender, fair and white,
　　Moved so far the warriors' stubborn hearts,
That on their shapes they gazed with delight;
　　The nymphs applied their sweet alluring arts,
And one of them above the waters quite
　　Lift up her head, her breasts, and higher parts,
And all that might weak eyes subdue and take;
Her lower beauties veil'd the gentle lake.

LX.

As when the morning star escap'd and fled
　　From greedy waves with dewy beams up flies,
Or as the queen of love, new born and bred
　　Of th' ocean's fruitful froth, did first arise;
So vented she, her golden locks forth shed
　　Round pearls and crystal moist therein which lies:
But when her eyes upon the knights she cast,
She start, and feign'd her of their sight aghast;

LXI.

And her fair locks, that on a knot were tied
　　High on her crown, she 'gan at large unfold;
Which falling long and thick, and spreading wide,
　　The ivory soft and white mantled in gold:
Thus her fair skin the dame would clothe and hide,
　　And that which hid it no less fair was hold:
Thus clad in waves and locks, her eyes divine
From them ashamed did she turn and twine:

LXII.

Withal she smiled, and she blush'd withal,
    Her blush her smiling, smiles her blushing graced ;
Over her face her amber tresses fall,
    Whereunder love himself in ambush placed :
At last she warbled forth a treble small,
    And with sweet looks her sweet songs interlaced :—
O happy men ! that have the grace (quoth she)
This bliss, this heav'n, this paradise to see.

LXIII.

This is the place wherein you may assuage
    Your sorrows past, here is that joy and bliss
That flourish'd in the antique golden age ;
    Here needs no law, here none doth aught amiss ;
Put off those arms, and fear not Mars his rage,
    Your sword, your shield, your helmet needless is ;
Then consecrate them here to endless rest,
You shall love's champions be and soldiers blest.

LXIV.

The fields for combat here are beds of down,
    Or heaped lilies under shady brakes :
But come and see our queen with golden crown,
    That all her servants blest and happy makes ;
She shall admit you gently for her own,
    Number'd with those that of her joy partakes :
But first within this lake your dust and sweat
Wash off, and at that table sit and eat.—

LXV.

While thus she sung, her sister lur'd them high,
    With many a gesture kind and loving show,
To music's sound as dames in court apply
    Their cunning feet, and dance now swift now slow.
But still the knights unmoved passed by,
    These vain delights for wicked charms they know ;
Nor could their heav'nly voice nor angel's look
Surprise their hearts, if eye or ear they took :

LXVI.

For if that sweetness once but touch'd their hearts,
    And proffer'd there to kindle Cupid's fire,
Straight armed reason to his charge upstarts,
    And quencheth lust and killeth fond desire :

Thus scorned were the dames, their wiles and arts,
  And to the palace gates the knights retire,
While in their streams the damsels dived sad,
Asham'd, disgrac'd, for that repulse they had.

BOOK XVI.

THE ARGUMENT.

The searchers pass through all the palace bright,
  Where in sweet prison lies Rinaldo pent,
And do so much, that full of rage and spite,
  With them he goes, sad, shamed, discontent.
With plaints and prayers to retain her knight
  Armida strives : he hears, but thence he went :
And she forlorn, her palace great and fair
Destroys for grief, and flies thence through the air.

I.

The palace great is builded rich and round,
  And in the centre of the inmost hold
There lies a garden sweet on fertile ground,
  Fairer than that where grew the trees of gold.
The cunning sprites had buildings rear'd around,
  With doors and entries false a thousand fold ;
A labyrinth they made that fortress brave,
Like Dedal's prison, or Porsenna's grave.

II.

The knights pass'd through the castle's largest gate
  (Though round about a hundred ports there shine),
The door leaves fram'd of carved silver plate
  Upon their golden hinges turn and twine :
They stay'd to view this work of wit and state,
  The workmanship excell'd the substance fine,
For all the shapes in that rich metal wrought,
Save speech, of living bodies wanted naught :

III.

Alcides there sat telling tales, and spun
  Among the feeble troops of damsels mild
(He that the fiery gates of hell had won,
  And heav'n upheld) ; false love stood by and smil'd ;

Arm'd with his club fair Iole forth run,
　His club with blood of monsters foul defil'd;
And on her back his lion's skin had she,
Too rough a bark for such a tender tree.

IV.

Beyond was made a sea, whose azure flood
　The hoary froth crush'd from the surges blue,
Wherein two navies great well ranged stood
　Of warlike ships, fire from their arms out flew;
The waters burnt about their vessels good,
　Such flames the gold therein enchased threw;
Cæsar his Romans hence, the Asian kings
Thence Antony and Indian princes, brings:

V.

The Cyclades seem'd to swim amid the main,
　And hill 'gainst hill and mount 'gainst mountain smote;
With such great fury met those armies twain,
　Here burnt a ship, there sunk a bark or boat;
Here darts and wildfire flew, there drown'd or slain
　Of princes dead the bodies fleet and float;
Here Cæsar wins, and yonder conquer'd been
The eastern ships, there fled th' Egyptian queen:

VI.

Antonius eke himself to fight betook,
　The empire lost to which he would aspire;
Yet fled not he, nor fight for fear forsook,
　But follow'd her, drawn on by fond desire:
Well might you see, within his troubled look,
　Strive and contend love, courage, shame and ire;
Oft look'd he back, oft gazed he on the fight,
But oft'ner on his mistress and her flight:

VII.

Then in the secret creeks of fruitful Nile,
　Cast in her lap he would sad death await,
And in the pleasure of her lovely smile
　Sweeten the bitter stroke of cursed fate.
All this did art with curious hand compile
　In the rich metal of that princely gate.
The knights these stories viewed first and last,
Which seen, they forward press'd and in they pass'd.

VIII.

As through his channel crook'd Meander glides
   With turns and twines, and rolls now to now fro,
Whose streams run forth there to the salt sea sides,
   Here back return, and to their spring-ward go:
Such crooked paths, such ways this palace hides;
   Yet all the maze their map described so,
That through the labyrinth they go in fine,
As Theseus did by Ariadne's line.

IX.

When they had passed all those troubled ways,
   The garden sweet spread forth her green to show,
The moving crystal from the fountains plays,
   Fair trees, high plants, strange herbs, and flow'rets new,
Sun-shiny hills, dales hid from Phœbus' rays,
   Groves, arbors, mossy caves, at once they view;
And that which beauty most, most wonder brought,
Nowhere appear'd the art which all this wrought.

X.

So with the rude the polish'd mingled was,
   That natural seem'd all, and every part
Nature would craft in counterfeiting pass,
   And imitate her imitator art.
Mild was the air, the skies were clear as glass,
   The trees no whirlwind felt nor tempest's smart,
But ere their fruit drop off the blossom comes;
This springs, that falls, that rip'neth, and this blooms.

XI.

The leaves upon the self-same bough did hide,
   Beside the young, the old and ripened fig;
Here fruit was green, there ripe with vermeil side,
   The apples new and old grew on one twig;
The fruitful vine her arms spread high and wide,
   That bended underneath their clusters big;
The grapes were tender here, hard, young and sour,
There purple, ripe, and nectar sweet forth pour.

XII.

The joyous birds, hid under greenwood shade
   Sung merry notes on every branch and bough;
The wind, that in the leaves and waters play'd,
   With murmur sweet now sang, and whistled now;

Ceased the birds, the wind loud answer made,
    And while they sung it rumbled soft and low :
Thus, were it hap or cunning, chance or art,
The wind in this strange music bore his part.

XIII.

With party-color'd plumes and purple bill,
    A wond'rous bird among the rest there flew,
That in plain speech sung lovelays loud and shrill,
    Her leden was like human language true ;
So much she talk'd, and with such wit and skill,
    That strange it seemed how much good she knew ;
Her feather'd fellows all stood hush'd to hear,
Dumb was the wind, the waters silent were.—

XIV.

The gently-budding rose (quoth she) behold,
    The first scant peeping forth with virgin beams,
Half ope, half shut, her beauties doth up-fold
    In their dear leaves, and less seen fairer seems,
And after spreads them forth more broad and bold,
    Then languisheth and dies in last extremes :
For seems the same that decked bed and bow'r
Of many a lady late and paramour :

XV.

So in the passing of a day doth pass
    The bud and blossom of the life of man,
Nor e'er doth flourish more, but like the grass
    Cut down, becometh withered, pale, and wan ;
O gather then the rose while time thou has,
    Short is the day, done when it scant began ;
Gather the rose of love while yet thou mayst,
Loving be lov'd, embracing be embrac'd.—

XVI.

She ceas'd ; and as approving all she spoke
    The choir of birds their heav'nly tunes renew ;
The turtles sigh'd and sighs with kisses broke,
    The fowls to shades unseen by pairs withdrew ;
It seem'd the laurel chaste and stubborn oak,
    And all the gentle trees on earth that grew,
It seem'd the land, the sea, and heav'n above,
All breath'd out fancy sweet and sigh'd out love.

XVII.

Through all this music rare and strong consent
    Of strange allurements, sweet 'bove mean and measure,
Severe, firm, constant, still the knights forth went,
    Hard'ning their hearts 'gainst false enticing pleasure,
'Twixt leaf and leaf their sight before they sent,
    And after crept themselves at ease and leisure,
Till they beheld the queen sit with their knight
Beside the lake, shaded with boughs from sight:

XVIII.

Her breasts were naked, for the day was hot,
    Her locks unbound wav'd in the wanton wind;
Some deal she sweat (tir'd with the game you wot),
    Her sweat-drops bright, white, round, like pearls of Inde:
Her humid eyes a fiery smile forth shot,
    That like sun-beams in silver fountains shin'd;
O'er him her looks she hung, and her soft breast
The pillow was where he and love took rest:

XIX.

His hungry eyes upon her face he fed,
    And feeding them so pin'd himself away;
And she, declining often down her head,
    His lips, his cheeks, his eyes kiss'd as he lay;
Wherewith he sigh'd, as if his soul had fled
    From his frail breast to hers, and there would stay
With her beloved sprite. The armed pair
These follies all beheld and this hot fair.

XX.

Down by the lovers' side there pendant was
    A crystal mirror, bright, pure, smooth, and neat;
He rose and to his mistress held the glass
    (A noble page grac'd with that service great);
She with glad looks, he with inflam'd (alas!),
    Beauty and love beheld both in one seat;
Yet them in sundry objects each espies,
She in the glass, he saw them in her eyes:

XXI.

Her to command, to serve it pleas'd the knight;
    He proud of bondage, of her empire she.—
My dear (she said), that blesseth with thy sight
    Even blessed angels, turn thine eyes to me,

For painted in my heart and portray'd right,
   Thy worth, thy beauties, and perfections be ;
Of which the form, the shape, and fashion best,
Not in this glass is seen, but in my breast ;

XXII.

And if thou me disdain, yet be content
   At least so to behold thy lovely hue,
That while thereon thy looks are fix'd and bent,
   Thy happy eyes themselves may see and view ;
So rare a shape no crystal can present,
   No glass contain that heav'n of beauties true :
O let the skies thy worthy mirror be,
And in clear stars thy shape and image see !—

XXIII.

And with that word she smil'd, and ne'ertheless
   Her love-toys still she us'd and pleasures bold.
Her hair, that done, she twisted up in tress,
   And looser locks in silken laces roll'd ;
Her curls in garland-wise she did up dress,
   Wherein (like rich enamel laid on gold)
The twisted flow'rets smil'd; and her white breast,
The lilies there that spring, with roses dress'd :

XXIV.

The jolly peacock spreads not half so fair
   The eyed feathers of his pompous train ;
Nor golden Iris so bends in the air
   Her twenty-color'd bow through clouds of rain :
Yet all her ornaments, strange, rich, and rare,
   Her girdle did in price and beauty stain ;
Not that (with scorn) which Tuscan Guilla lost,
Nor Venus' ceston could match this for cost :

XXV.

Of mild denays, of tender scorns, of sweet
   Repulses, war, peace, hope, despair, joy, fear,
Of smiles, jests, mirth, wo, grief, and sad regret,
   Sighs, sorrows, tears, embracements, kisses dear,
That mixed first by weight and measure meet,
   Then at an easy fire attemper'd were,
This wond'rous girdle did Armida frame,
And when she would be loved wore the same :

XXVI.

But when her wooing fit was brought to end,
   She congee took, kiss'd him, and went her way ;
For once she used every day to wend
   'Bout her affairs, her spells and charms to say.
The youth remain'd, yet had no power to bend
   One step from thence, but used there to stray
'Mongst the sweet birds, through every walk and grove,
Alone, save for a hermit false call'd Love :

XXVII.

And when the silence deep and friendly shade
   Recall'd the lovers to their wonted sport,
In a fair room for pleasure built they lay'd,
   And longest nights with joys made sweet and short.
Now while the queen her household things survey'd,
   And left her lord, her garden, and disport,
The twain that hidden in the bushes were,
Before the Prince in glist'ring arms appear.

XXVIII.

As the fierce steed for age withdrawn from war,
   Wherein the glorious beast had always won,
That in vile rest, from fight sequester'd far,
   Feeds with the mares at large, his service done ;
If arms he see, or hear the trumpet's jar,
   He neigheth loud, and thither fast doth run,
And wisheth on his back the armed knight,
Longing for jousts, for tournaments, and fight :

XXIX.

So far'd Rinaldo when the glorious light
   Of their bright harness glister'd in his eyes,
His noble sprite awaked at that sight,
   His blood began to warm, his heart to rise ;
Though drunk with ease, devoid of wonted might,
   On sleep till then his weaken'd virtue lies.
Ubaldo forward stept, and to him held
Of diamonds clear that pure and precious shield :

XXX.

Upon the targe his looks amaz'd he bent,
   And therein all his wanton habit spied,
His civet, balm, and perfumes redolent,
   How from his locks they smok'd and mantle wide ;

His sword, that many a Pagan stout had shent,
  Bewrapt with flow'rs hung idly by his side,
So nicely decked that it seem'd the knight
Wore it for fashion sake, but not for fight.

XXXI.

As when from sleep and idle dreams abray'd
  A man awak'd calls home his wits again,
So in beholding his attire he play'd,
  But yet to view himself could not sustain ;
His looks he downward cast and naught he said,
  Griev'd, shamed, sad, he would have died fain ;
And oft he wish'd the earth or ocean wide
Would swallow him, and so his errors hide.

XXXII.

Ubaldo took the time and thus begun :—
  All Europe now and Asia be in war ;
And all that Christ adore, and fame have won
  In battaile strong, in Syria fighting are :
But thee alone (Bertoldo's noble son)
  This little corner keeps, exiled far
From all the world, buried in sloth and shame,
A carpet champion for a wanton dame !

XXXIII.

What letharge hath in drowsiness uppend
  Thy courage thus ?   What sloth doth thee infect ?
Up ! up ! our camp and Godfrey for thee send,   •
  Thee fortune, praise, and victory expect :
Come, fatal champion, bring to happy end
  This enterprise begun, and all that sect
(Which oft thou shaken hast) to earth full low
With thy sharp brand strike down, kill, overthrow.—

XXXIV.

This said, the noble infant stood a space
  Confused, speechless, senseless, ill, ashamed ;
But when that shame to just disdain gave place,
  To fierce disdain, from courage sprung untamed,
Another redness blushed through his face,
  Whence worthy anger shone, displeasure flamed ;
His nice attire in scorn he rent and tore,
For of his bondage vile that witness bore :

XXXV.

That done, he hasted from the charmed fort,
　　And through the maze pass'd with his searchers twain.
Armida of her mount and chiefest port
　　Wonder'd to find the furious keeper slain ;
Awhile she feared, but she knew in short
　　That her dear lord was fled ; then saw she plain
(Ah, woful sight !) how from her gates the man
In haste, in fear, in wrath, in anger ran.

XXXVI.

Whither, O cruel ! leav'st thou me alone ?—
　　She would have cried ; her grief her speeches stay'd,
So that her woful words are backward gone,
　　And in her heart a bitter echo made :
Poor soul ! of greater skill than she was one
　　Whose knowledge from her thus her joy convey'd ;
This wist she well, yet had desire to prove
If art could keep, if charms recall her love :

XXXVII.

All what the witches of Thessalia land
　　With lips unpure yet ever said or spake,
Words that could make heav'n's rolling circles stand,
　　And draw the damned ghosts from Limbo lake,
All well she knew, but yet no time she fand
　　To use her knowledge or her charms to make,
But left her arts, and forth she ran to prove
If single beauty were best charm for love :

XXXVIII.

She ran, nor of her honor took regard
　　(Oh where be all her vaunts and triumphs now ?
Love's empire great of late she made or mar'd,
　　To her his subjects humbly bend and bow,
And with her pride mix'd was a scorn so hard,
　　That to be lov'd she lov'd ; yet whilst they woo,
Her lovers all she hates ; that pleas'd her will,
To conquer men, and conquer'd, so to kill) :

XXXIX.

But now herself disdain'd, abandoned,
　　Ran after him that from her fled in scorn,
And her despised beauty labored
　　With humble plaints and prayers to adorn ;

She ran and hasted after him that fled,
  Through frost and snow, through brier, bush, and thorn ;
And sent her cries on message her before,
That reach'd not him till he had reach'd the shore.—

XL.

O thou that leav'st but half behind (quoth she)
  Of my poor heart, and half with thee dost carry,
O take this part, or render that to me,
  Else kill them both at once : ah ! tarry, tarry,
Hear my last words ; no parting kiss of thee
  I crave, for some more fit with thee to marry
Keep them : unkind ! what fear'st thou if thou stay ?
Thou may'st deny as well as run away.—

XLI.

At this Rinaldo stopp'd, stood still, and stay'd.
  She came, sad, breathless, weary, faint, and weak,
So wo-begone was never nymph or maid ;
  And yet her beauty's pride grief could not break :
On him she look'd, she gaz'd, but naught she said ;
  She would not, could not, or she durst not speak.
At her he look'd not, glanc'd not ; if he did,
Those glances shamefast were, close, secret, hid.

XLII.

As cunning singers, ere they strain on high
  In loud melodious tunes their gentle voice,
Prepare the hearers' ears to harmony,
  With feignings sweet, low notes, and warbles choice ;
So she, not having yet forgot pardie
  Her wonted shifts and sleights in Cupid's toys,
A sequence first of sighs and sobs forth cast
To breed compassion dear, then spake at last :—

XLIII.

Suppose not, cruel ! that I come to woo
  Or pray, as ladies do their loves and lords ;
Such were we late, if thou disdain it now,
  Or scorn to grant such grace as love affords,
At least yet as an en'my listen thou,
  Sworn foes sometime will talk and chaffer words ;
For what I ask thee may'st thou grant right well,
And lessen naught thy wrath and anger fell :

XLIV.

If me thou hate, and in that hate delight,
   I come not to appease thee, hate me still ;
It 's like for like ; I bore great hate and spite
   'Gainst Christians all, chiefly I wish'd thee ill :
I was a pagan born, and all my might
   Against Godfredo bent, mine art and skill ;
I follow'd thee, took thee, and bore thee far
To this strange isle, and kept thee safe from war ;

XLV.

And more, which more thy hate may justly move,
   More to thy loss, more to thy shame and grief,
I thee enchanted and allur'd to love ;
   Wicked deceit, craft worthy sharp reprief !
Mine honor gave I thee, all gifts above,
   And of my beauty made thee lord and chief,
And to my suitors old what I denay'd,
That gave I thee, my lover new, unpray'd :

XLVI.

But reckon that among my faults, and let
   Those many wrongs provoke thee so to wrath
That hence thou run, and that at naught thou set
   This pleasant house, so many joys which hath :
Go, travel, pass the seas, fight, conquest get,
   Destroy our faith ; what, shall I say our faith ?
Ah, no ! no longer ours ; before thy shrine
Alone I pray, thou cruel saint of mine :

XLVII.

Ah ! only let me go with thee, unkind !
   A small request although I were thy foe ;
The spoiler seldom leaves the prey behind,
   Who triumphs lets his captives with him go ;
Among thy pris'ners poor Armida bind,
   And let the camp increase thy praises so,
That thy beguiler so thou couldst beguile,
And point at me thy thrall and bondslave vile ;

XLVIII.

Despised bondslave, since my lord doth hate
   These locks, why keep I them or hold them dear ?
Come, cut them off, that to my servile state
   My habit answer may, and all my gear :

I follow thee in spite of death and fate
   Through battles fierce where dangers most appear ;
Courage I have and strength enough, perchance,
To lead thy courser spare and bear thy lance :

XLIX.

I will or bear or be myself thy shield,
   And to defend thy life will lose mine own !
This breast, this bosom soft, shall be thy bield
   'Gainst storms of arrows, darts, and weapons thrown ;
Thy foes pardie encount'ring thee in field,
   Will spare to strike thee (mine affection known),
Lest me they wound, nor will sharp veng'ance take
On thee, for this despised beauty's sake.

L.

O wretch ! dare I still vaunt or help invoke
   From this poor beauty, scorned and disdained ?—
She said no more, her tears her speeches broke,
   Which from her eyes like streams from springs down rained ;
She would have caught him by the hand or cloak,
   But he stepp'd backward and himself restrained ;
Conquer'd his will, his heart ruth soften'd not,
There plaints no issue, love no entrance, got :

LI.

Love enter'd not to kindle in his breast
   (Which reason late had quench'd) his wonted flame ;
Yet enter'd pity in the place at least
   (Love's sister, but a chaste and sober dame),
And stirr'd him so that hardly he suppress'd
   The springing tears that to his eyes up came ;
But yet e'en there his plaints repressed were,
And (as he could) he look'd and feigned cheer.—

LII.

Madam (quoth he), for your distress I grieve,
   And would amend it if I might or could ;
From your wise heart that fond affection drive ;
   I cannot hate nor scorn you, though I would ;
I seek no vengeance, wrongs I all forgive,
   Nor you my servant nor my foe I hold ;
Truth is, you err'd, and your estate forgot ;
Too great your hate was, and your love too hot :

LIII.

But these are common faults, and faults of kind
    Excus'd by nature, by your sex, and years :
I erred likewise ; if I pardon find,
    None can condemn you that our trespass hears.
Your dear remembrance will I keep in mind,
    In joys, in woes, in comforts, hopes and fears ;
Call me your soldier and your knight, as far
As Christian faith permits and Asia's war.

LIV.

Ah ! let our faults and follies here take end,
    And let our errors past you satisfy ;
And in this angle of the world ypend,
    Let both the fame and shame thereof now die :
From all the earth where I am known and kend
    I wish this fact should yet concealed lie ;
Nor yet in following me, poor knight, disgrace
Your worth, your beauty, and your princely race :

LV.

Stay here in peace : I go, nor wend you may
    With me, my guide your fellowship denies ;
Stay here, or hence depart some better way,
    And calm your thoughts ; you are both sage and wise.
While thus he spoke, her passions found no stay,
    But here and there she turn'd and roll'd her eyes,
And staring on his face awhile, at last
Thus in foul terms her bitter wrath forth brast :—

LVI.

Of Sophia fair thou never wert the child,
    Nor of the Azzaine race ysprung thou art ;
The mad sea waves thee bore, some tigress wild
    On Caucasus' cold crags nurs'd thee apart :
Ah cruel man ! in whom no token mild
    Appears of pity, ruth, or tender heart,
Could not my griefs, my woes, my plaints and all,
One sigh strain from thy breast, one tear make fall ?

LVII.

What shall I say, or how renew my speech ?
    He scorns me, leaves me, bids me call him mine ;
The victor hath his foe within his reach,
    Yet pardons her that merits death and pine ;

Hear how he counsels me, how he 'gan preach
   (Like chaste Xenocrates) 'gainst love divine :
Oh heav'ns ! oh gods ! why do these men of shame
Thus spoil your temples and blaspheme your name ?

LVIII.

Go, cruel, go ! go with such peace, such rest,
   Such joy, such comfort as thou leav'st me here ;
My angry soul, discharg'd from this weak breast,
   Shall haunt thee ever and attend thee near,
And fury-like, in snakes and fire-brands dress'd,
   Shall aye torment thee whom it late held dear :
And if thou 'scape the seas, the rocks, and sands,
And come to fight amid the pagan bands,

LIX.

There lying wounded 'mongst the hurt and slain,
   Of these my wrongs thou shalt the vengeance bear,
And oft Armida shalt thou call in vain
   At thy last gasp ; this hope I soon to hear.—
Here fainted she, with sorrow, grief, and pain,
   Her latest words scant well expressed were,
But in a swoon on earth outstretch'd she lies,
Stiff were her frozen limbs, clos'd were her eyes.

LX.

Thou clos'd thine eyes, Armida ; heav'n envied
   Ease to thy grief or comfort to thy wo :
Ah open them again, see tears down slide
   From his kind eyes whom thou esteem'st thy foe ;
If thou hadst heard, his sighs had mollify'd
   Thine anger hard, he sigh'd and mourned so ;
And, as he could, with sad and rueful look
His leave of thee and last farewell he took.

LXI.

What should he do ?   Leave on the naked sand
   This woful lady, half alive, half dead ?
Kindness forbade, pity did that withstand ;
   But hard constraint, alas ! did thence him lead.
Away he went, the west wind blew from land
   'Mongst the rich tresses of their pilot's head,
And with that golden sail the waves she cleft :
To land he look'd till land unseen he left.

LXII.

Wak'd from her trance, forsaken, speechless, sad,
  Armida wildly star'd and gaz'd about :—
And is he gone (quoth she), nor pity had,
  To leave me thus 'twixt life and death in doubt ?
Could he not stay ? could not the traitor lad
  From this last trance help or recall me out ?
And do I love him still, and on this sand
Still unreveng'd, still mourn, still weeping stand ?

LXIII.

Fie ! no : complaints farewell ! with arms and art
  I will pursue to death this spiteful knight ;
Not earth's low centre, nor sea's deepest part,
  Nor heav'n, nor hell, can shield him from my might ;
I will o'ertake him, take him, cleave his heart ;
  Such veng'ance fits a wronged lover's spite :
In cruelty that cruel knight surpass
I will : but what avail vain words, alas !

LXIV.

O fool ! thou shouldest have been cruel then
  (For then this cruel well deserved thine ire),
When thou in prison hadst entrapp'd the man ;
  Now, dead with cold, too late thou askest fire :
But though my wit, my cunning nothing can,
  Some other means shall work my heart's desire :
To thee, my beauty, thine be all these wrongs,
Vengeance to thee, to thee revenge belongs ;

LXV.

Thou shalt be his reward, with murd'ring brand
  That dare this traitor of his head deprive.
O you my lovers, on this rock doth stand
  The castle of her love for whom you strive ;
I, the sole heir of all Damascus' land,
  For this revenge myself and kingdom give :
If by this price my will I cannot gain,
Nature gives beauty, fortune wealth, in vain.

LXVI.

But thee, vain gift ! vain beauty ! thee I scorn,
  I hate the kingdom which I have to give,
I hate myself, and rue that I was born ;
  Only in hope of sweet revenge I live.—

Thus raging with fell ire she 'gan return
    From that bare shore in haste and homeward drive,
And as true witness of her frantic ire,
    Her locks wav'd loose, face shone, eyes sparkled fire.

LXVII.

When she came home, she call'd with outcries shrill
    A thousand devils in Limbo deep that won ;
Black clouds the skies with horrid darkness fill,
    And pale for dread became th' eclipsed sun :
The whirlwind bluster'd big on every hill,
    And hell to roar under her feet begun ;
You might have heard how through the palace wide
Some spirits howl'd, some bark'd, some hiss'd, some cry'd.

LXVIII.

A shadow blacker than the mirkest night
    Environ'd all the place with darkness sad,
Wherein a firebrand gave a dreadful light,
    Kindled in hell by Tisiphone the mad.
Vanish'd the shade, the sun appear'd in sight,
    Pale were his beams, the air was nothing glad,
And all the palace vanish'd was and gone,
Not of so great a work was left one stone.

LXIX.

As oft the clouds frame shapes of castles great
    Amid the air, that little time do last,
But are dissolv'd by wind or Titan's heat,
    Or like vain dreams soon made and sooner pass'd ;
The palace vanish'd so, nor in his seat
    Left aught but rocks and crags by kind there plac'd :
She in her coach, which two old serpents drew,
Sat down, and as she us'd away she flew :

LXX.

She broke the clouds and cleft the yielding sky,
    And 'bout her gather'd tempest, storm, and wind ;
The lands that view the south pole flew she by,
    And left those unknown countries far behind ;
The straits of Hercules she pass'd, which lie
    'Twixt Spain and Afric ; nor her flight inclin'd
To north or south, but still did forward ride,
O'er seas and streams, till Syria's coasts she spy'd :

LXXI.

Nor went she forward to Damascus fair,
    But of her country dear she fled the sight,
And guided to Asphalte's lake her chair,
    Where stood her castle, there she ends her flight;
And from her damsels fair she made repair
    To a deep vault, far from resort and light,
Where in sad thoughts a thousand doubts she cast,
Till grief and shame to wrath gave place at last.—

LXXII.

I will not hence (quoth she) till Egypt's Lord
    In aid of Sion's King his host shall move,
Then will I use all helps that charms afford,
    And change my shape or sex if so behove;
Well can I handle bow, or lance, or sword,
    The worthies all will aid me for my love:
I seek revenge, and to obtain the same,
Farewell regard of honor, farewell shame:

LXXIII.

Nor let mine uncle and protector me
    Reprove for this, he most deserves the blame;
My heart and sex (that weak and tender be)
    He bent to deeds that maidens ill became;
His niece a wand'ring damsel first made he,
    He spurr'd my youth, and I cast off my shame;
His be the fault, if aught 'gainst mine estate
I did for love, or shall commit for hate.—

LXXIV.

This said, her knights, her ladies, pages, squires,
    She all assembleth, and for journey fit,
In such fair arms and vestures them attires,
    As show'd her wealth and well declar'd her wit;
And forward marched full of strange desires;
    Nor rested she by day or night one whit,
Till she came there where all the eastern bands,
Their kings and princes, lay on Gaza's sands.

BOOK XVII.

THE ARGUMENT.

Egypt's great host, in battle 'ray forth brought,
    The Caliph sends with Godfrey's pow'r to fight.
Armida, who Rinaldo's ruin sought,
    To them adjoins herself and Syria's might;
To satisfy her cruel will and thought,
    She gives herself to him that kills her knight.
He takes his fatal arms, and in his shield
His ancestors and their great deeds beheld.

I.

GAZA (the city) on the frontier stands
    Of Judah's realm, as men to Egypt ride,
Built near the sea; beside it of dry sands
    Huge wildernesses lie and deserts wide,
Which the strong winds lift from the parched lands,
    And toss like roaring waves in roughest tide,
That from those storms poor passengers almost
No refuge find, but there are drown'd and lost.

II.

Within this town, won from the Turks of yore,
    Strong garrison the king of Egypt plac'd;
And, for it nearer was and fitted more
    That high emprize to which his thoughts he cast,
He left great Memphis, and to Gaza bore
    His regal throne; and there, from countries vast
Of his huge empire, all the puissant host
Assembled he, and muster'd on the coast.

III.

Come say, my Muse! what manner times these were,
    And in those times how stood the state of things;
What pow'r this monarch had, what arms they bear,
    What nations subject, and what friends he brings;

For from all lands the southern ocean near
  Or morning star, came princes, dukes, and kings ;
And only thou, of half the world well-nigh,
The armies, lords, and captains canst descry.

IV.

When Egypt from the Greekish emperor
  Rebelled first and Christ's true faith deny'd,
Of Mahomet's descent a warrior
  There set his throne and rul'd that kingdom wide ;
Caliph he hight, and caliphs since that hour
  Are his successors named all beside :
So Nilus old his kings long time had seen,
That Ptolemies and Pharaohs call'd had been.

V.

Establish'd was that kingdom in short while,
  And grew so great, that over Asia's lands
And Lybia's realms it stretched many a mile,
  From Syria's coasts as far as Cyrene stands ;
And southward passed 'gainst the course of Nile,
  Through the hot clime where burnt Syene sands ;
Hence bounded in with sandy deserts waste,
And thence with Euphrates' rich flood embrac'd :

VI.

Maremma, myrrh and spices that doth bring,
  And all the rich Red Sea it comprehends ;
And to those lands toward the morning spring,
  That lie beyond that gulf, it far extends.
Great is that empire, greater by the king
  That rules it now, whose worth the land amends
And makes more famous ; lord thereof by blood,
By wisdom, valor, and all virtues good.

VII.

With Turks and Persians war he oft did wage,
  And oft he won, and sometime lost the field ;
Nor could his adverse fortune aught assuage
  His valor's heat, or make his proud heart yield ;
But when he grew unfit for war through age,
  He sheath'd his sword. and laid aside his shield ;
But yet his warlike mind he laid not down,
Nor his great thirst of rule, praise, and renown ;

VIII.

But by his knights still cruel wars maintain'd :
  So wise his words, so quick his wit appears,
That of the kingdom large o'er which he reign'd
  The charge seem'd not too weighty for his years :
His greatness Africk's lesser kings constrain'd
  To tremble at his name ; all Inde him fears ;
And other realms that would his friendship hold,
Some armed soldiers sent, some gifts, some gold.

IX.

This mighty prince assembled had the flow'r
  Of all his realms against the Frenchmen stout,
To break their rising empire and their pow'r,
  Nor of sure conquest had he fear or doubt.
To him Armida came, ev'n at the hour
  When in the plains (old Gaza's walls without)
The lords and leaders all their armies bring
In battle 'ray, muster'd before their king.

X.

He on his throne was set, to which on hight
  Who clomb an hundred ivory stairs first told,
Under a pentise wrought of silver bright,
  And trod on carpets made of silk and gold ;
His robes were such as best beseemen might
  A king so great, so grave, so rich, so old ;
And twin'd of sixty ells of lawn and more,
A turban strange adorn'd his tresses hoar :

XI.

His right hand did his precious sceptre wield,
  His beard was grey, his looks severe and grave ;
And from his eyes (not yet made dim with eild)
  Sparkled his former worth and vigor brave ;
His gestures all the majesty upheild
  And state, as his old age and empire crave.
So Phidias carv'd, Apelles so, pardie,
Erst painted Jove, Jove thund'ring down from sky.

XII.

On either side him stood a noble lord,
  Whereof the first held in his upright hand
Of severe justice the unpartial sword ;
  The other bore the scale and causes scann'd,

Keeping his folk in peace and good accord,
  And termed was Lord Chancellor of the land :
But Marshal was the first, and us'd to lead
His armies forth to war oft with good speed.

XIII.

Of bold Circassians with their halberds long
  About his throne his guard stood in a ring,
All richly arm'd in golden corslets strong,
  And by their sides their crooked swords down hing.
Thus set, thus seated, his grave lords among,
  His hosts and armies great beheld the king ;
And every band, as by his throne it went,
Their ensigns low inclin'd and arms down bent.

XIV.

Their squadrons first the men of Egypt show
  In four troops, and each his several guide ;
Of the high country two, two of the low,
  Which Nile had won out of the salt sea side ;
His fertile slime first stopp'd the water's flow,
  Then harden'd to firm land the plough to bide ;
So Egypt still increas'd, within far plac'd
That part is now where ships erst anchor cast.

XV.

The foremost band the people were that dwell'd
  In Alexandria's rich and fertile plain,
Along the western shore, whence Nile expell'd
  The greedy billows of the swelling main ;
Araspes was their guide, who more excell'd
  In wit and craft than strength or warlike pain ;
To place an ambush close, or to devise
A treason false, was none so sly, so wise.

XVI.

The people next that 'gainst the morning rays,
  Along the coast of Asia have their seat ;
Arontes led them, whom no warlike praise
  Ennobled, but high birth and titles great ;
His helm ne'er made him sweat in toilsome frays,
  Nor was his sleep e'er broke with trumpet's threat ;
But from soft ease to try the toil of fight,
His fond ambition brought this carpet knight.

XVII.

The third seem'd not a troop or squadron small,
 But a huge host, nor seem'd it so much grain
In Egypt grew as to sustain them all ;
 Yet from one town thereof came all that train,
A town in people to huge shires equal,
 That did a thousand streets and more contain ;
Great Cair it hight, whose commons from each side
Came swarming out to war, Campson their guide.

XVIII.

Next under Gazel marched they that plough
 The fertile lands above that town which lie,
Up to the place where Nilus tumbling low,
 Falls from his second cataract on high.
Th' Egyptians weapon'd were with sword and bow,
 No weight of helm or hawberk list they try ;
And richly arm'd in their strong foes no dread
Of death, but great desire of spoil, they bred.

XIX.

The naked folk of Barca these succeed,
 Unarmed half ; Alarcon led that band,
That long in deserts liv'd in extreme need,
 On spoils and preys purchas'd by strength of hand.
To battle strong unfit, their king did lead
 His army next brought from Zumara land.
Then he of Tripoli, for sudden fight
And skirmish short, both ready, bold, and light.

XX.

Two captains next brought forth their bands to show,
 Whom Stony sent and Happy Arabie,
Which never felt the cold of frost and snow,
 Or force of burning heat, unless fame lie ;
Where incense pure and all sweet odors grow,
 Where the sole phœnix doth revive, not die ;
And midst the perfumes rich and flow'rets brave,
Both birth and burial, cradle hath and grave ;

XXI.

Their clothes not rich, their garments were not gay,
 But weapons like th' Egyptian troops they had.
Th' Arabians next that have no certain stay,
 No house, no home, no mansion good or bad,

But ever (as the Scythian hordas stray)
    From place to place their wand'ring cities gad :
These have both voice and stature feminine,
Hair long and black, black face, and fiery eine.

XXII.

Long Indian canes, with iron arm'd, they bear,
    And as upon their nimble steeds they ride,
Like a swift storm their speedy troops appear,
    If winds so fast bring storms from heavens wide.
By Syphax led the first Arabians were ;
    Aldine the second squadron had to guide ;
And Abiazar proud brought to the fight
The third, a thief, a murd'rer, not a knight.

XXIII.

The islanders came then their prince before,
    Whose lands Arabia's gulf inclos'd about,
Wherein they fish and gather oysters store,
    Whose shells great pearles rich and round pour out:
The Red Sea sent with them from his left shore,
    Of negroes grim a black and ugly rout :
These Agricalt, and those Osmida brought,
A man that set law, faith, and truth at naught.

XXIV.

The Ethiops next which Meroe doth breed
    (That sweet and gentle isle of Meroe),
'Twixt Nile and Astrabore that far doth spread,
    Where two religions are, and kingdoms three :
These Assamiro and Canario lead,
    Both kings, both pagans, and both subject be
To the great caliph ; but the third king kept
Christ's sacred faith, nor to these wars outstepp'd.

XXV.

After two kings (both subject also) ride,
    And of two bands of archers had the charge :
The first Soldan of Orms, plac'd in the wide
    Huge Persian bay, a town rich, fair and large :
The last of Bœcan, which at every tide
    The sea cuts off from Persia's southern marge,
And makes an isle ; but when it ebbs again,
The passage there is sandy, dry, and plain.

XXVI.

Nor thee, great Altamore! in her chaste bed
　　Thy loving queen kept with her dear embrace;
She tore her locks, she smote her breast, and shed
　　Salt tears to make thee stay in that sweet place:—
Seem the rough seas more calm, cruel! she said,
　　Than the mild looks of thy kind spouse's face?
Or is thy shield, with blood and dust defil'd,
A dearer armful than thy tender child?—

XXVII.

This was the mighty king of Sarmachand,
　　A captain wise, well skill'd in feats of war;
In courage fierce, matchless for strength of hand,
　　Great was his praise, his force was noised far;
His worth right well the Frenchmen understand,
　　By whom his virtues fear'd and loved are:
His men were arm'd with helms and hauberks strong,
And by their sides broad swords and masses long.

XXVIII.

Then from the mansions bright of fresh Aurore
　　Adrastus came, the glorious king of Inde,
A snake's green skin spotted with black he wore,
　　That was made rich by art and hard by kind;
An elephant this furious giant bore,
　　He fierce as fire, his mounture swift as wind;
Much people brought he from his kingdoms wide,
'Twixt Indus, Ganges, and the salt sea side.

XXIX.

The king's own troops came next, a chosen crew,
　　Of all the camp the strength, the crown, the flow'r,
Wherein each soldier had with honors due
　　Rewarded been for service ere that hour;
Their arms were strong for need and fair for show;
　　Upon fierce steeds well mounted rode this pow'r,
And heav'n itself with the clear splendor shone
Of their bright armor, purple, gold, and stone.

XXX.

'Mongst these Alarco fierce, and Odemare
　　The muster-master was, and Hidraort,
And Rimedon, whose rashness took no care
　　To shun death's bitter stroke in field or fort;

Tigranes, Rapold stern, the men that fare
    By sea, that robbed in each creek and port:
Ormond, and Marlabust th' Arabian nam'd,
Because that land rebellious he reclaim'd.

XXXI.

There Pirga, Arimon Orindo are,
    Brimarte the scaler, and with him Swifant
The breaker of wild horses brought from far:
    Then the great wrestler, strong Aridamante;
And Tisapherne, the thunderbolt of war,
    Whom none surpass'd, whom none to match durst vaunt
At tilt, at tournay, or in combat brave,
With spear or lance, with sword, with mace or glaive.

XXXII.

A false Armenian did this squadron guide,
    That in his youth from Christ's true faith and light
To the blind lore of paganism did slide,
    That Clement late, now Emireno hight;
Yet to his king he faithful was and try'd,
    True in all causes, his in wrong and right;
A cunning leader and a soldier bold,
For strength and courage young, for wisdom old.

XXXIII.

When all these regiments were pass'd and gone,
    Appear'd Armide, and came her troop to show;
Set in a chariot bright with precious stone,
    Her gown tuck'd up, and in her hand a bow:
In her sweet face her new displeasures shone
    Mix'd with the native beauties there which grow,
And quicken'd so her looks, that in sharp-wise
It seems she threats, and yet her threats entice:

XXXIV.

Her chariot, like Aurora's glorious wain,
    With carbuncles and yacinths glister'd round;
Her coachman guided with the golden rein
    Four unicorns, by couples, yoked and bound:
Of squires and lovely ladies hundreds twain
    (Whose rattling quivers at their backs resound)
On milk-white steeds wait on the chariot bright,
Their steeds to manage ready, swift to flight:

XXXV.

Follow'd her troop, led forth by Aradin,
  Which Hidraort from Syria's kingdom sent.
As when the new-born phœnix doth begin
  To fly to Ethiop-ward at the fair bent
Of her rich wings, strange plumes, and feathers thin,
  Her crowns and chains with native gold besprent;
The world amazed stands, and with her fly
A host of wond'ring birds, that sing and cry:

XXXVI.

So pass'd Armida, look'd on, gaz'd on so,
  A wond'rous dame in habit, gesture, face;
There liv'd no wight to love so great a foe,
  But wish'd and long'd those beauties to embrace;
Scant seen, with anger sullen, sad for wo,
  She conquer'd all the lords and knights in place;
What would she do (her sorrows past) think you,
When her fair eyes, her looks, and smiles shall woo?

XXXVII.

She past, the king commanded Emiren
  Of his rich throne to mount the lofty stage,
To whom his host, his army, and his men,
  He would commit, now in his graver age.
With stately grace the man approached then,
  His looks his coming honor did presage:
The guard asunder cleft and passage made;
He to the throne up went, and there he stay'd;

XXXVIII.

To earth he cast his eyes, and bent his knee.
  To whom the king thus 'gan his will explain:—
To thee this sceptre, Emiren! to thee
  These armies I commit; my place sustain
'Mongst them; go set the King of Judah free,
  And let the Frenchmen feel my just disdain;
Go, meet them, conquer them, leave none alive,
Or those that 'scape from battle bring captive.—

XXXIX.

Thus spake the tyrant, and the sceptre laid
  With all his sovereign power upon the knight.—
I take this sceptre at your hand (he said),
  And with your happy fortune go to fight;

And trust, my lord, in your great virtue's aid,
    To 'venge all Asia's harms, her wrongs to right;
Nor e'er but victor will I see your face,
Our overthrow shall bring death, not disgrace:

XL.

Heav'ns grant, if ill (yet no mishap I dread)
    Or harm they threaten 'gainst this camp of thine,
That all that mischief fall upon my head,
    Theirs be the conquest, and the danger mine;
And let them safe bring home their captain dead,
    Buried in pomp of triumph's glorious shrine.—
He ceas'd, and then a murmur loud up went,
With noise of joy and sound of instrument:

XLI.

Amid the noise and shout up rose the king,
    Environed with many a noble peer,
That to his royal tent the monarch bring,
    And there he feasted them and made them cheer;
To him and him he talk'd, and carv'd each thing,
    The greatest honor'd, meanest graced were;
And while this mirth, this joy, and feast doth last,
Armida found fit time her nets to cast.

XLII.

But when the feast was done, she (that espy'd
    All eyes on her fair visage fix'd and bent,
And by true notes and certain signs descry'd,
    How love's imprison'd fire their entrails brent)
Arose; and where the king sat in his pride,
    With stately pace and humble gestures went;
And, as she could, in looks, in voice, she strove
Fierce, stern, bold, angry, and severe to prove.—

XLIII.

Great emperor, behold me here (she said),
    For thee, my country, and my faith to fight;
A dame, a virgin, but a royal maid,
    And worthy seems this war a princess' height;
For by the sword the sceptre is upstay'd,
    This hand can use them both with skill and might;
This hand of mine can strike, and at each blow
Thy foes and ours kill, wound, and overthrow: ·

XLIV.

Nor yet suppose this is the foremost day
    Wherein to war I bent my noble thought,
But for the surety of thy realms, and stay
    Of our religion true, ere this I wrought.
Yourself best know if this be true I say,
    Or if my former deeds rejoic'd you aught,
When Godfrey's hardy knights and princes strong
I captive took, and held in bondage long :

XLV.

I took them, bound them, and so sent them bound
    To thee, a noble gift, with whom they had
Condemned low in dungeon under ground
    For ever dwelt, in wo and torment sad ;
So might thine host an easy way have found
    To end this doubtful war with conquest glad,
Had not Rinaldo fierce my knights all slain,
And set those lords (his friends) at large again :

XLVI.

Rinaldo is well known (and there a long
    And true rehearsal made she of his deeds) ;
This is the knight that since hath done me wrong,
    Wrong yet untold, that sharp revengement needs :
Displeasure, therefore, mix'd with reason strong,
    This thirst of war in me, this courage breeds ;
Nor how he injur'd me time serves to tell,
Let this suffice, I seek revengement fell ;

XLVII.

And will procure it, for all shafts that fly
    Light not in vain, some work the shooter's will ;
And Jove's right hand, with thunders cast from sky,
    Takes open vengeance oft for secret ill :
But if some champion dare this knight defy
    To mortal battle, and by fight him kill,
And with his hateful head will me present,
That gift my soul shall please, my heart content :

XLVIII.

So please, that for reward enjoy he shall
    (The greatest gift I can or may afford)
Myself, my beauty, wealth, and kingdoms all,
    To marry him and take him for my lord,

This promise will I keep, whate'er befall,
    And thereto bind himself by oath and word:
Now he that deems this purchase worth his pain,
Let him step forth and speak, I none disdain.—

XLIX.

While thus the princess said, his hungry eyne
    Adrastus fed on her sweet beauty's light:—
The gods forbid (quoth he) one shaft of thine
    Should be discharg'd 'gainst that discourteous knight;
His heart unworthy is, shootress divine!
    Of thine artillery to feel the might;
To wreak thine ire behold me prest and fit,
I will his head cut off, and bring thee it;

L.

I will his heart with this sharp sword divide,
    And to the vultures cast his carcass out.—
Thus threaten'd he, but Tisaphere envy'd
    To hear his glorious vaunt and boasting stout,
And said—But who art thou, that so great pride
    Thou show'st before the king, me, and this rout?
Pardie, here are some such whose worth exceeds
Thy vaunting much, yet boast not of their deeds.—

LI.

The Indian fierce reply'd—I am the man
    Whose acts his words and boasts have aye surpass'd;
But if elsewhere the words thou now began
    Had utter'd been, that speech had been thy last.—
Thus quarrell'd they; the monarch stay'd them then,
    And 'twixt the angry knights his sceptre cast:
Then to Armida said:—Fair queen, I see
Thy heart is stout, thy thoughts courageous be;

LII.

Thou worthy art that their disdain and ire
    At thy commands these knights should both appease,
That 'gainst thy foe their courage hot as fire
    Thou may'st employ, both when and where thou please;
There all their pow'r and force, and what desire
    They have to serve thee, may they show at ease.—
The monarch held his peace when this was said,
And they new proffer of their service made:

LIII.

Nor they alone, but all that famous were
   In feats of arms, boast that he shall be dead ;
All offer her their aid, all say and swear
   To take revenge on his condemned head.
So many arms mov'd she against her dear,
   And swore her darling under foot to tread.
But he, since first th' enchanted isle he left,
Safe in his barge the roaring waves still cleft.

LIV.

By the same way return'd the well-taught boat
   By which it came, and made like haste, like speed :
The friendly wind, upon her sail that smote,
   So turn'd as to return her ship had need.
The youth sometime the pole or bear did note,
   Or wand'ring stars which clearest nights forth spread ;
Sometimes the floods, the hills, or mountains steep,
Whose woody fronts o'ershade the silent deep.

LV.

Now of the camp the man the state inquires,
   Now asks the customs strange of sundry lands ;
And sail'd till clad in beams and bright attires
   The fourth day's sun on th' eastern threshold stands ;
But when the western seas had quench'd those fires,
   Their frigate struck against the shore and sands.
Then spoke their guide—The land of Palestine
This is ; here must your journey end and mine.—

LVI.

The knights she set upon the shore all three,
   And vanish'd thence in twinkling of an eye.
Up rose the night, in whose deep blackness be
   All colors hid of things in earth or sky ;
Nor could they house, or hold, or harbor see,
   Or in that desert sign of dwelling spy ;
Nor track of man or horse, or aught that might
Inform them of some path or passage right.

LVII.

When they had mus'd what way they travel should,
   From the waste shore their steps at last they twin'd ;
And, lo ! far off at last their eyes behold
   Something, they wist not what, that clearly shin'd,
VOL. II.   11

With rays of silver and with beams of gold,
　　Which the dark folds of night's black mantle lin'd ;
Forward they went and marched 'gainst the light,
To see and find the thing that shone so bright.

LVIII.

High on a tree they saw an armor new,
　　That glister'd bright 'gainst Cinthia's silver ray ;
Therein, like stars in skies, the diamonds show
　　Fret in the gilden helm and hauberk gay ;
The mighty shield all scored full they view
　　Of pictures fair, ranged in meet array ;
To keep them sat an aged man beside,
Who to salute them rose when them he spy'd.

LIX.

The twain who first were sent in this pursuit,
　　Of their wise friend well knew the aged face ;
But when the wizard sage their first salute
　　Receiv'd, and quitted had with kind embrace,
To the young prince, that silent stood and mute,
　　He turn'd his speech :—In this unused place
For you alone I wait, my lord (quoth he),
My chiefest care your state and welfare be ;

LX.

For, though you wot it not, I am your friend,
　　And for your profit work, as these can tell ;
I taught them how Armida's charms to end,
　　And bring you hither from love's hateful cell :
Now to my words (though sharp perchance) attend,
　　Nor be aggriev'd although they seem too fell ;
But keep them well in mind, till in the truth
A wise and holier man instruct thy youth.

LXI.

Not underneath sweet shades and fountains shrill,
　　Among the nymphs, the fairies, leaves, and flow'rs ;
But on the steep, the rough, and craggy hill
　　Of virtue, stand this bliss, this good of ours ;
By toil and travail, not by sitting still
　　In pleasure's lap, we come to honor's bow'rs :
Why will you thus in sloth's deep valley lie ?
The royal eagles on high mountains fly :

LXII.

Nature lifts up thy forehead to the skies,
   And fills thy heart with high and noble thought,
That thou to heav'nward aye shouldst lift thine eyes,
   And purchase fame by deeds well done and wrought;
She gives thee ire, by which hot courage flies
   To conquest; not through brawls and battles fought
For civil jars, nor that thereby you might
Your wicked malice wreak and cursed spite;

LXIII.

But that your strength spurr'd forth with noble wrath,
   With greater fury might Christ's foes assault;
And that your bridle should with lesser scath
   Each secret vice, and kill each inward fault;
For so his godly anger ruleth hath
   Each righteous man beneath heav'n's starry vault;
And at his will makes it now hot, now cold,
Now lets it run, now doth it fetter'd hold.—

LXIV.

Thus parled he.   Rinaldo, hush'd and still,
   Great wisdom heard in those few words compil'd;
He mark'd his speech; a purple blush did fill
   His guilty cheeks; down went his eyesight mild.
The hermit by his bashful looks his will
   Well understood, and said:—Look up, my child,
And painted in this precious shield behold
The glorious deeds of thy forefathers old;

LXV.

Thine elders' glory herein see and know,
   In virtue's path how they trod all their days,
Whom thou art far behind, a runner slow
   In this true course of honor, fame, and praise.
Up! up! thyself incite by the fair show
   Of knightly worth which this bright shield bewrays;
That be thy spur to praise.—At last the knight
Look'd up, and on those portraits bent his sight.

LXVI.

The cunning workman had in little space
   Infinite shapes of men there well express'd;
For there described was the worthy race,
   And pedigree of all the house of Este;

Come from a Roman spring, o'er all the place
  Flowed pure streams of crystal east and west ;
With laurel crowned stood the princess old,
Their wars the hermit and their battles told ;

LXVII.

He show'd him Caius first, when first in prey
  To people strange the falling empire went,
First Prince of Este, that did the sceptre sway
  O'er such as chose him lord by free consent ;
His weaker neighbors to his rule obey,
  Need made them stoop, constraint doth force content.
After, when Lord Honorius call'd the train
Of savage Goths into his land again,

LXVIII.

And when all Italy did burn and flame
  With bloody war, by this fierce people made,
When Rome a captive and a slave became,
  And to be quite destroy'd was most afraid,
Aurelius, to his everlasting fame,
  Preserv'd in peace the folk that him obey'd.
Next whom was Forrest, who the rage withstood
Of the bold Huns, and of their tyrant proud :

LXIX.

Known by his look was Attila the fell
  Whose dragon eyes shone bright with anger's spark ;
Worse faced than a dog, who view'd him well
  Suppos'd they saw him grin and heard him bark ;
But when in single fight he lost the bell,
  How through his troops he fled there might you mark ;
And how Lord Forrest after fortified
Aquilia's town, and how for it he died ;

LXX.

For there was wrought the fatal end and fine
  Both of himself and of the town he kept :
But his great son, renowned Acarine,
  Into his father's place and honors stepp'd.
To cruel fate, not to the Huns, Altine
  Gave place ; and when time serv'd again forth leapt,
And in a vale of Po built for his seat,
Of many a village small, a city great :

LXXI.

Against the swelling flood he bank'd it strong ;
   And thence up rose the fair and noble town
Where they of Este should by succession long
   Command, and rule in bliss and high renown.
'Gainst Odoacer then he fought ; but wrong
   Oft spoileth right, fortune treads courage down,
For there he died for his dear country's sake,
And of his fathers' praise did so partake :

LXXII.

With him died Alphorisio ; Azzo was
   With his dear brother into exile sent :
But homewards they in arms again repass
   (The Herule king oppress'd) from banishment.
His front through pierced with a dart (alas !),
   Next them of Este th' Epaminondas went,
That smiling seem'd to cruel death to yield,
When Totila was fled, and safe his shield.

LXXIII.

Of Boniface I speak. Valerian,
   His son, in praise and pow'r succeeded him,
Who durst sustain, in years though scant a man,
   Of the proud Goths an hundred squadrons trim.
Then he that 'gainst the Sclaves much honor won,
   Ernesto, threat'ning stood with visage grim ;
Before him Aldoard, the Lombard stout
Who from Monscelces boldly erst shut out.

LXXIV.

There Henry was, and Berengare the bold,
   That serv'd Great Charles in his conquests high,
Who in each battle gave the onset would,
   A hardy soldier and a captain sly.
After, Prince Lewis did he well uphold
   Against his nephew, king of Italy ;
He won the field, and took that king alive.
Next him stood Otho with his children five.

LXXV.

Of Almerike the image next they view,
   Lord Marquis of Ferrara first create,
Founder of many churches, that upthrew
   His eyes like one that used to contemplate.

'Gainst him the second Azzo stood in rew,
  With Berengarius that did long debate,
Till after often change of fortune's stroke,
He won, and on all Italy laid the yoke.

Albert, his son, the Germans warr'd among,
  And there his praise and fame was spread so wide,
That having foil'd the Danes in battle strong,
  His daughter young became great Otho's bride.
Behind him Hugo stood, with warfare long
  That broke the horn of all the Romans' pride,
Who of all Italy the Marquis hight,
And Tuscane whole possessed as his right.

LXXVII.

After Tedaldo, puissant Boniface
  And Beatrice his dear possess'd the stage;
Nor was there left heir male of that great race
  T' enjoy the sceptre, state, and heritage;
The Princess Maude alone supplied the place,
  Supplied the want in number, sex, and age;
For far above each sceptre, throne, and crown,
The noble Dame advanc'd her veil and gown.

LXXVIII.

With manlike vigour shone her noble look,
  And more than manlike wrath her face o'erspread;
There the fell Normans, Guichard there forsook
  The field, till then who never fear'd nor fled;
Henry the Fourth she beat, and from him took
  His standard, and in church it offered;
Which done, the Pope back to the Vatican
She brought, and plac'd in Peter's chair again.

LXXIX.

As he that honor'd her and held her dear,
  Azzo the Fifth stood by her lovely side:
But the Fourth Azzo's offspring far and near
  Spread forth, and through Germania fructify'd:
Sprung from that branch did Guelpho bold appear,
  Guelpho his son by Cunigond his bride;
And in Bavaria's field transplanted new,
This Roman graft flourish'd, increas'd, and grew.

LXXX.

A branch of Este there in the Guelfian tree
  Ingraffed was, which of itself was old,
Whereon you might the Guelphos fairer see
  Renew their sceptres and their crowns of gold ;
On which heav'n's good aspects so bended be,
  That high and broad it spread and flourish'd bold,
Till underneath his glorious branches laid
Half Germany, and all under his shade :

LXXXI.

This regal plant from his Italian root
  Sprung up as high and blossom'd fair above.
For nenst Lord Guelpho, Bertold issued out,
  With the Sixth Azzo, whom all virtues love.
This was the pedigree of worthies stout,
  Who seem'd in that bright shield to live and move.
Rinaldo waked up and cheer'd his face,
To see these worthies of his house and race.

LXXXII.

To do like acts his courage wish'd and sought,
  And with that wish transported him so far,
That all those deeds which filled aye his thought
  (Towns won, forts taken, armies kill'd in war),
As if they were things done indeed and wrought,
  Before his eyes he thinks they present are ;
He hastily arms him, and with hope and haste
Sure conquest met, prevented, and embrac'd.

LXXXIII

But Charles, who had told the death and fall
  Of the young Prince of Danes, his late dear lord,
Gave him the fatal weapon, and withal—
  Young knight (quoth he), take with good luck this sword,
Your just, strong, valiant hand, in battle shall
  Employ it long, for Christ's true faith and word ;
And of its former lord revenge the wrongs,
Who lov'd you so, that deed to you belongs.—

LXXXIV.

He answered :—God for his mercy sake
  Grant that this hand which holds this weapon good,
For thy dear master may sharp vengeance take,
  May cleave the Pagan's heart and shed his blood.—

To this but short reply did Charles make,
    And thank'd him much, nor more on terms they stood ;
For, lo ! the wizard sage that was their guide,
On their dark journey hastes them forth to ride :—

LXXXV.

High time it is (quoth he) for you to wend
    Where Godfrey you awaits and many a knight,
There may we well arrive ere night doth end,
    And through this darkness can I guide you right.—
This said, up to his coach they all ascend,
    On its swift wheels forth roll'd the chariot light ;
He gave his coursers fleet the rod and rein,
And gallop'd forth and eastward drove amain.

LXXXVI.

While silent so through night's dark shade they fly,
    The hermit thus bespake the young man stout :—
Of thy great house, thy race, thine offspring high,
    Here hast thou seen the branch, the bole, the root,
And as these worthies born to chivalry
    And deeds of arms it hath tofore brought out ;
So is it, so it shall be fertile still,
Nor time shall end, nor age that seed shall kill.

LXXXVII.

Would God, as drawn from the forgetful lap
    Of antique time I have thine elders shown,
That so I could the catalogue unwrap
    Of thy great nephews yet unborn, unknown ;
That ere this light they view, their fate and hap
    I might foretell, and how their chance is thrown ;
That like thine elders so thou might'st behold
Thy children many, famous, stout and bold :

LXXXVIII.

But not by art or skill of things future
    Can the plain truth revealed be and told,
Although some knowledge doubtful, dark, obscure,
    We have of coming haps in clouds up-roll'd ;
Nor all which in this cause I know for sure
    Dare I foretell ; for of that father old,
The hermit Peter, learn'd I much, and he,
Withouten veil heav'n's secrets great doth see :

LXXXIX.

But this (to him reveal'd by grace divine)
　　By him to me declar'd, to thee I say,
Was never race, Greek, Barb'rous, or Latine,
　　Great in times past, or famous at this day,
Richer in hardy knights than this of thine :
　　Such blessings heav'n shall on thy children lay,
That they in fame shall pass, in praise o'ercome
The worthies old of Sparta, Carthage, Rome :

XC.

But 'mongst the rest I choose Alphonsus bold,
　　In virtue first, second in place and name,
He shall be born when this frail world grows old,
　　Corrupted, poor, and bare of men of fame ;
Better than he none shall, none can, or could
　　The sword or sceptre use, or guide the same,
To rule in peace, or to command in fight,
Thine offspring's glory and thy house's light :

XCI.

His younger age foretokens true shall yield
　　Of future valor, puissance, force, and might ;
From him no rock the savage beast shall shield ;
　　At tilt or tournay match him shall no knight ;
After he conquer shall in pitched field
　　Great armies, and win spoils in single fight ;
And on his locks (rewards for knightly praise)
Shall garlands wear of grass, of oak, of bays.

XCII.

His graver age, as well that eild it fits,
　　Shall happy peace preserve and quiet blest,
And from his neighbors strong 'mongst whom he sits,
　　Shall keep his cities safe in wealth and rest,
Shall nourish arts, and cherish pregnant wits,
　　Make triumphs great, and feast his subjects best ;
Reward the good, the ill with pains torment,
Shall dangers all foresee, and seen prevent :

XCIII.

But if it hap, against those wicked bands
　　That sea and earth infest with blood and war,
And in these wretched times to noble lands
　　Give laws of peace false and unjust that are,

That he be sent to drive their guilty hands
    From Christ's pure altars and high temples far ;
O what revenge, what vengeance shall he bring
On that false sect and their accursed king !

XCIV.

Too late the Moors, too late the Turkish king,
    'Gainst him should arm their troops and legions bold ;
For he beyond great Euphrates should bring,
    Beyond the frozen tops of Taurus cold,
Beyond the land where is perpetual spring,
    The cross, the eagle white, the lily of gold,
And, by baptizing of the Ethiops brown,
Of aged Nile reveal the springs unknown.—

XCV.

Thus said the hermit, and his prophecy
    The Prince accepted with content and pleasure,
The secret thought of his posterity,
    Of his concealed joys heap'd up the measure.
Meanwhile the morning bright was mounted high,
    And chang'd heav'n's silver wealth to golden treasure,
And high above the Christian tents they view
How the broad ensigns trembled, wav'd, and blew ;

XCVI.

When thus again their leader sage begun :—
    See how bright Phœbus clears the darksome skies,
See how with gentle beams the friendly sun
    The tents, the towns, the hills and dale descries ;
Through my well guiding is your voyage done,
    From danger safe in travel oft which lies ;
Hence, without fear of harm or doubt of foe,
March to the camp ; I may no nearer go.—

XCVII.

Thus took he leave, and made a quick return ;
    And forward went the champions three on foot,
And marching right against the rising morn,
    A ready passage to the camp found out.
Meanwhile had speedy fame the tidings borne
    That to the tents approach'd these barons stout,
And starting from his throne and kingly seat,
To entertain them rose Godfredo great.

BOOK XVIII.

I.

ARRIV'D where Godfrey to embrace him stood :—
   My sovereign lord, Rinaldo meekly said,
To 'venge my wrongs against Gernando proud,
   My honor's care provok'd my wrath unstay'd :
But that I you displeas'd, my chieftain good,
   My thoughts yet grieve, my heart is still dismay'd ;
And here I come, prest all exploits to try,
To make me gracious in your gracious eye.—

II.

To him that kneel'd (folding his friendly arms
   About his neck) the Duke this answer gave :—
Let pass such speeches sad of passed harms,
   Remembrance is the life of grief, his grave
Forgetfulness ; and for amends, in arms
   Your wonted valor use and courage brave ;
For you alone to happy end must bring
The strong enchantments of the charmed spring.

III.

That aged wood whence heretofore we got
   To build our scaling engines timber fit,
Is now the fearful seat, but how none wot,
   Where ugly fiends and damned spirits sit ;

To cut one twist thereof adventureth not
   The boldest knight we have ; nor without it
This wall can batter'd be : where others doubt
There venture thou, and show thy courage stout.—

IV.

This said he ; and the knight in speeches few
   Proffer'd his service to attempt the thing.
To hard assays his courage willing flew,
   To him praise was no spur, words were no sting.
Of his dear friends then he embrac'd the crew
   To welcome him which came ; for in a ring
About him Guelpho, Tancred, and the rest
Stood, of the camp the greatest, chief, and best.

V.

When with the Prince these lords had iterate
   Their welcomes oft, and oft their dear embrace ;
Towards the rest of lesser worth and state
   He turn'd, and them received with gentle grace :
The merry soldiers 'bout with shout and prate,
   With cries as joyful and as cheerful face,
As if in triumph's chariot bright as sun
He had return'd, Afric or Asia won.

VI.

Thus marched to his tent the champion good,
   And there sat down with all his friends around :
Now of the war he asks, now of the wood,
   And answer'd each demand they list propound.
But when they left him to his ease, upstood
   The hermit, and fit time to speak once found :
My lord, he said, your travels wond'rous are,
Far have you strayed, erred, wander'd far :

VII.

Much are you bound to God above, who brought
   You safe from false Armida's charmed hold ;
And thee a straying sheep whom once he bought,
   Hath now again reduced to his fold ;
And 'gainst his heathen foes, those men of naught,
   Hath chosen thee in place next Godfrey bold :
Yet may'st thou not, polluted thus with sin,
In his high service war or fight begin :

VIII.

The world, the flesh, with their infections vile
    Pollute thy thoughts impure, thy spirit stain ;
Not Po, not Ganges, nor sev'n-mouthed Nile,
    Not the wide seas can wash thee clean again ;
Only to purge all faults which thee defile
    His blood hath power who for thy sins was slain :
His help therefore invoke, to him bewray
Thy secret faults, mourn, weep, complain, and pray.—

IX.

This said, the knight first with the witch unchaste
    His idle loves and follies vain lamented ;
Then kneeling low, with heavy looks down cast,
    His other sins confess'd, and all repented,
And meekly pardon crav'd for first and last.
    The hermit with his zeal was well contented,
And said—On yonder hill next morn go pray,
That turns his forehead 'gainst the morning ray ;

X.

That done, march to the wood, whence each one brings
    Such news of furies, goblins, fiends and sprites ;
The giants, monsters, and all dreadful things
    Thou shalt subdue, which that dark grove unites ;
Let no strange voice that mourns or sweetly sings,
    Nor beauty whose glad smile frail hearts delights,
Within thy breast make ruth or fury rise,
But their false looks and prayers false despise.—

XI.

Thus he advis'd him, and the hardy knight
    Prepar'd him gladly to this enterprise ;
Thoughtful he past the day, and sad the night ;
    And ere the silver morn began to rise,
His arms he took, and in a coat him dight
    Of color strange, cut in the warlike guise ;
And on his way, sole, silent, forth he went
Alone, and left his friends, and left his tent.

XII.

It was the time when 'gainst the breaking day
    Rebellious night yet strove, and still repined ;
For in the east appear'd the morning grey,
    And yet some lamps in Jove's high palace shined ;

When to mount Olivet he took his way,
 And saw (as round about his eyes he twined)
Night's shadows hence, from thence the morning's shine ;
This bright, that dark ; that earthly, this divine.

XIII.

Thus to himself he thought : how many bright
 And splendid lamps shine in heav'n's temple high ;
Day hath his golden sun, her moon the night,
 Her fix'd and wand'ring stars the azure sky ;
So framed all by their Creator's might,
 That still they live and shine, and ne'er shall die,
Till (in a moment) with the last day's brand
They burn, and with them burns sea, air, and land.

XIV.

Thus as he mused to the top he went,
 And there kneel'd down with reverence and fear,
His eyes upon heav'n's eastern face he bent,
 His thoughts above all heav'ns uplifted were :—
The sins and errors (which I now repent)
 Of mine unbridled youth, O Father dear !
Remember not, but let thy mercy fall,
And purge my faults, and mine offences all.

XV.

Thus prayed he. With purple wings up flew,
 In golden weed, the morning's lusty queen,
Begilding, with the radiant beams she threw,
 His helm, his harness, and the mountain green :
Upon his breast and forehead gently blew
 The air, that balm and nardus breath'd unseen ;
And o'er his head, let down from clearest skies,
A cloud of pure and precious dew there flies :

XVI.

The heav'nly dew was on his garments spread,
 To which compar'd his clothes pale ashes seen,
And sprinkled so that all that paleness fled,
 And thence of purest white bright rays out-stream.
So cheered are the flow'rs, late withered,
 With the sweet comfort of the morning beam ;
And so, return'd to youth, a serpent old
Adorns herself in new and native gold.

XVII.

The lovely whiteness of his changed weed
   The Prince perceived well and long admir'd :
Towards the forest march'd he on with speed,
   Resolv'd as such adventures great requir'd :
Thither he came whence shrinking back for dread
   Of that strange desert's sight the first retir'd ;
But not to him fearful or loathsome made
That forest was, but sweet with pleasant shade.

XVIII.

Forward he pass'd, and in the grove before
   He heard a sound that strange, sweet, pleasing was ;
There roll'd a crystal brook with gentle roar,
   There sigh'd the winds as through the leaves they pass,
There did the nightingale her wrongs deplore,
   There sung the swan, and singing died, alas !
There lute, harp, cittern, human voice he heard,
And all these sounds one sound right well declar'd.

XIX.

A dreadful thunderclap at last he heard,
   The aged trees and plants well-nigh that rent ;
Yet heard he nymphs and syrens afterward,
   Birds, winds, and waters, sing with sweet consent :
Whereat amaz'd he stay'd, and well prepar'd
   For his defence, heedful and slow forth went :
Nor in his way his passage aught withstood,
Except a quiet, still, transparent flood :

XX.

On the green banks which that fair stream in-bound,
   Flowers and odors sweetly smil'd and smell'd,
Which reaching out its stretched arms around,
   All the large desert in its bosom held ;
And through the grove one channel passage found,
   That in the wood, in that the forest dwell'd ;
Trees clad the streams, streams green those trees aye made,
And so exchang'd their moisture and their shade.

XXI.

The knight some way sought out the flood to pass,
   And, as he sought, a wondrous bridge appear'd,
A bridge of gold, a huge and weighty mass,
   On arches great of that rich metal rear'd :

When through that golden way he enter'd was,
  Down fell the bridge, swelled the stream, and wear'd
The work away, nor sign left where it stood,
And of a river calm became a flood.

XXII.

He turn'd, amaz'd to see it troubled so,
  Like sudden brooks increas'd with molten snow ;
The billows fierce that tossed to and fro,
  The whirlpools suck'd down to their bosoms low :
But on he went to search for wonders mo,
  Through the thick trees, there high and broad which grow ;
And in that forest huge and desert wide
The more he sought, more wonders still he spy'd :

XXIII.

Whereso he stepp'd, it seem'd the joyful ground
  Renew'd the verdure of her flowery weed ;
A fountain here, a well-spring there he found ;
  Here bud the roses, there the lilies spreed ;
The aged wood o'er and about him round
  Flourish'd with blossoms new, new leaves, new seed ;
And on the boughs and branches of those treen
The bark was soften'd, and renew'd the green :

XXIV.

The manna on each leaf did pearled lie,
  The honey stilled from the tender rind,
Again he heard that wond'rous harmony,
  Of songs and sweet complaints of lovers kind ;
The human voices sung a treble high,
  To which respond the birds, the streams, the wind ;
But yet unseen those nymphs, those singers were,
Unseen the lutes, harps, viols, which they bear.

XXV.

He look'd, he listen'd, yet his thoughts deny'd
  To think that true which he both heard and see :
A myrtle in an ample plain he spy'd,
  And thither by a beaten path went he :
The myrtle spread her mighty branches wide,
  Higher than pine, or palm, or cypress tree ;
And far above all other plants was seen
That forest's lady, and that desert's queen.

XXVI.

Upon the tree his eyes Rinaldo bent,
    And there a marvel great and strange began ;
An aged oak beside him cleft and rent,
    And from his fertile hollow womb forth ran
(Clad in rare weeds and strange habiliment)
    A nymph for age able to go to man ;
An hundred plants beside, even in his sight,
Childed an hundred nymphs, so great, so dight ;

XXVII.

Such as on stages play, such as we see
    The Dryads painted, whom wild Satyrs love ;
Whose arms half naked, locks untrussed be,
    With buskins laced on their legs above,
And silken robes tuck'd short above their knee ;
    Such seem'd the Sylvan daughters of this grove,
Save that, instead of shafts and boughs of tree,
She bore a lute, a harp or cittern she ;

XXVIII.

And wantonly they cast them in a ring,
    And sung and danc'd to move his weaker sense ;
Rinaldo round about environing,
    As centres are with their circumference :
The tree they compass'd eke, and 'gan to sing,
    That woods and streams admir'd their excellence :
Welcome, dear lord ! welcome to this sweet grove ;
Welcome, our lady's hope ! welcome her love !

XXIX.

Thou com'st to cure our princess, faint and sick
    For love ; for love of thee, faint, sick, distressed ;
Late black, late dreadful, was this forest thick,
    Fit dwelling for sad folk with grief oppressed ;
See, with thy coming how the branches quick
    Revived are, and in new blossoms dressed.—
This was their song ; and after from it went
First a sweet sound, and then the myrtle rent.

XXX.

If antique times admir'd Silenus old,
    That oft appear'd set on his lazy ass,
How would they wonder if they did behold
    Such sights as from the myrtle high did pass !

Thence came a lady fair, with locks of gold,
  That like in shape, in face, and beauty was
To sweet Armida : Rinald thinks he spies
Her gestures, smiles, and glances of her eyes.

XXXI.

On him a sad and smiling look she cast,
  Which twenty passions strange at once bewrays :—
And art thou come (quoth she), return'd at last
  To her from whom but late thou ran'st thy ways ?
Com'st thou to comfort me for sorrows past,
  To ease my widow'd nights and careful days ?
Or comest thou to work me grief and harm ?
Why nilt thou speak ? why not thy face disarm ?

XXXII.

Com'st thou a friend or foe ?   I did not frame
  That golden bridge to entertain my foe ;
Nor open'd flow'rs and fountains as you came,
  To welcome him with joy that brings me wo.
Put off thy helm ; rejoice me with the flame
  Of thy bright eyes, whence first my fires did grow ;
Kiss me, embrace me, if you further venture,
Love keeps the gate, the fort is eath to enter.—

XXXIII.

Thus as she woos, she rolls her rueful eyes
  With piteous look, and changeth oft her cheer ;
An hundred sighs from her false heart up flies,
  She sobs, she mourns, it is great ruth to hear ;
The hardest breast sweet pity mollifies,
  What stony heart resists a woman's tear ?
But yet the knight, wise, wary, not unkind,
Drew forth his sword, and from her careless twin'd.

XXXIV.

Towards the tree he march'd ; she thither start,
  Before him stepp'd, embrac'd the plant, and cry'd—
Ah ! never do me such a spiteful part,
  To cut my tree, this forest's joy and pride ;
Put up thy sword, else pierce therewith the heart
  Of thy forsaken and despis'd Armide ;
For through this breast, and through this heart, unkind !
To this fair tree thy sword shall passage find.—

XXXV.

He lift his brand, nor car'd, though oft she pray'd ;
  And she her form to other shape did change ;
Such monsters huge, when men in dreams are laid,
  Oft in their idle fancies roam and range ;
Her body swell'd, her face obscure was made,
  Vanish'd her garments rich and vestures strange ;
A giantess before him high she stands,
Like Briareus armed with an hundred hands.

XXXVI.

With fifty swords and fifty targets bright,
  She threaten'd death, she roared, cry'd, and fought :
Each other nymph, in armor likewise dight,
  A cyclops great became. He fear'd them naught,
But on the myrtle smote with all his might,
  That groan'd like living souls to death nigh brought ;
The sky seem'd Pluto's court, the air seem'd hell,
Therein such monsters roar, such spirits yell :

XXXVII.

Lighten'd the heav'n above, the earth below
  Roared aloud ; that thunder'd, and this shook :
Bluster'd the tempests strong, the whirlwinds blow,
  The bitter storm drove hailstones in his look :
But yet his arm grew neither weak nor slow,
  Nor of that fury heed or care he took,
Till low to earth the wounded tree down bended ;
Then fled the spirits all, the charms all ended :

XXXVIII.

The heav'ns grew clear, the air wax'd calm and still,
  The wood returned to its wonted state ;
Of witchcrafts free, quite void of spirits ill,
  Of horror full, but horror there innate :
He further prov'd if aught withstood his will
  To cut those trees as did the charms of late ;
And finding naught to stop him, smil'd and said—
O shadows vain ! O fools, of shades afraid !—

XXXIX.

From thence home to the camp-ward turn'd the knight,
  The hermit cry'd, up starting from his seat—
Now of the wood the charms have lost their might,
  The sprites are conquer'd, ended is the feat :

See where he comes.—In glist'ring white all dight
    Appear'd the man, bold, stately, high, and great ;
His eagle's silver wings to shine begun
With wond'rous splendor 'gainst the golden sun.

XL.

The camp receiv'd him with a joyful cry,
    A cry the dales and hills about that fill'd ;
Then Godfrey welcom'd him with honors high,
    His glory quench'd all spite, all envy kill'd.—
To yonder dreadful grove (quoth he), went I,
    And from the fearful wood, as me you will'd,
Have driven the sprites away ; thither let be
Your people sent, the way is safe and free.—

XLI.

Sent were the workmen thither, thence they brought
    Timber enough, by good advice select ;
And though by skilless builders fram'd and wrought,
    Their engines rude and rams were late erect,
Yet now the forts and tow'rs from whence they fought
    Were framed by a cunning architect ;
William, of all the Genoas lord and guide,
Which late rul'd all the seas from side to side ;

XLII.

But forced to retire from it at last,
    The Pagan fleet the sea's moist empire won ;
His men with all their stuff and store in haste
    Home to the camp with their commander run :
In skill, in wit, in cunning, him surpass'd
    Yet never engineer beneath the sun ;
Of carpenters an hundred large he brought,
That what their lord devised made and wrought.

XLIII.

This man began with wondrous art to make,
    Not rams, not mighty brakes, not slings alone,
Wherewith the firm and solid walls to shake,
    To cast a dart or throw a shaft or stone ;
But fram'd of pines and firs, did undertake
    To build a fortress huge, to which was none
Yet ever like ; whereof he cloth'd the sides,
Against the balls of fire, with raw bulls' hides :

XLIV.

In mortisses and sockets framed just,
  The beams, the studs, and puncheons join'd he fast;
To beat the city's wall, beneath forth burst
  A ram with horned front; about her waist
A bridge the engine from her side out-thrust,
  Which on the wall when need required she cast;
And from her top a turret small up stood,
Strong, surely arm'd, and builded of like wood:

XLV.

Set on an hundred wheels the rolling mass
  On the smooth lands went nimbly up and down,
Though full of arms and armed men it was,
  Yet with small pains it ran as it had flown.
Wonder'd the camp so quick to see it pass,
  They prais'd the workmen and their skill unknown;
And on that day two tow'rs they builded more,
Like that which sweet Clorinda burnt before.

XLVI.

Yet wholly were not from the Saracines
  Their works concealed and their labors hid,
Upon that wall which next the camp confines,
  They placed spies who marked all they did:
They saw the ashes wild and squared pines,
  How to the tents, trail'd from the grove, they slid;
And engines huge they saw, yet could not tell
How they were built, their forms they saw not well.

XLVII.

Their engines eke they rear'd, and with great art
  Repair'd each bulwark, turret, port, and tow'r,
And fortify'd the plain and easy part,
  To bide the storm of every warlike stour;
Till as they thought, no sleight or force of mart
  To undermine or scale the same had pow'r;
And false Ismeno 'gan new balls prepare
Of wicked fire, wild, wond'rous, strange, and rare.

XLVIII.

He mingled brimstone with bitumen fell,
  Fetch'd from that lake where Sodom erst did sink;
And from that flood which nine times compass'd hell,
  Some of the liquor hot he brought, I think,

Wherewith the quenchless fire he temper'd well,
  To make it smoke and flame and deadly stink ;
And for his wood cut down the aged sire
Would thus revengement take with flame and fire.

XLIX.

While thus the camp, and thus the town were bent,
  These to assault, these to defend the wall,
A speedy dove through the clear welkin went,
  Straight o'er the tents, seen by the soldiers all ;
With nimble fans the yielding air she rent,
  Nor seem'd it that she would alight or fall,
Till she arriv'd near that besieged town,
Then from the clouds at last she stooped down :

L.

But, lo ! from whence I nolt, a falcon came,
  Armed with crooked bill and talons long,
And 'twixt the camp and city cross'd her game,
  That durst not bide her foe's encounter strong,
But right upon the royal tent down came,
  And there the lords and princes great among,
When the sharp hawk nigh touch'd her tender head,
In Godfrey's lap she fell, with fear half dead :

LI.

The Duke receiv'd her, saved her, and spy'd,
  As he beheld the bird, a wond'rous thing ;
About her neck a letter close was tied
  By a small thread, and thrust under her wing ;
He loosed forth the writ and spread it wide,
  And read th' intent thereof :—To Judah's king
(Thus said the schedule) honors high increase,
Th' Egyptian chieftain wisheth health and peace :

LII.

Fear not, renowned Prince, resist, endure
  Till the third day, or till the fourth at most ;
I come, and your deliverance will procure,
  And kill your coward foes and all their host.—
This secret in that brief was clos'd up sure,
  Writ in strange language, to the winged post
Giv'n to transport ; for in their warlike need,
The East such message us'd oft with good speed.

LIII.

The Duke let go the captive dove at large,
    And she that had his counsel close bewray'd,
Trait'ress to her great lord, touch'd not the marge
    Of Salem's town, but fled far thence afraid.
The Duke, before all those which had or charge
    Or office high, the letter read, and said—
See how the goodness of the Lord foreshows
The secret purpose of our crafty foes;

LIV.

No longer then let us protract the time,
    But scale the bulwarks of this fortress high;
Through sweat and labor 'gainst those rocks sublime
    Let us ascend, which to the southward lie:
Hard will it be that way in arms to climb,
    But yet the place and passage both know I;
And that high wall, by site strong on that part,
Is least defenc'd by arms, by work, and art.

LV.

Thou, Raimond, on this side with all thy might
    Assault the wall, and by those crags ascend;
My squadrons with mine engines huge shall fight,
    And 'gainst the northern gate my puissance bend;
That so our foes, beguiled with the sight,
    Our greatest force and pow'r shall there attend,
While my great tow'r from thence shall nimbly slide,
And batter down some worse-defended side:

LVI.

Camillo, thou not far from me shalt rear
    Another tow'r, close to the walls ybrought.—
This spoken, Raimond old that sat him near
    (And while he talk'd great things tost in his thought),
Said—To Godfredo's counsel given us here
    Naught can be added, from it taken naught;
Yet this I further wish, that some were sent
To spy their camp, their secret, and intent;

LVII.

That may their number and their squadrons brave
    Describe, and through their tents disguised mask.—
Quoth Tancred—Lo! a subtle squire I have,
    A person fit to undertake this task;

A man, quick, ready, bold, sly to deceive,
   To answer wise, and well advis'd to ask ;
Well languaged ; and that with time and place
Can change his look, his voice, his gait, his grace.—

LVIII.

Sent for, he came ; and when his lord him told
   What Godfrey's pleasure was, and what his own,
He smiled and said, forthwith he gladly would :
   I go (quoth he), careless what chance be thrown,
And where encamped be these Pagans bold ;
   Will walk in every tent, a spy unknown,
Their camp even at noon day I enter shall,
And number all their horse and footmen all ;

LIX.

How great, how strong, how arm'd this army is,
   And what their guide intends, I will declare ;
To me the secrets of that heart of his
   And hidden thoughts shall open lie and bare.—
Thus Vafrine spoke, nor longer stay'd on this,
   But for a mantle chang'd the coat he ware ;
Nak'd was his neck, and 'bout his forehead bold
Of linen white full twenty yards he roll'd :

LX.

His weapons were a Syrian bow and quiver,
   His gestures barb'rous like the Turkish train ;
Wonder'd all they that heard his tongue deliver
   Of every land the language true and plain ;
In Tyre, a born Phœnician, by the river
   Of Nile, a knight bred in th' Egyptian main,
Both people would have thought him : forth he rides
On a swift steed o'er hills and dales that glides.

LXI.

But ere the third day came the French forth sent
   Their pioneers to even the rougher ways,
And ready made each warlike instrument,
   Nor aught their labor interrupts or stays ;
The nights in busy toil they likewise spent,
   And with long evenings lengthen'd forth short days ;
Till naught was left the hosts that hinder might
To use their utmost power and strength in fight.

LXII.

That day which of th' assault the day forerun,
  The godly Duke in prayer spent well nigh,
And all the rest, because they had misdone,
  The sacrament receive, and mercy cry ;
Then oft the Duke his engines great begun
  To show, where least he would their strength apply.
His foes rejoic'd, deluded in that sort,
To see him bent against their surest port :

LXIII.

But after, aided by the friendly night,
  His greatest engine to that side he brought
Where plainest seem'd the wall, where with their might
  The flankers least could hurt them as they fought ;
And to the southern mountain's greatest height,
  To raise his turret old Raimondo sought :
And thou, Camillo, on that part had'st thine,
Where from the north the walls did westward twine.

LXIV.

But when amid the eastern heav'n appear'd
  The rising morning bright as shining glass,
The troubled Pagans saw, and seeing fear'd,
  How the great tow'r stood not where late it was ;
And here and there tofore unseen was rear'd,
  Of timber strong, a huge and fearful mass ;
And numberless with beams, with ropes, and strings,
They view the iron rams, the brakes, and slings.

LXV.

The Syrian people now were no whit slow
  Their best defences to that side to bear
Where Godfrey did his greatest engine show,
  From thence where late in vain they placed were ;
But he who at his back right well did know
  The host of Egypt to be 'proaching near,
To him call'd Guelpho and the Roberts twain,
And said—On horseback look you still remain,

LXVI.

And have regard, while all our people strive
  To scale this wall where weak it seems and thin,
Lest unawares some sudden host arrive,
  And at our backs unlook'd-for war begin.—

This said, three fierce assaults at once they give,
  The hardy soldiers all would die or win;
And on three parts resistance makes the King,
And rage 'gainst strength, despair 'gainst hope doth bring;

LXVII.

Himself upon his limbs, with feeble cild
  That shook unwieldy with their proper weight,
His armor laid, and long unused shield,
  And march'd 'gainst Raimond to the mountain's height.
Great Soliman 'gainst Godfrey took the field;
  Forenenst Camillo stood Argantes straight,
Where Tancred strong he found; so fortune will
That this good Prince his wonted foe shall kill.

LXVIII.

The archers shot their arrows sharp and keen,
  Dipp'd in the bitter juice of poison strong,
The shady face of heav'n was scantly seen,
  Hid with the clouds of shafts and quarries long;
Yet weapons sharp with greater fury been
  Cast from the towers the Pagan troops among,
For thence flew stones and clifts of marble rocks,
Trees shod with iron, timber, logs, and blocks:

LXIX.

A thunderbolt seem'd every stone, it brake
  His limbs and armors so on whom it light,
That life and soul it did not only take,
  But all his shape and face disfigured quite:
The lances stay'd not in the wounds they make,
  But through the gored body took their flight,
From side to side, through flesh, through skin and rind
They flew, and flying left sad death behind.

LXX.

But yet not all this force and fury drove
  The Pagan people to forsake the wall,
But to revenge these deadly blows they strove,
  With darts that fly, with stones and trees that fall:
For need so cowards oft courageous prove,
  For liberty they fight, for life and all,
And oft with arrows, shafts, and stones that fly,
Give bitter answer to a sharp reply.

LXXI.

This while the fierce assailants never cease,
  But sternly still maintain a threefold charge,
And 'gainst the clouds of shafts draw nigh at ease,
  Under a pentise made of many a targe,
The armed towers close to the bulwarks prease,
  And strive to grapple with the battled marge,
And launch their bridges out ; meanwhile below
With iron fronts the rams the walls down throw.

LXXII.

Yet still Rinaldo unresolved went,
  And far unworthy him this service thought,
If 'mongst the common sort his pains he spent ;
  Renown so got the Prince esteemed naught ;
His angry looks on every side he bent,
  And where most harm, most danger was, he sought :
And where the wall high, strong, and surest was,
That part would he assault, and that way pass:

LXXIII.

And turning to the worthies him behind,
  All hardy knights, whom Dudon late did guide :
O shame ! (quoth he) this wall no war doth find,
  When batter'd is elsewhere each part, each side ;
All pain is safety to a valiant mind,
  Each way is eath to him that dares abide ;
Come, let us scale this wall, though strong and high,
And with your shields keep off the darts that fly.—

LXXIV.

With him united all while thus he spake,
  Their targets hard above their heads they threw,
Which join'd in one an iron pentise make,
  That from the dreadful storm preserv'd the crew ;
Defended thus their speedy course they take,
  And to the wall without resistance drew,
For that strong penticle protected well
The knights from all that flew and all that fell.

LXXV.

Against the fort Rinaldo 'gan up-rear
  A ladder huge, an hundred steps of height,
And on his arm the same did eas'ly bear
  And move, as winds do reeds or rushes light ;

Sometimes a tree, a rock, a dart or spear,
    Fell from above, yet forward climb'd the knight,
And upward fearless preased, careless still
Though mount Olympus fell or Ossa hill:

LXXVI.

A mount of ruins, and of shafts a wood,
    Upon his shoulders and his shield he bore,
One hand the ladder held whereon he stood,
    The other bare his targe his face before;
His hardy troop, by his ensample good
    Provok'd, with him the place assaulted sore,
And ladders long against the walls they clap,
Unlike in courage yet, unlike in hap:

LXXVII.

One died, another fell, he forward went,
    And these he comforts and he threat'neth those,
Now with his hand outstretch'd the battlement
    Well nigh he reach'd, when all his armed foes
Ran thither, and their force and fury bent
    To throw him headlong down, yet up he goes;
A wond'rous thing, one knight whole armed bands,
Alone, and hanging in the air, withstands!

LXXVIII.

Withstands, and forceth his great strength so far,
    That like a palm whereon huge weight doth rest,
His forces so resisted stronger are,
    His virtues higher rise the more oppress'd,
Till all that would his entrance bold debar
    He backward drove, upleaped, and possess'd
The wall, and safe and easy with his blade
To all that after came the passage made.

LXXIX.

There killing such as durst and did withstand,
    To noble Eustace, that was like to fall,
He reached forth his friendly conqu'ring hand,
    And next himself help'd him to mount the wall.
This while Godfredo and his people fand
    Their lives to greater harms and dangers thrall;
For there not man with man, nor knight with knight
Contend, but engines there with engines fight:

LXXX.

For in that place the Paynims rear'd a post,
    Which late had serv'd some gallant ship for mast,
And over it another beam they cross'd,
    Pointed with iron sharp, to it made fast
With ropes, which, as men would, the dormant tost
    Now out, now in, now back, now forward cast;
In its swift pulleys oft the men withdrew
The tree, and oft the riding balk forth threw;

LXXXI.

The mighty beam redoubled oft its blows,
    And with such force the engine smote and hit,
That her broad side the tow'r wide open throws,
    Her joints were broke, her rafters cleft and split:
But yet, 'gainst every hap whence mischief grows
    Prepar'd, the peece ('gainst such extremes made fit)
Launch'd forth two scythes, sharp, cutting, long, and broad,
And cut the ropes whereon the engine rode.

LXXXII.

As an old rock, which age or stormy wind
    Tears from some craggy hill or mountain steep,
Doth break, doth bruise, and into dust doth grind
    Woods, houses, hamlets, herds, and folds of sheep;
So fell the beam, and down with it all kind
    Of arms, of weapons, and of men did sweep,
Wherewith the towers once or twice did shake,
Trembled the walls, the hills and mountains quake.

LXXXIII.

Victorious Godfrey boldly forward came,
    And had great hope even then the place to win:
But, lo! a fire, with stench, with smoke, and flame,
    Withstood his passage, stopp'd his entrance in:
Such burnings Ætna yet could never frame,
    When from her entrails hot her fires begin;
Nor yet in summer, on the Indian plain,
Such vapors warm from scorching air down rain.

LXXXIV.

Here balls of wildfire, there fly burning spears,
    This flame was black, that blue, this red as blood;
Stench well-nigh choketh them, noise deafs their ears,
    Smoke blinds their eyes, fire kindleth on the wood;

Nor those raw hides, which for defence it wears,
  Could save the tow'r, in such distress it stood ;
For now they wrinkle, now it sweats and fries,
Now burns, unless some help come down from skies.

LXXXV.

The hardy Duke before his folk abides,
  Nor chang'd he color, countenance, or place,
But comforts those that from the scaldred hides
  With water strove th' approaching flames to chase :
In these extremes, the Prince and those he guides
  Half roasted stood before fierce Vulcan's face ;
When, lo ! a sudden and unlook'd-for blast
The flames against the kindlers backward cast ;

LXXXVI.

The winds drove back the fire where heaped lie
  The Pagans' weapons, where their engines were :
Which kindling quickly in that substance dry,
  Burnt all their store and all their warlike gear.
O glorious captain ! whom the Lord from high
  Defends, whom God preserves and holds so dear ;
For thee heav'n fights, to thee the winds from far,
Call'd with thy trumpet's blast, obedient are.

LXXXVII.

But wicked Ismen to his harm that saw
  How the fierce blast drove back the fire and flame,
By art would nature change, and thence withdraw
  Those noisome winds, else calm and still the same :
'Twixt two false wizards, without fear or awe,
  Upon the walls in open sight he came ;
Black, grisly, loathsome, grim, and ugly faced,
Like Pluto old betwixt two furies placed :

LXXXVIII.

And now the wretch those dreadful words begun,
  Which tremble make deep hell and all her flock ;
Now troubled is the air, the golden sun
  His fearful beams in clouds did close and lock :
When from the tow'r, which Ismen could not shun,
  Out flew a mighty stone, late half a rock,
Which light so just upon the wizards three,
That driv'n to dust their bones and bodies be ;

LXXXIX.

To less than naught their members old were torn,
  And shiver'd were their heads to pieces small,
As small as are the bruised grains of corn,
  When from the mill resolv'd to meal they fall ;
Their damned souls to deepest hell down borne,
  Far from the joy and light celestial,
The furies plunged in th' infernal lake :
O mankind ! at their ends ensample take.

XC.

This while the engine, which the tempest cold
  Had sav'd from burning with his friendly blast
Approached had so near the batter'd hold,
  That on the walls her bridge at ease she cast ;
But Soliman ran thither fierce and bold,
  To cut the plank whereon the Christians pass'd,
And had perform'd his will, save that up-rear'd
High in the skies a turret new appear'd ;

XCI.

Far in the air up-climb'd the fortress tall,
  Higher than house, than steeple, church, or tower ;
The Pagans trembled to behold the wall
  And city subject to its shot and power :
Yet kept the Turk his stand, though on him fall
  Of stones and darts a sharp and deadly shower ;
And still to cut the bridge he hopes and strives,
And those that fear with cheerful speech revives.

XCII.

The angel Michael, to all the rest
  Unseen, appear'd before Godfredo's eyes,
In pure and heav'nly armor richly dress'd,
  Brighter than Titan's rays in clearest skies :
Godfrey (quoth he), this is the moment bless'd
  To free this town that long in bondage lies ;
See ! see what legions in thine aid I bring,
For heav'n assists thee, and heav'n's glorious King :

XCIII.

Lift up thine eyes and in the air behold
  The sacred armies how they muster'd be ;
That cloud of flesh in which from times of old
  All mankind wrapped is I take from thee,

And from thy senses their thick mist unfold,
   That face to face thou mayst these spirits see,
And for a little space right well sustain
   Their glorious light, and view those angels plain:

XCIV.

Behold the souls of every lord and knight
   That late bore arms and died for Christ's dear sake,
How on thy side against this town they fight,
   And of thy joy and conquest will partake:
There where the dust and smoke blind all men's sight,
   Where stones and ruins such a heap do make,
There Hugo fights, in thickest cloud embar'd,
And undermines that bulwark's groundwork hard:

XCV.

See Dudon yonder, who with sword and fire
   Assails and helps to scale the northern port,
That with bold courage doth thy folk inspire,
   And rears their ladders 'gainst th' assaulted fort:
He that high on the mount in grave attire
   Is clad, and crowned stands in kingly sort,
Is Bishop Ademare, a blessed spirit,
Bless'd for his faith, crown'd for his death and merit:

XCVI.

But higher lift thy happy eyes, and view
   Where all the sacred hosts of heav'n appear.—
He look'd, and saw where winged armies flew,
   Innumerable, pure, divine, and clear;
A battaile round of squadrons three they shew,
   And all by threes those squadrons ranged were,
Which spreading wide in rings still wider go;
Mov'd with a stone, calm water circleth so.

XCVII.

With that he wink'd, and vanish'd was and gone
   That wond'rous vision when he look'd again;
His worthies fighting view'd he one by one,
   And on each side saw signs of conquest plain;
For with Rinaldo 'gainst his yielding fone
   His knights were enter'd and the Pagans slain:
This seen, the Duke no longer stay could brook,
But from the bearer bold his ensign took,

XCVIII.

And on the bridge he stepp'd, but there was stay'd
  By Soliman, who entrance all denied :
That narrow tree to virtue great was made
  The field, as in few blows right soon was try'd :—
Here will I give my life for Sion's aid,
  Here will I end my days (the Soldan cry'd) ;
Behind me cut or break this bridge, that I
May kill a thousand Christians first, then die.—

XCIX.

But thither fierce Rinaldo threatening went,
  And at his sight fled all the Soldan's train.—
What shall I do ? If here my life be spent,
  I spend and spill (quoth he) my blood in vain.—
With that his steps from Godfrey back he bent,
  And to him let the passage free remain,
Who threatening follow'd as the Soldan fled,
And on the walls the purple cross dispread ;

C.

About his head he toss'd, he turn'd, he cast
  That glorious ensign, with a thousand twines,
Thereon the wind breathes with his sweetest blast,
  Thereon with golden rays glad Phœbus shines,
Earth laughs for joy, the streams forbear their haste,
  Floods clap their hands, on mountains dance the pines,
And Sion's towers and sacred temples smile
For their deliverance from that bondage vile.

CI.

And now the armies rear'd the happy cry
  Of victory, glad, joyful, loud, and shrill,
The hills resound, the echo shouteth high,
  And Tancred bold, that fights and combats still
With proud Argantes, brought his tower so nigh,
  That on the wall, against the boaster's will,
In his despite his bridge he also laid,
And won the place, and there the cross display'd.

CII.

But on the southern hill, where Raimond fought
  Against the townsmen and their aged King,
His hardy Gascoignes gained small or naught,
  Their engine to the walls they could not bring ;

For thither all his strength the Prince had brought,
    For life and safety sternly combatting ;
And for the wall was feeblest on that coast,
There were his soldiers best and engines most.

CIII.

Besides, the tow'r upon that quarter found
    Unsure, uneasy, and uneven the way,
Nor art could help, but that the rougher ground
    The rolling mass did often stop and stay :
But now of victory the joyful sound
    The King and Raimond heard amid their fray,
And by the shout they and their soldiers know
The town was enter'd on the plain below.

CIV.

Which heard, Raimondo thus bespake this crew :—
    The town is won, my friends, and doth it yet
Resist ?   Are we kept out still by these few ?
    Shall we no share in this high conquest get ?
But from that part the King at last withdrew,
    He strove in vain their entrance there to let,
And to a stronger place his folk he brought,
Where to sustain th' assault awhile he thought.

CV.

The conquerors at once now enter'd all,
    The walls were won, the gates were open'd wide ;
Now bruised, broken down, destroyed fall
    The ports and towers that battery durst abide :
Rageth the sword, death murd'reth great and small,
    And proud 'twixt wo and horror sad doth ride ;
Here runs the blood, in ponds there stands the gore,
And drowns the knights in whom it liv'd before.

BOOK XIX.

~~~~~~~~~

~~~~~~~~~

I.

Now death, or fear, or care to save their lives,
　　From their forsaken walls the Pagans chase ;
Yet neither force, nor fear, nor wisdom drives
　　The constant knight Argantes from his place ;
Alone against ten thousand foes he strives,
　　Yet dreadless, doubtless, careless seem'd his face ;
Not death, not danger, but disgrace he fears,
And still unconquer'd (though beset) appears.

II.

But 'mongst the rest upon his helmet gay
　　With his broad sword Tancredie came and smote :
The Pagan knew the Prince by his array,
　　By his strong blows, his armor, and his coat ;
For once they fought, and when night stay'd that fray,
　　New time they chose to end their combat hot,
But Tancred fail'd, wherefore the Pagan knight
Cry'd—Tancred, com'st thou thus, thus late to fight ?

III.

Too late thou com'st, and not alone, to war,
　　But yet the fight I neither shun nor fear,
Although from knighthood true thou errest far,
　　Since like an engineer thou dost appear,

That tower, that troop, thy shield and safety are;
   Strange kind of arms in single fight to bear!
Yet shalt thou not escape (O conqueror strong
Of ladies fair!) sharp death to 'venge that wrong.—

IV.

Lord Tancred smiled with disdain and scorn,
   And answer'd thus :—To end our strife (quoth he)
Behold at last I come, and my return
   (Though late) perchance will be too soon for thee;
For thou shalt wish, of hope and help forlorn,
   Some sea or mountain plac'd 'twixt thee and me;
And well shalt know, before we end this fray,
No fear or cowardice hath caus'd my stay;

V.

But come aside, thou by whose prowess dies
   The monsters, knights, and giants in all lands,
The killer of weak women thee defies.—
   This said, he turned to his fighting bands
And bids them all retire :—Forbear (he cries)
   To strike this knight; on him let none lay hands,
For mine he is, more than a common foe,
By challenge new and promise old also.—

VI.

Descend (the fierce Circassian 'gan reply)
   Alone, or all this troop for succor take,
To deserts waste, or place frequented high,
   For 'vantage none I will the fight forsake.—
Thus given and taken was the bold defy,
   And through the prease (agreed so) they brake;
Their hatred made them one, and as they wend,
Each knight his foe did for despite defend.

VII.

Great was his thirst of praise, great the desire
   That Tancred had the Pagan's blood to spill,
Nor could that quench his wrath or calm his ire,
   If other hand his foe should foil or kill;
He sav'd him with his shield, and cry'd—Retire
   (To all he met), and do this knight none ill.—
And thus defending 'gainst his friends his foe,
Through thousand angry weapons safe they go.

VIII.

They left the city, and they left behind
   Godfredo's camp, and far beyond it pass'd ;
And came, where into creeks and bosoms blind
   A winding hill his corners turn'd and cast ;
A valley small and shady dale they find
   Amid the mountains steep, so laid and plac'd
As if some theatre or closed place
Had been, for men to fight or beasts to chase :

IX.

There stay'd the champions both.   With rueful eyes
   Argantes 'gan the fortress won to view.
Tancred his foe withouten shield espies,
   And far away his target therefore threw,
And said—Whereon doth thy sad heart devise ?
   Think'st thou this hour must end thy life untrue ?
If this thou fear, and dost foresee thy fate,
Thy fear is vain, thy foresight comes too late.—

X.

I think (quoth he) on this distressed town,
   The aged queen of Judah's ancient land,
Now lost, now sacked, spoil'd and trodden down,
   Whose fall in vain I strived to withstand ;
A small revenge, for Sion's fort o'erthrown,
   That head can be cut off by my strong hand.—
This said, together with great heed they flew,
For each his foe for bold and hardy knew.

XI.

Tancred of body active was and light,
   Quick, nimble, ready both of hand and foot :
But higher by the head the Pagan knight
   Of limb far greater was, of heart as stout.
Tancred laid low and travers'd in his fight,
   Now to his ward retir'd, now struck out ;
Oft with his sword his foe's fierce blows he broke,
And rather chose to ward than bear his stroke.

XII.

But bold and bolt upright Argantes fought,
   Unlike in gesture, like in skill and art ;
His sword outstretch'd before him far he brought,
   Nor would his weapon touch, but pierce his heart :

To catch his point Prince Tancred strove and sought,
  But at his breast or helm's unclosed part
He threaten'd death, and would with stretch'd-out brand
His entrance close and fierce assaults withstand.

XIII.

With a tall ship so doth a galley fight,
  When the still winds stir not th' unstable main,
Where this in nimbleness as that in might
  Excels ; that stands, this goes and comes again,
And shifts from prow to poop with turnings light :
  Meanwhile the other doth unmov'd remain,
And on her nimble foe approacheth nigh,
Her weighty engines tumbleth down from high.

XIV.

The Christian sought to enter on his foe,
  Voiding his point, which at his breast was bent ;
Argantes at his face a thrust did throw,
  Which while the Prince awards and doth prevent,
His ready hand the Pagan turned so,
  That all defence his quickness far o'erwent,
And pierc'd his side ; which done, he said, and smil'd—
The craftsman is in his own craft beguil'd.—

XV.

Tancredie bit his lips for scorn and shame,
  Nor longer stood on points of fence and skill,
But to revenge so fierce and fast he came,
  As if his hand could not o'ertake his will ;
And at his vizor aiming just, 'gan frame
  To his proud boast an answer sharp ; but still
Argantes broke the thrust ; and at half-sword,
Swift, hardy, bold, in stept the Christian lord ;

XVI.

With his left foot fast forward 'gan he stride,
  And with his left the Pagan's right arm hent ;
With his right hand meanwhile the man's right side
  He cut, he wounded, mangled, tore, and rent ;—
To his victorious teacher (Tancred cry'd),
  His conquer'd scholar hath this answer sent.—
Argantes chafed, struggled, turn'd, and twin'd,
Yet could not so his captive arm unbind :

XVII.

His sword at last he let hang by the chain,
   And grip'd his hardy foe in both his hands;
In his strong arms Tancred caught him again,
   And thus each other held and wrapt in bands.
With greater might Alcides did not strain
   The giant Anteus on the Lybian sands;
On hold-fast knots their brawny arms they cast,
And whom he hateth most each held embrac'd:

XVIII.

Such was their wrestling, such their shocks and throws,
   That down at once they tumbled both to ground;
Argantes (were it hap or skill, who knows)
   His better hand loose and in freedom found;
But the good Prince, his hand more fit for blows,
   With his huge weight the Pagan underbound;
But he, his disadvantage great that knew,
Let go his hold, and on his feet up flew.

XIX.

Far slower rose th' unwieldy Saracine,
   And caught a rap ere he was rear'd upright:
But as against the blust'ring winds a pine
   Now bends his top, now lifts his head on height,
His courage so, when it 'gan most decline,
   The man reinforced and advanc'd his might,
And with fierce change of blows renew'd the fray,
Where rage for skill, horror for art bore sway.

XX.

The purple drops from Tancred's sides down railed,
   But from the Pagan ran whole streams of blood,
Wherewith his force grew weak, his courage quailed,
   As fires decay which fuel want or food.
Tancred, that saw his feeble arm now failed
   To strike his blows, that scant he stirr'd or stood,
Assuag'd his anger and his wrath allay'd,
And stepping back, thus gently spoke and said:—

XXI.

Yield, hardy knight, and chance of war, or me,
   Confess to have subdued thee in this fight;
I will no trophy, triumph, spoil of thee,
   Nor glory wish, nor seek a victor's right.—

More terrible than erst herewith grew he,
  And all awak'd his fury, rage, and might,
And said—Dar'st thou of 'vantage speak or think,
Or move Argantes once to yield or shrink?

XXII.

Use, use thy vantage; thee and fortune both
  I scorn, and punish will thy foolish pride.—
As a hot brand flames most ere it forth go'th,
  And dying blazeth bright on every side;
So he (when blood was lost) with anger wroth
  Reviv'd his courage, when his puissance died;
And would his latest hour, which now drew nigh,
Illustrate with his end, and nobly die:

XXIII.

He join'd his left hand to her sister strong,
  And with them both let fall his weighty blade.
Tancred to ward his blow his sword up flung,
  But that it smote aside, nor there it stay'd,
But from his shoulder to his side along
  It glanc'd, and many wounds at once it made:
Yet Tancred feared naught, for in his heart
Found coward dread no place, fear had no part.

XXIV.

His fearful blow he doubled, but he spent
  His force in waste, and all his strength in vain;
For Tancred from the blow against him bent,
  Leaped aside, the stroke fell on the plain:
With thine own weight o'erthrown to earth thou went,
  Argantes stout, nor could'st thyself sustain,
Thyself thou threwest down, O happy man!
Upon whose fall none boast or triumph can.

XXV.

His gaping wounds the fall set open wide,
  The streams of blood about him made a lake;
Help'd with his left hand, on one knee he tried
  To rear himself, and new defence to make.
The courteous Prince stepp'd back, and—Yield thee, cried,
  No hurt he proffer'd him, no blow he strake.
Meanwhile, by stealth, the Pagan false him gave
A sudden wound, threat'ning with speeches brave.

XXVI.

Herewith Tancredie furious grew, and said—
    Villain ! dost thou my mercy so despise ?—
Therewith he thrust and thrust again his blade,
    And through his vental pierc'd his dazzled eyes.
Argantes died, yet no complaint he made,
    But as he furious liv'd he careless dies ;
Bold, proud, disdainful, fierce, and void of fear,
His motions last, last looks, last speeches were.

XXVII.

Tancred put up his sword and praises glad
    Gave to his God, that sav'd him in this fight ;
But yet this bloody conquest feebled had
    So much the conqueror's force, his strength, and might,
That through the way he fear'd, which homeward led,
    He had not strength enough to walk upright ;
Yet, as he could, his steps from thence he bent,
And foot by foot a heavy pace forth went :

XXVIII.

His legs could bear him but a little stound,
    And more he hastes (more tir'd) less was his speed ;
On his right hand at last, laid on the ground,
    He lean'd, his hand weak like a shaking reed ;
Dazzled his eyes, the world on wheels ran round,
    Day wrapt her brightness up in sable weed ;
At length he swooned, and the victor knight
Naught differ'd from his conquer'd foe in sight.

XXIX.

But while these lords their private fight pursue,
    Made fierce and cruel through their secret hate,
The victors' ire destroy'd the faithless crew
    From street to street, and chas'd from gate to gate.
But of the sacked town the image true
    Who can describe, or paint the woful state ;
Or with fit words this spectacle express
Who can, or tell the city's great distress ?

XXX.

Blood, murder, death, each street, house, church defil'd,
    There heaps of slain appear, there mountains high ;
There, underneath th' unburied hills up-pil'd
    Of bodies dead, the living buried lie ;

There the sad mother with her tender child
    Doth tear her tresses loose, complain, and fly ;
And there the spoiler, by her amber hair,
Draws to his lust the virgin chaste and fair.

XXXI.

But through the way that to the west hill yood,
    Whereon the old and stately temple stands,
All soil'd with gore and wet with lukewarm blood,
    Rinaldo ran and chas'd the pagan bands ;
Above their heads he heav'd his curtlax good,
    Life in his grace, and death lay in his hands ;
Nor helm nor target strong his blows off bears,
Best armed there seem'd he no arms that wears,

XXXII.

For 'gainst his armed foes he only bends
    His force, and scorns the naked folk to wound ;
Them whom no courage arms, no arms defends,
    He chased with his looks and dreadful sound :
O ! who can tell how far his force extends,
    How these he scorns, threats those, lays them on ground ?
How with unequal harm, with equal fear,
Fled all, all that well arm'd or naked were !

XXXIII.

Fast fled the people weak, and with the same
    A squadron strong is to the temple gone,
Which burnt and builded oft, still keeps the name
    Of the first founder, wise king Solomon ;
That prince this stately house did whilome frame
    Of cedar trees, of gold and marble stone ;
Now not so rich, yet strong and sure it was,
With turrets high, thick walls, and doors of brass.

XXXIV.

The knight arrived where in warlike sort
    The men that ample church had fortify'd,
And closed found each wicket, gate, and port,
    And on the top defences ready spy'd ;
He lift his frowning looks, and twice that fort
    From its high top down to the groundwork ey'd,
And entrance sought, and twice with his swift foot
The mighty place he measured about.

XXXV.

Like as a wolf about the closed fold
    Rangeth by night his hoped prey to get,
Enrag'd with hunger and with malice old,
    Which kind 'twixt him and harmless sheep hath set :
So search'd he high and low about that hold,
    Where he might enter without stop or let ;
In the great court he stay'd : his foes above
Attend th' assault, and would their fortune prove.

XXXVI.

There lay by chance a posted tree thereby,
    Kept for some needful use : whate'er it were,
The armed galleys not so thick nor high
    Their tall and lofty masts at Genes up-rear:
This beam the knight against the gates made fly
    From his strong hands, all weights which lift and bear ;
Like a light lance the tree he shook and toss'd,
And bruis'd the gate, the threshold, and the post :

XXXVII.

No marble stone, no metal strong out-bore
    The wond'rous might of that redoubled blow,
The brazen hinges from the walls it tore,
    It broke the locks, and laid the doors down low ;
No iron ram, no engine could do more,
    Nor cannons great that thunderbolts forth throw :
His people like a flowing stream in throng,
And after them enter'd the victor strong.

XXXVIII.

The woful slaughter black and loathsome made
    That house, sometime the sacred house of God.
O Heav'nly Justice ! if thou be delay'd,
    On wretched sinners sharper falls thy rod ;
In them, this place profaned which invade,
    Thou kindled ire, and mercy all forbade,
Until with their hearts' blood the Pagans vile
This temple wash'd, which they did late defile.

XXXIX.

But Soliman this while himself fast sped
    Up to the fort, which David's Tower is named,
And with him all the soldiers left he led,
    And 'gainst each entrance new defences framed :

The tyrant Aladine eke thither fled,
    To whom the Soldan thus (far off) exclaimed—
Come, come, renowned king ! up to this rock,
Thyself within this fortress safe up-lock ;

XL.

For well this fortress shall thee and thy crown
    Defend ; awhile here may we safe remain.—
Alas ! (quoth he) alas ! for this fair town,
    Which cruel war beats down ev'n with the plain :
My life is done, mine empire trodden down ;
    I reign'd, I liv'd, but now nor live nor reign ;
For now, alas ! behold the fatal hour
That ends our lives, and ends our kingly pow'r.—

XLI.

Where is your virtue, where your wisdom grave,
    And courage stout ? (the angry Soldan said)
Let chance our kingdoms take which erst she gave,
    Yet in our hearts our kingly worth is laid ;
But come, and in this fort your person save.
    Refresh your weary limbs and strength decay'd.—
Thus counsell'd he, and did to safety bring
Within that fort the weak and aged king.

XLII.

His iron mace in both his hands he hent,
    And on his thigh his trusty sword he tied,
And to the entrance fierce and fearless went,
    And kept the strait, and all the French defy'd :
The blows were mortal which he gave or lent,
    For whom he hit he slew, else by his side
Laid low on earth, that all fled from the place
Where they beheld that great and dreadful mace.

XLIII.

But old Raimondo with his hardy crew
    By chance came thither, to his great mishap ;
To that defended path the old man flew,
    And scorn'd his blows and him that kept the gap ;
He struck his foe, his blow no blood forth drew,
    But on the front with that he caught a rap,
Which in a swoon low in the dust him laid,
Wide open, trembling, with his arms display'd.

XLIV.

The Pagans gather'd heart at last, though fear
  Their courage weak had put to flight but late,
So that the conquerors repulsed were
  And beaten back, else slain before the gate.
The Soldan ('mongst the dead beside him near
  That saw Lord Raimond lie in such estate)
Cry'd to his men—Within these bars (quoth he)
Come draw this knight, and let him captive be.—

XLV.

Forward they rush'd to execute his word,
  But hard and dang'rous that emprise they found,
For none of Raimond's men forsook their lord,
  But to their guide's defence they flocked round ;
Thence fury fights, hence pity draws the sword,
  Nor strive they for vile cause or on light ground ;
The life and freedom of that champion brave,
Those spoil, these would preserve, those kill, these save.

XLVI.

But yet at last, if they had longer fought,
  The hardy Soldan would have won the field,
For 'gainst his thund'ring mace availed naught,
  Or helm of temper fine, or seven-fold shield ;
But from each side great succor now was brought
  To his weak foes, now fit to faint and yield ;
And both at once, to aid and help the same,
The sovereign Duke and young Rinaldo came.

XLVII.

As when a shepherd, raging round about
  That sees a storm with wind, hail, thunder, rain
(When gloomy clouds have day's bright eye put out),
  His tender flock drives from the open plain
To some thick grove or mountain's shady foot,
  Where heav'n's fierce wrath they may unhurt sustain :
And with his hook, his whistle, and his cries,
Drives forth his fleecy charge, and with them flies ;

XLVIII.

So fled the Soldan when he 'gan descry
  This tempest come from angry war forth cast ;
The armors clash'd and lighten'd 'gainst the sky,
  And from each side swords, weapons, fire, out brast :

He sent his folk up to the fortress high
    To shun the furious storm, himself stay'd last;
Yet to the danger he gave place at length,
For wit his courage, wisdom rul'd his strength.

XLIX.

But scant the knight was safe the gate within,
    Scant closed were the doors, when having broke
The bars, Rinaldo doth assault begin
    Against the port, and on the wicket stroke
His matchless might; his great desire to win,
    His oath and promise, doth his wrath provoke;
For he had sworn, nor should his word be vain,
To kill the man that had Prince Sweno slain.

L.

And now his armed hand that castle great
    Would have assaulted and had shortly won,
Nor safe pardie the Soldan there a seat
    Had found, his fatal foe's sharp wrath to shun
Had not Godfredo sounded the retreat,
    For now dark shades to shroud the earth begun;
Within the town the Duke would lodge that night,
And with the morn renew th' assault and fight.

LI.

With cheerful look thus to his folk he said—
    High God hath holpen well his children dear;
This work is done, the rest this night delay'd
    Doth little labor bring, less doubt, no fear;
This tower, our foes' weak hope and latest aid,
    We conquer will when sun shall next appear;
Meanwhile, with love and tender ruth, go see
And comfort those which hurt and wounded be;

LII.

Go cure their wounds who boldly ventured
    Their lives, and spilt their good to get this hold;
That fitteth more this host for Christ forth led,
    Than thirst of vengeance or desire of gold:
Too much, ah! too much blood this day is shed;
    In some we too much haste to spoil behold;
But I command no more you spoil and kill,
And let a trumpet publish forth my will.—

LIII.

This said, he went where Raimond panting lay,
  Wak'd from the swoon wherein he late had been.
Nor Soliman, with countenance less gay
  Bespake his troops, and kept his grief unseen :
My friends, you are unconquered this day,
  In spite of fortune still our hope is green,
For underneath great shows of harm and fear,
Our dangers small, our losses little were :

LIV.

Burnt are your houses, and your people slain,
  Yet safe your town is though your walls be gone,
For in yourselves and in your sovereign
  Consists your city, not in lime and stone :
Your king is safe, and safe is all his train,
  In this strong fort defended from their fone ;
And on this empty conquest let them boast,
Till with this town again their lives be lost ;

LV.

And on their heads the loss at last will light,
  For with good fortune proud and insolent,
In spoil and murder spend they day and night,
  In riot, drinking, lust, and ravishment ;
And may amid their preys, with little fight,
  At ease be overthrown, kill'd, slain, and spent ;
If in this carelessness th' Egyptian host
Upon them fall, which now draws near this coast :

LVI.

Meanwhile, the highest buildings of this town
  We may shake down with stones about their ears,
And with our darts and spears from engines thrown
  Command that hill Christ's sepulchre that bears.—
Thus comforts he their hopes and hearts cast down,
  Awakes their valors, and exiles their fears.
But while these things hap'd thus, Vafrino goes
Unknown amid ten thousand armed foes.

LVII.

The sun nigh set had brought to end the day,
  When Vafrine went the Pagan host to spy ;
He past unknown, a close and secret way,
  A traveller, false, cunning, crafty, sly ;

Past Ascalon he saw the morning grey
  Step o'er the threshold of the eastern sky,
And ere bright Titan half his course had run,
That camp, that mighty host, to show begun :

LVIII.

Tents infinite and standards broad he spies,
  This red, that white, that blue, this purple was ;
And hears strange tongues, and stranger harmonies
  Of trumpets, clarions, and well-sounding brass ;
The elephant there brays, the camel cries,
  The horses neigh, as to and fro they pass ;
Which seen and heard, he said within his thought—
Hither all Asia is, all Afric brought.—

LIX.

He view'd the camp awhile, her site and seat,
  What ditch, what trench it had, what rampire strong ;
Nor close nor secret ways to work his feat
  He longer sought, nor hid him from the throng,
But enter'd through the gates, broad, royal, great,
  And oft he ask'd, and answer'd oft among ;
In questions wise, in answers short and sly ;
Bold was his look, eyes quick, front lifted high.

LX.

On every side he pryed here and there,
  And mark'd each way, each passage, and each tent :
The knights he notes, their steeds, and arms they bear,
  Their names, their armors, and their government ;
And greater secrets hopes to learn, and hear
  Their hidden purpose and their close intent.
So long he walk'd and wander'd, till he spy'd
The way t' approach the great pavilion's side :

LXI.

There, as he look'd, he saw the canvas rent,
  Through which the voice found eath and open way
From the close lodgings of the regal tent,
  And inmost closet where the captain lay ;
So that if Emireno spake, forth went
  The sound to them that listen what they say ;
There Vafrine watch'd, and those that saw him thought
To mend the breach that there he stood and wrought.

LXII.

The captain great within bare-headed stood,
   His body arm'd, and clad in purple weed ;
Two pages bore his shield and helmet good ;
   He, leaning on a bending lance, gave heed
To a big man, whose looks were fierce and proud,
   With whom he parled of some haughty deed ;
Godfredo's name, as Vafrine watch'd, he heard,
Which made him give more heed, take more regard.

LXIII.

Thus spake the chieftain to that surly sire :—
   Art thou so sure that Godfrey shall be slain ?
I am (quoth he), and swear ne'er to retire,
   Except he first be kill'd, to court again :
I will prevent those that with me conspire ;
   Nor other guerdon ask I for my pain,
But that I may hang up his harness brave
At Caire, and under them these words engrave :

LXIV.

These arms Ormondo took in noble fight
   From Godfrey proud, that spoil'd all Asia's lands,
And with them took his life ; and here on height,
   In memory thereof, this trophy stands.—
The Duke reply'd—Ne'er shall that deed, bold knight,
   Pass unrewarded at our sov'reign's hands ;
What thou demandest shall he gladly grant,
Nor gold nor guerdon shalt thou wish or want :

LXV.

Those counterfeited armors then prepare,
   Because the day of fight approacheth fast.—
They ready are (quoth he).—Then both forbear
   From further talk, these speeches were the last.
Vafrine (these great things heard) with grief and care
   Remain'd astound, and in his thoughts oft cast
What treason false this was, how feigned were
Those arms, but yet that doubt he could not clear.

LXVI.

From thence he parted, and broad waking lay
   All that long night, nor slumber'd once nor slept ;
But when the camp by peep of springing day
   Their banners spread, and knights on horseback leapt,

With them he marched forth in meet array,
    And where they pitched lodg'd, and with them kept ;
And then from tent to tent he stalk'd about,
To hear and see, and learn this secret out.

LXVII.

Searching about, on a rich throne he fand
    Armida sat, with dames and knights around ;
Sullen she sat and sigh'd, it seem'd she scand
    Some weighty matters in her thought profound ;
Her rosy cheek lean'd on her lily hand,
    Her eyes (love's twinkling stars) she bent to ground ;
Weep she or no he knows not, yet appears
Her humid eyes e'en great with child with tears.

LXVIII.

He saw before her set Adrastus grim,
    That seemed scant to live, move, or respire,
So was he fixed on his mistress trim,
    So gazed he, and fed his fond desire :
But Tisipherne beheld now her, now him,
    And quak'd sometime for love, sometime for ire ;
And in his cheeks the color went and came,
For there wrath's fire now burnt, now shone love's flame.

LXIX.

Then from the garland fair of virgins bright,
    'Mongst whom he lay enclos'd, rose Altamore ;
His hot desire he hid and kept from sight,
    His looks were rul'd by Cupid's crafty lore ;
His left eye view'd her hand, her face ; his right
    Both watch'd her beauty's hid and secret store,
And entrance found where her thin veil bewray'd
The milken way between her breasts that laid.

LXX.

Her eyes Armida lift from earth at last,
    And clear'd again her front and visage sad,
'Midst clouds of wo, her looks which overcast,
    She lighten'd forth a smile, sweet, pleasant, glad :—
My lord (quoth she), your oath and promise past,
    Hath freed my heart of all the griefs it had,
That now in hope of sweet revenge it lives,
Such joy, such ease, desired vengeance gives.—

LXXI.

Cheer up thy looks (answer'd the Indian king),
   And for sweet beauty's sake appease thy wo,
Cast at your feet, ere you expect the thing,
   I will present the head of thy strong foe ;
Else shall this hand his person captive bring,
   And cast in prison deep.—He boasted so :
His rival heard him well, yet answer'd naught,
But bit his lips, and grieved in secret thought.

LXXII.

To Tisipherne the damsel turning right—
   And what say you, my noble lord ?—(quoth she.)
He taunting said—I, that am slow to fight,
   Will follow far behind, the worth to see
Of this your terrible and puissant knight.—
   In scornful words this bitter scoff gave he.—
Good reason (quoth the king) thou come behind,
Nor e'er compare thee with the Prince of Inde.—

LXXIII.

Lord Tisiphernes shook his head and said—
   Oh had my power free like my courage been,
Or had I liberty to use this blade,
   Who slow, who weakest is, soon should be seen ;
Nor thou nor thy great vaunts make me afraid,
   But cruel love I fear and this fair queen.—
This said, to challenge him the king forth leap'd,
But up his mistress start and 'twixt them stepp'd.—

LXXIV.

Will you thus rob me of that gift (quoth she)
   Which each hath vow'd to give by word and oath ?
You are my champions, let that title be
   The bond of love and peace between you both ;
He that displeas'd is, is displeas'd with me,
   For which of you is griev'd, and I not wroth ?—
Thus warn'd she them, their hearts (for ire nigh broke)
In forced peace and rest thus bore love's yoke.

LXXV.

All this heard Vafrine as he stood beside,
   And having learn'd the truth, he left the tent.
That treason was against the Christians' guide
   Contriv'd, he wist, yet wist not how it went ;

By words and questions far off he try'd
   To find the truth ; more difficult, more bent
Was he to know it, and resolv'd to die,
Or of that secret close th' intent to spy.

LXXVI.

Of sly intelligence he prov'd all ways,
   All crafts, all wiles that in his thoughts abide ;
Yet all in vain the man by wit assays
   To know that false compact and practice hid :
But chance (what wisdom could not tell) bewrays,
   Fortune of all his doubt the knots undid ;
So that prepar'd for Godfrey's last mishap,
At ease he found the net, and spy'd the trap.

LXXVII.

Thither he turn'd again where seated was
   The angry lover 'twixt her friends and lords,
For in that troop much talk he thought would pass,
   Each great assembly store of news affords :
He sided there a lusty lovely lass,
   And with some courtly terms the wench he boards ;
He feigns acquaintance, and as bold appears
As he had known that virgin twenty years.

LXXVIII.

He said—Would some sweet lady grace me so,
   To choose me for her champion, friend, and knight,
Proud Godfrey's or Rinaldo's head, I trow,
   Should feel the sharpness of my curtlax bright :
Ask me the head, fair mistress, of some foe,
   For to your beauty vowed is my might.—
So he began, and meant in speeches wise
Further to wade, but thus he brake the ice.

LXXIX.

Therewith he smil'd, and smiling 'gan to frame
   His looks so to their old and native grace,
That towards him another virgin came,
   Heard him, beheld him, and with bashful face
Said—For thy mistress choose no other dame
   But me, on me thy love and service place ;
I take thee for my champion, and apart
Would reason with thee, if my knight thou art.—

LXXX.

Withdrawn, she thus began :—Vafrine, pardie,
  I know thee well, and me thou know'st of old.—
To his last trump this drove the subtle spy,
  But smiling towards her he turn'd him bold :—
Ne'er that I wot I saw thee erst with eye,
  Yet for thy worth all eyes should thee behold ;
This much I know right well, for from the same
Which erst you gave me different is my name :

LXXXI.

My mother bore me near Biserta's wall,
  Her name was Lesbine, mine is Almansore.—
I knew long since (quoth she) what men thee call,
  And thine estate, dissemble it no more,
From me thy friend hide not thyself at all,
  If I bewray thee let me die therefore ;
I am Erminia, daughter to a prince,
But Tancred's slave, thy fellow-servant since :

LXXXII.

Two happy months within that prison kind,
  Under thy guard, rejoiced I to dwell,
And thee a keeper meek and good did find ;
  The same, the same I am ; behold me well.—
The squire her lovely beauty call'd to mind,
  And mark'd her visage fair.—From thee expel
All fear (she says), for me live safe and sure,
I will thy safety, not thy harm procure.

LXXXIII.

But yet I pray thee, when thou dost return,
  To my dear prison lead me home again ;
For in this hateful freedom even and morn
  I sigh for sorrow, mourn and weep for pain :
But if to spy perchance thou here sojourn,
  Great hap thou hast to know their secrets plain,
For I their treasons false, false trains can say,
Which few beside can tell, none will bewray.—

LXXXIV.

On her he gaz'd, and silent stood this while,
  Armida's sleights he knew, and trains unjust,
Women have tongues of craft, and hearts of guile,
  They will, they will not, fools that on them trust,

For in their speech is death, hell in their smile;
   At last he said—If hence depart you lust,
I will you guide, on this conclude we here,
And further speech till fitter time forbear.—

LXXXV.

Forthwith (ere thence the camp remove) to ride
   They were resolv'd, their flight that season fits.
Vafrine departs; she to the dames beside
   Returns, and there on thorns awhile she sits;
Of her new knight she talks, till time and tide
   To 'scape unmark'd she finds, then forth she gets,
Thither where Vafrine her unseen abode,
There took she horse, and from the camp they rode.

LXXXVI.

And now in deserts waste and wild arrived,
   Far from the camp, far from resort and sight,
Vafrine began—'Gainst Godfrey's life contrived,
   The false compacts and trains unfold aright.—
Then she, those treasons, from their spring derived,
   Repeats, and brings their hid deceits to light :—
Eight knights (she says), all courtiers brave, there are,
But Ormond strong the rest surpasseth far;

LXXXVII.

These, whether hate or hope of gain them move,
   Conspired have and fram'd their treason so,
That day when Emiren by fight shall prove
   To win lost Asia from his Christian foe;
These, with the cross scor'd on their arms above,
   And arm'd like Frenchmen, will disguised go
Like Godfrey's guard that gold and white do wear,
Such shall their habit be, and such their gear;

LXXXVIII.

Yet each will bear a token in his crest,
   That so their friends for Pagans may them know;
But in close fight when all the soldiers best
   Shall mingled be, to give the fatal blow
They will creep near, and pierce Godfredo's breast,
   While of his faithful guard they bear false show,
And all their swords are dipt in poison strong,
Because each wound shall bring sad death ere long :

LXXXIX.

And for their chieftain wist I knew their guise,
    What garments, ensigns, and what arms you carry,
Those feigned arms he forc'd me to devise,
    So that from yours but small or naught they vary :
But these unjust commands my thoughts despise,
    Within their camp therefore I list not tarry,
My heart abhors I should this hand defile
With spot of treason or with act of guile.

XC.

This is the cause, but not the cause alone.—
    And there she ceas'd and blush'd, and on the main
Cast down her eyes ; these last words scant out-gone,
    She would have stopt, nor durst pronounce them plain.
The squire what she conceal'd would know, as one
    That from her breast her secret thoughts could strain.—
Of little faith (quoth he), why wouldst thou hide
Those causes true from me thy squire and guide ?

XCI.

With that she fetch'd a sigh, sad, sore, and deep,
    And from her lips her words slow, trembling came :—
Fruitless (she said), untimely hard to keep,
    Vain modesty farewell, and farewell shame :
Why hope you, restless love, to bring on sleep ?
    Why strive your fires to quench sweet Cupid's flame ?
No, no, such cares and such respects beseem
Great ladies, wand'ring maids them naught esteem.

XCII.

That night, fatal to me and Antioch town,
    Then made a prey to her commanding foe,
My loss was greater than was seen or known,
    There ended not, but thence began my wo :
Light was the loss of friends, of realm or crown ;
    But with my state I lost myself also
Ne'er to be found again, for then I lost
My wit, my sense, my heart, my soul almost.

XCIII.

Through fire and sword, through blood and death, Vafrine
    (Which all my friends did burn, did kill, did chase ,
Thou know'st I run to thy dear lord and mine,
    When first he enter'd had my father's place,

And kneeling with salt tears in my swollen eyne—
   Great prince (quoth I) grant mercy, pity, grace ;
Save not my kingdom, not my life, I said,
But save mine honor, let me die a maid.—

XCIV.

He lift me by the trembling hand from ground,
   Nor stay'd he till my humble speech was done ;
But said—A friend and keeper hast thou found,
   Fair virgin, nor to me in vain you run :
A sweetness strange from that sweet voice's sound
   Pierced my heart, my breast's weak fortress won,
Which creeping through my bosom soft, became
A wound, a sickness, and a quenchless flame.

XCV.

He visits me ; with speeches kind and grave
   He sought to ease my griefs, and sorrow's smart :
He said—I give thee liberty, recave
   All that is thine, and at thy will depart :
Alas ! he robb'd me when he thought he gave,
   Free was Erminia, but captiv'd her heart ·
Mine was the body, his the soul and mind,
He gave the cage, but kept the bird behind.

XCVI.

But who can hide desire, or love suppress ?
   Oft of his worth with thee in talk I strove,
Thou (by my trembling fit that well couldst guess
   What fever held me) said'st, Thou art in love ;
But I denied, for what can maids do less ?
   And yet my sighs thy sayings true did prove ;
Instead of speech, my looks, my tears, mine eyes,
Told in what flame, what fire, thy mistress fries.

XCVII.

Unhappy silence ! well I might have told
   My woes, and for my harms have sought relief,
Since now my pains and plaints I utter bold,
   Where none that hears can help or ease my grief.
From him I parted, and did close up-fold
   My wounds within my bosom, death was chief
Of all my hopes and helps, till love's sweet flame
Pluck'd off the bridle of respect and shame,

XCVIII.

And caus'd me ride to seek my lord and knight,
    For he that made me sick could make me sound ;
But on an ambush I mischanc'd to light
    Of cruel men in armor clothed round ;
Hardly I 'scap'd their hands by mature flight,
    And fled to wilderness and desert ground,
And there I liv'd in groves and forests wild,
With gentle grooms and shepherds' daughters mild :

XCIX.

But when hot love, which fear had late suppress'd,
    Reviv'd again, there nould I longer sit,
But rode the way I came, nor ere took rest
    Till on like danger, like mishap I hit :
A troop, to forage and to spoil address'd,
    Encounter'd me, nor could I fly from it :
Thus was I ta'en, and those that had me caught
Egyptians were, and me to Gaza brought !

C.

And for a present to their captain gave,
    Whom I entreated and besought so well,
That he mine honor had great care to save,
    And since with fair Armida let me dwell.
Thus taken oft, escaped oft I have ;
    Ah ! see what haps I pass'd, what dangers fell !
So often captive, free so oft again,
Still my first bands I keep, still my first chain ;

CI.

And he that did this chain so surely bind
    About my heart, which none can loose but he,
Let him not say, Go, wand'ring damsel ! find
    Some other home, thou shalt not bide with me ;
But let him welcome me with speeches kind,
    And in my wonted prison set me free.—
Thus spake the princess, thus she and her guide
Talk'd day and night, and on their journey ride.

CII.

Through the highways Vafrino would not pass,
    A path more secret, safe, and short he knew ;
And now close by the city's wall he was
    When sun was set, night in the east up-flew ;

With drops of blood besmear'd he found the grass,
   And saw where lay a warrior murder'd new,
That all be-bled the ground ; his face to skies
He turns, and seems to threat though dead he lies ;

CIII.

His harness and his habit both bewray'd
   He,was a Pagan.   Forward went the squire,
And saw whereas another champion laid
   Dead on the land, all soil'd with blood and mire :
This was some Christian knight, Vafrino said ;
   And, marking well his arms and rich attire,
He loos'd his helm and saw his visage plain,
And cry'd—Alas ! here lies Tancredie slain !—

CIV.

The woful virgin tarried and gave heed
   To the fierce looks of that proud Saracine,
Till that high cry, full of sad fear and dread,
   Pierc'd through her heart with sorrow, grief, and pine ;
At Tancred's name thither she ran with speed,
   Like one half mad or drunk with too much wine ;
And when she saw his face, pale, bloodless, dead,
She lighted, nay, she tumbled from her steed :

CV.

Her springs of tears she looseth forth, and cries—
   Hither why bring'st thou me, ah fortune blind !
Where dead, for whom I liv'd, my comfort lies,
   Where war for peace, travail for rest I find :
Tancred, I have thee, see thee, yet thine eyes
   Look not upon thy love and handmaid kind ;
Undo their doors, their lids fast closed sever ;
Alas ! I find thee for to lose thee ever.

CVI.

I never thought that to mine eyes (my dear)
   Thou couldst have grievous or unpleasant been,
But now would blind or rather dead I were,
   That thy sad plight might be unknown, unseen :
Alas ! where is thy mirth and smiling cheer ?
   Where are thine eyes' clear beams and sparkles sheen ?
Of thy fair cheek where is the purple red,
And forehead's whiteness ? are all gone, all dead ?

CVII.

Tho' gone, tho' dead, I love thee still ; behold
    Death wounds but kills not love ; yet if thou live,
Sweet soul, still in his breast, my follies bold
    Ah pardon, love's desires and stealth forgive ;
Grant me from his pale mouth some kisses cold,
    Since death doth love of just reward deprive ;
And of thy spoils, sad death, afford me this,
Let me his mouth, pale, cold, and bloodless, kiss :

CVIII.

O gentle mouth ! with speeches kind and sweet
    Thou didst relieve my grief, my wo, and pain ;
Ere my weak soul from this frail body fleet,
    Ah comfort me with one dear kiss or twain ;
Perchance, if we alive had hap'd to meet,
    They had been giv'n which now are stol'n : O vain,
O feeble life, betwixt his lips out fly !
O let me kiss thee first, then let me die !

CIX.

Receive my yielded spirit, and with thine
    Guide it to heav'n, where all true love hath place.—
This said, she sigh'd and tore her tresses fine,
    And from her eyes two streams pour'd on his face.
The man, revived with those show'rs divine,
    Awak'd, and opened his lips a space ;
His lips were open, but fast shut his eyes,
And with her sighs one sigh from him up-flies.

CX.

The dame perceiv'd that Tancred breath'd and sight,
    Which calm'd her griefs some deal and eas'd her fears :
Unclose thine eyes (she says), my lord and knight,
    See my last services, my plaints, and tears ;
See her that dies to see thy woful plight,
    That of thy pain her part and portion bears ;
Once look on me, small is the gift I crave,
The last which thou canst give, or I can have.—

CXI.

Tancred look'd up, and clos'd his eyes again,
    Heavy and dim, and she renew'd her wo.
Quoth Vafrine—Cure him first and then complain,
    Med'cine is life's chief friend, plaint her worst foe.—

They pluck'd his armor off, and she each vein,
    Each joint, and sinew felt and handled so,
And search'd so well each thrust, each cut, and wound,
That hope of life her love and skill soon found.

CXII.

From weariness and loss of blood she spy'd
    His greatest pains and anguish most proceed,
Naught but her veil amid those deserts wide
    She had to bind his wounds in so great need ;
But love could other bands (though strange) provide,
    And pity wept for joy to see that deed,
For with her amber locks, cut off, each wound
She tied ; (O happy man, so cur'd, so bound !)

CXIII.

For why ? her veil was short and thin, those deep
    And cruel hurts to fasten, roll, and bind ;
Nor salve nor simple had she ; yet to keep
    Her knight alive strong charms of wondrous kind
She said, and from him drove that deadly sleep,
    That now his eyes he lifted, turn'd, and twin'd,
And saw his squire, and saw that courteous dame
In habits strange, and wonder'd whence she came.

CXIV.

He said—O Vafrine, tell me whence com'st thou,
    And who this gentle surgeon is disclose.—
She smil'd, she sigh'd, she look'd she wist not how,
    She wept, rejoic'd, she blush'd as red as rose :—
You shall know all (she says) ; your surgeon now
    Commands your silence, rest, and soft repose,
You shall be sound, prepare my guerdon meet.—
His head then laid she in her bosom sweet.

CXV.

Vafrine devis'd this while how he might bear
    His master home ere night obscur'd the land,
When, lo ! a troop of soldiers did appear,
    Whom he descry'd to be Tancredie's band :
With him, when he and Argant met, they were ;
    But when they went to combat hand for hand
He bade them stay behind, and they obey'd ;
But came to seek him now, so long he stay'd.

CXVI.

Besides them, many follow'd that inquest,
  But these alone found out the rightest way.
Upon their friendly arms the men addrest
  A seat, wherein he sat, he lean'd, he lay.
Quoth Tancred—Shall the strong Circassian rest
  In this broad field, for wolves and crows a prey ?
Ah ! no ; defraud not you that champion brave
Of his just praise, of his due tomb and grave :

CXVII.

With his dead bones no longer war have I,
  Boldly he died, and nobly was he slain ;
Then let us not that honor him deny,
  Which after death alonely doth remain.—
The Pagan dead they lifted up on high,
  And after Tancred bore him through the plain.
Close by the virgin chaste did Vafrine ride,
As he that was her squire, her guard, her guide.—

CXVIII.

Not home (quoth Tancred) to my wonted tent,
  But bear me to this royal town, I pray ;
That if, cut short by human accident,
  I die, there I may see my latest day ;
The place where Christ upon his cross was rent,
  To heav'n perchance may easier make the way ;
And ere I yield to death's and fortune's rage,
Perform'd shall be my vow and pilgrimage.—

CXIX.

Thus to the city was Tancredie borne,
  And fell on sleep, laid on a bed of down.
Vafrino, where the damsel might sojourn
  A chamber got, close, secret, near his own.
That done, he came the mighty Duke beforne,
  And entrance found ; for till his news were known,
Naught was concluded 'mongst those knights and lords,
Their counsel hung on his report and words.

CXX.

Where weak and weary wounded Raimond laid,
  Godfrey was set upon his couch's side,
And round about the man a ring was made
  Of lords and knights, that fill'd the chamber wide :

There, while the squire his late discov'ry said,
    To break his talk none answer'd, none reply'd:
My lord (he said), at your command I went,
And view'd their camp, each cabin, booth, and tent;

CXXI.

But of that mighty host the number true
    Expect not that I can or should descry,
All cover'd with their armies might you view
    The fields, the plains, the dales, and mountains high;
I saw what way soe'er they went and drew
    They spoil'd the land, drank floods and fountains dry;
For not whole Jordan could have giv'n them drink,
Nor all the grain in Syria bread, I think:

CXXII.

But yet amongst them many bands are found,
    Both horse and foot, of little force and might,
That keep no order, know no trumpet's sound,
    That draw no sword, but far off shoot and fight;
But yet the Persian army doth abound
    With many a footman strong and hardy knight;
So doth the king's own troop, which all is framed
Of soldiers old, th' Immortal Squadron named;

CXXIII.

Immortal called is that band of right,
    For of that number never wanteth one,
But in his empty place some other knight
    Steps in, when any man is dead or gone,
This army's leader Emireno hight,
    Like whom in wit and strength are few or none,
Who hath in charge, in plain and pitched field,
To fight with you, to make you fly or yield:

CXXIV.

And well I know their army and their host
    Within a day or two will here arrive.
But thee, Rinaldo, it behoveth most
    To keep thy noble head for which they strive,
For all the chief in arms or courage boast
    They will the same to Queen Armida give,
And for the same she gives herself in price;
Such hire will many hands to work entice.

CXXV.

The chief of these that have thy murder sworn
  Is Altamore, the king of Sarmachand :
Adrastus then, whose realm lies near the morn,
  A hardy giant, bold, and strong of hand ;
This king upon an elephant is borne,
  For under him no horse can stir or stand :
The third is Tisipherne, as brave a lord
As ever put on helm or girt on sword.——

CXXVI.

This said, from young Rinaldo's angry eyes
  Flew sparks of wrath, flames in his visage shin'd,
He long'd to be amid those enemies,
  Nor rest nor reason in his heart could find.
But to the Duke Vafrine his talk applies :
  The greatest news, my lord, are yet behind,
For all their thoughts, their crafts, and counsels tend,
By treason false to bring thy life to end.

CXXVII.

Then all from point to point he 'gan expose
  The false compact, how it was made and wrought ;
The arms and ensigns feigned, poison close,
  Ormondo's vaunt, what praise, what thank he sought,
And what reward ; and satisfy'd all those
  That would demand, inquire, or ask of aught.
Silence was made awhile, when Godfrey thus :——
Raimondo, say, what counsel giv'st thou us ?——

CXXVIII.

Not, as we purpos'd late, next morn (quoth he)
  Let us not scale, but round besiege this tow'r,
That those within may have no issue free
  To sally out and hurt us with their pow'r :
Our camp well rested and refreshed see,
  Provided well 'gainst this last storm and show'r ;
And then in pitched field fight if you will ;
If not, delay, and keep this fortress still :

CXXIX

But lest you be endanger'd, hurt, or slain,
  Of all your cares take care yourself to save ;
By you this camp doth live, doth win, doth reign,
  Who else can rule or guide these squadrons brave ?

And, for the traitors shall be noted plain,
　　Command your guard to change the arms they have;
So shall their guile be known; in their own net
So shall they fall, caught in the snare they set.—

CXXX.

As it hath ever (thus the Duke begun),
　　Thy counsel shows thy wisdom and thy love,
And what you left in doubt shall thus be done;
　　We will their force in pitched battle prove;
Clos'd in this wall and trench the fight to shun,
　　Doth ill this camp beseem and worse behove;
But we their strength and manhood will assay
And try, in open field and open day:

CXXXI.

The fame of our great conquests to sustain,
　　Or bide our looks and threats, they are not able;
And when this army is subdued and slain,
　　Then is our empire settled, firm and stable;
The tow'r shall yield, or but resist in vain,
　　For fear her anchor is, despair her cable.—
Thus he concludes, and rolling down the west
Fast set the stars, and call'd them all to rest.

BOOK XX.

I.

THE sun call'd up the world from idle sleep,
    And of the day ten hours were gone and past,
When the bold troop that had the tower to keep
    Espy'd a sudden mist, that overcast
The earth with mirksome clouds and darkness deep,
    And saw it was th' Egyptian camp at last
Which rais'd the dust for hills and valleys broad
That host did overspread and overload.

II.

Therewith a merry shout and joyful cry
    The Pagans rear'd from their besieged hold ;
The cranes from Thrace with such a rumor fly,
    His hoary frost and snow when Hyems old
Pours down, and fast to warmer regions high,
    From the sharp winds, fierce storms, and tempests cold ;
And quick and ready this new hope and aid,
Their hands to shoot, their tongues to threaten made.

III.

From whence their ire, their wrath, and hardy threat
    Proceeds, the French well knew and plain espy'd,
For from the walls and ports the army great
    They saw, her strength, her number, pomp, and pride ;

Swelled their breasts with valor's noble heat,
　　Battle and fight they wish'd ; Arm ! arm ! they cry'd :
The youth to give the sign of fight all pray'd
Their duke, and were displeas'd because delay'd

IV.

Till morning next, for he refus'd to fight ;
　　Their haste and heat he bridled, but not brake ;
Nor yet, with sudden fray or skirmish light,
　　Of these new foes would he vain trial make :—
After so many wars (he says), good right
　　It is that one day's rest at least you take.—
For thus in his vain foes he cherish would
The hope which in their strength they have and hold.

V.

To see Aurora's gentle beam appear,
　　The soldiers armed, prest, and ready lay ;
The skies were never half so fair and clear
　　As in the breaking of that blessed day ;
The merry morning smil'd, and seem'd to wear,
　　Upon her silver crown, sun's golden ray ;
And, without cloud, heav'n his redoubled light
Bent down to see this field, this fray, this fight.

VI.

When first he saw the day break, show, and shine,
　　Godfrey his host in good array brought out ;
And to besiege the tyrant Aladine,
　　Raimond he left, and all the faithful rout
That from the towns was come of Palestine
　　To serve and succor their deliv'rer stout ;
And with them left a hardy troop beside
Of Gascoignes strong, in arms well prov'd, oft try'd.

VII.

Such was Godfredo's count'nance, such his cheer,
　　That from his eye sure conquest flames and streams,
Heav'n's gracious favors in his looks appear,
　　And great and goodly more than erst he seems ;
His face and forehead full of noblesse were,
　　And on his cheek smiled youth's purple beams ;
And in his gait, his grace, his acts, his eyes,
Somewhat far more than mortal lives and lies.

VIII.

He had not marched far, ere he espied
　　Of his proud foes the mighty host draw nigh ;
A hill at first he took and fortified
　　At his left hand, which stood his army by ;
Broad in the front, behind more strait up tied,
　　His army ready stood the fight to try,
And to the middle-ward well arm'd he brings
His footmen strong, his horsemen serv'd for wings.

IX.

To the left wing, spread underneath the bent
　　Of the steep hill that sav'd their flank and side,
The Roberts twain, two leaders good, he sent ;
　　His brother had the middle-ward to guide ;
To the right wing himself in person went,
　　Down where the plain was dang'rous, broad, and wide,
And where his foes with their great numbers would
Perchance environ round his squadrons bold.

X.

There all his Lorrainers and men of might,
　　All his best arm'd he plac'd, and chosen bands,
And with those horse some footmen armed light,
　　That archers were (us'd to that service), stands :
Th' advent'rers then, in battle and in fight
　　Well try'd, a squadron famous through all lands,
On the right hand he set, somedeal aside,
Rinaldo was their leader, lord, and guide.

XI.

To whom the duke—In thee our hope is laid
　　Of victory, thou must the conquest gain ;
Behind this mighty wing so far display'd,
　　Thou with thy noble squadron close remain ;
And when the Pagans would our backs invade,
　　Assail them then, and make their onset vain ;
For, if I guess aright, they have in mind
To compass us, and charge our troops behind.—

XII.

Then through his host, that took so large a scope
　　He rode and view'd them all, both horse and foot ;
His face was bare, his helm unclos'd and ope ;
　　Lighten'd his eyes, his looks bright fire shot out ;

He cheers the fearful, comforts them that hope,
   And to the bold recounts his boasting stout,
And to the valiant his adventures hard,
These bids he look for praise, those for reward.

XIII.

At last he stay'd, whereof his squadrons bold
   And noblest troops assembled was best part ;
There from a rising bank his will he told,
   And all that heard his speech thereat took heart ;
And as the molten snow from mountains cold
   Runs down in streams, with eloquence and art,
So from his lips his words and speeches fell,
Shrill, speedy, pleasant, sweet, and placed well :—

XIV.

My hardy host, you conquerors of the east,
   You scourge wherewith Christ whips his heathen fone,
Of victory behold the latest feast,
   See the last day for which you wish'd alone ;
Not without cause the Saracens, most and least,
   Our gracious Lord hath gather'd here in one,
For all your foes and His assembled are,
That one day's fight may end seven years of war :

XV.

This fight shall bring us many victories ;
   The danger none ; the labor will be small :
Let not the number of your enemies
   Dismay your hearts, grant fear no place at all ;
For strife and discord through their army flies,
   Their bands ill rank'd themselves entangle shall,
And few of them to strike or fight shall come,
For some want strength, some heart, some elbow room :

XVI.

This host, with whom you must encounter now,
   Are men half-naked, without strength or skill :
From idleness or following the plough,
   Late pressed forth to war against their will ;
Their swords are blunt, shields thin, soon pierced thro',
   Their banners shake, their bearers shrink ; for ill
Their leaders heard, obey'd, or follow'd be,
Their loss, their flight, their death, I well foresee :

XVII.

Their captain, clad in purple, arm'd in gold,
    That seems so fierce, so hardy, stout, and strong
The Moors or weak Arabians vanquish could,
    Yet can he not resist your valors long ;
What can he do, tho' wise, tho' sage, tho' bold,
    In that confusion, trouble, thrust, and throng ?
Ill known is he, and worse he knows his host ;
Strange lords ill fear'd are, ill obey'd of most :

XVIII.

But I am captain of this chosen crew,
    With whom I oft have conquer'd, triumph'd oft ;
Your lands and lineages long since I knew,
    Each knight obeys my rule, mild, easy, soft ;
I know each sword, each dart, each shaft I view,
    Although the quarry fly in skies aloft ;
Whether the same of Ireland be or France,
And from what bow it comes, what hand perchance :

XIX.

I ask an easy and an usual thing,
    As you have oft, this day so win the field ;
Let zeal and honor be your virtue's sting ;
    Your lives, my fame, Christ's faith, defend and shield ;
To earth these Pagans slain and wounded bring,
    Tread on their necks, make them all die or yield :
What need I more exhort you ? from your eyes
I see how victory, how conquest flies ?—

XX.

Upon the captain, when his speech was done,
    It seem'd a lamp and golden light down came,
As from night's azure mantle oft doth run,
    Or fall, a sliding star or shining flame ;
But from the bosom of the burning sun
    Proceeded this, and garland-wise the same
Godfredo's noble head encompass'd round,
And (as some thought) foreshow'd he should be crown'd.

XXI.

Perchance (if man's proud thought or saucy tongue
    Have leave to judge or guess at heav'nly things)
This was the angel which had kept him long,
    That now came down and hid him with his wings.

While thus the duke bespeaks his armies strong,
    And every troop and band in order brings,
Lord Emiren his host disposed well,
And with bold words whet on their courage fell.

XXII.

The man brought forth his army great with speed,
    In order good his foes at hand he spy'd ;
Like the new moon his host two horns did spread,
    In midst the foot, the horse were on each side ;
The right wing kept he for himself to lead,
    Great Altamore receiv'd the left to guide ;
The middle-ward led Muleasses proud,
And in that battaile fair Armida stood.

XXIII.

On the right quarter stood the Indian grim,
    With Tisipherne and all the king's own band ;
But where the left wing spread her squadrons trim,
    O'er the large plain did Altamoro stand,
With African and Persian kings with him,
    And two that came from Meroe's hot sand ;
And all his cross-bows and his slings he plac'd
Where room best serv'd to shoot, to throw, to cast.

XXIV.

Thus Emiren his host put in array,
    And rode from band to band, from rank to rank ;
His truchmen now, and now himself doth say,
    What spoil his folk shall gain, what praise, what thank
To him that feared—Look up, ours is the day,
    (He says) vile fear to bold hearts never sank ;
How dareth one against an hundred fight ?
Our cry, our shade, will put them all to flight.—

XXV.

But to the bold—Go, hardy knight (he says),
    His prey out of this lion's paws go tear.—
To some before his thoughts the shape he lays,
    And makes therein the image true appear,
How his sad country him entreats and prays,
    His house, his loving wife, and children dear :
Suppose (quoth he) thy country doth beseech
And pray thee thus ; suppose this is her speech :

XXVI.

Defend my laws, uphold my temples brave,
 My blood from washing of my streets withhold ;
From ravishing my virgins keep, and save
 Thine ancestors' dead bones and ashes cold ;
To thee thy fathers' dear and parents' grave
 Show their uncover'd heads, white, hoary, old ;
To thee thy wife, her breasts with tears o'erspread,
Thy sons their cradles show, thy marriage bed.—

XXVII.

To all the rest—You, for her honor's sake,
 Whom Asia makes her champions, by your might
Upon these thieves, weak, feeble, few, must take
 A sharp revenge, yet just, deserv'd, and right.—
Thus many words in several tongues he spake,
 And all his sundry nations to sharp fight
Encouraged.   But now the dukes had done
Their speeches all, the hosts together run.

XXVIII.

It was a great, a strange, and wond'rous sight,
 When front to front those noble armies met,
How every troop, how in each troop each knight
 Stood prest to move, to fight, and praise to get.
Loose in the wind waved their ensigns light,
 Trembled the plumes that on their crests were set ;
Their arms, impresses, colors, gold, and stone,
'Gainst the sun-beams smil'd, flamed, sparkled, shone :

XXIX.

Of dry-top'd oaks they seem'd two forests thick,
 So did each host with spears and pikes abound :
Bent were their bows, in rest their lances stick,
 Their hands shook swords, their slings held cobles roun l.
Each steed to run was ready, prest, and quick
 At his commander's spur, his hand, his sound ;
He chafes, he stamps, careers, and turns about ;
He foams, snorts, neighs, and fire and smoke breathes out.

XXX.

Horror itself in that fair sight seem'd fair,
 And pleasure flew amid sad dread and fear ;
The trumpets shrill that thunder'd in the air
 Were music mild and sweet to every ear ;

The faithful camp, though less, yet seem'd more rare
    In that strange noise, more warlike, shrill, and clear,
In notes more sweet; the pagan trumpets jar:
These sung, their armors shin'd; those glister'd far.

XXXI.

The Christian trumpets give the deadly call,
    The Pagans' answer, and the fight accept.
The godly Frenchmen on their knees down fall
    To pray, and kiss'd the earth, and then up-leapt
To fight: the land between was vanish'd all;
    In combat close each host to other stepped;
For now the wings had skirmish hot begun,
And with their battles forth the footmen run.

XXXII

But who was first of all the Christian train
    That gave the onset first, first won renown?
Gildippes, thou wert she; for, by thee slain,
    The King of Orms, Hircano, tumbled down;
The man's breast-bone thou clov'st and rent in twain,
    So heav'n with honor would thee bless and crown:
Pierc'd through he fell, and, falling, heard withall
His foe prais'd for her strength, and for his fall.

XXXIII.

Her lance thus broke, the hardy dame forth drew,
    With her strong hand, a fine and trenchant blade;
And 'gainst the Persians fierce and bold she flew,
    And in their troop wide streets and lanes she made;
Even in the girdling steed divided new
    In pieces twain, Zopire on earth she laid;
And then Alcaro's head she swept off clean,
Which like a foot-ball tumbled on the green.

XXXIV.

A blow fell'd Artaxerxes; with a thrust
    Was Argeus slain: the first lay in a trance.
Ismael's left hand cut off fell in the dust,
    For on his wrist her sword fell down by chance:
The hand let go the bridle where it lust;
    The blow upon the courser's ears did glance,
Who felt the reins at large, and with the stroke
Half-mad, the ranks disorder'd, troubled, broke.

XXXV.

All these, and many more, by time forgot,
  She slew and wounded; when against her came
The angry Persians all, cast on a knot,
  For on her person would they purchase fame;
But her dear spouse and husband wanted not,
  In so great need, to aid the noble dame .
Thus join'd, the haps of war unhurt they prove,
Their strength was double, double was their love.

XXXVI.

The noble lovers use, well might you see,
  A wond'rous guise, till then unseen, unheard;
To save themselves forgot both he and she,
  Each other's life did keep, defend, and guard;
The strokes that 'gainst her lord discharged be,
  The dame had care to bear, to brake, to ward;
His shield kept off the blows bent on his dear,
Which, if need be, his naked head should bear.

XXXVII.

So each sav'd other, each for other's wrong
  Would vengeance take, but not revenge their own.
The valiant Soldan, Artabano strong,
  Of Boccan isle, by her was overthrown;
And by his hand (the bodies dead among)
  Alvante, that durst his mistress wound, fell down;
And she between the eyes hit Arimonte,
(Who hurt her lord) and cleft in twain his front.

XXXVIII.

But Altamore, who had that wing to lead,
  Far greater slaughter on the Christians made;
For where he turn'd his sword or twin'd his steed,
  He slew, or man and beast on earth down laid;
Happy was he that was at first struck dead,
  That fell not down alive, for whom his blade
Had spar'd, the same cast in the dusty street
His horse tore with his teeth, bruis'd with his feet.

XXXIX.

By this brave Persian's valor kill'd and slain
  Were strong Brunello and Ardonio great;
The first his head and helm had cleft in twain;
  The last in stranger wise he did entreat,

For through his heart he pierc'd, and through the vein
   Where laughter had his fountain and his seat,
So that (a dreadful thing, believ'd uneath!)
He laugh'd for pain, and laugh'd himself to death.

XL.

Nor these alone with that accursed knife
   Of this sweet light and breath deprived lie;
But with that cruel weapon lost their life
   Gentonio, Guascar, Rosimond, and Guye.
Who knows how many in that fatal strife
   He slew?   What knights his courser fierce made die?
The names and countries of the people slain
Who tells?   Their wounds and deaths who can explain?

XLI.

With this fierce king encounter durst not one,
   Not one durst combat him in equal field;
Gildippes undertook that task alone;
   No doubt could make her shrink, no danger yield;
By Thermodonte was never Amazone,
   That manag'd steeled axe or carried shield,
That seem'd so bold as she, so strong, so light,
When forth she run to meet that dreadful knight.

XLII.

She hit him where with gold and rich aumaile
   His diadem did on his helmet flame,
She broke and cleft the crown, and caus'd him vail
   His proud and lofty top, his crest down came;
Strong seem'd her arm that could so well assail:
   The Pagan shook for spite, and blush'd for shame;
Forward he rush'd, and would at once requite
Shame with disgrace; and with revenge, despite.

XLIII.

Right on the front he gave that lady kind
   A blow, so huge, so strong, so great, so sore,
That out of sense and feeling down she twin'd;
   But her dear knight his love from ground upbore.
Were it their fortune, or his noble mind,
   He stay'd his hand, and struck the dame no more:
A lion so stalks by, and with proud eyes
Beholds, but scorns to hurt, a man that lies.

XLIV.

This while Ormondo false, whose cruel hand
   Was arm'd and prest to give the trait'rous blow,
With all his fellows 'mongst Godfredo's band
   Enter'd unseen, disguised that few them know :
The thievish wolves, when night o'ershades the land,
   That seem like faithful dogs in shape and show,
So to the closed folds in secret creep,
And entrance seek, to kill some harmless sheep.

XLV.

He 'proached nigh, and to Godfredo's side
   The bloody Pagan now was placed near ;
But when his colors gold and white he spy'd,
   And saw the other signs that forged were—
See ! see ! this traitor false (the captain cry'd),
   That like a Frenchman would in show appear ;
Behold how near his mates and he are crept.—
This said, upon the villain forth he leap'd :

XLVI.

Deadly he wounded him ; and that false knight
   Nor strikes, nor wards, nor striveth to be gone ;
But (as Medusa's head were in his sight)
   Stood like a man new turn'd to marble stone.
All lances broke, unsheath'd all weapons bright,
   All quivers emptied were, on them alone ;
In parts so many were the traitors cleft,
That those dead men had no dead bodies left.

XLVII.

When Godfrey was with Pagan blood bespread,
   He enter'd then the fight, and that was past
Where the bold Persian fought and combatted,
   Where the close ranks he open'd, cleft, and brast ;
Before the knight the troops and squadrons fled,
   As Afric's dust before the southern blast :
The Duke recall'd them, in array them plac'd,
Stay'd those that fled, and him assail'd that chas'd.

XLVIII.

The champions strong there fought a battle stout,
   Troy never saw the like by Xanthus old.
A conflict sharp there was meanwhile on foot
   'Twixt Baldwin good and Muleasses bold.

The horsemen also (near the mountain's root,
  And in both wings) a furious skirmish hold,
And where the barb'rous Duke in person stood,
'Twixt Tisiphernes and Adrastus proud.

XLIX.

With Emiren, Robert the Norman strove,
  Long time they fought, yet neither lost nor won.
The other Robert's helm the Indian clove,
  And broke his arms, their fight would soon be done.
From place to place did Tisiphernes rove,
  And found no match, against him none durst run,
But where the prease was thickest thither flew
The knight, and at each stroke fell'd, hurt or slew.

L.

Thus fought they long, yet neither shrink nor yield,
  In equal balance hung their hope and fear :
All full of broken lances lay the field,
  All full of arms that clov'n and shatter'd were ;
Of swords, some to the body nail the shield,
  Some cut men's throats, and some their bellies tear,
Of bodies, some upright, some grovelling lay,
And for themselves eat graves out of the clay.

LI.

Beside his lord slain lay the noble steed ;
  There friend with friend lay kill'd, like lovers true ;
There foe with foe, the live under the dead,
  The victor under him whom late he slew.
A hoarse unperfect sound did each where spread,
  Whence neither silence, nor plain outcries flew ;
There fury roars, ire threats, and wo complains,
One weeps, another cries, he sighs for pains.

LII.

The arms that late so fair and glorious seem,
  Now soil'd and slubber'd, sad and sullen grow ;
The steel his brightness lost, the gold his beam,
  The colors had no pride nor beautȳ's show ;
The plumes and feathers on their crests that stream,
  Are strewed wide upon the earth below :
The hosts both clad in blood, in dust and mire,
Had chang'd their cheer, their pride, their rich attire.

LIII.

But now the Moors, Arabians, Æthiops black
  (Of the left wing that held the utmost marge)
Spread forth their troops, and purpos'd at the back
  And side their heedless foes t' assail and charge :
Slingers and archers were not slow nor slack
  To shoot and cast ; when with his battle large
Rinaldo came, whose fury, haste, and ire
Seem'd earthquake, thunder, tempest, storm and fire.

LIV.

The first he met was Asimire, his throne
  That set in Meroe's hot sun-burnt land ;
He cut his neck in twain, flesh, skin and bone,
  The sable head down tumbled on the sand ;
But when by death of this black Prince alone
  The taste of blood and conquest once he fand,
Whole squadrons then, whole troops to earth he brought,
Things wond'rous, strange, incredible, he wrought ;

LV.

He gave more deaths than strokes, and yet his blows
  Upon his feeble foes fell oft and thick ;
To move three tongues as a fierce serpent shows,
  Which rolls the one she hath, swift, speedy, quick ;
So thinks each Pagan, each Arabian trows,
  He wields three swords all in one hilt that stick ;
His readiness their eyes so blinded hath,
Their dread that wonder bred, fear gave it faith.

LVI.

The Afric tyrants and the Negro kings
  Fell down on heaps, drown'd each in other's blood ;
Upon their people ran the knights he brings,
  Prick'd forward by their guide's ensample good,
Kill'd were the Pagans, broke their bows and slings ;
  Some died, some fell, some yielded, none withstood :
A massacre was this, no fight ; these put
Their foes to death ; those hold their throats to cut.

LVII.

Small while they stood with heart and hardy face
  On their bold breasts deep wounds and hurts to bear,
But fled away, and troubled in the chase,
  Their ranks disorder'd be with too much fear :

Rinaldo follow'd them from place to place,
    Till quite discomfit and dispers'd they were ;
That done, he stays, and all his knights recalls,
And scorns to strike his foe that flies or falls.

LVIII.

Like as the wind, stopp'd by some wood or hill,
    Grows strong and fierce, tears boughs and trees in twain ;
But with mild blasts, more temperate, gentle, still,
    Blows through the ample field, or spacious plain ;
Against the rocks as sea-waves murmur shrill,
    But silent pass amid the open main :
Rinaldo so, when none his force withstood,
Assuag'd his fury, calm'd his angry mood ;

LIX.

He scorn'd upon their fearful backs that fled
    To wreak his ire, and spend his force in vain,
But 'gainst the footmen strong his troops he led,
    Whose side the Moors had open left and plain ;
The Africanes, that should have succored
    That battaile, all were run away or slain ;
Upon their flank with force and courage stout
His men at arms assail'd the bands on foot :

LX.

He brake their pikes, and brake their close array,
    Enter'd their battaile, fell'd them down around :
So wind or tempest with impetuous sway
    The ears of ripen'd corn strikes flat to ground :
With blood, arms, bodies dead, the harden'd clay
    Plaster'd the earth, no grass nor green was found ;
The horsemen running thro' and thro' their bands,
Kill, murder, slay ; few 'scape, not one withstands.

LXI.

Rinaldo came where his forlorn Armide
    Sat in her golden chariot mounted high,
A noble guard she had on every side
    Of lords, of lovers, and much chivalry :
She knew the man when first his arms she spy'd ;
    Love, hate, wrath, sweet desire, strove in her eye.
He chang'd some deal his look and count'nance bold ;
She chang'd from frost to fire, from heat to cold.

LXII.

The Prince past by the chariot of his dear,
    Like one that did his thoughts elsewhere bestow,
Yet suffer'd not her knights and lovers near
    Their rival so to 'scape withouten blow :
One drew his sword, another couched his spear ;
    Herself an arrow sharp set in her bow,
Disdain her ire new sharp'd and kindled hath,
But love appeas'd her, love assuag'd her wrath :

LXIII.

Love bridled fury, and reviv'd of new
    His fire, not dead, though buried in displeasure ;
Three times her angry hand the bow up drew,
    And thrice again let slack the string at leisure ;
But wrath prevail'd at last, the reed out flew,
    For love finds mean, but hatred knows no measure ;
Out flew the shaft, but with the shaft this charm,
This wish she sent—Heav'ns grant it do no harm.—

LXIV.

She bids the reed return the way it went,
    And pierce her heart which so unkind could prove,
Such force had love, though lost and vainly spent ;
    What strength hath happy. kind, and mutual love !
But she that gentle thought did straight repent,
    Wrath, fury, kindness, in her bosom strove ;
She would, she would not, that it miss'd or hit ;
    Her eyes, her heart, her wishes follow'd it.

LXV.

But yet in vain the quarry lighted not,
    For on his hawberk hard the knight it hit,
Too hard for woman's shaft or woman's shot,
    Instead of piercing there it broke and split.
He turn'd away ; she burnt with fury hot,
    And thought he scorn'd her power, and in that fit
Shot oft and oft, her shafts no entrance found,
And while she shot, love gave her wound on wound.—

LXVI.

And is he then unpierceable (quoth she),
    That neither force nor foe he needs regard ?
His limbs (perchance) arm'd with that hardness be,
    Which makes his heart so cruel and so hard ;

No shot that flies from eye or hand I see
   Hurts him, such rigor doth his person guard ;
Arm'd or disarm'd, his foe or mistress kind,
Despis'd alike, like hate, like scorn I find.

LXVII.

But what new form is left, device, or art,
   By which, to which exchang'd, I might find grace ?
For in my knights and all that take my part
   I see no help, no hope, no trust I place :
To his great prowess, might, and valiant heart,
   All strength is weak, all courage vile and base.—
This said she, for she saw how, through the field,
Her champions fly, faint, tremble, fall and yield.

LXVIII.

Nor left alone can she her person save,
   But to be slain or taken stands in fear,
Though with her bow a javelin long she have,
   Yet weak was Phœbe's bow, blunt Pallas' spear,
But as the swan, that sees the eagle brave
   Threat'ning her flesh and silver plumes to tear,
Falls down to hide her 'mongst the shady brooks ;
Such were her fearful motions, such her looks.

LXIX.

But Altamore, this while that strove and sought
   From shameful flight his Persian host to stay,
That was discomfit and destroy'd to naught,
   Whilst he alone maintain'd the fight and fray,
Seeing distress'd the goddess of his thought,
   To aid her ran, nay flew, and laid away
All care both of his honor and his host ;
If she were safe, let all the world be lost.

LXX.

To the ill-guarded chariot swift he flew,
   His weapon made him way with bloody war.
Meanwhile Lord Godfrey and Rinaldo slew
   His feeble bands, his people murder'd are.
He saw their loss, but aided not his crew,
   A better lover than a leader far.
He set Armida safe, then turn'd again
With tardy succor, for his folk were slain :

LXXI.

And on that side the woful Prince beheld
  The battle lost, no help nor hope remain'd.
But on the other wing the Christians yield,
  And fly, such 'vantage there the Egyptians gain'd :
One of the Roberts was nigh slain in field ;
  The other by the Indian strong constrain'd
To yield himself his captive and his slave.
Thus equal loss and equal foil they have.

LXXII.

Godfredo took the time and season fit
  To bring again his squadrons in array,
And either camp well order'd, rang'd and knit,
  Renew'd the furious battle, fight and fray :
New streams of blood were shed, new swords them hit ;
  New combats fought, new spoils were borne away ;
And unresolv'd and doubtful, on each side,
Did praise and conquest, Mars and Fortune ride.

LXXIII.

Between the armies twain while thus the fight
  Wax'd sharp, hot, cruel, though renew'd but late,
The Soldan climb'd up to the tower's height,
  And saw far off their strife and fell debate ;
As from some stage or theatre, the knight
  Saw play'd the tragedy of human state,
Saw death, blood, murder, wo and horror strange,
And the great acts of fortune, chance and change.

LXXIV.

At first astonish'd and amaz'd he stood,
  Then burnt with wrath, and self-consuming ire
Swelled his bosom like a raging flood ;
  To be amid that battle, such desire,
Such haste he had, he don'd his helmet good,
  His other arms he had before entire—
Up, up (he cried), no more, no more within
  This fortress stay ; come follow, die or win.—

LXXV.

Whether the same were Providence Divine
  That made him leave the fortress he possess'd,
For that the empire proud of Palestine
  This day should fall, to rise again more bless'd ;

Or that he breaking felt the fatal line
    Of life, and would meet death with constant breast ;
Furious and fierce he did the gates unbar,
And sudden rage brought forth, and sudden war ;

LXXVI.

Nor stay'd he till the folk on whom he cry'd
    Assemble might, but out alone he flies,
A thousand foes the man alone defy'd,
    And ran among a thousand enemies ;
But with his fury call'd from every side,
    The rest ran out, and Aladine forth hies ;
The cowards had no fear, the wise no care ;
This was not hope nor courage, but despair.

LXXVII.

The dreadful Turk with sudden blows down cast
    The first he met, nor gave them time to plain
Or pray, in murd'ring them he made such haste,
    That dead they fell ere one could see them slain.
From mouth to mouth, from eye to eye, forth past
    The fear and terror, that the faithful train
Of Syrian folk, not us'd to dang'rous fight,
Were broken, scatter'd, and nigh put to flight.

LXXVIII.

But with less terror and disorder less,
    The Gascoignes kept array, and kept their ground,
Though most the loss and peril them oppress,
    Unwares assail'd they were, unready found :
No rav'ning tooth or talon hard I guess
    Of beast, or eager hawk, doth slay and wound
So many sheep, or fowls, weak, feeble, small,
As his sharp sword kill'd knights and soldiers tall ;

LXXIX.

It seem'd his thirst and hunger 'suage he would
    With their slain bodies and their blood pour'd out.
With him his troops and Aladino old
    Slew the besiegers, kill'd the Gascoigne rout.
But Raimond ran to meet the Soldan bold,
    Nor to encounter him had fear or doubt,
Though his right hand by proof too well he know,
Which laid him late for dead, at one huge blow :

LXXX.

They met, and Raimond fell amid the field,
    This blow again upon his forehead light ;
It was the fault and weakness of his eild,
    Age is not fit to bear strokes of such might.
Each one lift up his sword, advanc'd his shield,
    Those would destroy, and these defend the knight.
On went the Soldan, for the man he thought
Was slain, or eas'ly might be captive brought.

LXXXI.

Among the rest he ran, he rag'd, he smote,
    And in small space, small time, great wonders wrought ;
And as his rage him led and fury hote
    To kill and murder, matter new he sought.
As from his supper poor, with hungry throat,
    A peasant hastes to a rich feast ybrought,
So from this skirmish to the battle great
He ran, and quench'd with blood his fury's heat.

LXXXII.

Where batter'd was the wall he sallied out,
    And to the field in haste and heat he goes,
With him went rage and fury, fear and doubt
    Remain'd behind, among his scatter'd foes :
To win the conquest strove his squadron stout,
    Which he unperfect left ; yet loth to lose
The day, the Christians fight, resist and die ;
And ready were to yield, retire and fly :

LXXXIII.

The Gascoigne bands retir'd, but kept array ;
    The Syrian people ran away outright.
The fight was near the place where Tancred lay,
    His house was full of noise and great affright ;
He rose and looked forth to see the fray,
    Though every limb was weak, faint, void of might ;
He saw the County lie, his men o'erthrown,
Some beaten back, some kill'd, some felled down.

LXXXIV.

Courage in noble hearts that ne'er is spent,
    Yet fainted not, though faint were every limb,
But re-enforc'd each member cleft and rent,
    And want of blood and strength supplied in him :

In his left hand his heavy shield he hent,
　　Nor seem'd the weight too great, his curtlax trim
His right hand drew, nor for more arms he stood
Or stay'd ; he needs no more whose heart is good ;

LXXXV.

But coming forth, cried—Whither will you run,
　　And leave your leader to his foes in prey ?
What ! shall these heathen of his armor won,
　　In their vile temples hang up trophies gay ?
Go home to Gascoigne then, and tell his son
　　That where his father died you ran away.—
This said, against a thousand armed foes
He did his breast, weak, naked, sick, oppose ;

LXXXVI.

And with his heavy, strong, and mighty targe
　　(That with sev'n hard bulls' hides was surely lin'd,
And strengthen'd with a cover thick and large
　　Of stiff and well-attemper'd steel behind)
He shielded Raimond from the furious charge,
　　From swords, from darts, from weapons of each kind,
And all his foes drove back with his sharp blade,
That sure and safe he lay as in a shade.

LXXXVII.

Thus sav'd, thus shielded, Raimond 'gan respire ;
　　He rose and rear'd himself in little space,
And in his bosom burnt the double fire
　　Of vengeance ; wrath his heart, shame filled his face :
He look'd around to spy (such was his ire)
　　The man whose stroke had laid him in that place,
Whom when he sees not, for disdain he quakes,
And on his people sharp revengement takes.

LXXXVIII.

The Gascoignes turn again ; their lord in haste
　　To 'venge their loss his band re-order'd brings ;
The troop that durst so much now stood aghast,
　　For where sad fear grew late now boldness springs ;
Now follow'd they that fled ; fled they that chas'd ;
　　So in one hour alt'reth the state of things :
Raimond requites his loss, shame, hurt, and all,
And with an hundred deaths reveng'd one fall.

LXXXIX.

Whilst Raimond wreaked thus his just disdain
  On the proud heads of captains, lords and peers,
He spies great Sion's King amid the train,
  And to him leaps, and high his sword he rears,
And on his forehead strikes and strikes again,
  Till helm and head he breaks, he cleaves, he tears;
Down fell the King, the guiltless land he bit,
That now keeps him because he kept not it.

XC.

Their guides, one murder'd thus, the other gone,
  The troops divided were in divers thought;
Despair made some run headlong 'gainst their fone,
  To seek sharp death, that comes uncall'd, unsought;
And some (that laid their hope on flight alone)
  Fled to their fort again; yet chance so wrought,
That with the fliers in the victors pass,
And so the fortress won and conquer'd was.

XCI.

The hold was won, slain were the men that fled,
  In courts, halls, chambers high, above, below.
Old Raimond fast up to the leads him sped,
  And there, of victory true sign and show,
His glorious standard to the wind he spread,
  That so both armies his success might know.
But Soliman saw not the town was lost,
For far from thence he was, and near the host:

XCII.

Into the field he came: the lukewarm blood
  Did smoke and flow through all the purple field;
There of sad death the court and palace stood,
  There did he triumphs lead and trophies bield.
An armed steed fast by the Soldan yood,
  That had no guide nor lord the reins to wield;
The tyrant took the bridle, and bestrode
The courser's empty back, and forth he rode.

XCIII.

Great, yet but short and sudden, was the aid
  That to the Pagans, faint and weak, he brought;
A thunderbolt he was, you would have said;
  Great, yet that comes and goes as swift as thought,

And of his coming swift, and flight unstay'd,
   Eternal signs in hardest rocks hath wrought:
For by his hand an hundred knights were slain,
But time forgot hath all their names but twain:

XCIV.

Gildippes fair, and Edward thy dear lord,
   Your noble death, sad end, and woful fate
(If so much pow'r our vulgar tongue afford),
   To all strange wits, strange ears, let me dilate,
That ages all your love and sweet accord,
   Your virtue, prowess, worth may imitate:
And some kind servant of true love that hears,
May grace your death, my verses, with some tears.

XCV.

The noble lady thither boldly flew,
   Where the fierce Soldan fought, and him defy'd;
Two mighty blows she gave the Turk untrue,
   One cleft his shield, the other pierc'd his side.
The Prince the damsel by her habit knew:—
   See, see this mankind strumpet! see (he cry'd)
This shameless whore! for thee fit weapons were
Thy neeld and spindle, not a sword and spear.—

XCVI.

This said, full of disdain, rage, and despite,
   A strong, a fierce, a deadly stroke he gave,
And pierc'd her armor, pierc'd her bosom white,
   Worthy no blows but blows of love to have:
Her dying hand let go the bridle quite,
   She faints, she falls, 'twixt life and death she strave.
Her lord to help her came, but came too late,
Yet was not that his fault, it was his fate.

XCVII.

What should he do? to divers parts him call
   Just ire and pity kind; one bids him go
And succor his dear lady, like to fall;
   The other calls for vengeance on his foe;
Love biddeth both, love says he must do all,
   And with his ire joins grief, with pity wo.
What did he then? with his left hand the knight
Would hold her up, revenge her with his right:

XCVIII.

But to resist against a knight so bold,
    Too weak his will and pow'r divided were ;
So that he could not his fair love uphold,
    Nor kill the cruel man that slew his dear.
His arm, that did his mistress kind enfold,
    The Turk cut off.   Pale grew his looks and cheer ;
He let her fall, himself fell by her side ;
And, for he could not save her, with her died.

XCIX.

As the high elm (whom his dear vine hath twin'd
    Fast in her hundred arms and holds embrac'd),
Bears down to earth his spouse and darling kind,
    If storm or cruel steel the tree down cast,
And her full grapes to naught doth bruise and grind,
    Spoils his own leaves, faints, withers, dies at last ;
And seems to mourn and die, not for his own
But for her death, with him that lies o'erthrown :

C.

So fell he mourning, mourning for the dame
    Whom life and death had made for ever his ;
They would have spoke, but not one word could frame,
    Deep sobs their speech, sweet sighs their language is ;
Each gaz'd on other's eyes, and, while the same
    Is lawful, join their hands, embrace, and kiss :
And thus sharp death their knot of life untied,
Together fainted they, together died.

CI.

But now swift fame her nimble wings dispread,
    And told each where their chance, their fate, their fall ;
Rinaldo heard the case by one that fled
    From the fierce Turk, and brought him news of all :
Disdain, good-will, wo, wrath, the champion led
    To take revenge ; shame, grief, for vengeance call.
But, as he went, Adrastus with his blade
Forestall'd the way, and show of combat made.

CII.

The giant cry'd—By sundry signs I note,
    That whom I wish, I search, thou, thou art he ;
I mark'd each worthy's shield, his helm, his coat,
    And all this day have call'd and cry'd for thee ;

To my sweet saint I have thy head devote,
　　Thou must my sacrifice, my offering be:
Come, let us here our strength and courage try,
Thou art Armida's foe, her champion I.—

CIII.

Thus he defy'd him: on his front before
　　And on his throat he struck him, yet the blow
His helmet neither bruised, cleft, nor tore,
　　But in his saddle made him bend and bow.
Rinaldo hit him on the flank so sore,
　　That neither art nor herb could help him now:
Down fell the giant strong; one blow such power,
Such puissance had: so falls a thunder'd tower.

CIV.

With horror, fear, amazedness, and dread,
　　Cold were the hearts of all that saw the fray;
And Soliman (that view'd that noble deed)
　　Trembled; his paleness did his fear bewray;
For in that stroke he did his end aread,
　　He wist not what to think, to do, to say;
A thing in him unused, rare, and strange;
But so doth heav'n men's hearts turn, alter, change.

CV.

As when the sick or frantic men oft dream
　　In their unquiet sleep and slumber short,
And think they run some speedy course, and seem
　　To move their legs and feet in hasty sort;
Yet feel their limbs far slower than the stream
　　Of their vain thoughts, that bears them in this sport,
And oft would speak, would cry, would call, or shout,
Yet neither sound, nor voice, nor word send out;

CVI.

So run to fight the angry Soldan would,
　　And diden force his strength, his might, his ire,
Yet felt not in himself his courage old,
　　His wonted force, his rage and hot desire;
His eyes, that sparkled wrath and fury bold,
　　'Grew dim and feeble, fear had quench'd that fire;
And in his heart an hundred passions fought,
Yet not on fear or base retire he thought.

CVII.

While unresolv'd he stood, the victor knight
   Arriv'd, and seem'd in quickness, haste, and speed,
In boldness, greatness, goodliness, and might,
   Above all princes born of human seed:
The Turk small while resists, not death, nor fight,
   Made him forget his state or race, through dread;
He fled no strokes, he fetch'd no groan nor sigh,
Bold were his motions last, proud, stately, high.

CVIII.

Now when the Soldan (in those battles past,
   That Antœus-like, oft fell, oft rose again,
Ever more fierce, more fell) fell down at last
   To lie for ever, when this Prince was slain,
Fortune, that seld is stable, firm or fast,
   No longer durst resist the Christian train,
But rang'd herself in row with Godfrey's knights;
With them she serves, she runs, she rides, she fights.

CIX.

The Pagan troops, the King's own squadron, fled,
   Of all the East the strength, the pride, the flow'r,
Late call'd Immortal, now discomfited,
   It lost that title proud, and lost all pow'r,
To him that with the royal standard fled,
   Thus Emireno said, with speeches sour—
Art not thou he to whom to bear I gave
My King's great banner and his standard brave?

CX.

This ensign, Rimedon, I gave not thee
   To be the witness of thy fear and flight;
Coward! dost thou thy lord and captain see
   In battle strong, and run'st thyself from fight?
What seek'st thou? safety? come, return with me
   The way to death is path to virtue right:
Here let him fight that would escape, for this
The way to honor, way to safety is.—

CXI.

The man return'd, and swell'd with scorn and shame:
   The Duke with speeches grave exhorts the rest;
He threats, he strikes sometime, till back they came,
   And rage 'gainst force, despair 'gainst death address'd.

Thus of his broken armies 'gan he frame
  A battle new, some hope dwelt in his breast;
But Tisiphernes bold reviv'd him most,
Who fought and seem'd to win when all was lost.

CXII.

Wonders that day wrought noble Tisipherne,
  The hardy Normans all he overthrew;
The Flemings fled before the champion stern,
  Gernier, Rogero, Gerard bold he slew;
His glorious deeds to praise and fame eterne,
  His life's short date prolong'd, enlarg'd, and drew;
And then, as he that set sweet life at naught,
The greatest peril, danger most he sought.

CXIII.

He spy'd Rinaldo, and although his field
  Of azure purple now and sanguine shows,
And though the silver bird amid his shield
  Were armed gules, yet he the champion knows,
And says—Here greatest peril is, heav'ns yield
  Strength to my courage, fortune to my blows,
That fair Armida her revenge may see;
Help, Macon! for his arms I vow to thee.—

CXIV.

Thus prayed he, but all his vows were vain,
  Macon was deaf, or slept in heaven above;
And as a lion strikes him with his train
  His native wrath to quicken and to move,
So he awak'd his fury and disdain
  And sharp'd his courage on the whetstone love;
Himself he sav'd behind his mighty targe,
And forward spurr'd His steed, and gave the charge.

CXV.

The Christian saw the hardy warrior come,
  And leaped forth to undertake the fight;
The people round about gave place and room,
  And wonder'd on that fierce and cruel sight:
Some prais'd their strength, their skill and courage some,
  Such and so desp'rate blows struck either knight,
That all that saw forgot both ire and strife,
Their wounds, their hurts, forgot both death and life.

CXVI.

One struck; the other did both strike and wound,
  His arms were surer, and his strength was more;
From Tisipherne the blood stream'd down around,
  His shield was cleft, his helm was rent and tore.
The dame (that saw his blood besmear the ground,
  His armor broke, limbs weak, wounds deep and sore,
And all her guard dead, fled, and overthrown)
Thought now her field lay waste, her hedge lay down:

CXVII.

Environ'd with so brave a troop but late,
  Now stood she in her chariot all alone,
She feared bondage, and her life did hate,
  All hope of conquest and revenge was gone;
Half-mad and half-amaz'd, from where she sat
  She leaped down, and fled from friends and fone;
On a swift horse she mounts, and forth she rides
Alone, save for disdain and love her guides.

CXVIII.

In days of old, Queen Cleopatra so
  Alone fled from the fight and cruel fray,
Against Augustus great, his happy foe,
  Leaving her lord to loss and sure decay:
And as that lord for love let honor go,
  Follow'd her flying sails, and lost the day;
So Tisipherne the fair and fearful dame
Would follow, but his foe forbids the same.

CXIX.

But when the Pagan's joy and comfort fled,
  It seem'd the sun was set, the day was night;
'Gainst the brave Prince with whom he combated
  He turn'd, and on the forehead struck the knight:
When thunders forged are in Typhon's bed,
  Not Bronte's hammer falls so swift, so right;
The furious stroke fell on Rinaldo's crest,
And made him bend his head down to his breast.

CXX.

The champion in his stirrups high up-start,
  And cleft his hawberk hard and tender side,
And sheath'd his weapon in the Pagan's heart,
  The castle where man's life and soul do bide;

The cruel sword his breast and hinder part
  With double wound unclos'd and open'd wide;
And two large doors made for his life and breath,
Which pass'd, and cur'd hot love with frozen death.

CXXI.

This done, Rinaldo stay'd and look'd around
  Where he should harm his foes, or help his friends;
Nor of the Pagans saw he squadron sound,
  Each standard falls, ensign to earth descends;
His fury quiet then and calm he found,
  There all his wrath, his rage, and rancor ends.
He call'd to mind how, far from help or aid,
Armida fled, alone, amaz'd, afraid:

CXXII.

Well saw he when she fled, and with that sight
  The Prince had pity, courtesy, and care;
He promis'd her to be her friend and knight,
  When erst he left her in the island bare:
The way she fled he ran and rode a-right,
  Her palfrey's feet signs in the grass out ware:
But she this while found out an ugly shade,
Fit place for death, where naught could life persuade.

CXXIII.

Well pleased was she with those shadows brown,
  And yet displeas'd with luck, with life, with love;
There from her steed she lighted, there laid down
  Her bow and shafts, her arms that helpless prove;—
There lie with shame (she says), disgrac'd, o'erthrown,
  Blunt are the weapons, blunt the arms I move;
Weak to revenge my harms, or harm my foe,
My shafts are blunt; ah, love! would thine were so!

CXXIV.

Alas! among so many, could not one,
  Not one draw blood, one wound or rend his skin?
All other breasts to you are marble stone,
  Dare you then pierce a woman's bosom thin?
See, see my naked heart! on this alone
  Employ your force, this fort is eath to win;
And love will shoot you from his mighty bow,
Weak is the shot that dripile falls in snow.

CXXV.

I pardon will your fear and weakness past;
  Be strong, mine arrows, cruel, sharp 'gainst me:
Ah wretch! how is thy chance and fortune cast,
  If plac'd in these thy good and comfort be!
But since all hope is vain, all help is waste,
  Since hurts ease hurts, wounds must cure wounds in thee!
Then with thine arrow's stroke cure strokes of love,
Death for thy heart must salve and surgeon prove:

CXXVI.

And happy me, if being dead and slain,
  I bear not with me this strange plague to hell:
Love, stay behind! come thou with me, disdain,
  And with my wronged soul for ever dwell;
Or else with it turn to the world again,
  And vex that knight with dreams and visions fell;
And tell him, when 'twixt life and death I strove,
My last wish was revenge, last word was love.—

CXXVII.

And with that word half-mad, half-dead, she seems;
  An arrow, poignant, strong, and sharp she took:
When her dear knight found her in these extremes,
  Now fit to die and pass the Stygian brook,
Now prest to quench her own and beauty's beams,
  Now death sat on her eyes, death in her look;
When to her back he stepp'd, and stay'd her arm,
Stretch'd forth to do that service last, last harm.

CXXVIII.

She turns, and, ere she knows, her lord she spies,
  Whose coming was unwish'd, unthought, unknown;
She shrieks, and twines away her 'sdeignful eyes
  From his sweet face; she falls dead in a swoon;
Falls as a flow'er half cut that bending lies:
  He held her up, and, lest she tumble down,
Under her tender side his arm he plac'd,
His hand her girdle loos'd, her gown unlac'd;

CXXIX.

And her fair face, fair bosom, he bedews
  With tears, tears of remorse, of ruth, of sorrow.
As the pale rose her color lost renews
  With the fresh drops fall'n from the silver morrow;

So she revives, and cheeks empurpled shows,
  Moist with their own tears, and with tears they borrow;
Thrice look'd she up, her eyes thrice closed she,
As who say, let me die ere look on thee.

CXXX.

And his strong arm, with weak and feeble hand,
  She would have thrust away, loos'd, and untwin'd:
Oft strove she, but in vain, to break that band,
  For he the hold he got not yet resign'd;
Herself fast bound in those dear knots she fand,
  Dear, though she feigned scorn, strove, and repin'd,
At last she speaks, she weeps, complains, and cries,
Yet durst not, did not, would not see his eyes:—

CXXXI.

Cruel at thy departure, at return
  As cruel! say, what chance thee hither guideth?
Wouldst thou prevent her death, whose heart forlorn
  For thee, for thee death's strokes each hour divideth?
Com'st thou to save my life? alas! what scorn,
  What torment for Armida poor abideth!
No, no; thy crafts and sleights I will descry,
But she can little do that cannot die.

CXXXII.

Thy triumph is not great, nor well array'd,
  Unless in chains thou lead a captive dame;
A dame now ta'en by force, before betray'd,
  This is thy greatest glory, greatest fame:
Time was that thee of love and life I pray'd,
  Let death now end my love, my life, my shame;
Yet let not thy false hand bereave this breath,
For if it were thy gift, hateful were death.

CXXXIII.

Cruel! myself an hundred ways can find
  To rid me from thy malice, from thy hate;
If weapons sharp, if poisons of all kind,
  If fire, if strangling fail in that estate,
Yet ways enough I know to stop this wind,
  A thousand entries hath the house of fate.
Ah, leave these flatt'ries! leave weak hope to move;
Cease, cease! my hope is dead, dead is my love.—

CXXXIV.

Thus mourned she, and from her watery eyes
    Disdain and love dropt down, roll'd up in tears.
From his pure fountains ran two streams likewise,
    Wherein chaste pity and mild ruth appears.
Thus with sweet words the Queen he pacifies :—
    Madam, appease your grief, your wrath, your fears,
For to be crown'd, not scorn'd, your life I save :
Your foe nay, but your friend, your knight, your slave.

CXXXV.

But if you trust no speech; no oath, no word,
    Yet in mine eyes my zeal, my truth behold ;
For to that throne, whereof thy sire was lord,
    I will restore thee, crown thee with that gold ;
And if high heav'n would so much grace afford
    As from thy heart this cloud, this veil unfold
Of Paganism, in all the East no dame
Should equalize thy fortune, state, and fame.—

CXXXVI.

Thus plaineth he, thus prays, and his desire
    Endears with sighs that fly, and tears that fall ;
That, as against the warmth of Titan's fire
    Snow drifts consume on tops of mountains tall,
So melts her wrath, but love remains entire :—
    Behold (she says) your handmaid and your thrall,
My life, my crown, my wealth, use at your pleasure.—
Thus death her life became, loss prov'd her treasure.

CXXXVII.

This while the captain of th' Egyptian host,
    That saw his royal standard laid on ground,
Saw Rimedon, that ensign's prop and post,
    By Godfrey's noble hand kill'd with one wound,
And all his folk discomfit, slain, and lost,
    No coward was in this last battle found,
But rode about and sought, nor sought in vain,
Some famous hand of which he might be slain :

CXXXVIII.

Against Lord Godfrey boldly out he flew,
    For nobler foe he wish'd not, could not spy ;
Of desp'rate courage show'd he tokens true,
    Where'er he join'd, or stay'd, or passed by ;

And cried to the Duke as near he drew—
   Behold of thy strong hand I come to die,
Yet trust to overthrow thee with my fall,
My castle's ruin shall break down thy wall.—

CXXXIX.

This said, forth spurr'd they both, both high advance
   Their swords aloft, both struck at once, both hit;
His left arm wounded had the knight of France,
   His shield was pierc'd, his vauntbrace cleft and split;
The Pagan backward fell, half in a trance,
   On his left ear his foe so hugely smit;
And as he sought to rise, Godfredo's sword
Pierced him through : so died that army's lord.

CXL.

Of his great host, when Emiren was dead,
   Fled the small remnant that alive remained.
Godfrey espied, as he turn'd his steed,
   Great Altamore on foot, with blood all stained,
With half a sword, half helm upon his head,
   'Gainst whom a hundred fought, yet not one gained :—
Cease, cease this strife, he cry'd ; and thou, brave knight,
Yield ; I am Godfrey, yield thee to my might.—

CXLI.

He that till then his proud and haughty heart
   To act of humbleness did never bend,
When that great name he heard, from the north part
   Of our wide world renown'd to Æthiop's end,
Answer'd—I yield to thee, thou worthy art,
   I am thy prisoner, fortune is thy friend :
On Altamoro great thy conquest bold
Of glory shall be rich, and rich of gold :

CXLII.

My loving queen, my wife and lady kind,
   Shall ransom me with jewels, gold, and treasure.—
God shield (quoth Godfrey) that my noble mind
   Should praise and virtue so by profit measure ;
All that thou hast from Persia and from Inde
   Enjoy it still, therein I take no pleasure ;
I set no rent on life, no price on blood ;
I fight, and sell not war for gold or good.—

CXLIII.

This said, he gave him to his knights to keep,
    And after those that fled his course he bent;
They to their rampires fled and trenches deep,
    Yet could not so death's cruel stroke prevent;
The camp was won, and all in blood doth steep,
    The blood in rivers stream'd from tent to tent;
It soil'd, defil'd, defaced all the prey,
Shields, helmets, armors, plumes, and feathers gay.

CXLIV.

Thus conquer'd Godfrey; and as yet the sun
    Div'd not in silver waves his golden wain,
But day-light serv'd him to the fortress won
    With his victorious host to turn again:
His bloody coat he put not off, but run
    To the high temple with his noble train,
And there hung up his arms, and there he bows
His knees, there pray'd, and there perform'd his vows.

THE END.

GLOSSARY.

Abrayed—awaked.
Affray—affright.
Algates—nevertheless.
Amating—terrifying.
Appaid—rewarded, paid.

Band—bound.
Bases—stockings.
Battaile—battle, battalion.
Batten—fat.
Beild—shelter.
Bewraied—discovered.
Blaised—published.
Bourgeon—shoot forth.
Brand—sword.
Brast—burst.
Brust—broken.
Busk'd—prepared.

Cade—domesticated.
Cantle—a piece, a fragment.
Carknet—a necklace.
Chevisance—achievement.
Cobles—stones used in slinging.
Cog—a boat.
Copes—covering for the head.
Cornet—company of horse.
Cumbers—embarrassments.

Desave—deceive.
Dictamnum—the plant dittany.
Dight—clothed.
Dormant—a large beam.
Dripile—weak.

Eame—uncle.
Eath—easy.
Eft—soon.
Eftsoons—quickly.
Eild—age, period of life.
Emprise—enterprise.

Fand—found.
Filed—smooth.

Foin—thrust.
Fone—foes.
Forenenst—opposite.
Foreslowed—slackened.
Forray'd—foraged.
Froarie—frothy.
Frushed—bruised, crushed.

Giglet-wise—wantonly.
Gite—a vest.
Glaive—sword.
Gnarring—growling.
Greaves—groves.
Gree—favor, good-will.

Hags—brambles.
Heban—ebon, of ebony.
Hent—taken, put on, seized upon.
Hings—hangs.
Hoult—a wood.
Hurtle—jostle, rush against.

Kest—cast.

Lear'd—learned.
Leasing—falsehood.
Leden—language.
Legier—craftily.
Liefer—dearer, better, rather.
Lite—little.

Mavors—Mars.
Mew—cage, enclosed place.
Mister—sort, or manner of.
Mo—more.
Mote—might, may.

Nar—near.
Nathless—nevertheless.
Nill—will not.
Nould—would not.

Pardie—a mincing oath, used familiarly.

Peece—a fortress.
Pheer—companion.
Pight—fixed.
Pine—pain.
Prease—press.
Prest—ready.
Pricked—spurred.

Quarel—an arrow.
Quarry—an arrow.

Raught—reached.
Remew—remove.
Rochets—surplices.
Ruth—compassion.
In rew—in row.

Scaldred—parched.
Scath—mischief.
Scissed—cut.
Seld—seldom.
Seely—foolish
Sell—saddle.
Semblant—figure, appearance.
Sendal—fine linen.
Shaw—thicket.
Sheen—bright.
Shend—injure, spoil.
Sight—sighed.
Sleeveless—useless.
Smook—smoke.
Sown—sound.
Spiall—spy.
Spring—a grove.
Stallworth—brave, stout.
Sterve—perish.

Stound—space of time.
Stour—fight.
Stowers—battles.

Teen—grief.
Thorpe—a village.
Tofore—before.
Tooting—peeping.
Tout –to look upon.
Truchmen—interpreters.

Ugly—terrific.
Uneath—scarcely, with difficulty.
Unwroken—unrevenged.
Ure—a wild ox.

Vamure—advanced wall.
Ventail—the fore part of a helmet,
  which lifts up.

Wannish—somewhat wan.
Warray'd—made war upon.
Ween—imagine.
Weet—to know.
Wend—go.
Whilere—some time before.
Windlays—windings.
Wist—knew.
Won—dwell.
Wond—inhabited.
Wood—furious, savage.

Ycleped—called.
Yode—went.
Yood—went.
Ypight—fixed.